John Joy
On the Ordinary
and Extraordinary Magisterium

D1599240

STUDIA OECUMENICA FRIBURGENSIA

(= New Series of ÖKUMENISCHEN BEIHEFTE)
Published by the Institute for Ecumenical Studies
Fribourg Switzerland

84

John Joy

On the Ordinary
and Extraordinary Magisterium
from Joseph Kleutgen
to the Second Vatican Council

Aschendorff
Verlag

Münster
2017

Veröffentlicht mit Unterstützung des Hochschulrates
der Universität Freiburg Schweiz

About the cover illustration:
The cover illustration shows the calling of the sons of Zebedee as represented on theBernward column
(circa 1020), a Romanesque bronze column in HildesheimCathedral. The detail shows Jesus with his
right hand outstretched to James andJohn. In his left hand, Jesus holds a book as a symbol of the Word
of Life, which ishimself. The design of the book in the form of an ear is echoed by the folds of therobes
of Jesus, emphasizing the unity of person and message. From the boat, thedisciple reaches out his hand
towards Jesus. Does he grasp the written letters orreach for the living Word? On this choice depends the
vitality of our theology andthe fertility of our commitment to the community of the Church.
For the letter kills, but the Spirit gives life ...
Now the Lord is the Spirit, and where the Spirit of the Lord is, there is freedom.

2 Cor 3:6 and 17

Satz: Institut für Ökumenische Studien der Universität Freiburg Schweiz

© 2017 Aschendorff Verlag GmbH & Co. KG, Münster

www.aschendorff-buchverlag.de

Printed in Germany 2017
Gedruckt auf säurefreiem, alterungsbeständigem Papier ∞
ISBN 978-3-402-12209-9
ISBN 978-3-402-12210-5 (E-Book-PDF)

Table of Contents

ABBREVIATIONS

AAS   *Acta Apostolica Sedis commentarium officiale.* Rome: Typis Polyglottis Vaticanis, 1909–.

AS   *Acta Synodalia Sacrosancti Concilii Oecumenici Vaticani Secundi.* Rome: Typis Polyglottis Vaticanis, 1970–1999.

Denz.   *Denzinger: Enchiridion symbolorum definitionum et declarationum de rebus fidei et morum,* 43rd edition. Edited by Peter Hünermann for the original bilingual edition. Edited by Robert Fastiggi and Anne Englund Nash for the bilingual English edition. San Francisco: Ignatius Press, 2012.

Mansi   *Sacrorum Conciliorum Nova et Amplissima Collectio.* Ed. Giovanni Domenico Mansi. Paris: Welter, 1901–1927.

ACKNOWLEDGMENTS

My thanks are due first of all to Prof. Dr. Barbara Hallensleben of the University of Fribourg for her patient direction of this work over the long course of its maturation. Her words of encouragement, advice, and direction were equally invaluable and equally appreciated.

I also want to thank Dr. Timothy Kelly of the International Theological Institute for helping me to see many of the difficulties involved in the question and Pater Dr. Rupert Mayer of the Dominican Priory in Vienna for helping me to see some of the deficiencies in my own initial understanding of the matter. Thanks to Dr. Alan Fimister of the St. John Vianney Theological Seminary in Denver for many fruitful conversations and helpful suggestions.

Thanks as well to the many friends and colleagues whose shared love of theology has made the work so much more enjoyable, especially Louis Bolin, Kyle Washut, David and Katie Hunt, Christopher Owens, and Peter DeWitt.

My most heartfelt gratitude, however, I owe to my lovely wife Lisa for her unwavering love, support, and encouragement, and to my beautiful children who patiently endured too many summer vacations spent by their father closeted in his office rather than with them playing catch and swimming in the cool waters of Lake Michigan as they would have preferred.

Words are not adequate to express such gratitude. But the printed page allows for nothing else, so it will have to suffice for the present. Thank you.

INTRODUCTION

1. The Question

The question of the meaning and use of the terms 'ordinary magisterium' and 'extraordinary magisterium' is a question pertaining to the ways in which the teaching authority of the Church is exercised. The term 'magisterium', in contemporary usage, refers to the Church's teaching power or office of teaching *(munus docendi)*, which pertains to matters of faith and morals.[1] This is distinguished from the Church's office of ruling *(munus regendi)*, which is related to the discipline and government of the Church, and from her office of sanctifying *(munus sanctificandi)*, which refers principally to her liturgical worship and the administration of the sacraments.[2] The magisterium is said to be 'authentic' (that is, 'authoritative') because those who exercise it within the Church speak with the authority of Christ and in his name.[3] This magisterium is hierarchical and pastoral; that is, it is exercised by the bishops in union with the pope for the sake of the salvation of souls.

For me personally, the question of the distinction between the ordinary and the extraordinary magisterium arose out of my research into the ordinary papal magisterium in the context of a study of the extension and limits of papal infallibility. In the period between the First Vatican Council (1869–1870) and the Second Vatican Council (1962–1965), many theologians advanced and

---

1   Derived from the Latin 'magister' ('teacher'), the term 'magisterium' (although not the concept) was introduced into official ecclesiastical parlance by Pope Gregory XVI, Encyclical Letter on Church and State to the Clergy of Switzerland *Commissum divinitus* (17 May 1835), § 4: "The Church has, by its divine institution, the power of the magisterium to teach and define matters of faith and morals and to interpret the Holy Scriptures without danger of error" (*The Papal Encyclicals, 1740–1981*, vol. 1, ed. Claudia Carlen [Ypsilanti: Pierian Press, 1990], 254). See also Yves Congar, "A Semantic History of the Term 'Magisterium'," in *The Magisterium and Morality*, Readings in Moral Theology, vol. 3, ed. Charles E. Curran and Richard A. McCormick, 297–313 (New York: Paulist Press, 1982).

2   See Vatican Council II, Session V, Dogmatic Constitution on the Church *Lumen gentium* (21 Nov. 1964), § 21. For a discussion of this threefold division of offices adopted by Vatican II, see Joseph Lécuyer, "La triple charge de l'évêque," in *L'Église de Vatican II*, vol. 3, ed. Guilherme Baraúna, Unam Sanctam 51c, 891–914 (Paris: Cerf, 1966).

3   See Vatican II, *Lumen gentium*, § 25: "[Bishops] are authentic teachers, that is, teachers endowed with the authority of Christ, who preach to the people committed to them the faith they must believe and put into practice and by the light of the Holy Spirit illustrate that faith" (Denz. 4149).

defended the thesis that the pope was able to teach infallibly not only in his extraordinary magisterium, but also, under certain conditions, in the exercise of his ordinary magisterium.[4] A prominent example of this appears in the voluminous French *Dictionnaire de théologie catholique*, in the article on papal infallibility contributed by Edmond Dublanchy. This is a scholarly treatise running to eighty columns, in the midst of which the author sets forth a clear and concise argument for the infallibility of the ordinary papal magisterium.

Dublanchy derives his two fundamental premises from the two decrees of the First Vatican Council. Firstly, the definition of papal infallibility in the dogmatic constitution *Pastor Aeternus* states that the pope, speaking *ex cathedra*, "possesses through the divine assistance promised to him in blessed Peter the infallibility with which the Divine Redeemer willed his Church to be endowed in defining the doctrine concerning faith or morals."[5] From this text Dublanchy infers the equality of, or even identity between, the infallibility possessed by the Church as a whole and the infallibility possessed by the pope as supreme head of the Church on earth. The Second Vatican Council provides additional support for this first premise of the argument. In the dogmatic constitution *Lumen gentium*, speaking of infallible papal definitions, the council teaches that, "Then the Roman pontiff is not pronouncing judgment as a private person; but, rather, as the supreme teacher of the universal Church, in whom the charism of infallibility of the Church herself is individually present, he is expounding or defending a doctrine of Catholic faith."[6] Here we see that the very same charism of infallibility possessed by the Church is also present in the pope as supreme teacher of the universal Church: as the Church

---

4   See especially Jean-Michel-Alfred Vacant, *Le magistère ordinaire de l'Eglise et ses organes* (Paris; Lyons: Delhomme et Briguet, 1887); Edmond Dublanchy, "Infaillibilité du Pape," in *Dictionnaire de théologie catholique*, vol. 7, 1638–1717 (Paris: Letouzey et Ané, 1927); Joseph C. Fenton, "The Doctrinal Authority of Papal Encyclicals," *American Ecclesiastical Review* 121 (1949): 136–50, 210–20; "Infallibility in the Encyclicals," *American Ecclesiastical Review* 128 (1953): 177–98; Joseph Salaverri, *Tractatus de Ecclesia Christi*, in *Sacrae theologiae summa*, vol. 1, 5th ed. (Madrid: Biblioteca de Autores Cristianos, 1962), 700–701; "Valor de las Encíclicas a la luz de 'Humani Generis'," *Miscelánea Comillas* 17 (1952): 135–72; Paul Nau, "Le Magistère pontifical ordinaire au premier concile du Vatican," *Revue Thomiste* 62 (1962): 341–97.

5   Vatican Council I, Session IV, First Dogmatic Constitution on the Church of Christ *Pastor Aeternus* (18 Jul. 1870), cap. 4: "Romanum pontificem, cum ex cathedra loquitur [...] per assisten-tiam divinam ipsi in beato Petro promissam, ea infallibilitate pollere, qua divinus Redemptor Ecclesiam suam in definienda doctrina de fide vel moribus instructam esse voluit" (Denz. 3074).

6   Vatican II, *Lumen gentium*, § 25: "Tunc enim Romanus Pontifex non ut persona privata sententiam profert, sed ut universalis Ecclesiae magister supremus, in quo charisma infallibilitatis ipsius Ecclesiae singulariter inest, doctrinam fidei catholicae exponit vel tuetur" (Denz. 4149).

is infallible, so the pope as head of the Church is infallible. Dublanchy's reasoning thus appears to be secure in establishing the premise that whatever infallibility is possessed by the Church is also possessed by the pope.

He then draws his next premise from the dogmatic constitution *Dei Filius*, where it reads: "All those things are to be believed with divine and Catholic faith that are contained in the word of God, written or handed down, and which by the Church, either in solemn judgment or through her ordinary and universal teaching office, are proposed for belief as having been divinely revealed."[7] From this text it appears that the Church is able to propose dogmas not only in her solemn judgments but also through her ordinary and universal magisterium. Nothing is said explicitly about infallibility in this text, but Dublanchy reasons that a power which is able to bind all of the faithful to make the act of divine faith must be infallible; else it would be able to lead the entire Church into heresy, which is impossible. This point – that the Church is able to teach infallibly through her ordinary magisterium – also receives additional support from the Second Vatican Council, where it speaks of the infallibility exercised by the college of bishops in union with the pope even in their state of dispersion throughout the world, which is commonly understood as pertaining to their ordinary magisterium.[8] Once again, therefore, Dublanchy's reasoning seems to be secure in establishing the premise that the Church possesses an infallible ordinary magisterium. His argument can thus be summarized in the following syllogism: (1) whatever infallibility is possessed by the Church is also possessed by the pope (implied in *Pastor Aeternus*, confirmed by *Lumen gentium*); (2) the Church possesses an infallible ordinary magisterium (implied in *Dei Filius*, confirmed by *Lumen gentium*); (3) therefore, the pope possesses an infallible ordinary magisterium.[9]

---

7 Vatican Council I, Session III, Dogmatic Constitution on the Catholic Faith *Dei Filius* (24 Apr. 1870), cap. 3: "Porro fide divina et catholica ea omnia credenda sunt, quae in verbo Dei scripto vel tradito continentur et ab Ecclesia sive solemni iudicio sive ordinario et universali magisterio tamquam divinitus revelata credenda proponuntur" (Denz. 3011).

8 See Vatican II, *Lumen gentium*, § 25: "Although the individual bishops do not enjoy the prerogative of infallibility, they nevertheless proclaim Christ's doctrine infallibly whenever, even though dispersed throughout the world, but still maintaining the bond of communion among themselves and with the successor of Peter, and authentically teaching matters of faith and morals, they are in agreement on one position as definitively to be held" (Denz. 4149).

9 Dublanchy sums up his argument in a single succinct sentence: "Puisque, selon le décret du concile du Vatican, le pape possède l'infaillibilité donnée par Jésus á son Église et que, pour l'Église, cette infaillibilité peut s'étendre aux actes du magistère ordinaire, dans la mesure et aux conditions précédemment indiquées, voir ÉGLISE, t. IV, col. 2193 sq., on doit affirmer que le pape

Despite such apparently strong arguments, however, the nearly unanimous consensus of contemporary theologians is firmly against the infallibility of the ordinary papal magisterium. The third edition of the renowned *Lexicon für Theologie und Kirche*, for example, simply asserts as a matter of fact: "an *infallible* ordinary magisterium of the pope does not exist."[10] And the authority of Pope John Paul II is also against the infallibility of the ordinary papal magisterium. Within a series of catechetical talks on the Creed delivered in general audience, he at one point contrasts the ordinary papal magisterium against the *ex cathedra* definitions of the pope, which he identifies with the extraordinary magisterium,[11] or the 'solemn' exercise of the magisterium,[12] and then later asserts that the pope speaks infallibly only ('*solo*') when he speaks *ex cathedra*.[13] Taken together these statements appear to exclude the infallibility of the ordinary papal magisterium entirely.

---

enseignant seul, en vertu de son magistère ordinaire, est infaillible dans la même mesure et aux mêmes conditions" (Dublanchy, "Infaillibilité," 1705).

10   Wolfgang Beinert, "Unfehlbarkeit," in *Lexicon für Theologie und Kirche*, vol. 10, 3rd ed., ed. Walter Kasper (Freiburg im Breisgau: Herder, 2001), 390: „Ein *unfehlbares* ordenl. Lehramt des Papstes existiert nicht." See also Joseph A. Komonchak, "Ordinary Papal Magisterium and Religious Assent," in *Contraception: Authority and Dissent*, ed. Charles E. Curran (New York: Herder and Herder, 1969), 106; Avery Dulles, *Magisterium: Teacher and Guardian of the Faith* (Naples: Sapientia Press, 2007), 70; Francis A. Sullivan, *Magisterium: Teaching Authority in the Catholic Church* (Eugene: Wipf and Stock, 2002), 172.

11   Pope John Paul II, General Audience on the Doctrinal Mission of the Successor of Peter (10 Mar. 1993): "L'esercizio di tale magistero può avvenire anche in modo *straordinario*, quando il successore di Pietro – da solo o con il concilio dei vescovi, quali successori degli Apostoli – si pronuncia *ex cathedra* su un determinato punto di dottrina o di morale cristiana." Text taken from the website of the Holy See (http://w2.vatican.va/content/john-paul-ii/es/audiences/1993/documents/hf_jp-ii_aud_19930310.html), accessed 6 June 2015.

12   Pope John Paul II, General Audience on the Divine Assistance in the Magisterium of the Successor of Peter (17 Mar. 1993): "Come è noto, ci sono dei casi nei quali il magistero pontificale si esercita solennemente su particolari punti di dottrina, appartenenti al deposito della rivelazione o ad essa strettamente connessi. È il caso delle *definizioni* 'ex cathedra', come quelle della Immacolata Concezione di Maria, fatta da Pio IX nel 1854, e della sua Assunzione al cielo, fatta da Pio XII nel 1950." Text taken from the website of the Holy See (http://w2.vatican.va/content/john-paul-ii/it/audiences/1993/documents/hf_jp-ii_aud_19930317.html), accessed 6 Jun. 2015.

13   Pope John Paul II, General Audience on the Divine Assistance in the Magisterium of the Successor of Peter (24 Mar. 1993): "Infine, egli non la possiede come se potesse disporne o contarvi in ogni circostanza, ma solo 'quando parla dalla cattedra', e solo in un campo dottrinale limitato alle verità di fede e di morale e a quelle che vi sono strettamente connesse." Text taken from the website of the Holy See (http://w2.vatican.va/content/john-paul-ii/it/audiences/1993/documents/hf_jp-ii_aud_19930324.html), accessed 6 June 2015.

If there is not an infallible ordinary papal magisterium, however, and I do not suggest that there is,[14] then the arguments proposed by Dublanchy and other defenders of the same thesis must have been flawed. But where was the flaw? It is hard to see how there could be any fallacy in a syllogism such as Dublanchy's. And the individual premises seem well established on the basis of both Vatican I and Vatican II. The only remaining possibility is that the argument goes awry due to an ambiguous use of terms. And it is my contention that there is a frequently overlooked ambiguity inherent in the term 'ordinary magisterium'.

What is the meaning of the term 'ordinary magisterium'? And how is the ordinary magisterium distinct from the extraordinary magisterium? The terminology of 'ordinary magisterium' and 'extraordinary magisterium' has a relatively brief history in theology, dating back only to the middle of the nineteenth century. The first use of the term 'ordinary magisterium' in the official documents of the Church can be found in the apostolic letter *Tuas libenter* (1863) of Pope Pius IX to the Archbishop of Munich-Freising. In the First Vatican Council's dogmatic constitution *Dei Filius* (1870), the 'ordinary and universal magisterium' is contrasted against the 'solemn judgments' of the Church, which thus appear to be 'extraordinary' by comparison. The term 'extraordinary magisterium' occurs in the encyclical letter *Mortalium animos* (1928) of Pope Pius XI; the encyclical letter *Humani generis* (1950) of Pope Pius XII makes reference to a papal exercise of the ordinary magisterium. Neither term is used in *Pastor Aeternus* (1870), nor in *Lumen gentium* (1964), although each of these deals to some extent with the concepts involved. This distinction has entered into the *Code of Canon Law* (1983)[15] and the *Catechism of the Catholic Church* (1997)[16]; and it appears in the documents of the Congregation for the Doctrine of the Faith.[17] Yet in all of this, relatively little explanation is given of the precise import of the terms or of their proper application in particular cases.

This lack of a full and clear exposition in the documents of the Church is reflected by (or perhaps reflects) the lack of a consensus among theologians. Although the terms are widely used and the distinction often appealed to,

---

14 Previously, I did argue in favor of an infallible ordinary papal magisterium (see John P. Joy, *Cathedra Veritatis: On the Extension of Papal Infallibility* [Licentiate Thesis, International Theological Institute, 2012], 51–89), but I have since revised my position.

15 *Code of Canon Law* [henceforth: CIC] (25 Jan. 1983), can. 750, § 1.

16 *Catechism of the Catholic Church* (15 Aug. 1997), § 2034.

17 See especially Congregation for the Doctrine of the Faith [henceforth: CDF], Instruction on the Ecclesial Vocation of the Theologian *Donum veritatis* (24 May 1990).

especially in controversies over the doctrinal weight of particular doctrines or acts of magisterial teaching, yet the nature of the distinction is understood in different ways by different theologians. Prefacing his own use of the terms, Richard Gaillardetz rightly notes: "The terminology employed here is by no means universally accepted among theologians. Indeed, contemporary discussions of issues related to the magisterium have been hampered considerably by a lack of terminological consistency."[18]

In an essay published more than half a century ago, commenting on Pope Pius XII's reference to the ordinary magisterium of the pope in *Humani generis*, Edmond Benard complains of this same terminological inconsistency, and raises many of the same questions – still largely unanswered – that have prompted my own research. He writes:

> While I do not believe that there is any real disagreement among Catholic theologians about the substance of their teaching on the Ordinary Magisterium, there definitely is a difference in the terminology employed – a difference that creates a difficulty in teaching the matter to theological students and might possibly be the cause of some confusion. Do we say, for instance, with Dublanchy, that the Pope can be infallible by virtue of his Ordinary Magisterium; or do we, with Dieckmann, make equivalent terms of "Ordinary" Magisterium and "non-infallible" Magisterium? Do we say, with Billot, that the Pope can speak infallibly without speaking *ex cathedra*; or do we, with Zapelena, Diekamp and others regard an infallible pronouncement as, inevitably, also an *ex cathedra* one? Are we to say that the Holy Father is infallible in his Ordinary Magisterium or that he is not? Are we to say that an infallible pronouncement is necessarily an *ex cathedra* pronouncement or that it is not? In what terms can we best express the reality involved? These, I submit, are questions that should be examined before we can discuss without nominal ambiguity the Ordinary Magisterium of the Pope.[19]

It is not my intention to attempt a definitive answer to all of the questions raised here by Benard; but I hope that a deeper analysis of the concepts at the heart of the matter will at least provide a starting point from which such answers could be attempted.

18 Richard R. Gaillardetz, *Teaching with Authority: A Theology of the Magisterium of the Church*, Theology and Life Series, vol. 41 (Collegeville: Liturgical Press, Michael Glazier, 1997), 162, n. 6.
19 Edmond D. Benard, "The Doctrinal Value of the Ordinary Teaching of the Holy Father in View of *Humani Generis*," *Proceedings of the Catholic Theological Society of America* 6 (1951): 78–79.

2. The Context of the Question

The question of a distinction between the ordinary and the extraordinary magisterium arises within the broader context of fundamental dogmatic ecclesiology. The more immediate context is the classification of doctrine such as can be found within the concluding formula of the Profession of Faith promulgated by the Congregation for the Doctrine of the Faith.[20] After the recitation of the Nicene Creed, the Profession of Faith concludes with these three additional paragraphs:

> With firm faith, I also believe everything contained in the Word of God, whether written or handed down in tradition, which the Church, either by a solemn judgment or by the ordinary and universal Magisterium, sets forth to be believed as divinely revealed.[21]

> I also [firmly] accept and hold each and everything definitively proposed by the Church regarding teaching on faith and morals.[22]

> Moreover, I adhere with religious submission of will and intellect to the teachings that either the Roman pontiff or the college of bishops enunciate when they exercise their authentic Magisterium, even if they do not intend to proclaim these teachings by a definitive act.[23]

---

20 CDF, *Professio fidei* (29 Jun. 1998). The predecessor of the *Professio fidei* in its current form was the 1564 Tridentine Profession of Faith (see Denz. 1862–70) together with the 1910 Oath against Modernism (see Denz. 3537–50). These were supplanted by a very brief formula in 1967, which was then expanded in 1988. This last version was then re-promulgated without alteration in 1998 shortly after Pope John Paul II's Motu Proprio *Ad tuendam fidem* (18 May 1998), by which he caused the contents of the extended formula of the Profession of Faith to be inserted into the *Code of Canon Law* and the *Code of Canons of the Eastern Churches*.

21 CDF, *Professio fidei* (1998): "Firma fide quoque credo ea omnia quae in verbo Dei scripto vel tradito continentur et ab Ecclesia sive sollemni iudicio sive ordinario et universali Magisterio tamquam divinitus revelata credenda proponuntur" (AAS 90 [1998]: 542; Denz. 5070). The words 'sive sollemni iudicio' are unaccountably missing from the Latin text in Denz. 5070, although the English equivalent is included. Cf. CIC, can. 750, § 1; *Code of Canons of the Eastern Churches* [henceforth: CCEO] (18 Oct. 1990), can. 598, § 1.

22 CDF, *Professio fidei* (1998): "Firmiter etiam amplector ac retineo omnia et singula quae circa doctrinam de fide vel moribus ab eadem definitive proponuntur" (AAS 90 [1998]: 542; Denz. 5070). The word 'firmly' is missing from the English translation in Denz. 5070, although the Latin 'firmiter' is included. Cf. CIC, can. 750, § 2; CCEO, can. 598, § 2.

23 CDF, *Professio fidei* (1998): "Insuper religioso voluntatis et intellectus obsequio doctrinis adhaereo quas sive Romanus Pontifex sive Collegium episcoporum enuntiant cum Magisterium authenticum exercent etsi non definitivo actu easdem proclamare intendant" (AAS 90 [1998]: 543; Denz. 5070). Cf. CIC, can. 752; CCEO, can. 599.

Cardinal Joseph Ratzinger and Archbishop Tarcisio Bertone, at that time the prefect and secretary, respectively, of the Congregation for the Doctrine of the Faith, also issued a doctrinal note providing commentary on this concluding formula.[24] This commentary is a very important point of reference for understanding the state of the question today. But while it certainly deserves respect and attention, it does not seem that it has any properly magisterial authority. It comes from the offices of the Congregation for the Doctrine of the Faith, and it is included in the *Acta Apostolicae Sedis* and in the most recent edition of Denzinger, but it was issued without the seal of papal approbation that accompanies the doctrinal decrees of the Roman Congregations as an indication of their participation in the authority of the papal magisterium. The Congregation for the Doctrine of the Faith itself, in the instruction *Donum veritatis*, refers to the importance of explicit papal approval for the authority of its own documents:

> The Roman Pontiff fulfills his universal mission with the help of the institutes of the Roman Curia and in a particular way with that of the Congregation for the Doctrine of the Faith in what pertains to doctrine of faith and morals. Thus it follows that the documents of this Congregation, expressly approved by the Roman Pontiff, participate in the ordinary magisterium of the successor of Peter.[25]

As Cardinal Avery Dulles explains: "The acts of congregations, though not issued in the name of the pope himself, gain juridical authority by being approved by him either in a general way *(in forma communi)* or specifically *(in forma specifica)*. In the latter case they are equivalently acts of the pope himself."[26] As far as I understand it then, since this doctrinal commentary was not formally approved by the pope, either generally or specifically, it does not have any properly juridical authority and thus does not require even that religious submission of will and intellect spoken of in the third paragraph of the

---

24 Joseph Ratzinger and Tarcisio Bertone, *Doctrinal Commentary on the Concluding Formula of the Profession of Faith* (29 Jun. 1998) (AAS 90 [1998]: 543–49; Denz. 5071–72).

25 CDF, *Donum veritatis*, § 18: "Romanus Pontifex missionem suam universalem adimplet auxilio institutorum Curiae Romanae, peculiarique modo Congregationis pro Doctrina Fidei quod attinet ad doctrinam fidei et morum. Exinde sequitur documenta huius Congregationis, expresse a Romano Pontifice approbata, participare Magisterium ordinarium successoris Petri" (AAS 82 [1990]: 1558). Cf. CIC, cann. 360–61; Pope Paul VI, Apostolic Constitution on the Roman Curia *Regimini Ecclesiae Universae* (15 Aug. 1967), §§ 29–40; Pope John Paul II, Apostolic Constitution *Pastor Bonus* (28 Jun. 1988).

26 Dulles, *Magisterium*, 53.

concluding formula.[27] Hence I follow Dulles' usage in referring the authorship of the commentary to Ratzinger and Bertone personally rather than to the Congregation for the Doctrine of the Faith as such.

According to this doctrinal commentary, dogmas belonging to the first paragraph of the concluding formula *(de fide credenda)* and truths of Catholic doctrine belonging to the second paragraph *(de fide tenenda)* may be defined by solemn judgments of popes or ecumenical councils or may be infallibly taught by the ordinary and universal magisterium.[28] And doctrines belonging to the third paragraph are said to be taught by the ordinary magisterium of the pope or the college of bishops.[29] In the context of the classification of doctrine, then, the distinction between the ordinary and the extraordinary magisterium is typically schematized as follows:

I.   Catholic Dogma *(de fide credenda)*
    a. Defined by Extraordinary Magisterium
        i. By the Pope speaking *ex cathedra*
        ii. By an Ecumenical Council
    b. Taught by Ordinary and Universal Magisterium
II. Definitive Catholic Doctrine *(de fide tenenda)*
    a. Defined by Extraordinary Magisterium
        i. By the Pope speaking *ex cathedra*
        ii. By an Ecumenical Council
    b. Taught by Ordinary and Universal Magisterium
III. Authentic Catholic Doctrine
    a. Taught by Ordinary Magisterium of Pope
    b. Taught by Ordinary Magisterium of Bishops

27 This is also the conclusion reached by Dulles (Ibid., 86, n. 7): "This commentary, since it does not emanate from the Congregation as such, is not an official document of the Church."

28 See Ratzinger and Bertone, *Doctrinal Commentary*, § 5: "These doctrines [of the first paragraph] *are contained in the Word of God, written or handed down, and defined with a solemn judgment as divinely revealed truths either by the Roman pontiff when he speaks 'ex cathedra' or by the college of bishops gathered in council or infallibly proposed for belief by the ordinary and universal Magisterium*" (Denz. 5071); § 6: "Such doctrines [of the second paragraph] *can be defined solemnly by the Roman pontiff when he speaks 'ex cathedra' or by the college of bishops gathered in council, or they can be taught infallibly by the ordinary and universal Magisterium of the Church as a 'doctrine definitively to be held'*" (Denz. 5071). Italics in the original.

29 See Ratzinger and Bertone, *Doctrinal Commentary*, § 10: "Such teachings are, however, an expression of the ordinary Magisterium of the Roman pontiff or of the college of bishops and therefore require *religious submission of will and intellect*" (Denz. 5072). Italics in the original.

A related context in which the same distinction often arises is that of general treatments of the magisterium, which are frequently divided into considerations of the subject, object, and act (or modes of operation) of the magisterium. Here, a schema such as the following is typical:

    I.   The Subject of the Magisterium
       a. The Pope
       b. The College of Bishops
          i.   Gathered in Ecumenical Council
          ii. Dispersed throughout the World
   II.   The Object of the Magisterium
       a. Divinely revealed matters of faith and morals
       b. Matters of faith and morals connected to divine revelation
  III. The Act of the Magisterium
       a. Defining (Extraordinary Magisterium)
       b. Teaching (Ordinary Magisterium)

The subject of the supreme magisterium of the Church is twofold: it can be exercised either by the pope or by the college of bishops, and by the college of bishops whether gathered in ecumenical council or dispersed throughout the world. Individual bishops may also exercise an authentic magisterium in their own dioceses.[30] Since the college of bishops includes the pope as its head, theologians have sometimes spoken in terms of two 'inadequately distinct' subjects of the magisterium, but many contemporary theologians prefer to speak of only one subject of the magisterium – namely, the college of bishops – which can be exercised in two ways: by the whole college acting collectively or by the pope acting individually as head of the college.[31]

The object of the magisterium is similarly twofold: matters of faith and morals directly revealed by God in Scripture or Tradition constitute the primary object of the magisterium. The term 'dogma', in the sense in which it

---

30 Useful summaries of the authority of individual bishops can be found in Dulles, *Magisterium*, 57–58; Sullivan, *Magisterium*, 52–55; Gaillardetz, *Teaching with Authority*, 34–43. On the more difficult question of the magisterial authority exercised by groups of bishops in episcopal conferences and synods, see Francis A. Sullivan, "The Teaching Authority of Episcopal Conferences," *Theological Studies* 63 (2002): 472–93.

31 See, for example, Yves Congar, *Fifty Years of Catholic Theology: Conversations with Yves Congar*, ed. Bernard Lauret (Philadelphia: Fortress, 1988), 51; Karl Rahner, "On the Relationship between the Pope and the College of Bishops," in *Theological Investigations*, vol. 10, trans. David Bourke (New York: Herder and Herder, 1973), 50–70; Gaillardetz, *Teaching with Authority*, 60. Sullivan accepts both ways of speaking as legitimate (Sullivan, *Magisterium*, 99–100).

is commonly used in contemporary theology, signifies such divinely revealed truths as are also proposed as such by the Church, whether by solemn judgment or by the ordinary and universal magisterium.[32] The dogmatic teaching of the Church is infallible and the dogmas of the Church are correspondingly said to be irreformable or immutable.[33] They require the assent of divine and Catholic faith (divine faith in response to God revealing and Catholic faith in response to the Church teaching), which Ratzinger and Bertone also identify as the assent of theological faith; denial or obstinate doubt of a dogma of the Church constitutes heresy.[34]

The secondary object of the magisterium extends to matters of faith or morals that are indirectly contained in the deposit of faith[35] in virtue of their necessary connection with divinely revealed truths. These are truths strictly connected to divine revelation by logical or historical relationships inasmuch as they are necessary for safeguarding and expounding the contents of the deposit of faith.[36] Commonly proposed examples of truths belonging to the

---

32 On the meaning of the term 'dogma' with reference to its historical development, see Francis A. Sullivan, *Creative Fidelity: Weighing and Interpreting the Documents of the Magisterium* (Eugene: Wipf and Stock, 2003), 28–40; cf. Richard R. Gaillardetz, *By What Authority? A Primer on Scripture, the Magisterium, and the Sense of the Faithful* (Collegeville: Liturgical Press, 2003), 90–99; *Teaching with Authority*, 92–99.

33 'Immutable' is the word used by Ratzinger and Bertone (*Doctrinal Commentary*, § 5); Vatican I and Vatican II refer to the definitions of the Church as 'irreformable' (*Pastor Aeternus*, cap. 4; *Lumen gentium*, § 25). Sullivan regards these terms as interchangeable, each signifying that the truth expressed is permanent and that the Church is permanently committed to it (Sullivan, *Magisterium*, 81). Dulles explains the term 'irreformable' in the same sense, noting that it does not rule out 'reformulations' of doctrine as long as the same meaning is expressed; he also notes that more recent statements of the magisterium tend to use the term 'definitive' rather than 'irreformable', apparently with the same meaning (Dulles, *Magisterium*, 66). Cf. CDF, Declaration *Mysterium Ecclesiae* (24 Jun. 1973), § 5.

34 Ratzinger and Bertone, *Doctrinal Commentary*, § 5: "In the first paragraph, [...] the object taught is constituted by all those doctrines of divine and Catholic faith that the Church proposes as divinely and formally revealed [...] These doctrines require the assent of theological faith by all members of the faithful. Thus, whoever obstinately places them in doubt or denies them falls under the censure of heresy, as indicated by the respective canons of the Codes of Canon Law" (Denz. 5071). Cf. Vatican I, *Dei Filius*, cap. 3; CIC, cann. 750, § 1, 751, 1364, § 1; CCEO, cann. 598, 1436.

35 The 'deposit of faith' (see 1 Tim 6:20; 2 Tim 1:12, 14) is a common metaphor for the Gospel itself.

36 See John Paul II, *Ad tuendam fidem*, § 3: "These truths, in the investigation of Catholic doctrine, illustrate the divine Spirit's particular inspiration for the Church's deeper understanding of a truth concerning faith or morals with which they are connected either for historical reasons or by a logical relationship" (Denz. 5066); cf. Vatican II, *Lumen gentium*, § 25; CDF, *Mysterium Ecclesiae*, § 3; *Donum veritatis*, § 23.

secondary object of the magisterium include the so-called 'preambles of faith' (e.g. the ability of the mind to know truth), dogmatic facts (such as the legitimacy of a papal election or an ecumenical council), theological conclusions (conclusions drawn partly from reason and partly from divine revelation), and the canonization of saints.[37]

Finally, the act of the magisterium is also twofold: ordinary and extraordinary. The state of the question as it pertains to this distinction shall be set forth in three parts: firstly, with regard to the extraordinary magisterium; secondly, the ordinary and universal magisterium; and thirdly, the 'non-universal' or 'merely' ordinary magisterium.

3.   The State of the Question

The basic source text for the distinction between the ordinary and the extraordinary magisterium is from the First Vatican Council's dogmatic constitution *Dei Filius*, where it reads:

> Further, all those things are to be believed with divine and Catholic faith that are contained in the word of God, written or handed down, and which by the Church, either in solemn judgment or through her ordinary and universal teaching office, are proposed for belief as having been divinely revealed.[38]

By way of contrast with the teaching of the ordinary and universal magisterium, the solemn judgments of the Church appear here as exercises of an implied extraordinary magisterium.

3.1 The Extraordinary Magisterium

With regard to the extraordinary magisterium, several questions arise immediately: firstly, is the extraordinary magisterium exercised only in the solemn judgments spoken of in *Dei Filius*? The more common opinion is that the extraordinary magisterium is indeed limited to the solemn judgments of the Church.[39] But John Boyle holds that the term 'extraordinary magisterium'

---

37 Cf. Ludwig Ott, *Fundamentals of Catholic Dogma*, ed. James Bastible, trans. Patrick Lynch (Rockford: Tan Books, 1974), 299; Dulles, *Magisterium*, 76–81; Sullivan, *Magisterium*, 135–36.

38 Vatican I, *Dei Filius*, cap. 3: "Porro fide divina et catholica ea omnia credenda sunt, quae in verbo Dei scripto vel tradito continentur et ab Ecclesia sive solemni iudicio sive ordinario et universali magisterio tamquam divinitus revelata credenda proponuntur" (Denz. 3011). The first paragraph of the concluding formula of the *Professio fidei* is drawn almost verbatim from this text.

39 See, for example, Gaillardetz, *Teaching with Authority*, 162; Sullivan, *Magisterium*, 120–21; Dulles, *Magisterium*, 67–73.

should be taken to refer to all teaching issued by ecumenical councils (whether in the form of solemn judgments or not), whereas the term 'ordinary magisterium' refers to the teaching of the Church dispersed throughout the world.[40] One possible interpretation of the distinction between the ordinary and the extraordinary magisterium, therefore, is that it refers essentially to a distinction between the teaching of the Church gathered in council and that of the Church dispersed throughout the world. On this view, the teaching of the Second Vatican Council, for example, contrary to common opinion, would represent an exercise of the extraordinary magisterium, although this would not necessarily imply that its teaching is infallible.

But if, on the other hand, the extraordinary magisterium is limited to the solemn judgments of the Church, it must be asked further whether this means that it is limited to judgments of external solemnity or whether all the definitive judgments of the Church are intrinsically solemn. In other words, is the term 'solemn' used here in a qualifying or limiting sense? Or is it merely descriptive of the Church's judgments? The more common opinion today takes the latter position, simply equating the solemn judgments of the Church with the doctrinal definitions of ecumenical councils and popes speaking *ex cathedra*, such that every definition of the Church is *ipso facto* a solemn and extraordinary definition.[41] But the former position has not been without its defenders. Joseph Fenton, for example, held that not every infallible *ex cathedra* definition is a solemn judgment; rather, there is also such a thing as an infallible definition of the ordinary papal magisterium.[42] What distinguishes the extraordinary magisterium from the ordinary, on this view, is the external solemnity attaching to the formulae employed in the pronunciation of the definition or the pomp and ceremony of its promulgation. But this has nothing to do with its infallibility: "Circumstantial solemnity, as such," writes Fenton, "has no absolutely necessary connection with the infallibility of a pontifical definition."[43] On this

---

40 John P. Boyle, *Church Teaching Authority: Historical and Theological Studies* (Notre Dame: University of Notre Dame Press, 1995), 189–90, n. 30.

41 Sullivan writes: "This teaching is exercised in a 'solemn' or 'extraordinary' way when a doctrine is *defined* by an ecumenical council, or by a pope speaking *ex cathedra*" (*Magisterium*, 120–21; italics in the original). Cf. Ibid., 60–63; Dulles, *Magisterium*, 67–73; Ratzinger and Bertone, *Doctrinal Commentary*, §§ 5–6.

42 Fenton, "Infallibility in the Encyclicals," 186–89. In fact, Fenton finds it "interesting to note" that there are some theologians who do not share this position, implying that he took himself to be holding the majority opinion (Ibid., 181).

43 Ibid., 188. He continues: "That solemnity, of course, is a good and glorious thing within the

interpretation, the teaching of the Second Vatican Council – to use again the same example – would represent an exercise of the ordinary magisterium, although, again contrary to common opinion, this would not necessarily rule out that some of its teaching could be infallible.

Setting to one side for the present the interpretations represented by Boyle and Fenton, the more common opinion prevailing today is that the exercise of the extraordinary magisterium consists always and only in the definitions of ecumenical councils or of popes speaking *ex cathedra*, while every other form of teaching represents an exercise of the ordinary magisterium; the basic distinction between the extraordinary and the ordinary magisterium, then, as it is most commonly understood in contemporary theology, is essentially a distinction between *defining* doctrine and *not-defining* doctrine.[44] Taking this as our present basis, we will look more closely at the state of the question as it regards the subject of the extraordinary magisterium (those who are able to exercise it, and under what conditions); the act of the extraordinary magisterium (that which constitutes a solemn judgment or definition as such); and the object of the extraordinary magisterium (that with regard to which it is able to be exercised).

Subject: Since the extraordinary magisterium is a power of the supreme magisterium of the Church, it can only be exercised by those who hold supreme power in the Church: the pope and the college of bishops in union with him.[45] With regards to the pope, it is a necessary condition for his exercise of the extraordinary magisterium that he should be acting officially in his capacity as

---

Church of God. Those who saw and heard the Holy Father solemnly define the dogma of Our Lady's bodily Assumption into heaven know from happy experience the spiritual good engendered by an act of this kind. Yet it remains obvious that the visible head of the universal Church militant does not require or depend upon such solemnities in order that he may speak effectively and infallibly to the flock for which he is responsible to Christ" (Ibid., 188–89).

44 Gaillardetz notes that he follows Francis Sullivan and Yves Congar in understanding the distinction in this way (Gaillardetz, *Teaching with Authority*, 162, n. 6); cf. Yves Congar, *The Meaning of Tradition* (New York: Hawthorn, 1964), 65; Sullivan, *Magisterium*, 120–21. See also Ratzinger and Bertone, *Doctrinal Commentary*, §§ 5–6, 9.

45 See Vatican II, *Lumen gentium*, § 22: "In virtue of his office, that is, as vicar of Christ and pastor of the whole Church, the Roman pontiff has full, supreme, and universal power over the Church. And he is always free to exercise this power. The order of bishops, which succeeds to the college of apostles and gives this apostolic body continued existence, is also the subject of supreme and full power over the universal Church, provided we understand this body together with its head, the Roman pontiff, and never without this head. This power can be exercised only with the consent of the Roman pontiff" (Denz. 4146).

supreme head of the universal Church and not merely as a private person.[46] Most authors hold that not only the private teaching of the pope is excluded by this condition, but also his official teaching when acting as local bishop of the diocese of Rome, primate of Italy, or Patriarch of the West.[47] With regards to the college of bishops, it is commonly held that the condition for their exercise of the extraordinary magisterium is that they should be physically gathered in ecumenical council, although this seems to be a merely practical requirement.[48]

Act: The act of the extraordinary magisterium is the definition of doctrine. What does it mean to define doctrine? According to Francis Sullivan:

> When we speak of a council as 'defining' a doctrine, the word 'define' does not mean to give the exact meaning of a term, but rather to give a definitive judgment on a question. The root word *finis* means 'end' or 'limit'; when a council 'defines' a doctrine, it puts an end to freedom of opinion on the matter, and sets limits to the communion of the faith, because what is defined becomes part of the *normative* faith of the community.[49]

A 'definition' of doctrine is a 'definitive judgment', which Sullivan also refers to elsewhere as a 'solemn judgment', a 'solemn definition', or a 'definitive decision'.[50] The essential note of the act of definition is precisely its definitiveness, in the sense of finality or conclusiveness. It is an act intended to end discussion by means of a final and permanently binding judgment. The principal condition for the exercise of the extraordinary magisterium is thus the manifest intention, on the part of the one issuing the definition, of requiring full, final, and irrevocable assent to the doctrine defined.

---

46 See Vatican II, *Lumen gentium*, § 25: "For then the Roman pontiff is not pronouncing judgment as a private person; but, rather, as the supreme teacher of the universal Church, in whom the charism of infallibility is individually present, he is expounding or defending a doctrine of Catholic faith" (Denz. 4149). Cf. Vatican I, *Pastor Aeternus*, cap. 4.

47 See, for example, Gaillardetz, *Teaching with Authority*, 178–80; Sullivan, *Magisterium*, 101. Fenton, on the other hand, argues that the pope acting as local bishop of Rome is also acting *ipso facto* as head of the universal Church, and that he is able to teach infallibly even in doctrinal judgments addressed directly only to the diocese of Rome. See Joseph C. Fenton, "The Local Church of Rome," *American Ecclesiastical Review* 122 (1950): 454–64; "The Doctrinal Authority of Papal Allocutions," *American Ecclesiastical Review* 134 (1956): 109–17.

48 Sullivan raises the question of whether the physical gathering of the episcopate is strictly necessary: Could advances in modern technology enable something like an ecumenical council via internet? Or could the college of bishops authorize a representative group of their members to define doctrine in their name and with their authority? See Sullivan, *Magisterium*, 100–101.

49 Ibid., 60. Italics in the original.

50 Ibid., 60–63.

Although it is commonly said that a solemn judgment or definition puts an end to controversy, an important question that arises here is whether it is strictly necessary for an exercise of the extraordinary magisterium that the doctrine in question be actually in dispute, and if so, whether it is also necessary that this dispute be legitimate. According to Sullivan's explanation, a definition of doctrine "puts an end to freedom of opinion."[51] Does this mean that there must actually be freedom of opinion on a question as a necessary precondition for a definition? Or would it be possible for a pope or an ecumenical council to make use of the extraordinary magisterium in issuing a solemn definition on a point of doctrine already taught by the Church and therefore not open to legitimate dispute? In other words, is the extraordinary magisterium limited to *new* definitions or are definitions of existing doctrine also possible?

The position of Ratzinger and Bertone seems to be that the extraordinary magisterium is indeed limited to new definitions; in other words, they appear to hold that it is a necessary precondition for the exercise of the extraordinary magisterium that there be legitimate freedom of opinion on a matter prior to the act of definition, such that one is able to conclude, for example, that the doctrinal declaration of Pope John Paul II in the apostolic letter *Ordinatio sacerdotalis* is an act of the ordinary papal magisterium (rather than an extra-ordinary definition) on the grounds that the doctrine had already been infallibly taught by the ordinary and universal magisterium of the Church. The relevant text of *Ordinatio sacerdotalis* reads as follows:

> Wherefore, in order that all doubt may be removed regarding a matter of great importance, a matter that pertains to the Church's divine constitution itself, in virtue of Our ministry of confirming the brethren [cf. Lk 22:32], We declare that the Church has no authority whatsoever to confer priestly ordination on women and that this judgment is to be definitively held by all the Church's faithful.[52]

Now the First Vatican Council laid down the following conditions for the exercise of papal infallibility: the pope is said to be infallible when, (1) acting in the

---

51 Sullivan uses the same phrase again in the context of dogmatic definitions: "We have already seen that the term 'define' in the present context means to give a definitive judgment which puts an end to freedom of opinion on a question and decisively establishes some truth as an element of the normative faith of the community" (Sullivan, *Magisterium*, 102).

52 Pope John Paul II, Apostolic Letter *Ordinatio sacerdotalis* (22 May 1994), § 4: "Ut igitur omne dubium auferatur circa rem magni momenti, quae ad ipsam Ecclesiae divinam constitutionem pertinet, virtute ministerii Nostri confirmandi fratres [cf. Lc 22:32], declaramus Ecclesiam facultatem nullatenus habere ordinationem sacerdotalem mulieribus conferendi, hancque sententiam ab omnibus Ecclesiae fidelibus esse definitive tenendam" (Denz. 4983).

office of shepherd and teacher of all Christians, (2) by virtue of his supreme
apostolic authority, (3) he defines (4) a doctrine concerning faith or morals (5)
to be held by the universal Church.[53] The question as to whether or not *Ordinatio sacerdotalis* is an exercise of papal infallibility is largely a question as to
whether it meets the third condition listed above – whether it is an act of
'defining' in the relevant sense.[54] For the other conditions seem to be indisputably fulfilled: (1) the letter is addressed to all the bishops of the Church, and
the central declaration is addressed to all the faithful. (2) The pope invokes his
ministry of confirming the brethren with reference to Luke 22:32, which is cited
in the Second Vatican Council's reformulation of the doctrine of papal
infallibility.[55] (4) the doctrine is said to pertain to the divine constitution of the
Church itself. And (5) the doctrine is explicitly proposed as definitively to be
held by all the faithful.[56] As for condition (3), however, Ratzinger and Bertone
deny that the declaration of *Ordinatio sacerdotalis* is an act of definition on the
grounds that the doctrine had already been infallibly taught by the ordinary and
universal magisterium.

In their doctrinal commentary, Ratzinger and Bertone address the possibility that a doctrine already taught infallibly by the ordinary and universal

---

53 See Vatican I, *Pastor Aeternus*, cap. 4: "Romanum Pontificem, cum ex cathedra loquitur, id est,
cum omnium Christianorum pastoris et doctoris munere fungens pro suprema sua Apostolica
auctoritate doctrinam de fide vel moribus ab universa Ecclesia tenendam definit, per assistentiam
divinam ipsi in beato Petro promissam, ea infallibilitate pollere, qua divinus Redemptor Ecclesiam
suam in definienda doctrina de fide vel moribus instructam esse voluit; ideoque eiusmodi Romani
Pontificis definitiones ex sese, non autem ex consensu Ecclesiae, irreformabiles esse" (Denz.
3074).

54 For further discussion of this question, see Francis A. Sullivan, "New Claims for the Pope," *The
Tablet* 248 (18 Jun. 1994): 767–69; Angel Antón, "*Ordinatio Sacerdotalis*: Algunas reflexiones de
'gnoseología teológica'," *Gregorianum* 75 (1994): 723–42; Peter Hünermann, "Schwerwiegende
Bedenken: Eine Analyse des Apostolischen Schreibens 'Ordinatio Sacerdotalis'," *Herder Korrespondenz* 48 (1994): 406–10; Ida Raming, "Endgültiges Nein zum Priestertum der Frau? Zum
Apostolischen Schreiben Papst Johannes Pauls II. Ordinatio Sacerdotalis," *Orientierung: Katholische Blätter für weltanschauliche Information* 58 (1994): 190–93.

55 Vatican II, *Lumen gentium*, § 25: "And this is the infallibility that the Roman pontiff, the head of
the college of bishops, enjoys in virtue of his office, when, as the supreme shepherd and teacher
of all the faithful, who confirms his brethren in their faith [*cf. Lk 22:32*], by a definitive act he
proclaims a doctrine of faith or morals" (Denz. 4149).

56 Were it not for the intervention of Cardinal Ratzinger maintaining the contrary, Sullivan appears
to have been ready to conclude that *Ordinatio sacerdotalis* does contain an infallible definition:
"This language comes very close to that of a solemn definition, but we are assured by Cardinal
Ratzinger that it was not the intention of John Paul II to speak *ex cathedra*" (Sullivan, *Creative
Fidelity*, 22).

magisterium should be formally confirmed or reaffirmed by the pope (presumably the same reasoning would apply to confirmations or reaffirmations of existing doctrine on the part of ecumenical councils). The authors state that, "The *declaration of confirmation* or *reaffirmation* by the Roman pontiff in this case is not a new dogmatic definition *(actus dogmatizationis novus)*, but a formal attestation of a truth already possessed and infallibly transmitted by the Church."[57] The language here echoes what Ratzinger had previously written in a contribution to *L'Osservatore Romano* on the subject of *Ordinatio sacerdotalis*:

> In view of a magisterial text of the weight of the present Apostolic Letter, inevitably another question is raised: how binding is this document? It is explicitly stated that what is affirmed here must be definitively held in the Church, and that this question is no longer open to the interplay of differing opinions. Is this therefore an act of dogmatizing? Here one must answer that the Pope is not proposing any new dogmatic formula, but is confirming a certainty which has been constantly lived and held firm in the Church. In the technical language one should say: here we have an act of the ordinary Magisterium of the Supreme Pontiff, an act therefore which is not a solemn definition *ex cathedra,* even though in terms of content a doctrine is presented which is to be considered definitive. In other words, a certainty already existing in the Church, but now questioned by some, is confirmed by the Pope's apostolic authority. It has been given a concrete expression, which also puts in a binding form what has always been lived.[58]

The emphasis here again is on a contrast between a new dogmatic formulation and a confirmation of existing doctrine. Elsewhere, this time in connection with the official reply of the Congregation for the Doctrine of the Faith to a question about the status of *Ordinatio sacerdotalis*,[59] Ratzinger writes:

---

57 Ratzinger and Bertone, *Doctrinal Commentary*, § 9: "Ergo Romani Pontificis *declaratio confirmandi* seu *iterum affirmandi* actus dogmatizationis novus non est, sed confirmatio formalis veritatis ab Ecclesia iam obtentae atque infallibiliter traditae" (Denz. 5072).

58 Joseph Ratzinger, "The Limits of Church Authority," *L'Osservatore Romano*, English Edition (29 Jun. 1994): 7.

59 See CDF, *Responsum ad dubium* (28 Oct. 1995): "*Question*: Is the teaching that the Church has no authority whatsoever to confer priestly ordination on women, which is presented in the apostolic letter *Ordinatio sacerdotalis* [as] to be held definitively *(tamquam definitive tenenda)*, to be understood as belonging to the deposit of faith? *Response*: Yes. This teaching requires definitive assent, since, founded on the written Word of God and from the beginning constantly preserved and applied in the tradition of the Church, it has been set forth infallibly by the ordinary and universal Magisterium. Thus, in the present circumstances, the Roman pontiff, exercising his

In response to this precise act of the Magisterium of the Roman Pontiff [...] all members of the faithful are required to give their assent to the teaching stated therein. To this end, the Congregation for the Doctrine of the Faith, with the approval of the Holy Father, has given an official Reply on the nature of this assent; it is a matter of full definitive assent, that is to say, irrevocable, to a doctrine taught infallibly by the Church [...] It should be emphasized that the definitive and infallible nature of this teaching of the Church did not arise with the publication of the Letter *Ordinatio Sacerdotalis*. In the Letter [...] the Roman Pontiff [...] has confirmed the same teaching by a formal declaration [...] In this case, an act of the ordinary Papal Magisterium, in itself not infallible, witnesses to the infallibility of the teaching of a doctrine already possessed by the Church.[60]

Here too the author equates the confirmation of existing doctrine with the exercise of the ordinary magisterium in such a way as to imply that the extra-ordinary magisterium is limited to 'new dogmatic formulae' or 'new acts of dogmatization'.

In the terminology of Ratzinger and Bertone, a 'new act of dogmatization' is a proposition of doctrine as 'to be believed as divinely revealed' or as 'definitively to be held' 'by a definitive act' *(actu definitivo)*; whereas the confirmation or reaffirmation of existing Catholic doctrine is proposed 'by a non definitive act' *(actu non definitivo)* even if proposed as 'to be believed as divinely revealed' or as 'definitively to be held'.[61] And only 'definitive acts' constitute solemn

---

proper office of confirming the brethren [*cf. Lk 22:32*], has handed on this same teaching by a formal declaration, explicitly stating what is to be held always, everywhere, and by all, as belonging to the deposit of the faith" (Denz. 5040–41).

60 Joseph Ratzinger, "Letter Concerning the CDF Reply Regarding *Ordinatio Sacerdotalis*," *L'Osservatore Romano*, English Edition (19 Nov. 1995): 2. Although Ratzinger appears to deny the *per se* infallibility of *Ordinatio sacerdotalis* (even while affirming the infallibility of the doctrine on other grounds), Bertone is less clear on this point. In his article, "Magisterial Documents and Public Dissent," *L'Osservatore Romano*, English Edition (29 Jan. 1997): 6, it is hard to tell whether Bertone intends to say that the papal confirmation of the teaching of the ordinary and universal magisterium merely participates in the infallibility of the concordant teaching of the college of bishops or whether he intends to say that such a papal act of confirmation, although belonging to the ordinary magisterium, is infallible *per se*. Sullivan interprets him in the latter sense. See Francis A. Sullivan, "Recent Theological Observations on Magisterial Documents and Public Dissent," *Theological Studies* 58 (1997): 513.

61 Ratzinger and Bertone, *Doctrinal Commentary*, § 9: "The Magisterium of the Church, however, teaches a doctrine to be *believed as divinely revealed* (first paragraph) or to be *held definitively* (second paragraph) with an act that is either *defining* or *non-defining*. In the case of a defining act, a truth is solemnly defined by an 'ex cathedra' pronouncement by the Roman pontiff or by the

definitions of the extraordinary magisterium. Any act of teaching other than a 'new act of dogmatization' belongs *ipso facto* to the ordinary magisterium. For Ratzinger and Bertone, then, the key to the distinction between the ordinary and the extraordinary magisterium appears to lie in this: that the former is essentially traditional, in the sense of handing on what has been believed always, everywhere, and by all, while the latter is essentially innovative, not in the sense of proposing new doctrines absolutely speaking, but in the sense of making what had previously been open to dispute now a matter of obligatory belief. In support of this interpretation, Bertone offers the following consideration:

> If we were to hold that the Pope must necessarily make an *ex cathedra* definition whenever he intends to declare a doctrine as definitive because it belongs to the deposit of faith, it would imply an underestimation of the ordinary, universal Magisterium, and infallibility would be limited to the solemn definitions of the Pope or a Council, in a way that differs from the teaching of Vatican I and Vatican II, which attribute an infallible character to the teachings of the ordinary, universal Magisterium.[62]

According to Bertone, then, it would seem to imply a denial of the infallibility of the ordinary and universal magisterium if one were to hold that a definitive papal confirmation of a doctrine already taught by the ordinary and universal magisterium were itself an infallible definition. It is hard to see why this should be the case, though, unless one were to assume that the same doctrine cannot be taught infallibly more than once or in more than one way, which is by no means self-evident.

---

action of an ecumenical council. In the case of a *non-defining* act, a doctrine is taught *infallibly* by the ordinary and universal Magisterium of the bishops dispersed throughout the world who are in communion with the successor of Peter. *Such a doctrine can be confirmed or reaffirmed by the Roman pontiff, even without recourse to a solemn definition,* by declaring explicitly that it belongs to the teaching of the ordinary and universal Magisterium as a truth that is divinely revealed (first paragraph) or as a truth of Catholic doctrine (second paragraph). Consequently, when there has not been a judgment on a doctrine in the solemn form of a definition, but this doctrine, belonging to the inheritance of the deposit of faith, is taught by the ordinary and universal Magisterium, which necessarily includes the pope, such a doctrine is to be understood as having been set forth infallibly. The *declaration of confirmation* or *reaffirmation* by the Roman pontiff in this case is not a new dogmatic definition, but a formal attestation of a truth already possessed and infallibly transmitted by the Church" (Denz. 5072). Italics in the original. The same distinctions appear in Bertone, "Magisterial Documents and Public Dissent," 6.

62 Bertone, "Magisterial Documents and Public Dissent," 6.

Object: That the extraordinary magisterium can be exercised with regard to the primary object of the magisterium is undisputed. Properly dogmatic definitions of doctrine require that the doctrine be defined specifically as to be believed as divinely revealed or as a dogma of divine and Catholic faith. In the language of Ratzinger and Bertone's doctrinal commentary, these would be definitions *de fide credenda*. In theory, the extension of the extraordinary magisterium to the secondary object of the magisterium would appear to be equally uncontroversial: that is, it would appear to be the case that merely doctrinal definitions of doctrine, qualified generically as definitively to be held rather than more specifically as to be believed as divinely revealed, are possible in addition to properly dogmatic definitions. But in practice, the possibility of non-dogmatic definitions *(de fide tenenda)*, is frequently denied or overlooked.[63]

Ratzinger and Bertone, for example, clearly affirm the possibility of definitions *de fide tenenda* in their commentary on the second paragraph of the concluding formula.[64] Yet at the same time, in their treatment of papal confirmations and reaffirmations of doctrines taught by the ordinary and universal

---

63 Sullivan, for example, adverts to the possibility of non-dogmatic definitions in *Creative Fidelity*, 16, 80–81; but in the main text of the book he discusses only defined dogmas, undefined dogmas, and non-definitive teaching. Similarly, the treatment of the extraordinary magisterium in Sullivan, *Magisterium*, 79–118, is restricted to dogmatic definitions, while the secondary object of the magisterium is considered only in the context of the ordinary and universal magisterium (Ibid., 119–52). At one point he also remarks that the ordinary and universal magisterium is called 'ordinary' in order "to distinguish it from the solemn or extraordinary act of defining a dogma of faith" (Ibid., 56). Cf. Gaillardetz, *Teaching with Authority*, 184: "All are exercises of the *ordinary* magisterium, as I have been applying the term, because all fall short of the fullest engagement of supreme teaching authority in the Church, the solemn and infallible definition of Church dogma." Gaillardetz also speaks only of dogmatic definitions in his section on the extra-ordinary magisterium in *By What Authority?*, 81–84. See also Dulles, *Magisterium*, 83–91. This narrowing of the extraordinary magisterium to properly dogmatic definitions – to the exclusion of merely doctrinal definitions – may have been prompted or reinforced by the 1917 CIC, can. 1323, § 3, which read: "Nothing is to be understood as dogmatically declared or defined unless this is clearly manifested." The 1983 CIC, can. 749, § 3, corrects this by replacing the term 'dogmatically' with 'infallibly': "Nothing is to be understood as infallibly defined unless this is manifestly the case."

64 Ratzinger and Bertone, *Doctrinal Commentary*, § 6: "The object taught by this formula includes *all those teachings belonging to the dogmatic or moral area that are necessary for faithfully keeping and expounding the deposit of faith, even if they have not been proposed by the Magisterium of the Church as formally revealed.* Such doctrines *can be defined solemnly by the Roman pontiff when he speaks 'ex cathedra' or by the college of bishops gathered in council, or they can be taught infallibly by the ordinary and universal Magisterium of the Church as a 'doctrine definitively to be held'"* (Denz. 5071). Italics in the original.

magisterium, there appears a tendency to reason from the premise that these declarations are not dogmatic to the conclusion that they are not solemn definitions, which could be taken to imply a denial (or at least neglect) of the possibility of non-dogmatic definitions *de fide tenenda*. Recall Ratzinger's comments in *L'Osservatore Romano*: "Is this therefore an act of dogmatizing? Here one must answer that the Pope is not proposing any new dogmatic formula, but is confirming a certainty which has been constantly lived and held firm in the Church."[65] Bertone strikes this note as well: "Although it is not *per se* a *dogmatic definition* (like the Trinitarian dogma of Nicaea, the Christo-logical dogma of Chalcedon or the Marian dogmas)".[66] And in their joint commentary: "The *declaration of confirmation* or *reaffirmation* by the Roman pontiff in this case is not a new dogmatic definition *(actus dogmatizationis novus)*, but a formal attestation of a truth already possessed and infallibly transmitted by the Church."[67] In order to belong to the extraordinary magisterium, must a definition therefore be not only new, but also dogmatic? If the term 'dogmatic' is being used in the technical theological sense of requiring the response of divine and Catholic faith, then there is here a serious conflict between principles and application. Perhaps for this reason it would be more generous to read Ratzinger and Bertone's use of the term 'dogmatic' in the more general, non-technical sense of 'firm and unyielding', which applies equally to the first and second paragraphs of the concluding formula.

But the same apparent restriction of the extraordinary magisterium to properly dogmatic definitions also appears in the common tendency to con-clude that the teaching of Vatican II as a whole belongs solely to the ordinary magisterium on the grounds that the council defined no new dogmas.[68] The Second Vatican Council's teaching on the sacramentality of the episcopate is an excellent test case for the possibility of a non-dogmatic definition of the extraordinary magisterium inasmuch as this teaching was apparently intended

---

65 Joseph Ratzinger, "The Limits of Church Authority," *L'Osservatore Romano* (29 Jun. 1994): 7.

66 Bertone, "Magisterial Documents and Public Dissent," 6. Italics in the original.

67 Ratzinger and Bertone, *Doctrinal Commentary*, § 9. Italics in the original.

68 Note the twofold emphasis on *dogma*, and on *new* dogma in these quotations: "Although the Second Vatican Council was an extraordinary event, its documents represent what we mean here by 'ordinary' teaching, since this council chose not to use the authority it had to define any new dogma of Catholic faith" (Sullivan, *Magisterium*, 121); "Since Vatican II nowhere expressed its intention to define a dogma, its exercise of magisterium belongs in the category of 'ordinary,' that is to say, non-defining magisterium" (Sullivan, *Creative Fidelity*, 167); "Vatican II, following the instructions of Pope John XXIII, abstained from invoking its own infallibility. It neither defined new dogmas nor anathematized new errors" (Dulles, *Magisterium*, 76).

to settle a question previously open to legitimate dispute.[69] According to Dulles, who cites Yves Congar, this teaching "ranks as a 'definitive judgment'," yet Dulles still attributes it to the ordinary and universal magisterium on the grounds that it is "not a dogmatic definition in the strict sense."[70] Similarly, according to Umberto Betti, this is not a definition "in the technical sense of the word" since it would not be heresy to reject it.[71] It is true that this doctrine was not proposed as a dogma of divine and Catholic faith, but if there is a definitive doctrinal judgment of an ecumenical council that settles a question hitherto freely disputed by theologians, why not acknowledge it as a solemn definition of the extraordinary magisterium, unless the latter is indeed restricted to the primary object of the magisterium and so to properly dogmatic definitions *de fide credenda* to the exclusion of definitions *de fide tenenda*?

3.2 The Ordinary and Universal Magisterium

By way of contrast with the extraordinary magisterium, every kind of magisterial teaching other than the solemn definitions of popes and ecumenical councils is usually understood as belonging to the ordinary magisterium. Commenting on the text of *Dei Filius*, Sullivan remarks: "In this statement of Vatican I the term 'solemn judgment' refers to the act by which a doctrine is defined; hence the term 'ordinary' refers to the kind of teaching by which doctrines are not defined."[72] It is worth noting immediately that the concept of

---

69 Vatican II, *Lumen gentium*, § 21: "And the sacred council teaches that by episcopal consecration the fullness of the sacrament of orders is conferred, that fullness of power, namely, which both in the Church's liturgical practice and in the language of the Fathers of the Church is called the high priesthood, the supreme power of the sacred ministry" (Denz. 4145).

70 Dulles, *Magisterium*, 69–70. Cf. Yves Congar, "En guise de conclusion," in *L'Église de Vatican II*, vol. 3, ed. Guilherme Baraúna, Unam Sanctam 51c (Paris: Cerf, 1967), 1367: "la façon de s'exprimer n'est pas celle d'une définition dogmatique, mais la matière est très importante, la place qu'elle occupe dans la doctrine de l'épiscopatsi decisive, qu'on voit mal comment le Concile n'aurait pas porté, ici, un jugement définitif."

71 Umberto Betti, "Qualification théologique de la Constitution," in *L'Église de Vatican II*, vol. 2, ed. Guilherme Baraúna, Unam Sanctam 51b (Paris: Cerf, 1967), 217: "L'unique différence, donc, entre la doctrine de Vatican I et celle de Vatican II, consiste dans le fait que celle-ci, à la différence de cella-là, n'équivaut pas à une définition au sens technique du mot; c'est pourquoi, sa négation n'entraîne pas *ipso facto* la privation de la communion ecclésiastique annexée à la profession d'une hérésie."

72 Sullivan, *Magisterium*, 123; cf. *Creative Fidelity*, 167: "Since Vatican II nowhere expressed its intention to define a dogma, its exercise of magisterium belongs in the category of 'ordinary,' that is to say, non-defining magisterium." For similar views, see also Gaillardetz, *Teaching with Authority*, 162–63; Dulles, *Magisterium*, 67–73.

the ordinary magisterium, understood in this way, is almost entirely negative. That is, it is understood primarily in terms of what it is not rather than in terms of what it is. I would suggest that this is one of the principal causes of the difficulties involved in the question at hand. A positive conception of the ordinary magisterium is needed for a satisfactory account of the distinction between the ordinary and the extraordinary magisterium. The ordinary (non-defining) magisterium is then commonly subdivided into the 'ordinary and universal magisterium' (which is infallible, at least under certain conditions) and the merely 'ordinary magisterium' (which is not infallible).[73] In this section we shall look at the subject, act, and object of the ordinary and universal magisterium, as it is commonly understood in contemporary theology.

Subject: The term 'ordinary and universal magisterium' appears, as seen above, in the text of *Dei Filius*, where it is contrasted against the solemn judgments of the Church. What does the term 'universal' add to the notion of the ordinary (non-defining) magisterium? There are at least three possible interpretations: one would be that the teaching authority itself is universal in the sense of pertaining to all the members of the Church (both the pope and the college of bishops exercise a 'universal' magisterium in this sense, although the term 'supreme magisterium' is often preferred as a means of conveying this notion); a second interpretation would be that the teaching authority is vested in a universal subject (namely, in the whole body of bishops including the pope rather than in the pope alone); and a third would be that it is vested in a subject that is universally dispersed geographically (that is, in the college of bishops apart from their occasional gatherings in ecumenical council).

At the First Vatican Council, when questions were raised about the meaning of the text under consideration, Bishop Martin explained on behalf of the deputation on faith that the term 'universal' was not to be understood as touching either directly or indirectly upon the magisterium of the pope, but rather with reference to the text of *Tuas libenter*, wherein Pope Pius IX speaks of the ordinary magisterium of the whole Church dispersed throughout the world.[74] On the basis of this explanation, the more common opinion today is

---

73 Gaillardetz uses the term 'nonuniversal' in order to distinguish this 'ordinary magisterium' more precisely from the 'ordinary and universal magisterium' (see, Gaillardetz, *Teaching with Authority*, 162–63).

74 See Salaverri, *De Ecclesia Christi*, 669: "Eiusdem definitionis sensum ulterius determinavit Episcopus Martin, nomine eiusdem Deputationis fidei, dicens 'Ratio quare vox *universali* apponitur, haec est, ut scilicet ne quis putet nos loqui hoc loco de Magisterio infallibili S. Sedis Apostolicae. Nam nullatenus ea fuit intentio Deputationis, quaestionem de infallibilitate Summi

that the pope alone is unable to exercise the ordinary and universal magisterium.[75] But opinion is more divided as to whether it can be exercised by the college of bishops only in the state of dispersion throughout the world (based, as it were, on a strict interpretation of Martin's explanation),[76] or whether it is also exercised by the college of bishops gathered in ecumenical council when not defining doctrine (based on an extension of the principles taken to be involved in Martin's explanation).[77]

Act: The teaching of the bishops dispersed throughout the world is declared to be infallible under certain conditions in the text of *Lumen gentium*, where it reads:

> Although the individual bishops do not enjoy the prerogative of infallibility, they nevertheless proclaim Christ's doctrine infallibly whenever, even though dispersed throughout the world, but still maintaining the bond of communion among themselves and with the successor of Peter, and authentically teaching matters of faith and morals, they are in agreement on one position as definitively to be held *(tamquam definitive tenendam)*.[78]

Pontificis sive directe sive indirecte tangere. Hoc igitur verbum 'universali' idem fere significat, quod Sanctissimus Pater in suis Litteris Apostolicis expressit, nempe Magisterium totius Ecclesiae per orbem disperse'."

75 Sullivan, *Magisterium*, 123: "It is also clear from the *Acta* of Vatican I that the term 'universal magisterium' refers to the teaching of the whole episcopate with the pope, and not to the teaching of the pope alone, even when this is directed at the universal Church." Cf. Gaillardetz, *Teaching with Authority*, 184; Dulles, *Magisterium*, 70. Fenton, however, holds that the pope does exercise an ordinary and universal magisterium in the relevant sense and that this is just as infallible as the ordinary and universal magisterium exercised by the bishops. See Joseph C. Fenton, "The *Humani generis* and the Holy Father's Ordinary Magisterium," *American Ecclesiastical Review* 125 (1951): 58.

76 This seems to be the position of Sullivan: "The term '*universal* ordinary magisterium' refers to the concordant teaching of the whole Catholic episcopate together with the Pope, apart from the rather rare occasions when the bishops are gathered in ecumenical council" (*Magisterium*, 122; cf. 25, 56, 79; *Creative Fidelity*, 14). This is also the understanding expressed in Richard R. Gaillardetz, *Witnesses to the Faith: Community, Infallibility, and the Ordinary Magisterium of Bishops* (New York; Mahwah, N.J.: Paulist Press, 1992), 4.

77 Contrary to his own earlier usage, Gaillardetz adopts this position in *Teaching with Authority*, 163, 184, 188–89; and in *By What Authority?*, 85. This also seems to be the position of Dulles, *Magisterium*, 67–70.

78 Vatican II, *Lumen gentium*, § 25: "Licet singuli praesules infallibilitatis praerogativa non polleant, quando tamen, etiam per orbem dispersi, sed communionis nexum inter se et cum Successore Petri servantes, authentice res fidei et morum docentes in unam sententiam tamquam definitive tenendam conveniunt, doctrinam Christi infallibiliter enuntiant" (Denz. 4149).

One interpretation holds that the bishops exercise their ordinary and universal magisterium only when they meet these conditions, so that the teaching of the ordinary and universal magisterium is always infallible. All 'non-definitive'[79] teaching is then relegated to the (merely) ordinary magisterium, to be considered below. Another possibility is that the concordant teaching of the bishops, at least when dispersed throughout the world, is always an exercise of the ordinary and universal magisterium, whether that teaching is proposed as definitively to be held or not. In this case, the teaching of the ordinary and universal magisterium would be infallible only in some cases, namely when it meets all the conditions specified in the above text of *Lumen gentium*.[80]

The act of the ordinary and universal magisterium, then, is the act of non-defining teaching, and it is either restricted to, or infallible only when, it is proposed 'as definitively to be held' *(tamquam definitive tenendam)*. The principal difficulty that arises here is how this concordant and definitive teaching of the bishops dispersed throughout the world can be adequately recognized. On the one hand, Karl Rahner holds that, "An absolutely strict and irreformable assent must be explicitly called for."[81] Other authors deny the necessity of such an explicit declaration.[82] Sullivan, based on his reading of *Tuas libenter*,

---

79 The term 'non-definitive' is generally used in order to express the absence of the definitive note required for strictly infallible teaching without giving the impression that this kind of teaching is essentially prone to error. The authentic magisterium, even when 'merely authentic', is always exercised in the name of Christ and with his authority, under the guidance of the Holy Spirit.

80 Dulles seems to hold the former interpretation (Dulles, *Magisterium*, 67). Sullivan takes the latter position (Sullivan, *Magisterium*, 57). Gaillardetz appears to have modified his position on the matter: in an earlier work he seems to interpret the term 'ordinary and universal magisterium' only in reference to the infallible teaching of the bishops dispersed throughout the world (Gaillardetz, *Witnesses to the Faith*, 4); but in later works he makes it clear that the same term also encompasses the 'non-definitive' teaching of the college of bishops, whether gathered in ecumenical council or dispersed throughout the world (Gaillardetz, *Teaching with Authority*, 163; *By What Authority?*, 85).

81 Karl Rahner, "Commentary on *Lumen gentium*," in *Commentary on the Documents of Vatican II*, vol. 1, ed. Herbert Vorgrimler, trans. Lalit Adolphus et al. (New York: Herder and Herder, 1967), 210. Cf. Karl Rahner, "Magisterium," in *Sacramentum Mundi: An Encyclopedia of Theology*, vol. 3, ed. Karl Rahner (New York: Herder and Herder, 1968), 356: "It is not enough that a doctrine be propounded with moral unanimity by the whole episcopate. It is further required that the doctrine be explicitly propounded 'tamquam definitive tenendam' (LG 25)." See also Sullivan's discussion of the issue in *Magisterium*, 125–27.

82 See, for example, Ratzinger and Bertone, *Doctrinal Commentary*, § 9, n. 1: "It should be noted that the infallible teaching of the ordinary and universal Magisterium is not only set forth with an explicit declaration of a doctrine to be believed or held definitively, but it is also expressed by a doctrine implicitly contained in a practice of the Church's faith, derived from revelation, or, in any

suggests that the consensus of theologians is the only sure way of recognizing the infallible teaching of the ordinary and universal magisterium.[83]

Object: It is generally admitted that the infallible teaching of the ordinary and universal magisterium extends to the secondary object of the magisterium, as is indicated by the use of the broader phrase 'as definitively to be held' in place of the more restrictive 'to be believed as divinely revealed' in the above text of *Lumen gentium*,[84] although there is some question as to the precise theological qualification of the doctrine of the Church's infallibility with regard to the secondary object of the magisterium.[85] And there is even more disagreement as

---

case, necessary for eternal salvation, and attested to by the uninterrupted tradition: such an infallible teaching is thus objectively set forth by the whole episcopal body, understood in a diachronic and not necessarily synchronic sense. Furthermore, the intention of the ordinary and universal Magisterium to set forth a doctrine as definitive is not generally linked to technical formulation of particular solemnity; it is enough that is be clear from the tenor of the words used and from their context" (Denz. 5072). Cf. Dulles, *Magisterium*, 67: "The unanimity of the episcopal body is sometimes difficult to verify, but in many cases it is apparent from what the bishops regularly do or knowingly permit in preaching, liturgical prayer, catechesis, confessional practice, and the like."

83 See especially Sullivan, *Creative Fidelity*, 99–106. Gaillardetz would appear to agree: "In fact, based on the wording of the papal brief, it would seem legitimate to conclude that where there is no universal and constant consensus of Catholic theologians the infallibility of the teaching of the ordinary magisterium might itself be called into question" (Gaillardetz, *Witnesses to the Faith*, 28). For a critique of this thesis, see Lawrence J. Welch, "The Infallibility of the Ordinary Universal Magisterium: A Critique of Some Recent Observations," *Heythrop Journal* 39 (1998): 18–36, and the whole exchange that followed: Richard R. Gaillardetz, "The Ordinary Universal Magisterium: Unresolved Questions," *Theological Studies* 63 (2002): 447–71; Lawrence J. Welch, "Reply to Richard Gaillardetz on the Ordinary Universal Magisterium and to Francis Sullivan," *Theological Studies* 64 (2003): 598–609; Francis A. Sullivan, "Reply to Lawrence J. Welch," *Theological Studies* 64 (2003): 610–15. See also the exchange between Sullivan and Germain Grisez: John C. Ford and Germain Grisez, "Contraception and the Infallibility of the Ordinary Magisterium," *Theological Studies* 39 (1978): 258–312; Sullivan, *Magisterium*, 143–52; Germain Grisez, "The Ordinary Magisterium's Infallibility: A Reply to Some New Arguments," *Theological Studies* 55 (1994): 720–32; Francis A. Sullivan, "Reply to Germain Grisez," *Theological Studies* 55 (1994): 732–37; Germain Grisez, "Response to Francis Sullivan's Reply," *Theological Studies* 55 (1994): 737–38.

84 Dulles, however, appears to limit the ordinary and universal magisterium to the primary object when he introduces the concept as follows: "The *ordinary* universal magisterium is engaged when the whole body of bishops, in hierarchical communion with the successor of Peter, is morally unanimous in teaching a certain doctrine as a matter of divine and Catholic faith, to be accepted by all as pertaining to the faith of the Church" (Dulles, *Magisterium*, 67).

85 Ratzinger and Bertone refer to this as a "Catholic doctrine" (Ratzinger and Bertone, *Doctrinal Commentary*, § 6); cf. CDF, *Mysterium Ecclesiae*, § 3: "According to Catholic doctrine, the infallibility of the Church's Magisterium extends not only to the deposit of faith but also to those

to just how far the secondary object itself extends, especially with regard to specific moral norms of the natural law. A common position among theologians in former times was that every matter of faith and morals is included at least in the secondary object as intrinsically connected to divine revelation, including the whole natural moral law.[86] But the position of many contemporary theologians is that, although the Church can teach authoritatively on all matters of faith and morals, which includes particular norms of the natural law, nevertheless her infallibility extends only as far as the secondary object of the magisterium, and this is restricted to those matters of faith and morals that are strictly necessary for the defense or exposition of divine revelation; and whereas particular norms of the natural law may be useful, the argument usually goes, they are not strictly necessary for this purpose.[87]

3.3 The (Merely) Ordinary Magisterium

How one describes the 'non-universal' ordinary magisterium depends very much on how one interprets the term 'ordinary and universal magisterium'; and, as we have seen, there is not unanimity on this point. If the ordinary and universal magisterium covers all the non-defining teaching of the college of bishops, then what remains is the ordinary teaching of individual bishops or groups of bishops and of the pope.[88] If, however, the ordinary and universal magisterium covers only the teaching of the bishops dispersed throughout the

---

matters without which that deposit cannot be rightly preserved and expounded" (Denz. 4536). Sullivan interprets it merely as the common opinion of theologians (Sullivan, *Magisterium*, 134); Dulles regards it as "theologically certain Catholic teaching" (Dulles, *Magisterium*, 74).

86 See, for example, Robert Bellarmine, *De summo pontifice* IV, 5; Joseph Kleutgen, *Die Theologie der Vorzeit vertheidigt*, vol. 1, 2nd ed. (Münster: Theissing, 1867), 146; Johann Baptist Franzelin, *Tractatus de divina traditione et scriptura* (Turin: Marietti, 1870), 110, 547–51. Contemporary defense of this position appears in John J. Reed, "Natural Law, Theology and the Church," *Theological Studies* 26 (1965): 55; Germain Grisez, "Infallibility and Specific Moral Norms: A Review Discussion," *The Thomist* 46 (1985): 248–87; Umberto Betti, "Considerazioni dottrinali," *Notitia* 25 (1989): 321–25.

87 This is the position taken by Francis A. Sullivan, "Some Observations on the New Formula for the Profession of Faith," *Gregorianum* 70 (1989): 552–54; "The Theologian's Ecclesial Vocation and the 1990 CDF Instruction," *Theological Studies* 52 (1991): 55–58; "The 'Secondary Object' of Infallibility," *Theological Studies* 54 (1993): 536–50. See also Sullivan, *Magisterium*, 136–52, wherein the author provides a long list of theologians who concur with him in the opinion that the Church is unable to teach infallibly with regard to specific moral norms apart from any that have been formally revealed. Some of the more prominent names include Hans Küng, Charles Curran, Josef Fuchs, John Boyle, Joseph Komonchak, Karl Rahner, and Gustave Thils.

88 This is how Gaillardetz divides the subject in *Teaching with Authority*, 163–84.

world, then the ordinary teaching of ecumenical councils will have to be included here.[89] And finally, if the ordinary and universal magisterium is exercised only in the infallible (definitive) teaching of the bishops dispersed throughout the world, then we have in this section to treat all the 'non-definitive' teaching of the pope and the bishops, whether gathered in council or dispersed.[90] I will follow what I take to be the more common approach in treating, under the heading of 'ordinary magisterium', the authoritative but 'non-definitive' teaching of the Church.[91] As previously, we will divide our consideration according to the subject, act, and object of this merely authentic ('non-definitive') ordinary magisterium.

Subject: The merely authentic or 'non-definitive' ordinary magisterium of the Church can be exercised by the pope or by the college of bishops. The third paragraph of the concluding formula requires a "religious submission of will and intellect to the teachings that either the Roman pontiff or the college of bishops enunciate when they exercise their authentic magisterium, even if they do not intend to proclaim these teaching by a definitive act."[92] The doctrinal commentary of Ratzinger and Bertone refers to such teachings as "an authentic expression of the ordinary Magisterium of the Roman pontiff or of the college of bishops."[93] The Second Vatican Council asks for the same religious submission in the context of the authentic magisterium of the pope and bishops:

---

89 This is the approach taken by Sullivan in *Magisterium*, 153–73, wherein the third category of magisterial teaching presented (after the extraordinary magisterium and the ordinary and universal magisterium) is the "non-definitive exercise of papal and conciliar teaching authority," which he also refers to as the exercise of the 'ordinary magisterium' without qualification (Sullivan, *Magisterium*, 154).

90 This is the position implied by Sullivan in *Creative Fidelity*, 19, where he explicitly equates the 'ordinary' magisterium with the 'authentic', 'non-definitive', 'non-infallible', and 'non-irreformable' magisterium of the pope or bishops, whether gathered in council or not.

91 Cf. Gaillardetz, *Teaching with Authority*, 163, n. 7: "In common usage today, the ordinary magisterium (as distinguished from the ordinary and universal magisterium) now refers to that teaching of the bishops that is proposed authoritatively but that does not exclude the possibility of error."

92 CDF, *Professio fidei* (1998): "Insuper religioso voluntatis et intellectus obsequio doctrinis adhaero quas sive Romanus Pontifex sive Collegium episcoporum enuntiant cum Magisterium authenticum exercent etsi non definitivo actu easdem proclamare intendant" (Denz. 5070).

93 Ratzinger and Bertone, *Doctrinal Commentary*, § 10: "Nihilominus tamen tales institutiones Magisterium ordinarium Romani Pontificis seu Collegii episcopalis authentice significant ideoque *obsequium religiosum voluntatis et intellectus* postulant" (Denz. 5072). Italics in the original.

In matters of faith and morals, the bishops speak in the name of Christ, and the faithful are to accept their teaching and adhere to it with a religious assent. This religious submission of mind and will must be shown in a special way to the authentic Magisterium of the Roman pontiff, even when he is not speaking *ex cathedra*; that is, it must be shown in such a way that his supreme Magisterium is acknowledged with reverence and that the judgments made by him are sincerely adhered to, according to his manifest mind and will. His mind and will in the matter may be principally known either from the character of the documents, from his frequent repetition of the same doctrine, or from his manner of speaking.[94]

The precise nature of this 'religious submission' has been a subject of much discussion,[95] but most authors conclude that it does leave room for some kind of legitimate dissent (or at least non-assent) from this kind of authoritative but 'non-definitive' teaching.[96]

From the text cited above, it appears that the ordinary ('non-definitive') magisterium of the pope includes every act of official papal teaching regarding matters of faith or morals that falls short of being an *ex cathedra* definition. The most commonly cited examples of this kind of teaching are papal encyclical letters.[97] The ordinary conciliar magisterium is generally understood along the same lines as the ordinary papal magisterium: the teaching of an ecumenical council is ordinary wherever its teaches falls short of being a solemn definition;

---

94 Vatican II, *Lumen gentium*, § 25 "fideles autem in sui Episcopi sententiam de fide et moribus nomine Christi prolatam concurrere, eique religioso animi obsequio adhaerere debent. Hoc vero religiosum voluntatis et intellectus obsequium singulari ratione praestandum est Romani Pontificis authentico magisterio etiam cum non ex cathedra loquitur; ita nempe ut magisterium euis supremum reverenter agnoscatur, et sententiis ab eo prolatis sincere adhaereatur, iuxta mentem et voluntatem manifestatam ipsius, quae se prodit praecipue sive indole documentorum, sive ex frequenti propositione euisdem doctrinae, sive ex dicendi ratione" (Denz. 4149).

95 John Boyle has made a useful study of the historical development of the concept of *obsequium mentis et voluntatis* in Boyle, *Church Teaching Authority*, 63–78.

96 What is asked for, according to Sullivan's reading, is a genuine internal assent that precludes the probability although not the possibility of error (Sullivan, *Magisterium*, 158–73; *Creative Fidelity*, 23–27). See also Gaillardetz, *Teaching with Authority*, 263–71; *By What Authority?*, 124–33; Dulles, *Magisterium*, 91–99. The "problem of dissent" in the Church is discussed at some length by the CDF in *Donum veritatis*, but the document does acknowledge some room at least for theologians to "raise questions regarding the timeliness, the form, or even the contents of magisterial interventions" (CDF, *Donum veritatis*, § 24; Denz. 4878).

97 This should not be taken to mean that it is impossible for an infallible definition to appear in a papal encyclical letter, but only that most of the teaching typical of papal encyclicals is not presented in such a definitive manner.

it is authoritative, but not infallible; and it requires the same religious submission of will and intellect.[98]

Act: The teaching of the 'ordinary magisterium' of a pope or an ecumenical council is found in any act of teaching that falls short of being a definition. Sullivan refers to this as the 'non-definitive exercise' of the papal or conciliar magisterium.[99] According to Ratzinger and Bertone, such teaching is characteristically presented "as true or at least as sure" *(tamquam vera aut saltem tamquam certa)*.[100] But does the act of the ordinary magisterium also include the proposition of doctrine 'as definitively to be held' *(tamquam definitive tenenda)*? This is a question that has already arisen in another connection: that is, whether a pope or an ecumenical council is able to propose a doctrine not only as 'true' or 'sure' but even as 'definitively to be held' without defining it, or whether such a proposition would simply be a definition *ipso facto*.

According to the position outlined by Ratzinger, which cannot but have considerable influence in theological circles due to his eminent position first as Cardinal Prefect of the Congregation for the Doctrine of the Faith and then later as Pope Benedict XVI, there is indeed a distinction between the act of defining a doctrine and the act of proposing a doctrine as definitively to be held, even with regard to the teaching of popes and ecumenical councils. This follows from the restriction of the extraordinary magisterium to 'new acts of dogmatization'. And it leads in turn to the conclusion that the proposition of a doctrine 'as definitively to be held' by a 'non-definitive' act is infallible if proceeding from the ordinary and universal magisterium of the bishops dispersed throughout the world, whereas the very same would be merely authoritative if proposed by the pope or by an ecumenical council.

---

98 The explanation of the Theological Commission at Vatican II regarding the theological qualification of its own teaching parallels the aforementioned text of *Lumen gentium*, § 25. It reads: "In view of conciliar practice and the pastoral purpose of the present Council, this sacred Synod defines matters of faith or morals as binding on the Church only when the Synod itself openly declares so. Other matters which the sacred Synod proposes as the doctrine of the supreme teaching authority of the Church, each and every member of the faithful is obliged to accept and embrace according to the mind of the sacred Synod itself, which becomes known either from the subject matter or from the language employed, according to the norms of theological interpretation" (Walter M. Abbott, ed., *The Documents of Vatican II* [Chicago: Association Press, 1966], 98; Latin text in AS III/8, 10).

99 See Sullivan, *Magisterium*, 153–73.

100 Ratzinger and Bertone, *Doctrinal Commentary*, § 10: "Ad hoc comma pertinet *omnis institutio de fide et de re morali tamquam vera aut saltem tamquam certa exhibita, licet iudicio sollemni non definita nec a Magisterio ordinario et univerali tamquam definita proposita*" (Denz. 5072). Italics in the original.

This then leads us back to the problem with which we began: although from the point of view of positive theology it would indeed be hard to establish the infallibility of an ordinary papal magisterium or of an ordinary conciliar magisterium (neither is explicitly affirmed in any document of the Church), it is nevertheless just as hard to see from a theoretical point of view why the proposition of a doctrine as definitively to be held by a non-defining act of the bishops dispersed throughout the world should be infallible when the same proposition of a doctrine with the same note (as definitively to be held) and in the same manner (by a non-defining act) by the pope or even by the bishops gathered in ecumenical council is not infallible. The former seems to imply a renewal of Gallicanism that goes well beyond the equality that Vatican II sought to establish between papal primacy (emphasized at Vatican I) and episcopal collegiality (emphasized at Vatican II); and the latter seems to make the physical geographical location of the bishops decisive for the degree of authority of their teaching, which would seem to be a new and strange kind of anticonciliarism. The ability to overcome this difficulty must be one of the principal requirements for a satisfactory conception of the distinction between the ordinary and extraordinary magisterium.

Object: It is generally admitted that the object of the 'non-definitive' ordinary magisterium extends to the entire field of faith and morals, including the whole of the natural moral law.[101] According to Ratzinger and Bertone, the object of the ordinary authentic magisterium includes "all those teachings on faith and morals [...] set forth in order to arrive at a deeper understanding of revelation or to recall the conformity of a teaching with the truths of faith or, lastly, to warn against ideas incompatible with these truths or against dangerous opinions that can lead to error."[102] From the viewpoint of those who hold that there are matters of faith or morals not sufficiently required for the defense or exposition of divine revelation and therefore not contained in the secondary object of the magisterium, these matters would constitute a tertiary object of the magisterium, to which the 'non-definitive' ordinary magisterium alone

---

101 Cf. CDF, *Donum veritatis*, § 16; Pope Paul VI, Encyclical Letter *Humanae vitae* (25 Jul. 1968), § 4.

102 Ratzinger and Bertone, *Doctrinal Commentary*, § 10: "Ad hoc comma pertinet *omnis institutio de fide et de re morali tamquam vera aut saltem tamquam certa exhibita, licet iudicio sollemni non definita nec a Magisterio ordinario et univerali tamquam definita proposita [...]*. Proponuntur quidem ad altiorem revelationis intelligentiam obtinendam vel ad confirmitatem alicuius doctrinae cum veritate fidei revocandam, vel tandem ad vigilantiam contra notiones ab iisdem veritatibus abhorrentes vel contra sententiae periculosas atque in errores inducentes excitandam" (Denz. 5072); cf. CDF, *Donum veritatis*, §§ 23–24.

extends.[103] For those who hold that the Church's infallibility extends as far as her teaching authority extends, and that all matters of faith and morals are contained either directly or indirectly in the deposit of faith, there would be no new and unique object of the 'non-definitive' ordinary magisterium.

4. The Purpose, Division, and Thesis of This Work

The purpose of this work is to make some contribution toward a clearer conception of the meaning of the terminology of ordinary and extraordinary magisterium in order to facilitate a more consistent use of the same. The principal means by which I hope to accomplish this is by a careful relection of the principal documents of the Church that either use this terminology or touch upon the basic concepts involved in light of the original conception of the ordinary and extraordinary magisterium found in the works of the nineteenth century Jesuit theologian Joseph Kleutgen.

I begin in the first part of the work by returning to the origins of the terminology of ordinary and extraordinary exercises of the magisterium in Kleutgen's treatise on the rule of faith. The importance of Kleutgen's work with respect to this question can hardly be overstated. His first introduction of the terms stands in the immediate background of the papal letter *Tuas libenter* in which this terminology was first introduced into official ecclesiastical parlance. The second edition of his work enlarges upon the first with the benefit of having seen the concept and terminology implicitly approved by papal usage; shortly thereafter, the term 'ordinary magisterium' was permanently enshrined in Catholic theology through the dogmatic constitution *Dei Filius* of the First Vatican Council – a constitution that Kleutgen himself helped to compose as a theological advisor at the council.

Kleutgen's understanding of the distinction differs in several important respects from contemporary conceptions. For him, the distinction between the Church gathered in council and the Church dispersed throughout the world does not hold the key to the distinction between the ordinary and extraordinary magisterium (as per Boyle), nor does the distinction between extrinsically solemn and non-solemn teaching (as per Fenton), nor between defining and non-defining teaching (as per Sullivan), nor again between traditional and innovative teaching (as per Ratzinger and Bertone). Rather, it is primarily based on the distinction between the explicitly documented teaching of the Church

---

103 Dulles appears to interpret it in this way (Dulles, *Magisterium*, 86).

(whether of pope or bishops, whether gathered in council or dispersed throughout the world) and the implicit or undocumented teaching of the Church – that is, the teaching of the Church *not* found in the documents of the hierarchical magisterium, but rather in Scripture, in the liturgy, in the fathers and doctors of the Church, in the consensus of the faithful, etc.

Though there are many points of agreement between Kleutgen's original conception and more contemporary ones, the differences have profound implications. The main parts of our consideration of Kleutgen's work will cover first, the extraordinary magisterium; secondly, the ordinary magisterium; thirdly, his conception of the nature of the distinction between them; and fourthly, the division between dogmatic and non-dogmatic teaching of the Church.

Part two will then consider the initial adoption of Kleutgen's terminology in the documents of the Church during the pontificate of Pius IX. These are the three foundational texts of the magisterium with respect to our topic. The apostolic letter *Tuas libenter* (1863) of Pope Pius IX and the dogmatic constitution *Dei Filius* (1870) of Vatican I introduce and permanently enshrine the term 'ordinary magisterium'. The dogmatic constitution *Pastor Aeternus* (1870) of Vatican I treats of the papal exercise of the extraordinary magisterium, although without using that term. All of these texts reveal a remarkable agreement with Kleutgen's understanding of the ordinary and extraordinary magisterium, and together they constitute the strongest argument for interpreting the distinction in light of Kleutgen's work.

Tuas libenter makes two principal points, both of which are also emphasized by Kleutgen: firstly, that divine faith is due not only to explicitly defined dogmas, but also to the undefined dogmas taught by the ordinary magisterium; and secondly, that submission is due not only to dogma but also to Catholic doctrine. The conciliar discussion and official explanation of the text of *Dei Filius* show that the intended context of the council's teaching (the rule of faith) and its intended target (dogmatic minimalism) are the same as in Kleutgen's work; the intended meaning of the term 'ordinary magisterium' is also clarified (by addition of the term 'universal') as referring to the magisterium of the whole Church dispersed throughout the world (as opposed to the magisterium exercised by the pope). Likewise, Bishop Gasser's official explanation of the intended sense of the definition of papal infallibility in *Pastor Aeternus* reveals three principal points about the extraordinary magisterium, each of which again agrees with Kleutgen: firstly, that the proper act of the extraordinary magisterium is the act of definition; secondly, that the exercise of the extraordinary magisterium is not limited to the definition of doctrine that is *de fide credenda* but extends to definitions *de fide tenenda* as well; and thirdly, that the exercise of the extraordinary magisterium is not limited to the settling of questions previously open to legitimate dispute.

The third and final part of the work then examines some of the more important developments of and departures from Kleutgen's conception and terminology that occurred in the period after the First Vatican Council up to and including the Second Vatican Council. One such departure was the idea of an infallible papal exercise of the ordinary magisterium that developed in the late nineteenth and early twentieth centuries. Although proposed and defended in various forms by various authors, we will confine our treatment of this idea to its origins in the writings of the French theologian J.-M.-A. Vacant, whose 1887 study on the ordinary magisterium proved to be highly influential for later theologians, and to its partial adoption in the encyclical letter *Humani generis* (1950) of Pope Pius XII. This adoption is partial rather than complete inasmuch as the letter does refer to a papal exercise of the ordinary magisterium but without attributing to it infallibility.

A second departure from Kleutgen's way of understanding the distinction between the ordinary and extraordinary magisterium lies in the idea that arose, apparently out of the writings of the French theologian Louis Billot, of a restriction of the extraordinary magisterium to the creation of new doctrinal obligations. In a well-known text often cited in support of the infallibility of the ordinary papal magisterium, Billot contrasts the 'new doctrinal judgments' that qualify as definitions in the strict sense with the kind of doctrinal instruction about matters in the preaching of the Church that is typically found in papal encyclical letters. And though Billot does not make it an explicit condition for the exercise of the extraordinary magisterium that the question defined must be one previously open to legitimate dispute, later authors do. Two later documents of the magisterium are especially relevant to this question. The encyclical letter *Mortalium animos* (1928) of Pope Pius XI contains the fullest treatment of the uses of the extraordinary magisterium. The apostolic constitution *Munificentissimus Deus* (1950) of Pope Pius XII contains an instructive consideration of the interplay between the extraordinary magisterium and the ordinary universal magisterium of the Church.

Finally, a third departure from the path marked out by Kleutgen can be seen in the deliberate choice of the Second Vatican Council to avoid the terminology of 'ordinary magisterium' and 'extraordinary magisterium' entirely. Whereas early drafts of the dogmatic constitution *Lumen gentium* (1964) contained such language, it was eliminated from the text in favor of a distinction between a (merely) authentic magisterium and the infallible magisterium of the Church, the latter of which is divided between the definitive teaching of the pope and of the college of bishops, whether gathered in council or dispersed throughout the world. While the teaching of *Lumen gentium* remains in substantial agreement with the basic positions defended by Kleutgen and in substantial continuity with the teaching of Vatican I, it is my contention that the terminological shift found therein represents a significant step forward – not yet sufficiently realized – toward a clearer conception of the various functions of the magisterium.

My hope throughout the work is to be able to show that the terminology of ordinary and extraordinary magisterium is best understood in light of Kleutgen's original conception; that the ambiguity inherent in this terminology led to its being applied over the course of time to two separate (but related) distinctions in two different (but related) contexts; and that this ambiguity can be resolved in a way that satisfactorily explains the apparent inequality between the infallibility of the 'ordinary magisterium' of the bishops dispersed throughout the world and the lack of strict infallibility of the 'ordinary magisterium' of popes and ecumenical councils without falling into a kind of semi-Gallicanism or anti-conciliarism.

Finally, I will close by suggesting that the conclusions reached in this work, if accepted, would have important implications for the theological evaluation of many important documents of the magisterium, including (and perhaps especially) the documents of Vatican II. And I will also propose what revisions I would consider useful in contemporary theological terminology regarding the magisterium in order to avoid unnecessary confusion.

PART I.

JOSEPH KLEUTGEN AND THE ORIGINS OF A TERMINOLOGY OF ORDINARY AND EXTRAORDINARY MAGISTERIUM

The use of the terms 'ordinary' and 'extraordinary' with regard to the magisterium appears to have originated with the Jesuit theologian Joseph Kleutgen in the middle of the nineteenth century.[1] Joseph Wilhelm Karl Kleutgen was born in 1811 at Dortmund in Westphalia. He studied philosophy at the University of Munich and theology at Münster and Paderborn. In order to avoid trouble with the Prussian government over military service, he changed his last name to Peters and obtained Swiss citizenship. He entered the Society of Jesus in 1834 at Brig, Switzerland, and was ordained to the priesthood in 1837. He taught ethics at Fribourg and then rhetoric at Brig before being called by his order to Rome in 1843.

It was during his time in Rome that Kleutgen published *Die Theologie der Vorzeit vertheidigt*, in which he introduces the terminology of an ordinary and an extraordinary exercise of the Church's magisterium. The work as a whole is a voluminous defense of scholastic theology against the modern theology of the nineteenth century, which consciously based itself on the methods of modern (post-Cartesian) philosophy. The first edition of this work was published at Münster in three volumes from 1853–1860; a second edition ("improved and much enlarged") was published in five volumes from 1867–1874.

Two noteworthy events occurred in between the publications of these two editions. In 1862 Kleutgen was suspended and banished from Rome on account of his connection with a scandal at the Benedictine Convent of St. Ambrose, where he served as a confessor.[2] And in 1863 the term 'ordinary magisterium' made its first appearance in a magisterial document, the apostolic letter *Tuas libenter* of Pope Pius IX to the Archbishop of Munich-Freising.

---

1   See Boyle, *Church Teaching Authority*, 30–42.
2   Relatively few details of this case were known until recent discoveries by Hubert Wolf in the archives of the Congregation for the Doctrine of the Faith, which were first made available to historians by Pope John Paul II. Wolf's publication of his findings revealed previously unimagined depths of scandalous activity amongst the nuns and their confessors, such that Kleutgen's previous reputation for sanctity has been cast very much into doubt. See Hubert Wolf, *Die Nonnen von Sant'Ambrogio. Eine wahre Geschichte* (Munich: Beck, 2013).

Kleutgen was recalled to Rome in time to serve as a theological advisor at the First Vatican Council (1869–1870), where he was instrumental in the drafting of the dogmatic constitution on the Catholic faith *Dei Filius*, in which the term 'ordinary magisterium' makes a prominent appearance. He was also a leading figure of the neo-scholastic revival and is widely believed to have been instrumental in the composition of *Aeterni Patris*, the 1879 encyclical letter of Pope Leo XIII on the restoration of Christian philosophy. His health declining, Kleutgen left Rome and died at Kaltern in the Southern Tyrol in 1883.

The volumes of Kleutgen's *Die Theologie der Vorzeit* together with the volumes of his subsequent work *Die Philosophie der Vorzeit* constitute a single project, the overarching aim of which was the vindication of the scholastic method in theology against the methods of modern (post-Cartesian) theology.[3] Just as Descartes represented a radical break in the history of philosophy, with his methodological doubt and his demand for absolute certainty, so the nineteenth century theology that used the methods of modern philosophy represented a radical break in the history of Catholic theology.

The Catholic theology of the nineteenth century German schools was divided into dogmatic theology, practical theology, and speculative theology, and in each of these areas Kleutgen found an outstanding representative of the methods of modern theology against whom he directed his critique. These were Georg Hermes (dogmatic theology),[4] Johann Baptist von Hirscher,[5] (practical theology), and Anton Günther (speculative theology).[6]

---

3 The understanding of Kleutgen's overarching neo-scholastic project that I present here is based largely on the research of Gerald A. McCool, *Nineteenth-Century Scholasticism: The Search for a Unitary Method* (New York: Fordham University Press, 1989), 167–215.

4 Hermes (1775–1831) was a priest and professor of theology at Bonn. In 1835, a few years after his death, his rationalistic system of theology was condemned by Pope Gregory XVI in the Brief *Dum acerbissimas* (26 Sep. 1835), Denz. 2738–40. Several of his works were also placed on the Index of Forbidden Books.

5 Hirscher (1788–1865), a contemporary of Kleutgen, was a priest and professor of theology at Tübingen and later at Freiburg in Breisgau. He was influential especially in the fields of morals and pastoral theology: his book on Christian morality ran through five editions, and his works on homiletics and catechetics were widely read as well. According to one biographer, "In the earlier editions some of the expressions and opinions of Hirscher, owing to the influence of the day, were deserving of censure; he corrected them by degrees and Kleutgen admits that the last editions are perfectly orthodox" (Georges Goyau, "Johann Baptist von Hirscher," in *The Catholic Encyclopedia*, vol. 7 [New York: Robert Appleton, 1910], 364).

6 Günther (1783–1863) was an Austrian priest, philosopher, and theologian, whose works were placed on the Index in 1857 and whose rationalism and other errors were condemned by Pope Pius IX in the Brief *Eximiam tuam* (15 Jun. 1857), Denz. 2828–31.

Gerald McCool describes the three-fold aim of Kleutgen's critique: "He had first to convince his readers that the German theologians simply did not know scholasticism and that the criticisms which they leveled against it were without historical foundation. An unwarranted prejudice against scholasticism was the basic reason for their unshakeable conviction that only their own method could cope with modern theological challenges."[7] Secondly, he wanted "to show that the modern theologians had failed to do justice to the demands of the Catholic faith in their theological exposition and defense of the Catholic mysteries and that the intrinsic deficiencies of their modern method accounted for their failure."[8] And finally, Kleutgen wanted "to show that, once it was properly understood, the scholastic method met the modern requirements for a rigorous scientific method while remaining free from the crippling deficiencies of post-Cartesian philosophy."[9]

The first part of *Die Theologie der Vorzeit* was organized as a series of comparisons of scholastic and modern theology on the major points of doctrine upon which they differed most sharply. These included the rule of faith, the divine essence, the Trinity, the freedom and purpose of creation, the supernatural order, grace, sin, original justice and original sin, the Redeemer and redemption. The second part of the work turned to the issue of theological method that was at the root of the divergence between scholastic and modern theology. Here Kleutgen discussed the history of Catholic theology, the use of philosophy in theology, the nature of faith and its place in theology, and the scientific character of scholastic theology, culminating in a "defense of its scientific unity, certainty, necessity, and completeness."[10]

Moreover, just as the root of the divergence on specific points of doctrine was rooted in a divergence of theological method, so the difference in theological method was rooted in an even more fundamental divergence of philosophical method, which could be traced back to Descartes. "Descartes' epistemology, his subjective starting point, his theory of certitude, his innatism, and his mathematical deductivism were the philosophical presuppositions on which modern philosophy was built."[11] The two volumes of *Die Philosophie der Vorzeit* were thus added in order to complete the project by a comparison of scholastic and post-Cartesian epistemology, metaphysics, and anthropology.

7   McCool, *Nineteenth-Century Scholasticism*, 171.
8   Ibid.
9   Ibid.
10 Ibid.
11 Ibid., 173.

The introduction of the terminology of ordinary and extraordinary magisterium occurs in the very first section of this massive project, in the opening treatise entitled *Von der Glaubensnorm* ('On the Rule of Faith').[12] The concept of a *regula fidei* was highly developed in the patristic age, going back as far as St. Irenaeus and Tertullian, but it finds its most famous expression in the rule of St. Vincent of Lérins: "In the Catholic Church all possible care must be taken to hold that faith which has been believed everywhere, always, and by all *(quod ubique, quod semper, quod ab omnibus creditum est)*."[13] Kleutgen defines it here as the highest principle by which to determine what the faithful are to believe as divinely revealed.[14] The principal target of his polemic here is Hirscher, although the views of Hermes, François Véron,[15] and (in the second edition) Philip Neri Chrismann are also considered.[16]

In the first edition, the treatise is divided into seven parts, which are as follows: (1) Essential and Non-Essential Points of Faith; (2) The Old Testament; (3) Judgments of the Church; (4) The Doctrine of the Church is not to be Sought in Her Judgments Alone; (5) Concept and Classification of Dogmas; (6) What Theologians Unanimously Declare as a Dogma is to be Regarded as Such; (7) Freedom of Thought and Teaching is not Restricted by Dogma Alone.[17]

The ordering of parts is dictated by the demands of the overall project. The headings are representative of what Kleutgen regards as the principal errors of modern theology with regard to the rule of faith rather than of the principal parts of a systematic exposition. This can be seen especially in that Kleutgen devotes an entire section of the work to a discussion of the Old Testament as a source of divine revelation without a corresponding treatment of the New

---

12 Joseph Kleutgen, *Die Theologie der Vorzeit vertheidigt*, vol. 1, 1st ed. (Münster: Theissing, 1853), 35–63; 2nd ed. (Münster: Theissing, 1867), 46–150. All translations are my own unless otherwise indicated.

13 St. Vincent of Lérins, *Commonitorium Primum*, § 2.

14 Kleutgen, *Die Theologie*, 1st ed., 35; 2nd ed., 46: "Unter Glaubensnorm versteht man den höchsten Grundsatz, nach welchem zu entscheiden ist, was zum Glauben der Kirche gehöre, und folglich von allen Katholiken als geoffenbarte Wahrheit angenommen und bekannt werden müsse."

15 Kleutgen refers to François Véron (1575–1649), a French Jesuit controversialist, by the Latin form of his name, 'Veronius'.

16 Chrismann (1751–1810) was a German Franciscan theologian. His main written work, *Regula Fidei Catholicae* (Lingg, 1792), was placed on the Index in 1869, two years after – and possibly on account of – the heavy criticism it received from Kleutgen in the work under consideration. See also the study of Johannes Beumer, "Die Regula Fidei Catholicae des Ph.N. Chrismann OFM und ihre Kritik durch J. Kleutgen SJ," *Franziskanische Studien* 46 (1964): 321–44.

17 For the complete text of this treatise on the rule of faith, transliterated into modern German typography, see Appendix A of this work.

Testament. He is responding here to Hirscher, who discusses Tradition and the New Testament as sources of revelation, but neglects the Old Testament, though Kleutgen admits that this may be mere oversight or deliberate short-hand on Hirscher's part, rather than a positive rejection of its authority.

The treatise is much lengthened in the second edition, from twenty-nine to one hundred and five pages. And it is more systematic in its organization. The whole treatise is now divided into two main chapters: (1) On the Word of God; and (2) On the Teaching of the Church. The chapter on the Word of God is then subdivided into two sections corresponding to the two traditional sources of revelation: (1.1) On the Holy Scriptures; and (1.2) On Tradition. The chapter on the teaching of the Church is subdivided into five sections: (2.1) On the Creeds and Judgments of the Church; (2.2) On the Ordinary Magisterium of the Church; (2.3) What the Theologians Unanimously Declare to be a Dogma is to be Regarded as Such; (2.4) On the Classification of Dogma; (2.5) On the Non-Dogmatic Teaching of the Church.[18]

The lack in the first edition of a distinct treatment of Sacred Tradition as a source of divine revelation has been supplied, and the treatment of Scripture has been expanded beyond a mere defense of the permanent authority of the Old Testament. One can also see that the term 'ordinary magisterium' now appears in the title of the section in which it is discussed. The section on the role of theologians bearing witness to the teaching of the ordinary magisterium has been moved to a more natural location following the section on the ordinary magisterium, whereas in the first edition these were separated by the section on the classification of dogma. The sections on the classification of dogma and on the non-dogmatic teaching of the Church are paired together at the end of the treatise rather than being separated by the section on the role of theologians. And finally, the discussion of a distinction between essential and non-essential points of faith, which was the topic of the first section in the first edition, has been subsumed here into a more fitting place within the section on the classification of dogma.

1.   The Extraordinary Judgments of the Church

In his treatise on the rule of faith, Kleutgen begins his consideration of the teaching of the Church with a section entitled *Entscheidungen der Kirche* ("Judgments of the Church"), which he will later identify as belonging to the

---

18   For the complete text of this chapter on the teaching of the Church, transliterated into modern German typography, see Appendix B of this work.

extraordinary magisterium. In the second edition the same discussion is placed under the title *Von den Bekenntnissen und Beschlüssen der Kirche* ("On the Creeds and Decisions of the Church").[19] As is already evident from these two headings, Kleutgen uses more than one term to refer to the characteristic exercise of the extraordinary magisterium. *'Entscheidung'* (judgment) and the verbal form *'entscheiden'* (to judge) are employed most frequently, followed by forms of *'Urtheile'* (judgment) and *'urtheilen'* (to judge). *'Beschluss'* (decision) and *'Erklärung'* (declaration) are also used, but less frequently. In Latin he regards the terms *'declaratio'* and *'definitio'* as equivalent, but chooses *'definitio'* for use within technical theological formulae. Thus, although I will usually use the term 'judgment', terms such as 'declaration', 'decision', 'determination', or 'definition' should be understood synonymously within the context of Kleutgen's terminology.

Throughout the entire treatise the principal question is always how to determine what a Catholic must believe. According to Kleutgen, the Catholic rule of faith is expressed in this formula: "To the faith belongs all that (and only that) which God has revealed (that is, what is contained in the written and orally transmitted word of God), and which is proposed as such by the Church for all to believe."[20] First and foremost, what must be believed is determined by divine revelation itself. For a Catholic, however, it is not divine revelation as privately interpreted that constitutes the rule of faith but rather divine revelation as authoritatively proposed by the Church. After treating of Scripture and Tradition as sources of divine revelation, the question at hand in Kleutgen's chapter on the Church is what suffices for this requisite proposition by the Church. There are first of all the Creeds, but these are not materially complete, for there have been dogmatic judgments made about doctrines which have not been added to the Creeds of the Church. The rule of faith, then, is determined not only by the Creeds but also by the judgments of the Church.

1.1 Judgments of the Church Gathered in Council

What constitutes a judgment of the Church? The first point that Kleutgen wants to make is that the judgments of the Church are not limited to those

19 Kleutgen, *Die Theologie*, 1st ed., 40–46; 2nd ed., 85–97.
20 Ibid., 1st ed., 46–47: "Alles das (und nur das) gehört zum Glauben, was Gott geoffenbart hat, (d. h. was in dem geschriebenen und mündlich überlieferten Worte Gottes enthalten ist), und als solches von der Kirche allen zu glauben vorgelegt wird." Cf. Ibid., 2nd ed., 98: "Gemäß dem oft erwähnten Grundsatz, in dem wir alle übereinstimmen, ist nur das katholische Glaubenslehre, was die Kirche als geoffenbarte Wahrheit allen zu glauben vorlegt."

imposed negatively by anathema, i.e. to the canons of the ecumenical councils. Such a limitation is "purely arbitrary," according to Kleutgen, who proposes instead this principle: "Whatever is proposed in the decrees of the councils in such a way that the intention of the fathers is unmistakably to declare before all Christendom what is the doctrine of the Church must certainly be accepted as a Catholic truth of faith."[21]

In the second edition, he defends this assertion at much greater length, contending that this restriction of the judgments of the Church to the canons of the ecumenical councils "is manifestly and entirely refuted both by the manner in which the decisions of the Church are composed as also by the explanations that accompany them."[22] With regard to the manner in which the judgments of the Church are formulated, Kleutgen points out that there are examples throughout Church history of conciliar judgments issued in positive as well as in negative forms. In some cases, it is true, councils have expressed the teaching of the Church only through the negative condemnation of errors, as at the Council of Trent in its decrees on original sin and on the sacraments,[23] at the Second Council of Constantinople against Origen,[24] and at the local synods of Milevum and Orange against the Pelagians.[25] But in other cases the councils have taken the opposite approach, expressing the teaching of the

---

21 Ibid., 1st ed., 41: "Aber diese Beschränkung ist eine rein willkürliche [...] Was immer also in den Decreten der Concilien so vorgetragen wird, daß die Absicht der Väter, was Lehre der Kirche sei, vor der ganzen Christenheit zu erklären, unverkennbar ist; das muß man gewiß als katholische Glaubenswahrheit annehmen."

22 Ibid., 2nd ed., 85: "Aber diese Beschränkung ist ganz gewiß rein willkürlich, und wird sowohl durch die Weise, in welcher die Beschlüsse der Kirche abgefaßt sind, als auch durch diesen beigefügte Erklärungen ganz offenbar widerlegt."

23 See the Council of Trent, Session V, *Decree on Original Sin* (17 Jun. 1546), Denz. 1510–16; Council of Trent, Session VII, *Decree on the Sacraments* (3 Mar. 1547), Denz. 1600–30.

24 It has long been a matter of debate whether the fifteen anathemas against Origen found in many older collections of the acts of the Second Ecumenical Council of Constantinople (553) were actually adopted by that council or whether they belong only to the acts of an earlier local council, the 543 Synod of Constantinople. The anathemas are not included in the collection *Decrees of the Ecumenical Councils*, ed. Norman P. Tanner (London: Sheed and Ward; Washington, D.C.: Georgetown University Press, 1990), which cites as justification the work of Franz Diekamp, *Die origenistischen Streitigkeiten im 6. Jahrhundert und das 5. allgemeine Konzil* (Münster: Aschendorff, 1899). The most recent edition of Denzinger includes nine anathemas against Origen from the 543 Synod of Constantinople that were later confirmed by Pope Vigilius (see Denz. 403–11).

25 The canons against the Pelagians often attributed to the Second Synod of Milevum (416) seem to belong instead to the Fifteenth (or Sixteenth) Synod of Carthage (418). See Denz. 222–30. For the canons against the Pelagians issued by the Second Synod of Orange (529), see Denz. 371–95.

Church only through positive declarations of the faith without any condemnations or with only a general condemnation of the opposing errors. As examples of this type, Kleutgen cites the famous Tome of Leo, which was received and adopted by the Council of Chalcedon,[26] the same Council of Chalcedon's definition of the union of two natures in Christ against the Nestorians and the Monophysites,[27] the Third Council of Constantinople's definition of the two wills in Christ against the Monothelites,[28] the decrees of the Council of Florence for union with the Greeks and the Armenians,[29] and the decree of the Council of Trent on Scripture and Tradition.[30] And in still further cases, the councils of the Church have combined the two modes of positive declaration and negative condemnation. This can be seen in the decrees of the Council of Vienne and the Fourth Lateran Council,[31] the decree of the Council of Florence for union with the Jacobites,[32] and especially in many of the decrees of the Council of Trent.

Since the question arises most frequently with regard to the decrees of Trent, Kleutgen offers a second argument drawn from these very decrees. First of all, he argues, the positive expositions of the faith found in the chapters of the decrees of Trent generally begin with the familiar formulas found in the definitions of many councils, such as 'this holy council declares', or 'teaches', or 'confesses', and such phrases recur frequently throughout the text; and then secondly, this positive exposition usually concludes with a statement explicitly obliging all Catholics to believe and firmly hold what has been set forth. Finally, the text itself also explains that the canons are given, not in order that the faithful might know what they are more strictly obliged to hold, but in order that they might know what they are to reject in addition to what they are to

---

26   Pope Leo I, Apostolic Letter to Bishop Flavian of Constantinople *Lectis dilectionis tuae* (13 Jun. 449), Denz. 290–95.

27   Council of Chalcedon, Session V, Definition of Faith *Sancta et magna* (22 Oct. 451), Denz. 300–303.

28   Council of Constantinople III, Session XVIII, Definition of Faith *Unigenitus Dei* (16 Sep. 681), Denz. 553–59.

29   Council of Florence, Session VI, Bull of Union with the Greeks *Laetentur caeli* (6 Jul. 1439), Denz. 1300–08; Council of Florence, Session VIII, Bull of Union with the Armenians *Exsultate Deo* (22 Nov. 1439), Denz. 1310–28.

30   Council of Trent, Session IV, *Decree on Scripture and Tradition* (8 Apr. 1546), Denz. 1501–1508.

31   For the decrees of the Council of Vienne (1311–1312), see Denz. 891–908; for the decrees of the Fourth Lateran Council (1215), see Denz. 800–20.

32   Council of Florence, Session XI, Bull of Union with the Copts and Ethiopians *Cantate Domino* (4 Feb. 1442), Denz. 1330–53.

accept.[33] "In the face of such explicit declarations," concludes Kleutgen, "it is hard to understand how one can claim that only the canons and not also the chapters of the Council of Trent have the force of ecclesiastical judgments."[34] Continuing in the same vein, he asks: "What then could still count as a defined doctrine of faith if not once more that which the Church openly and solemnly confesses as Catholic truth, and proposes as a doctrine contained in Scripture and Tradition to be believed by all who want to be saved?"[35] With this conclusion he returns to the same principle already expressed in the first edition of his treatise for the identification of dogmatic judgments or definitions:

> We may therefore express a general principle: whatever is presented in the decisions of the councils in such a way that the intention of the fathers is unmistakably to declare before all Christendom what is the revealed doctrine and faith of the Church; that must be acknowledged as a Catholic truth of faith.[36]

Here we have, then, the proper note of a dogmatic definition according to Kleutgen: the manifest intention to declare for the whole Church what belongs to the faith of the Church. And this can be realized in the positive teaching of ecumenical councils just as much as in their negative condemnations.[37]

---

33 As examples he cites the decrees on justification, on the holy Eucharist, on penance and extreme unction, and on the holy sacrifice of the Mass (see Denz. 1550, 1650, 1700, 1750).

34 Kleutgen, *Die Theologie*, 2nd ed., 87: "Wie man also bei solchen ausdrücklichen Erklärungen hat behaupten können, daß nur die *Canones* und nicht auch die *Capita* des tridentinischen Concils die Kraft kirchlicher Entscheidungen haben, ist kaum begreiflich."

35 Ibid., 2nd ed., 87–88: "Was könnte denn noch als entschiedener Glaubenssatz gelten, wenn nicht einmal mehr das, was die Kirche öffentlich und feierlich als katholische Wahrheit bekennt, und als in der Schrift und Tradition enthaltene Lehre allen, die selig werden wollen, zu glauben vorlegt?"

36 Ibid., 2nd ed., 88: "Wir dürfen demnach als allgemeinen Grundsatz aussprechen: Was immer in den Beschlüssen der Concilien so vorgetragen wird, daß die Absicht der Väter, was geoffenbarte Lehre und Glaube der Kirche sei, vor der ganzen Christenheit zu erklären, unverkennbar ist; das muß als katholische Glaubenswahrheit anerkannt werden."

37 At this point in the second edition of his treatise, Kleutgen adds another lengthy discussion, not found in the first edition, in response to a claim of Chrismann to the effect that those judgments of councils for which reasons are adduced only from the human sciences (and not from divine revelation) are not certain and infallible, thus requiring only human and not divine faith. Although Kleutgen admits that the reasons adduced in favor of a dogmatic definition should not be understood as also dogmatically defined (unless the Church declares that these reasons themselves are certainly contained in divine revelation), he still maintains that the definition itself must be accepted as certain and infallible regardless of the reasons given for it. Chrismann's approach represents an inversion of the proper order: we are not to decide whether a judgment

1.2 Judgments of the Church Dispersed throughout the World

The next step for Kleutgen is to counter the position of those who are willing to admit that the positive declarations of the ecumenical councils are to be counted as judgments of the Church along with their negative condemnations, but who still insist that no judgments of the Church are to be found outside of the teaching of ecumenical councils. Against this assertion, he poses the following rhetorical questions:

> But can they claim that the supreme power of judging in disputes of faith was given to the Church under the condition of a particular form of judgment? Or can they deny, without falling away from Catholicism, that the Church dispersed throughout the world *(Ecclesia per orbem dispersa)* is just as infallible as the Church gathered in council *(Ecclesia in concilio congregata)?*[38]

It should be noted here that, although Pope Pius IX later applies this phrase '*Ecclesia per orbem dispersa*' to the ordinary magisterium,[39] Kleutgen is not here distinguishing between the ordinary and the extraordinary magisterium, but rather between two ways in which the extraordinary magisterium itself is exercised. For this reason I cannot agree with the interpretation that equates Kleutgen's distinction between the ordinary and the extraordinary magisterium with this distinction between the Church gathered in council and the Church dispersed throughout the world.[40] Kleutgen is arguing that the Church is

---

of the Church is infallible on the basis of our own prior opinion of the contents of divine revelation, but to accept that something is contained in divine revelation on the basis of the Church's infallible judgment. See Kleutgen, *Die Theologie*, 2nd ed., 88–93.

38 Ibid., 1st ed., 41–42; 2nd ed., 93: "Aber können sie behaupten, daß die Vollmacht in Glaubensstreitigkeiten zu richten, der Kirche unter der Bedingung einer bestimmten Form des Gerichtes, ertheilt sei? oder ohne vom Katholicismus abzufallen, läugnen, daß die *Ecclesia per orbem dispersa* eben so unfehlbar ist, als die *Ecclesia in concilio congregata*?"

39 See Pope Pius IX, Apostolic Letter to the Archbishop of Munich-Freising *Tuas libenter* (21 Dec. 1863): "For even if it were a matter of that submission which must be manifested by an act of divine faith, nevertheless, this would not have to be limited to those matters that have been defined by explicit decrees of ecumenical councils or by the Roman pontiffs and by this Apostolic See, but would also have to be extended to those matters transmitted as divinely revealed by the ordinary Magisterium of the whole Church dispersed throughout the world and, for that reason, held by the universal and constant consensus of Catholic theologians as belonging to the faith" (Denz. 2879).

40 See Boyle, *Church Teaching Authority*, 189–90, n. 30; Sullivan reads Kleutgen in the same way: "Kleutgen had distinguished between the extraordinary magisterium, exercised by ecumenical councils in defining doctrine, and the 'ordinary and perpetual' magisterium exercised by the popes with the bishops when they are dispersed around the world" (Sullivan, *Creative Fidelity*, 100).

capable of exercising the (extraordinary) power of judgment outside of as well as inside of ecumenical councils. He sees no reason why the same body cannot exercise the same authority whether gathered together or dispersed; and just as the Church gathered in council can exercise its office of judging in two ways – by declaring the doctrine of the Church in decrees and by excluding errors in canons – so the Church dispersed throughout the world has also two modes of exercising judgment: by the reception of the judgments of particular councils and by the reception of papal judgments.[41]

As examples of the former, Kleutgen cites the provincial synods held against the Pelagians (e.g. the Second Synod of Orange),[42] the decisions of which, he says, have the same authority as those of ecumenical councils, since they were received by the whole Church afterwards, even though they were not approved by the whole Church beforehand. And as for the acceptance of papal judgments, the consent of the bishops can be given beforehand, as was happening at that time in the activity leading up to the papal definition of the Immaculate Conception,[43] or it can be given afterwards, as happened most clearly and explicitly with the papal condemnations of Baius and the Jansenists.[44] Although writing before the definition of papal infallibility at the First Vatican Council, and although he admits that the infallibility of the pope is not an article of faith (despite thinking that there are very good reasons in its favor), Kleutgen still insists that papal judgments must be counted as infallible judgments of the Church (that is, of the whole college of bishops[45]) insofar as they have been

41 Here again, if Boyle's interpretation of Kleutgen on the nature of the distinction were correct it would imply that solemn papal definitions *ex cathedra* do not belong to the extraordinary magisterium; whereas Kleutgen is at pains here precisely to show that these are to be counted (at least once received by the Church) as judgments of the extraordinary magisterium of the Church in its state of dispersion throughout the world.

42 For the decisions of the Second Synod of Orange (529), confirmed by Pope Boniface II in 531, see Denz. 370–400.

43 The first edition of Kleutgen's treatise on the rule of faith was published in 1853, one year before the papal definition of the Immaculate Conception. But Pope Pius IX had already begun to seek out the opinions of all the bishops as to the definability of the doctrine, and Kleutgen regards their positive response as an antecedent reception on their part of the ensuing definition.

44 See especially Pope Pius V, Bull *Ex omnibus afflictionibus* (1 Oct. 1567), Denz. 1901–80; Pope Innocent X, Apostolic Constitution *Cum occasione* (31 May 1653), Denz. 2001–07; Pope Clement XI, Apostolic Constitution *Vineam Domini Sabaoth* (16 Jul. 1705), Denz. 2390; Apostolic Constitution *Unigenitus Dei Filius* (8 Sep. 1713), Denz. 2400–2502; Pope Pius VI, Apostolic Constitution *Auctorem fidei* (28 Aug. 1794), Denz. 2600–2700.

45 Immediately after distinguishing between the Church gathered in council and the Church dispersed throughout the world, Kleutgen remarks: "Wir verstehen hier unter Kirche den

received and accepted by the Church. So to move, as Hirscher, Chrismann, and Veronius do,[46] from the premise that the infallibility of the pope is not an article of faith, to the conclusion that papal judgments can be straightforwardly discounted as infallible judgments of the Church, overlooks something which is admitted even by the strictest Gallican: namely, that such judgments are irrevocable once they receive the consent of the Church.[47]

2. The Ordinary Teaching of the Church

Kleutgen introduces the concept of the ordinary magisterium of the Church in opposition to the dogmatic minimalism of theologians such as Hirscher who would allow nothing to restrict one's freedom of opinion other than the solemn judgments of the Church: "Everyone," says Hirscher, "is allowed, without in the least ceasing to be a faithful Catholic, to follow that view which seems right to him, in all questions in which the doctrine has not been fixed by the Church,"[48] and by 'fixed' it seems clear that he intends the Creeds and other judgments of the Church. But according to Kleutgen, this is simply an error spread abroad by modern theologians, especially in Germany. His own view can be seen already from the title of the relevant section in the first edition of his treatise: *Nicht in den Entscheidungen der Kirche allein ist ihr Lehrbegriff zu suchen* ("The Doctrine of the Church is not to be Sought in Her Judgments Alone"). In the second edition this title is changed to: *Von dem ordentlichen Lehramt der Kirche* ("On the Ordinary Magisterium of the Church").[49]

Lehrkörper, dem alle Gläubigen unterworfen sind, also die Bischöfe in Vereinigung mit ihrem Haupte, dem Papste" (Kleutgen, *Die Theologie*, 1st ed., 42; 2nd ed., 93).

46 Kleutgen believes that the aim of these theologians to restrict as much as possible the field of infallible teaching is motivated by the desire to ease the way for Protestants who might consider returning to the Church. Admirable as such a motive may be, he is concerned that such a strategy may end up betraying parts of the faith or deceiving someone into returning to the Church under false pretenses.

47 The First Vatican Council famously excluded the necessity of reception by the Church as a condition for papal infallibility with its '*ex sese*' clause.

48 Kleutgen, *Die Theologie*, 1st ed., 40; 2nd ed., 98: "Jeder, sagt er, darf, ohne im geringsten auf-zuhören, ein glaubenstreuer Katholik zu sein, in allen Fragen, über welche der Lehrbegriff nicht kirchlich fixirt ist, jener Ansicht folgen, welche ihm nun eben die richtige zu sein scheint." Kleutgen's citation is taken from Johann Baptist von Hirscher, *Die kirchlichen Zustände der Gegenwart* (Mainz: Kirchheim and Schott, 1849), 68.

49 Kleutgen, *Die Theologie*, 1st ed., 46–53; 2nd ed., 97–115.

In setting forth his own position against the dogmatic minimalism represented by Hirscher, Kleutgen appeals to the existence of a twofold exercise of the magisterium:

> The Church exercises a twofold magisterium *(ein doppeltes Lehramt)*. The one is ordinary and perpetual *(ordentliche und immerwährende)*, and it consists in precisely those ongoing apostolates, about which Hirscher speaks in the passage quoted. The other is extraordinary *(außerordentlich)*, used only at special times, namely when false teachers disturb the Church, and it is not simply a teaching office *(Lehramt)*, but also a judging office *(Richteramt)*. With the latter, the Church only fends off the hostile attacks upon the sanctuary she preserves; with the former, she opens to her children the rich treasure deposited with her.[50]

Here we have the first explicit use of the terms 'ordinary' and 'extraordinary' with regard to the exercise of the magisterium, together with some description of their characteristic differences. But although using an innovative terminology, Kleutgen is using a traditional concept in order to oppose what he views as a substantive theological innovation.[51]

---

50 Ibid., 1st ed., 47: "Es übt nämlich die Kirche ein doppeltes Lehramt aus. Das eine ist das ordentliche und immerwährende, und besteht in eben jenen fortdauernden Apostolate, von dem Hirscher an der angeführten Stelle redet. Das andere ist außerordentlich, wird nur zu besonderen Zeiten, wenn nämlich Irrlehrer die Kirche beunruhigen, geübt, und ist nicht schlichtweg Lehramt, sondern zugleich Richteramt. In diesem wehrt die Kirche nur die feindseligen Angriffe auf das Heiligthum, das sie bewahret, ab; in jenem öffnet sie ihren Kindern den reichen Schatz, der bei ihr hinterlegt ist." Cf. Ibid., 2nd ed., 98.

51 As Sullivan writes: "[T]he idea which it intended to express can hardly be described as new. It is essentially the same as what Augustine meant by '*securus iudicat orbis terrarum*,' and what St. Thomas meant by saying: 'It is impossible for the judgment of the universal church to err in matters that pertain to faith,' and what Bellarmine meant by saying: 'What all the bishops teach as of faith is necessarily true and of faith.' It is likewise what the bishops at Trent had in mind when they appealed to 'what the Catholic Church has always believed and taught' as the sure ground for their dogmatic decrees. It is absurd to think that the Tridentine dogmas were merely pious opinions until the council defined them" (Sullivan, *Creative Fidelity*, 100). Kleutgen himself, in support of the antiquity of his thesis, adds at this point in the second edition a reference to the famous dictum of St. Vincent of Lérins. See Kleutgen, *Die Theologie*, 2nd ed., 99: "Und fanden wir nicht schon beim h. Vincenz diese selbe Lehre? Welches war die erste Regel, die er vorschrieb? Wir sollen an dem festhalten, was in allen Sprengeln rings auf dem Erdkreis gelehrt und bekannt wird, und erst, wann die Uebereinstimmung in der Gegenwart zu fehlen scheint, werden wir angewiesen zu untersuchen, ob sich die Kirche in der Vergangenheit über den fraglichen Punkt ausgesprochen habe."

2.1 Authority of the Ordinary Magisterium

As a first proof of his thesis – namely, that the doctrine of the Church is not to be sought in her judgments alone – Kleutgen appeals to the practice of the ancient fathers of the Church, who did not hesitate to accuse Marcion, Arius, Nestorius, and many others of heresy even before their doctrines had been condemned by a judgment of the Church; in fact, it was precisely this vigorous opposition that eventually led to their formal condemnation. Yet how could this be if the faith of the Church were unable to be known with certitude apart from her judgments? The fathers of the Church who opposed Arius, for example, seem to have acted on the assumption that the co-equal divinity of Father and Son was sufficiently taught by the Church such that its denial constituted heresy even prior to its solemn definition at the First Council of Nicaea.[52] In Kleutgen's terminology, it was already infallibly proposed as a dogma of faith by the ordinary magisterium prior to its solemn definition by the extraordinary magisterium.

At this point Kleutgen anticipates two objections. Firstly, many fathers and eminent doctors have expressed the principle that one must await the judgment of the Church before accusing a dissenter of heresy, from which it would seem to follow that Catholics are not strictly obliged to believe anything beyond what is found in the judgments of the Church (as Hirscher holds). In response to this, Kleutgen argues that the principle applies only to cases of questions legitimately disputed by the faithful children of the Church. Although he cites no examples here, it is clear elsewhere that he regards the question of the infallibility of the pope at that time in exactly this light. One could perhaps think also of the sixteenth century controversy over grace or the medieval disagreements about the Immaculate Conception of Mary. In these cases, where the truth was not sufficiently clear in Scripture or Tradition, or where contrary opinions were defended by eminent figures on both sides, it was necessary to await the judgment of the Church before accusing one's opponents of heresy.

---

52 Kleutgen, *Die Theologie*, 1ˢᵗ ed., 47–48; 2ⁿᵈ ed., 99: "Die h. Väter weisen fast immer auf die in der Kirche allgemeine Lehre, als auf die sicherste Glaubensnorm hin. Wenn sie nun aber der Meinung gewesen wären, was allgemeine Lehre der Kirche sei, lasse sich nur aus den Entscheidungen der Kirche erkennen: wie hätte sie dann so manche Neuerer, als den Marcion, den Arius, den Nestorius ausdrücklich und öffentlich der Ketzerei beschuldigen, wie hätten auch die Hirten einzelner Sprengel sie aus demselben Grunde mit dem Bannfluche belegen können, ehe die Kirche über jene Irrlehrer irgend eine Entscheidung erlassen hatte? Und doch sind das Thatsachen, die um so weniger eines Beweises bedürfen, als sie im Laufe der folgenden Jahrhunderte sich oft wiederholt haben."

But according to Kleutgen not every dispute is of such a nature.[53] The co-equal divinity of the Father and the Son was not a matter legitimately disputed by faithful children of the Church but rather a matter wherein the truth could be adequately known from the general faith of the Church.

A second objection arises from the fact that even with regard to heretics such as Arius or Nestorius, the Church did in fact issue judgments, and one would not want to hold that these were unnecessary. Kleutgen's reply to this is to say that all the judgments of the Church were and are necessary, but not all in the same way. In some cases, indeed, the judgment of the Church may be necessary for ascertaining the true doctrine of the Church (as it is necessary in questions of legitimate dispute); but in other cases, its purpose may be simply the solemn proclamation of doctrine already known and believed. Or again, Kleutgen says: "the doctrine of the innovators, in the main, could be spotted with certainty as erroneous, and yet for the identification of many individual points the advice of the fathers was desirable."[54] Then he continues:

> Something can be generally taught and believed in the Church as revealed truth, and therefore the error opposing it can be rejected with certainty as heretical, and yet even about this matter a judgment of the Church can be necessary. Namely, when the innovators succeed in winning a following, and in seducing even a single prominent member of the Church or other men of great prestige, so that it is, especially for the multitude of the faithful, slightly doubtful upon which side the truth lies. And this, basically, is the true story of all heresies. So we do not deny that, in order to identify the doctrine of the faith with certainty, the explicit judgment of the Church is necessary in some questions and in some times; we deny only that it is necessary in all questions and at all times.[55]

53　Ibid., 1st ed., 48; 2nd ed., 99–100: "Wohl begegnet man, sowohl in den Schriften der hh. Väter, als der späteren Theologen Aeußerungen, die jenen, welche wir bekämpfen, ähnlich lauten: man müsse, bevor man Andersdenkende der Ketzerei bezüchtige, das Urtheil der Kirche abwarten. Aber sie reden dann von einzelnen Fragen, über welche auch unter den treuen und erleuchteten Kindern der Kirche Streit obwaltete; nie aber haben sie den allgemeinen Satz ausgestellt, jeder dürfe in allen Stücken, über welche die Kirche nicht entscheiden habe, der Ansicht folgen, die ihm nun eben die richtigste zu sein scheine."

54　Ibid., 1st ed., 48; 2nd ed., 100: "So konnte die Lehre der Neuerer der Hauptsache nach mit Sicherheit als irrig erkannt werden, und doch zur Feststellung mancher einzelnen Punkte die Berathung der Väter erwünschlich sein."

55　Ibid., 1st ed., 48–49; 2nd ed., 100: "Ja, es kann etwas in der Kirche als geoffenbarte Wahrheit allgemein gelehrt und geglaubt, und deßhalb der ihr entgegenstehende Irrthum mit Zuversicht als Ketzerei verworfen, und dennoch über eben diesen Gegenstand eine kirchliche Entscheidung nothwendig werden. Wenn es nämlich den Neuerern gelingt, einen Anhang zu gewinnen, und

In other words, the true doctrine of the Church – infallibly taught by the ordinary magisterium – may be adequately knowable in itself, but inadequately known to some members of the faithful. In such cases the judgment of the Church is not necessary for making the truth identifiable in itself, but it is necessary for making the truth known to those shaken by doubt.

For Kleutgen, therefore, unlike Ratzinger and Bertone, there appears to be no restriction of the extraordinary magisterium to innovative definitions – to definitions of questions open to legitimate dispute; nor does the necessity for an extraordinary judgment regarding a matter already taught infallibly by the ordinary magisterium arise from (or imply) any inadequacy in the teaching of the ordinary magisterium itself; rather, it arises from an inadequate grasp of its teaching on the part of some of the faithful. What must not be overlooked, from Kleutgen's point of view, is that the extraordinary magisterium – like the Church itself – is primarily pastoral in nature: solemn judgments that merely confirm or reaffirm existing Catholic doctrine are indeed unnecessary for the advance of theology; but they may be necessary for the salvation of souls.

Confirmation that Kleutgen recognizes the possibility of extraordinary definitions of doctrines already taught infallibly by the ordinary magisterium can also be seen in his treatment of the development of dogma. The question he sets out to address is how it is that one often hears it said both that the Church in her formal judgments declares what is a dogma rather than makes new dogmas, and at the same time that something is a dogma because of and since it was defined by the Church. The former way of speaking implies that the doctrine was already a dogma before it was declared or defined as such by the Church; the latter implies that it was not a dogma until its definition. In order to show how both ways of speaking can be justified, Kleutgen distinguishes between what is a dogma 'in itself' and what is a dogma 'for us'. In the first sense, every dogma is contained at least implicitly in revelation from the beginning and so the Church, speaking absolutely, makes no new dogmas but only hands on what she has received. In other words, everything that is now or ever will be a dogma has always been a dogma at least in itself. But in the second sense, says Kleutgen, "insofar as we often cannot know, without her

---

wohl gar einzelne Vorsteher der Kirche oder andere Männer von großem Ansehen zu verführen, so wird es, besonders für die Menge der Gläubigen, leicht zweifelhaft, auf welcher Seite die Wahrheit sei. Und im Grunde ist ja dies die wahre Geschichte aller Ketzereien. Wir läugnen also nicht, daß, um die Glaubenslehre mit gewißheit zu erkennen, die ausdrückliche Entscheidung der Kirche in manchen Fragen und in manchen Zeiten nöthig ist; wir läugnen nur, daß sie es in allen Fragen und immer sei."

explicit declarations, whether a doctrine belongs to the contents of that revelation, we also say with truth that this doctrine is a dogma (for us) first through the declaration of the Church."[56] However, there are also cases in which we are able to know with certainty that a doctrine belongs to the contents of revelation even without an explicit declaration of the Church on account of the fact that it is universally believed and taught in the Church as a divinely revealed truth. In such cases the doctrine is already a dogma for us even prior to its definition.

Regarding the stages of dogmatic development, therefore, certain doctrines may pass immediately from being dogmas only in themselves to being defined as dogmas for us, as happened (according to Kleutgen) with the doctrine of the Immaculate Conception. Other doctrines may have been dogmas both in themselves and for us long before their definition as dogmas at a later stage. Here Kleutgen mentions the Eucharist and the other sacraments, predestination, justification, and the necessity of good works for salvation. These dogmas, he says, "remained without the seal of a formal judgment of the Church until later centuries precisely because they were generally taught and believed."[57] Still other doctrines may already be dogmas for us without yet being defined, although fully capable of being defined (as that Christians have the duty to love their neighbor).

Returning to the distinction between the ordinary and the extraordinary magisterium, he concludes: "that proclamation of the Church *(propositio Ecclesiae)* by which a revealed truth becomes a dogma for us can occur in two ways: through the enactment of formal judgments and through the usual doctrinal presentation."[58] Then he adds:

> Very many truths obtain certainty for us by one way as by the other; some, however, only through the explicit judgment, others only through the concurring teaching. Although no truth can be declared as a dogma by the Church which is not contained in revelation; yet it does not follow that any truth was

---

56 Ibid., 2nd ed., 106: "Insofern wir aber oftmals ohne ihre ausdrückliche Erklärung nicht wissen können, ob eine Lehre zum Inhalt jener Offenbarung gehöre; sagen wir auch mit Wahrheit, daß diese Lehre (für uns) erst durch die Erklärung der Kirche zum Dogma wird."

57 Ibid., 2nd ed., 107: "Aber wie viele Wahrheiten von hoher Bedeutung blieben eben deßhalb, weil sie allgemein gelehrt und geglaubt wurden, bis in die späteren Jahrhunderte ohne dieses Siegel eines förmlichen Urtheils der Kirche."

58 Ibid., 2nd ed., 108: "Dem gemäß dürfen wir nun wiederholen, was wir im Anfange sagten: jene Verkündigung der Kirche *(propositio Ecclesiae)*, wodurch eine geoffenbarte Wahrheit für uns zum Dogma wird, kann in doppelter Weise stattfinden, durch die Erlassung förmlicher Entscheidungen und durch den gewöhnlichen Lehrvortrag."

universally preached and believed already before the declaration so explicitly and precisely as it is now expressed.[59]

Thus some dogmas are made known to us through the teaching of the ordinary magisterium alone (as that Christians have the duty to love their neighbor); others are made known to us only through the extraordinary magisterium (as the Immaculate Conception of Mary); while still others are made known to us through both the ordinary and the extraordinary magisterium (as that good works are necessary for salvation). This implies once again that for Kleutgen, whether or not a doctrine has or has not already been taught infallibly by the ordinary magisterium is irrelevant to determining whether or nor a doctrinal declaration constitutes a solemn definition. For there is nothing to exclude a doctrine being proposed infallibly both by the ordinary and by the extra-ordinary magisterium.

2.2 Identifying the Teaching of the Ordinary Magisterium

How to identify or verify the teaching of the ordinary and universal magisterium is much discussed as a problem without an easy solution. And it must be admitted that it is often quite difficult to know what the bishops in their state of dispersion throughout the world agree upon as a doctrine definitively to be held.[60] From Kleutgen's point of view, however, this problem is not felt so sharply, in large part because he is not focused exclusively (or even primarily) on the teaching activity of the individual bishops dispersed throughout the world; for him, the teaching of the ordinary magisterium may be seen in many places, but perhaps most clearly in Scripture itself. He writes:

> The Church, initially through her constant and ordinary magisterium *(beständiges und ordentliches Lehramt)*, subsequently also through explicit conciliar definitions, has declared that the Holy Scriptures, as we have them now, are the genuine and unadulterated word of God. Thus she has also proposed to us for belief their entire contents as the revelation of God. Therefore, as soon as we cannot doubt that something is contained in the Scriptures, so we are also certain that this is taught by the Church as revealed truth.[61]

59 Ibid., 2nd ed., 108–109: "Sehr viele Wahrheiten erhalten für uns auf dem einen wie auf dem andern Wege Gewißheit; einige jedoch nur durch das ausdrückliche Urtheil, andere nur durch die übereinstimmende Lehre. Obgleich nämlich keine Wahrheit von der Kirche für dogmatisch erklärt werden kann, welche nicht in der Offenbarung enthalten ist; so folgt doch nicht, daß jedwede schon vor der Erklärung so ausdrücklich und bestimmt, als diese sie ausspricht, allgemein verkündigt und geglaubt wurde."

60 Cf. Vatican II, *Lumen gentium*, § 25.

61 Kleutgen, *Die Theologie*, 1st ed., 49; 2nd ed., 100–101: "Die Kirche hat, anfangs durch jenes ihr

According to Kleutgen, then, every doctrine clearly contained in Scripture is also *ipso facto* proposed as divinely revealed by the ordinary magisterium of the Church without any need to consult the individual bishops dispersed throughout the world. Immediately the objection arises that this approach must lead to arbitrary interpretations of Scripture being treated as dogma. Kleutgen responds that some language must be sufficiently clear in itself if communication through words is to be possible at all; and if this were not possible, then it would also be impossible to understand the Church's judgments without additional clarifications *ad infinitum*, in which case there would be no end of doubt about every doctrine – a conclusion which he finds absurd. In addition, the assertion that some (though certainly not all) truths contained in Scripture are sufficiently clear to be recognized as dogmas of faith is not the same as the Protestant principle of private interpretation, according to Kleutgen, for "the Catholic bases himself, even in the explanation of these individual places, upon the authority of the Church, namely upon her teaching that can be adequately known even without explicit judgments."[62] And what is more, Catholics recognize a living teacher and judge who can correct erroneous interpretations of Scripture. As examples of dogmas sufficiently proposed by the ordinary magisterium directly in Scripture, Kleutgen cites the historical nature of the sacrifice of Abraham and the swallowing of Jonah by the whale, the genuinely miraculous character of the miracles worked by Jesus and the Apostles, and the fact that property and marriage are to be held as sacred in human communities.[63]

What about those passages in Scripture which are not sufficiently clear in themselves? Even here, says Kleutgen, the Council of Trent refers the faithful not to the explicit judgments of the Church but to "that meaning which she has always held and holds" and to "the unanimous interpretation of the fathers,"[64] or in other words, to the living tradition. Hirscher is right, says Kleutgen, to

---

beständiges und ordentliches Lehramt, in der Folge auch durch ausdrückliche Concilien-beschlüsse, die h. Schrift, wie wir sie jetzt haben, für das ächte und unverfälschte Wort Gottes erklärt. Sie hat uns also auch den ganzen Inhalt derselben als Offenbarung Gottes zu glauben vorgelegt. Sobald wir demnach nicht zweifeln können, daß etwas in der Schrift enthalten ist; so sind wir auch gewiß, daß dies von der Kirche als geoffenbarte Wahrheit gelehrt wird."

62   Ibid., 1ˢᵗ ed., 50; 2ⁿᵈ ed., 101: "Aber wir können nun überdies behaupten, daß sich der Katholik, auch bei Erklärung dieser einzelnen Stellen, auf das Ansehen seiner Kirche, nämlich auf ihre auch ohne ausdrückliche Entscheidung hinlänglich bekannte Lehre stützt."

63   The examples may seem eclectic in the twenty-first century, but these were issues beginning to be heavily disputed in the middle of the nineteenth century. The last is a direct attack on Marxist socialism, which Kleutgen claims is not only irrational but also heretical.

64   See the Council of Trent, *Decree on Scripture and Tradition*, Denz. 1507.

understand the tradition "as those oral teachings, that apostolate upon which the Church was founded, and which continues in her infallibly by the assistance of the Holy Spirit, authenticating the Holy Scriptures as the word of God, preserving them unadulterated, explaining them and supplementing them."[65] Then follows an important remark: "Thus it would be the same as that which we named above the constant and ordinary magisterium *(beständige und ordentliche Lehramt)* of the Church."[66] Here Kleutgen explicitly equates the ordinary magisterium of the Church with the living tradition of the Church. Thus to say that Catholics are bound not only by the extraordinary but also by the ordinary magisterium is, for him, the same as saying that Catholics are bound not only by the judgments of the Church, but also by the word of God itself handed down in the Church through her living tradition. In addition to the plain sense of Scripture, therefore, one ought to look for the teaching of the ordinary magisterium in the teaching of the fathers, who are the privileged witnesses of the Church's tradition, and then also in the writings of other prominent doctors and theologians, the monuments of antiquity (e.g. graves with their inscriptions, churches with their altars and paintings), the customs, laws, and liturgies of the Church, and the decrees of individual bishops and local councils.[67] In other words, the teaching of the ordinary magisterium is to be sought in all the traditional *loci theologici*; and the statements of individual bishops comes only at the end of the list.

---

65   Kleutgen, *Die Theologie*, 1st ed., 50: "Dies nun führt uns auf die andere Quelle der Offenbarungslehre, die Tradition. Hirscher faßt dieselbe, wie schon bemerkt worden ist, als jenes mündliche Lehrwort, als jenes Apostolat auf, durch das die Kirche gegründet wurde, und das, durch den Beistand des h. Geistes unfehlbar, in ihr fortdauert, die h. Schrift als Gottes Wort beglaubigend, unverfälscht bewahrend, erklärend und ergänzend."

66   Ibid., 1st ed., 51: "So wäre sie dasselbe, was wir oben das beständige und ordentliche Lehramt der Kirche nannten."

67   Ibid., 1st ed., 51; 2nd ed., 102: "Aber die Apostel haben die ganze Heilslehre mündlich verkündigt, und in ihren schriftlichen Aufsätzen nur das widerholt, was für den jedesmaligen besonderen Zweck nothwendig war. Diese mündliche, die ganze Offenbarung umfassende Unterweisung dauert aber in der Kirche bis ans Ende der Zeiten fort. Ist nun dies die Tradition, so hat man sie nicht ausschließlich in den Schriften der hh. Väter zu suchen. Nicht bloß aus diesen, sondern auch aus den übrigen in der Kirche geschätzten Schriftstellern, ferner aus den Denkmalen des christlichen Alterthums, den Gräbern mit ihren Inschriften und symbolischen Verzierungen, den Kirchen mit ihren Altären und ihren Gemälden, vor allen aber aus der Handlungsweise der Kirche, ihrem Verfahren in der Leitung der Gläubigen ihren Gebräuchen beim Gottesdienst, ihren liturgischen Büchern, und endlich aus den öffentlichen Erlassen ihrer Hirten, besonders wenn dieselben in Partikular-Synoden versammelt waren, läßt sich ohne Zweifel erkennen, was in der Kirche allgemein gelehrt und geglaubt werde."

Finally, because the investigation of all the sources of theology may often be long and arduous, Kleutgen also proposes "a short and easy path for recognizing, even in difficult cases, whether something belongs to the general faith of the Church."[68] This is the unanimous consensus of the most prestigious theologians. Kleutgen devotes an entire section of his treatise to this topic, which is entitled: *Was die Theologen einstimmig für ein Dogma erklären, ist als (ein) solches zu betrachten* ("What the Theologians Unanimously Declare as a Dogma is to be Regarded as Such").[69] His basic claim is that, when all the most prestigious theologians agree that something is a dogma of faith, even though not determined by a solemn judgment of the Church, they are witnesses of the fact that it belongs to the general faith of the Church. And although the theologians themselves are certainly not infallible, "their testimony, when it is so explicit and unanimous, must be held as unobjectionable."[70] Of course, which theologians are to be counted as among the most prestigious will be difficult to determine decisively.

Nevertheless, in the second edition Kleutgen provides some examples of dogmas which can be known from the unanimous testimony of theologians, including: "that God is infinite according to his nature, that he is all good and all knowing, and that he foresees the free actions of men; that he freely created and rules the world, that creatures not only receive their existence from him, but are also held in being by him, and that his providence extends over everything."[71] Or again: "that the fallen angels are all damned and that the departed while atoning for their sins in purgatory are nevertheless unable to grow in virtue and merit."[72] Are we unable to present all eight beatitudes with confidence as doctrines of our Lord or must we choose only those few which

---

68 Ibid., 1ˢᵗ ed., 57; 2ⁿᵈ ed., 116: "so wollen wir doch hier noch auf einen kurzen und sicheren Weg, auch in schwierigen Fällen zu erkennen, ob etwas zum allgemeinen Glauben der Kirche gehöre, aufmerksam machen."

69 Ibid., 1ˢᵗ ed., 57–59; 2ⁿᵈ ed., 115–25.

70 Ibid., 1ˢᵗ ed., 58; 2ⁿᵈ ed., 116: "Sie treten also als Zeugen dieser Thatsache auf, und es muß ihr Zeugniß, wenn es so ausdrücklich und einstimmig ist, als unverwerflich gelten."

71 Ibid., 2ⁿᵈ ed., 119–20: "Man frage ihn, ob er lehre, daß Gott seinem Wesen nach unendlich, daß er allgütig, allwissend ist, daß er auch die freien Handlungen der Menschen vorhersieht; daß er die Welt mit Freiheit erschaffen hat und regiert, daß die Geschöpfe durch ihn nicht nur das Dasein empfangen haben, sondern auch in demselben erhalten werden, daß seine Vorsehung sich über alles erstreckt."

72 Ibid., 2ⁿᵈ ed., 120: "Man frage ihn ferner, ob er lehre, daß die gefallenen Engel alle verdammt sind, daß die Abgeschiedenen zwar im Fegfeuer ihre Sünden büßen, an Tugend und Verdienst jedoch nicht mehr wachsen können."

are partially reflected in judgments of the Church? Can we not present the flight of our Lord to Egypt as part of the faith with as much confidence as his birth and crucifixion? May we not believe in the sending of the Holy Spirit on Pentecost and our Lord's prior promise of this sending just as we believe in the divinity of the Holy Spirit as divinely revealed truths?[73] According to Kleutgen, we can and indeed we must.

Thus from an investigation of Scripture and Tradition through all the classical *loci theologici*, but most easily and directly from the consensus of eminent theologians, Kleutgen is convinced that one can know with certainty what the Church teaches about some things (not all things), even apart from or prior to an explicit judgment of the Church. As further examples, he refers to purgatory and prayers for the dead, the invocation and veneration of the saints, the sacraments, and the spiritual power of the pope and bishops. Many centuries passed before these things were explicitly determined by a judgment of the Church. To him it would be incredible to say that the Catholic faithful of all those earlier centuries were not able to believe these things with full certainty on the basis of Scripture and Tradition transmitted by the living tradition of the Church. In the second edition he also stresses that many moral doctrines especially must be held on the basis of the ordinary magisterium, as there have not been many explicit judgments about morals. For example, that it is the duty of Christians to love their enemies, or that pride is a sin and humility a virtue, are doctrines that have never been defined yet are universally believed and taught as divinely revealed truths; he is convinced that we can thus be certain that these are moral dogmas proposed by the ordinary magisterium of the Church.

---

73 Ibid.: "Und um ihn mehr und mehr zu überzeugen, führe man ihn auf das Gebiet der Sittenlehre und erinnere ihn an jene Glaubenspunkte, deren wir oben erwähnten, ihn z.B. fragend, ob er Bedenken trage, alle acht Seligpreisungen als Lehren des Herrn zu wiederholen oder etwa aus ihnen jene zwei oder drei wähle, die sich – wenigstens einigermaßen – in kirchlichen Entscheidungen wiederfinden. Ebenso darf man ihn aufmerksam machen, daß er die Flucht nach Aegypten mit derselben Zuversicht wie die Geburt und die Kreuzigung Christi vortrage, daß er nicht bloß die Gottheit des h. Geistes, sondern auch seine wunderbare Sendung am Pfingsttage, und nicht bloß diese Sendung, sondern auch die vorhergegangene Verheißung derselben als geoffenbarte Wahrheiten verkündige. – Und wo würden wir ein Ende finden, wenn wir hier fortfahren wollten?"

3.   The Nature of the Distinction

How, then, does Kleutgen understand the precise nature of the distinction between the ordinary and the extraordinary magisterium? The terms 'solemn' and 'solemnly' *(feierlich)* appear occasionally in Kleutgen's descriptions of the extraordinary magisterium, but his usage seems to be simply descriptive. That is, there is no evidence that he intends to make a distinction, such as Fenton makes, between solemn and non-solemn judgments of the Church. Rather, he appears to regard the judgments of the Church as intrinsically solemn. The term that Kleutgen employs most frequently in describing the extraordinary judgments of the Church is 'explicit' or 'explicitly' *(ausdrücklich)*, and this is especially in those places where he wants to emphasize the contrast between the extraordinary and the ordinary magisterium. By contrast, then, the distinguishing feature of the ordinary magisterium of the Church would appear to lie in the implicitness or intangibility of its teaching. Note the constant emphasis in this catena of quotations:

> "We now come back to the aforementioned assertion of newer theologians, that nothing belongs to the Catholic faith other than what has been explicitly decided *(ausdrücklich entscheiden sei)* by the Church."[74]

> "So we do not deny that, in order to identify the doctrine of the faith with certainty, the explicit judgment *(ausdrückliche Entscheidung)* of the Church is necessary in some questions and in some times; we deny only that it is necessary in all questions and at all times."[75]

> "So now the question is whether we can attain this certainty only through the explicit judgments *(ausdrücklichen Entscheidungen)* of the Church."[76]

> "The Church initially through her constant and ordinary magisterium *(beständiges und ordentliches Lehramt)*, subsequently also through explicit conciliar decisions *(ausdrückliche Concilienbeschlüsse)*, has explained the Holy Scriptures, as we have them now, as the genuine and unadulterated word of God."[77]

---

74 Ibid., 1ˢᵗ ed., 46: "Wir kommen nun auf die oben erwähnte Behauptung neuerer Theologen, es gehöre nichts anders zum katholischen Glauben, als was von der Kirche ausdrücklich entscheiden sei, zurück."

75 Ibid., 49; 2ⁿᵈ ed., 100: "Wir läugnen also nicht, daß, um die Glaubenslehre mit gewißheit zu erkennen, die ausdrückliche Entscheidung der Kirche in manchen Fragen und in manchen Zeiten nöthig ist; wir läugnen nur, daß sie es in allen Fragen und immer sei."

76 Ibid., 1ˢᵗ ed., 49; 2ⁿᵈ ed., 100: "Nun fragt es sich also, ob wir nur durch die ausdrücklichen Entscheidungen der Kirche zu dieser Gewißheit gelangen können."

77 Ibid., 49; 2ⁿᵈ ed., 100–01: "Die Kirche hat, anfangs durch jenes ihr beständiges und ordentliches Lehramt, in der Folge auch durch ausdrückliche Concilienbeschlüsse, die h. Schrift, wie wir sie jetzt haben, für das ächte und unverfälschte Wort Gottes erklärt."

"Thus are we able to claim, without waiting for an explicit judgment *(ausdrückliche Entscheidung)* of the Church, but relying on the words of Holy Scripture, that most of the facts of salvation history and many doctrines about God, virtue, and vice, have been proposed as truths of faith."[78]

"But regarding this we can now say that the Catholic bases himself, even in the explanation of these individual places, upon the authority of the Church, namely upon her teaching that can be adequately known even without an explicit judgment *(ausdrückliche Entscheidung)*."[79]

"But now we also ask here whether from such sources, before an explicit judgment *(ausdrücklichen Entscheidung)* of the Church, one cannot arrive at full certainty regarding what the Catholic Church teaches."[80]

"If nothing belongs to the faith except what has been fixed by the Church through an explicit judgment *(ausdrückliche Entscheidung)*, then one could, in the Church, make no act of faith for many centuries about the most important mysteries and moral doctrines of the religion, and each one could follow the view which seemed to him to be the most correct."[81]

"As for the other definition introduced by Hermes, which recognizes nothing as a dogma other than what has been explicitly determined *(ausdrücklich entschieden ist)* by the Church; this must be referred to as thoroughly erroneous."[82]

The constant emphasis on the explicitness of the extraordinary magisterium indicates that there is something implicit about the teaching of the ordinary

---

78   Ibid., 1st ed., 49; 2nd ed., 101: "So können wir dagegen behaupten, daß man nichtsdestoweniger von jeher die meisten Thatsachen der h. Geschichte und gar viele Lehren über Gott, Tugend and Laster, ohne eine ausdrückliche Entscheidung der Kirche abzuwarten, auf die Worte der Schrift gestützt, als Glaubenswahrheiten vorgetragen hat."

79   Ibid., 1st ed., 50; 2nd ed., 101: "Aber wir können nun überdies behaupten, daß sich der Katholik, auch bei Erklärung dieser einzelnen Stellen, auf das Ansehen seiner Kirche, nämlich auf ihre auch ohne ausdrückliche Entscheidung hinlänglich bekannte Lehre stützt."

80   Ibid., 1st ed., 51; 2nd ed., 102: "Nun aber fragen wir auch hier, ob man aus solchen Quellen nicht vor jeder ausdrücklichen Entscheidung der Kirche zur vollen Gewißheit gelangen könne, was die katholische Kirche, wie über viele andere Wahrheiten, so besonders über jene Punkte, die mit dem christlichen und kirchlichen Leben in nächster Beziehung stehen, lehre."

81   Ibid., 1st ed., 52; 2nd ed., 103: "Wenn nichts zum Glauben gehört, als was die Kirche durch ausdrückliche Entscheidung festgesetzt hat; so konnte man in der Kirche viele Jahrhunderte lang über die wichtigsten Geheimnisse und Sittenlehren der Religion keinen Glaubensact erwecken, und jeder der Ansicht folgen, die ihm nun eben die richtigste zu sein schien."

82   Ibid., 1st ed., 56: "Was nun die andere, von Hermes angeführte Definition, welche nichts als Dogma anerkennt, als was von der Kirche ausdrücklich entschieden ist, betrifft; so mußte sie durchaus als irrthümlich bezeichnet werden."

magisterium; yet this does not mean that the teaching of the ordinary magisterium can be entirely implicit or hidden. For example, a doctrine taught by the ordinary magisterium may very well be explicit in Scripture; but it is thereby also implicitly taught by the Church inasmuch as the Church proposes Scripture as the word of God. A doctrine may be taught explicitly by each of the fathers of the Church; but in that it is taught by all of them, we are able to perceive that it is also taught implicitly by the Church of whose tradition they are privileged witnesses. Likewise, a doctrine may be explicitly in the minds and hearts of all the faithful, or explicitly on the lips of all the bishops; and as such it would be clear that it was taught by the Church; yet none of these individually would be an explicit declaration of the Church, since no one of them speaks for the whole Church.

Another illuminating term that Kleutgen uses twice in the second edition of his treatise in reference to the extraordinary judgments of the Church is '*Urkundlich*' (documented):

> Thus if one wants to restrict the teaching of the Church by which we know with certainty what is revealed to those propositions by which she has rejected false doctrines or expressed her faith in documents *(urkundlich)*, so one establishes thereby in the first place an assertion unheard of up until our times.[83]

And again:

> When the shepherds of the Church, whether through the instruction which they impart themselves or through that which is imparted by the clergy in their name and under their supervision, universally proclaim a doctrine as a doctrine of faith, we then have in this a factual testimony of the universal Church that this doctrine is contained in the transmitted revelation, in the *depositum fidei*, and it would be purely arbitrary to acknowledge this testimony as fully valid only under the condition that it is at the same time formulated by the Church in documents *(urkundlich)*.[84]

---

83 Ibid., 2nd ed., 98–99: "Wenn man also die Lehre der Kirche, durch welche wir, was geoffenbart ist, mit Gewißheit erkennen, auf jene Sätze beschränken will, durch welche sie Irrlehren verworfen oder ihren Glauben urkundlich ausgesprochen hat; so stellt man dadurch erstlich eine bis auf unsere Zeiten unerhörte Behauptung auf."

84 Ibid., 2nd ed., 106–07: "Wenn die Hirten der Kirche, sei es nun durch die Unterweisung, die sie selbst ertheilen, sei es durch jene, die in ihrem Namen und unter ihrer Aufsicht von der Geistlichkeit ertheilt wird, allgemein eine Lehre als Glaubenslehre verkündigen; so haben wir hierin ein thatsächliches Zeugniß der allgemeinen Kirche, daß diese Lehre in der ihr überlieferten Offenbarung, dem *depositum fidei*, enthalten ist, und es wäre reine Willkür dieses Zeugniß nur unter der Bedingung, daß es zugleich urkundlich von der Kirche formulirt sei, als vollgültig anerkennen wollen."

The judgments of the extraordinary magisterium are formulated in the documents of the Church; by contrast, the teaching of the ordinary magisterium is not formulated in documents of the Church. From this point of view, the contemporary way of speaking of a pope or an ecumenical council exercising the ordinary magisterium in their explicit teaching documents would be quite foreign.

4. Dogma and Doctrine

Since the context of Kleutgen's discussion of the ordinary and extraordinary magisterium is the rule of faith, he is concerned primarily with dogma as the object of the Church's teaching – that is, with the Church's proposition of doctrines as divinely revealed truths requiring the response of divine and Catholic faith. A section of his treatise is thus given over to the classification of dogmas, in the first edition under the title of *Begriff und Eintheilung der Dogmen* ("Notion and Classification of Dogmas") and in the second edition under the title of *Von der Eintheilung der Dogmen* ("On the Classification of Dogmas").[85] A final section treats afterwards of the non-dogmatic teaching of the Church, under the title: *Die Denk- und Lehrfreiheit ist nicht bloß durch das Dogma beschränkt* ("The Freedom of Thought and Teaching is not Restricted only by Dogma"); in the second edition this is simplified to: *Von den nicht dogmatischen Lehren der Kirche* ("On the Non-Dogmatic Teaching of the Church").[86] Kleutgen's treatment of these topics is worth closer examination both for the additional light that can be shed on his understanding of the ordinary and extraordinary magisterium through situating them more firmly in their proper context and for the approach that it provides to the question of a 'non-definitive' exercise of the magisterium of the Church.

4.1 Divisions of Dogma

In the second edition of his treatise, Kleutgen opens his section on the classification of dogmas by noting that they may be divided either according to their contents or according to their causes. According to their contents, that is according to the truths which they express, dogmas may be divided into necessary truths and historical truths (that is, into truths having their reason in the eternal nature of God and truths presupposing the free works of God and

---

85   Ibid., 1st ed., 53–57; 2nd ed., 125–31.
86   Ibid., 1st ed., 60–63; 2nd ed., 132–50.

men); or they may be divided into theoretical dogmas and practical dogmas (that is, those which express what we ought to believe and those which express what we ought to do).[87]

Of more interest for our question, is the division of dogmas according to their causes, which comprises the entirety of the corresponding section in the first edition. Dogma, in a general sense, refers to any truth revealed by God, that is, any truth contained in the written (Scripture) or unwritten (Tradition) word of God. Now some of these truths have not been specifically determined by the judgment of the Church whereas others have been so determined. Thus Hermes proposes to call the former 'revealed dogmas' *(dogmata revelata)*, in the sense of 'merely' revealed, and the latter 'declared or defined dogmas' *(dogmata declarata v. definita);* and then he draws the conclusion that one falls away from the Church only by rejecting a defined dogma, and not by rejecting a revealed dogma, since, he says, we cannot be certain that it is revealed without the definition of the Church.

Kleutgen accepts the distinction but not the conclusion. As we have seen, he is convinced that some (though not all) truths are so plainly contained in Scripture or Tradition that one can know with objective certainty that they are dogmas of the faith even if they have not been defined as such. Now it is also possible that one comes to a subjective certainty that something is contained in revelation (as Melchior Cano and others regarding the infallibility of the pope)[88] without being able to verify that it is universally believed and taught as such in the Church. If one cannot show both that it is revealed by God and that it is proposed as such by the Church to be believed by all the faithful, then one cannot put it forward as a dogma, even if one is subjectively certain that it is revealed, since both divine revelation and ecclesiastical proposition are required for dogma in the strict sense. Such a doctrine may be a dogma materially,

---

87 A further division is made between dogmas necessary to believe by an absolute necessity of means (without believing which salvation is impossible), dogmas necessary to believe by divine command (such that invincible ignorance may excuse one), and dogmas that are not necessary to believe. With regard to this last point, Kleutgen transposes a discussion from the first section of the first edition of the treatise, entitled *Wesentliche und unwesentliche Glaubenspunkte* (see Kleutgen, *Die Theologie*, 1st ed., 35–37), wherein he argues against Hirscher that, although not obliged to know every last dogma of the Church, one would still fall away from the Church if one knowingly rejects even one of the least important dogmas taught by the infallible magisterium, since this would imply a rejection of the formal principle of faith. The traditional maxim, he remarks, is not *libertas in parvis*, but *libertas in dubiis*.

88 Both editions of Kleutgen's treatise on the rule of faith were published before the definition of papal infallibility at the First Vatican Council in 1870.

insofar as it is revealed, but without the proposition of the Church it lacks the formal account of a dogma. Hence one may accept it with divine faith *(fides divina)* but not with divine and Catholic faith *(fides divina et catholica)*.

Nevertheless, Kleutgen is careful to note that this should not be taken to contradict what he said above about the possibility of knowing with full certitude what the Church teaches on certain matters even without a judgment of the Church. Thus his own proposal is to divide dogmas at first into 'revealed dogmas' *(dogmata revelata)* and 'proposed dogmas' *(dogmata proposita)*, the former of which are dogmas materially or in themselves and the latter of which are dogmas also formally or with regard to us; and then to divide the proposed dogmas into "doctrines of revelation which are proposed to be believed as such through the usual magisterium of the Church *(dogmata communi Ecclesiae magisterio proposita)*" and "doctrines of revelation which are proposed to be believed as such by the explicit judgment of the Church *(dogmata definitione Ecclesiae proposita)*."[89] Interestingly, these technical Latin formulations of the ordinary and extraordinary exercise of the magisterium disappear in the second edition, perhaps because in the interim Pope Pius IX chose to make use of the term *'magisterium ordinarium'* rather than *'magisterium communis'* which appears here.

In any case, with regard to the formal or proposed dogmas, both the defined and the undefined are fully and equally dogmas of faith; each requires the same response of divine and Catholic faith; the denial of either constitutes heresy. According to Kleutgen, anyone who denies, for example, that our Lord was transfigured on Mount Tabor or that the Apostle Paul journeyed to Rome, despite these things not having been the subject of explicit judgments by the Church, would be just as much a heretic as one who denies the divinity of Christ, whether before or after the First Council of Nicaea. With regards to dogma, therefore, Kleutgen makes a double distinction, resulting in a threefold division: (1) in the broad sense, any truth contained in revelation is at least materially a dogma (a dogma in itself); (2) in order to be counted as a dogma in the strict sense (a dogma with regard to us) such a truth must also be proposed as such by the Church; but this proposition can occur in two ways:

---

89 Kleutgen, *Die Theologie*, 1st ed., 56: "Hieraus folgt denn nun, daß man die Dogmen nicht, wie Hermes vorschlägt, in Offenbarungslehren und erklärte Offenbarungslehren *(dogmata revelata et dogmata definita)* eintheilen kann, sondern, wenn man nun ja eine derartige Eintheilung will, in Offenbarungslehren, die als solche durch das gewöhnliche Lehramt der Kirche, und in Offenbarungslehren, die durch ausdrückliche Entscheidung der Kirche zu glauben vorgelegt werden. *(Dogmata communi Ecclesiae magisterio et dogmata definitione Ecclesiae proposita.)*"

(2a) by an explicit definition of the Church or (2b) by the common magisterium of the Church. One could thus speak of material dogmas *(dogmata revelata)*, formal dogmas *(dogmata proposita)*, and defined dogmas *(dogmata definita)*.

4.2 The Non-Dogmatic Teaching of the Church

The final part of Kleutgen's treatise on the rule of faith takes up the non-dogmatic teaching of the Church. The focus again is how far freedom of opinion extends for Catholics with respect to the teaching of the Church. Are Catholics permitted to hold whichever view seems best to them in all matters beyond the realm of dogma? Kleutgen is not willing to concede even this. To differ from the Church in a non-dogmatic matter is not heresy, but neither is it permissible or blameless. He refers here to the various grades of censure less than heresy which the Church has used in order to condemn various propositions. These include such censures as *erroneous, proximate to heresy, suspect of heresy* or *smacking of heresy, evil sounding, offensive to pious ears, scandalous, seditious, temerarious,* etc.[90] The condemnation of a proposition as heretical implies that the contradictory proposition is a dogma of the faith; censures less than heresy do not imply this, but they do imply that the contradictory proposition is at least connected with divine revelation. According to Kleutgen, therefore, the doctrine of the Church in the strict sense refers to that which the Church proposes as divinely revealed; but the doctrine of the Church in a broader sense also includes "that which, although not explicitly revealed, is yet bound together with what is revealed, and is taught and held as true in the Church with great agreement."[91] In the second edition, he adds a clarifying note: "It is understood that this is valid only of doctrines which relate to the Christian religion and stand therefore in connection with the revealed truth."[92]

---

90 Such censures were first used at the Council of Constance against John Wycliffe and Jan Hus, and have been used by many popes since, although they have largely fallen out of use since the Second Vatican Council.

91 Kleutgen, *Die Theologie,* 1st ed., 61: "Zur Lehre der Kirche im weiteren Sinne aber auch das, was obgleich nicht ausdrücklich geoffenbart, doch mit dem Geoffenbarten in Verbindung steht, und in der Kirche mit großer Uebereinstimmung für wahr gehalten und gelehrt wird." Cf. Ibid., 2nd ed., 140–41: "Zur Lehre der Kirche im engeren Sinne gehört, was von der Kirche als geoffenbarte Wahrheit geglaubt und bekannt wird; zur Lehre der Kirche im weiteren Sinne, was in ihr außerdem, sei es nun in Folge der erwähnten Erlasse oder auch ohne dieselben mit Uebereinstimmung angenommen und vorgetragen wird."

92 Ibid., 2nd ed., 141: "Es versteht sich, daß dies nur von Lehren gilt, welche sich auf die christliche Religion beziehen, und daher mit der geoffenbarten Wahrheit in Verbindung stehen."

Thus the Church's authority to teach extends beyond what is directly revealed (the primary object of the magisterium) to all those things which are intrinsically connected to revelation (the secondary object of the magisterium). And this, according to Kleutgen, is on account of the purpose of revelation, which is not only to teach us certain truths, but to order all our thoughts and actions insofar as they touch upon religion. "But this cannot happen," he says, "without sometimes determining the revealed doctrines more closely, sometimes developing their contents, sometimes following their inferences, and judging many other things according to them."[93]

Two questions can be raised here about Kleutgen's understanding of the merely doctrinal or non-dogmatic teaching of the Church. Firstly, does such teaching emanate from the extraordinary magisterium, from the ordinary magisterium, from both, or from some third thing? And secondly, does the Church's infallibility extend to this non-dogmatic teaching? Richard Gaillardetz interprets Kleutgen as referring in this connection to the exercise of a non-infallible 'pastoral magisterium' that is distinct from both the ordinary and the extraordinary magisterium. According to Gaillardetz:

> The Jesuit did recognize that the church might teach a doctrine with a lesser note than that of infallibility. He wrote in this regard of a *Hirtenamt* which applied revealed truth to particular circumstances. This application of revealed doctrine was not, properly speaking, an exercise in the teaching of the ordinary or extraordinary magisterium but was a matter of applying what was already revealed. In point of fact, the relationship between the teaching office and the pastoral office was unclear in Kleutgen's thought, and indeed was often unclear in the writings of Pius IX. That is to say, nowhere does one find clear criteria for distinguishing that teaching which is an expression of its pastoral office and that which belongs to the Church's teaching and judging office *(Lehramt und Richteramt)*."[94]

This seems to me to rest on a misunderstanding of Kleutgen's words. I would suggest that the reason why one might find it hard to distinguish between the teaching of the pastoral office and that of the teaching office in Kleutgen's thought is because Kleutgen did not think they were distinct. It is true that Kleutgen only uses the term *Hirtenamt* (pastoral office) in the context of the non-dogmatic teaching of the Church, but what he says is only this:

93　Ibid., 1st ed., 63; 2nd ed., 143: "Dies kann aber nicht geschehen, ohne bald die geoffenbarten Lehren näher zu bestimmen, bald ihren Inhalt zu entwicklen, bald aus ihnen zu folgern, und viele andere Gegenstände nach ihnen zu beurtheilen."

94　Gaillardetz, *Witnesses to the Faith*, 27.

Now the Church is commissioned by the power of her pastoral office *(Hirtenamtes)* to spread abroad the divine light as far as is required for the purpose of revelation; so we are also directed to her as our teacher for this closer determination, development and application or use of the revealed truths for the sciences and for life.[95]

I believe that what Kleutgen is saying here is simply that the Church's teaching office itself is essentially pastoral, on account of which it extends as far as is required to achieve the pastoral purpose of divine revelation, which is human salvation. And thus the teaching office extends both to the truths contained in the deposit of faith (its primary object) and to those truths connected to divine revelation (its secondary object).

Moreover, in the first edition of his treatise, there is already some evidence that the Church's non-dogmatic teaching is not envisaged as a third mode of teaching alongside the ordinary and extraordinary exercises of the magisterium. On the one hand, he refers to the censures less than heresy employed by the Church as 'judgments' *(Urtheile)*,[96] which is consistent with his terminology for the exercise of the extraordinary magisterium; and on the other hand, he speaks of the obligation binding on Catholics to accept non-dogmatic doctrines which are "taught and held as true in the Church with great agreement,"[97] which corresponds to his usual way of speaking about the ordinary magisterium. Thus it would appear that the difference between the merely doctrinal teaching of the Church and her properly dogmatic teaching lies only in this, that she proposes something (whether by her ordinary or extraordinary magisterium) only as a truth connected with divine revelation or she proposes something (again, whether by her ordinary or extraordinary magisterium) as a divinely revealed truth.

---

95 Kleutgen, *Die Theologie*, 1st ed., 63; 2nd ed., 143: "Ist nun die Kirche kraft ihres Hirtenamtes bestellt, das göttliche Licht, so weit als es der Zweck der Offenbarung erfordert, zu verbreiten; so sind wir auch bei dieser näheren Bestimmung, Entwicklung und Anwendung oder Benutzung der geoffenbarten Wahrheiten für die Wissenschaften und das Leben auf sie als unsere Lehrerin hingewiesen."

96 Ibid., 1st ed., 61: "Die Kirche erkennt also jene Freiheit, die man in Anspruch nimmt, alles, was nicht häretisch ist, lehren zu dürfen, durchaus nicht an, und rechtfertigt durch jene ihre Urtheile die Unterscheidung, welche die Theologen zwischen Lehre der Kirche im strengen und im weitern Sinne des Wortes machen."

97 Ibid.: "Zur Lehre der Kirche im weitern Sinne aber auch das, was obgleich nicht ausdrücklich geoffenbart, doch mit dem Geoffenbarten in Verbindung steht, und in der Kirche mit großer Uebereinstimmung für wahr gehalten und gelehrt wird."

In the second edition, however, this is even more explicit. The section on the non-dogmatic teaching of the Church opens with these words:

> There is no doubt that the Church, exercising her ordinary magisterium *(ordentliches Lehramt)*, presents some truths that are not to be regarded as sentences of faith: for example, the Assumption of Mary and the perfect wisdom which was given to the human soul of Christ in the first moment of its existence. But not even all of the doctrines established by explicit decisions *(ausdrückliche Entscheidungen)* are declared by her as truths of faith.[98]

It seems clear that Kleutgen is referring here to non-dogmatic truths proposed by the ordinary and extraordinary magisterium of the Church. His reference to the Assumption of Mary as a non-dogmatic doctrine taught by the ordinary magisterium is an interesting example, as this has since been defined as a dogma of faith. At the time of his writing it was (according to Kleutgen) universally held and taught in the Church that the blessed Virgin was assumed body and soul into heaven, but although this was proposed as certainly true it was not proposed as divinely revealed. As examples of the merely doctrinal or non-dogmatic definitions of the extraordinary magisterium, Kleutgen goes on here to speak especially of all those condemnations that utilize censures below the grade of heresy.

A second problem with Gaillardetz's interpretation of Kleutgen's treatment of the non-dogmatic teaching of the Church lies in the implication that Kleutgen regarded this teaching as being less than infallible. In the first edition, it is true, Kleutgen nowhere asserts the infallibility of this kind of non-dogmatic teaching; but neither does he deny it. In the second edition, however, he discusses the matter at length, arguing quite clearly and explicitly for the infallibility of this non-dogmatic teaching of the Church. At first he asks whether we can be sure that a definite judgment about the falsity of a doctrine is intended in the various forms of censure less than heresy. Considering the various censures in turn, he concludes that a judgment of falsity is included in each censure employed by the Church, with the exception of the *propositio temeraria* (temerarious or rash proposition) and with the provision that the *propositio captioso* (captious or ambiguous proposition) is rejected as false not absolutely

---

98 Ibid., 2ⁿᵈ ed., 132: "Es unterliegt keinem Zweifel, daß die Kirche ihr ordentliches Lehramt übend, manche Wahrheiten vorträgt, welche nicht als Glaubenssätze zu betrachten sind: die Auferstehung z.B. und die Himmelfahrt Maria's, die vollkommene Weisheit, welche der menschlichen Seele Christi im ersten Augenblick ihres Daseins verliehen wurde. Aber auch nicht alle Lehren, welche sie durch ausdrückliche Entscheidungen feststellt, werden von ihr für Glaubenswahrheiten erklärt."

but only in the sense that the words usually have or in the sense intended by their author. From the fact that the judgments whereby the Church bans various doctrines with such censures are definitively pronounced by the highest teaching authority in the Church for the whole of Christendom, Kleutgen concludes that they must be infallible: "Just as it is certain that an opinion is heretical which is declared as heretical by such a judgment, so it is certain that those are erroneous, irksome, and false, which are designated as such in the same judgments."[99] One may see Kleutgen's position on the extension of infallibility to the secondary object of the magisterium most clearly in the words with which he concludes the entire treatise:

> Certainly it is true that the authority of the Church has its limits: for it has been given to teach about the religion of Jesus Christ and not about everything that is able to be known by man. But what follows from this, if not that the Church teaches nothing and judges about nothing other than what belongs to the religion of Jesus Christ? If she were not given the infallible insight as to how far her authority to teach reached then her infallibility itself would obviously be void and meaningless. Thus whenever the bearer of this supreme authority judges about a doctrine in such a way that he obliges the whole of Christendom to submit to his judgment, then is the certainty of this judgment beyond doubt.[100]

Apparently, then, for Kleutgen, the dogmatic and the merely doctrinal teaching of the Church are equally infallible, just as the ordinary and the extraordinary magisterium are equally infallible. But inasmuch as these appear to be exhaustive divisions of the magisterium, this raises the question of whether he would recognize any exercise of the magisterium that would be anything less than infallible.

---

99 Ibid., 2nd ed., 143: "So gewiß es ist, daß eine Meinung häretisch ist, welche durch ein solches Urtheil für häretisch erklärt wird; so gewiß ist es, daß jene irrthumlich, ärgerlich, falsch sind, welche in demselben als solche bezeichnet werden."

100 Ibid., 2nd ed., 150: "Wohl ist es wahr, daß die Lehrgewalt der Kirche ihre Gränzen hat: denn sie ist gegeben, um die Religion Jesu Christi und nicht um alles, was von Menschen gewußt werden kann, zu lehren. Aber was folgt daraus, wenn nicht, daß die Kirche nichts lehrt, und über nichts entscheidet, als was zur Religion Jesu Christi gehört? Wäre ihr nicht die unfehlbare Einsicht verliehen, wie weit sich ihre Vollmacht zu lehren erstrecke, dann wäre ja offenbar die Unfehlbarkeit selbst nichtig und bedeutungslos. Wenn immer also der Träger dieser Vollmacht über eine Lehre so urtheilt, daß er die ganze Christenheit verpflichtet, seinem Urtheil sich zu unterwerfen, so ist auch die Untrüglichkeit dieses Urtheils außer Zweifel."

4.3 A Non-Definitive Magisterium?

Does Kleutgen recognize a 'non-definitive' exercise of the magisterium? Although he says very little about teaching of this kind, and although he insists on the infallibility of both the ordinary and the extraordinary magisterium both with regard to the dogmatic and non-dogmatic teaching of the Church, a crucial point to be kept in mind is that the context of his consideration is the rule of faith; it is not directly or principally the operations of the magisterium as such. His distinction between an ordinary and an extraordinary exercise of the magisterium is a division of the ways in which the certain and infallible teaching of the Church is communicated to the faithful. It is not intended as a global division of the operations of the magisterium as such, but as a division within the modes of operation of the infallible magisterium alone. Hence, if Kleutgen would recognize a 'non-definitive' exercise of the magisterium by popes and ecumenical councils, and at least one remark may be taken to indicate that he would,[101] it seems quite possible that he would not classify this as belonging either to the ordinary or to the extraordinary magisterium of the Church, but refer it instead to a more basic distinction between the infallible magisterium of the Church and a merely authoritative or 'non-definitive' magisterium of the pope and bishops. The non-definitive teaching of the pope or of an ecumenical council (such as appears most voluminously in papal encyclical letters and in the documents of Vatican II) can not easily be made to fit into either of his categories: although explicit, it does not belong to the extraordinary magisterium inasmuch as it falls short of being definitive; but because it is explicit and documented neither does it seem to belong to the ordinary magisterium.

Thus I do not agree with the assessment of John Boyle where, near the end of his study of the origins of the concept of an ordinary magisterium, he concludes:

---

101 He refers at one point to the commonly recognized distinction between the definition itself and the things which are added in a text in order to ground or illuminate the actual object of the declaration. See Kleutgen, *Die Theologie*, 1st ed., 41: "Was immer also in den Decreten der Concilien so vorgetragen wird, daß die Absicht der Väter, was Lehre der Kirche sei, vor der ganzen Christenheit zu erklären, unverkennbar ist; das muß man gewiß als katholische Glaubenswahrheit annehmen; obwohl deßhalb nicht auch alles, was zur Begründung oder Beleuchtung derselben zuweilen hinzugefügt wird." Cf. Ibid., 2nd ed., 88: "Was immer in den Beschlüssen der Concilien so vorgetragen wird, daß die Absicht der Väter, was geoffenbarte Lehre und Glaube der Kirche sei, vor der ganzen Christenheit zu erklären, unverkennbar ist; das muß als katholische Glaubenswahrheit anerkannt werden: — obwohl deßhalb nicht auch alles, was zur Begründung oder Beleuchtung der Lehre, welche eigentlicher Gegenstand der Erklärung ist, hinzugefügt wird."

The infallibility of the Church promised it by Christ is thus extended at least in principle to virtually every act and utterance of the ordinary magisterium. And – at least by implication – the doctrinal statements and condemnations of popes, bishops and curial offices acting under papal authority are all included under the notion of an ordinary magisterium."[102]

Firstly, it seems to me that the doctrinal statements and condemnations of popes (and perhaps of the sacred congregations of the Holy See, although this is a point which Kleutgen does not discuss) would actually be included in his way of thinking under the extraordinary magisterium as judgments of the Church – at least if they are given in a definitive manner to the universal Church. But even if Boyle has in mind only those statements that fall short of being definitive judgments, and even if Kleutgen would view such non-definitive yet explicit teaching as belonging to the ordinary magisterium (which is not at all clear from my reading of his texts), it would still be hard to see why infallibility would be attributed, even in principle, to any of the individual acts and utterances of the ordinary magisterium. When Kleutgen speaks of the infallibility of the ordinary magisterium he is speaking of the infallibility of the whole living tradition, or the infallible certainty one may have that a doctrine thus taught is true; he is not speaking of individually infallible acts of teaching such as occur in the extraordinary judgments of the Church. This is why, when speaking of the ordinary magisterium, it would seem better to me to speak in terms of the immutability of the doctrine rather than the infallibility of the act of teaching. For the truth of the doctrine is guaranteed in this case not by the fact that any single act of teaching is preserved from error but by the fact that they cannot all be false.

In any case, however, I believe that a schema such as the following more accurately represents the manner in which Kleutgen would divide the total operations of the magisterium:

1. Infallible Magisterium
    1.1 Ordinary Magisterium
    1.2 Extraordinary Magisterium
2. Merely Authentic Magisterium

This schema contrasts strongly with the way in which contemporary theologians tend to place the distinction between the extraordinary and the ordinary magisterium (understood in terms of 'defining' and 'non-defining'

---

102 Boyle, *Church Teaching Authority*, 38.

teaching) at the first level of division, with the distinction between infallible and merely authentic ('non-definitive') teaching at the second level, as follows:

1. Extraordinary Magisterium
2. Ordinary Magisterium
    2.1 Infallible Ordinary Magisterium
    2.2 Merely Authentic Ordinary Magisterium

The importance of this difference in the schematization of the operations of the magisterium will be seen more fully when we return to the question of the apparent inequality between pope and bishops in the exercise of the ordinary magisterium.

5.   Concluding Observations

5.1 Summary of Kleutgen's Theology of the Magisterium

According to Kleutgen, the Church exercises a twofold magisterium: ordinary and extraordinary. The extraordinary magisterium is the judging office *(Richteramt)* of the Church. It is exercised in the act of defining or declaring the doctrine of the Church. He makes no essential distinction in this regard between judgments, definitions, declarations, determinations, or decisions of the Church. These various terms are for him merely so many ways of expressing the definitive or irrevocable nature of the Church's judgments. The distinguishing feature of the extraordinary as compared to the ordinary magisterium lies in the explicitness of these judgments: they are visibly and tangibly enshrined in the public documents of the Church.

   In order for these extraordinary judgments to have binding authority on the universal Church, they must proceed from or at least be confirmed or received by the bearer or bearers of a universal authority. Thus, they may emanate from ecumenical councils, whose judgments are binding of themselves and immediately; from the popes, whose judgments are binding, if not of themselves and immediately (which is Kleutgen's opinion, later confirmed by Vatican I), then at least once they have been received by the Church; and finally, from local councils, whose judgments are not binding on the whole Church of themselves, but may become so if received as such by the universal Church.

   The judgments of the Church can be properly dogmatic, when a doctrine pertaining to faith or morals is declared or defined in an unambiguous way as a revealed truth to be believed as such by all the faithful. Or they may be merely doctrinal (non-dogmatic), as occurs when a doctrine pertaining to faith or morals is declared or defined as a certain truth to be held as such by all. But to say that a doctrinal definition is not dogmatic is not to say that it is any less definitive or infallible. Dogmatic and merely doctrinal definitions are equally infallible, which means in practice that they guarantee, in the former case, the fact that the doctrine defined is a truth contained directly in divine revelation, or in the latter case, that the doctrine defined is a truth at least connected to divine revelation. Thus the defined dogmas of the Church require the definitive assent of divine and Catholic faith, and their rejection constitutes heresy, while the defined doctrines of the Church require an equally definitive assent, but their rejection constitutes only error and not heresy, although this is still a blameworthy fault.

The characteristic note of judgment – that by which the extraordinary judgments of the Church can be recognized – is the manifest intention of declaring for the whole Church what the Church holds and teaches as certain truth. No particular form of words (e.g. *anathema sit or definimus)* is required. And although Kleutgen occasionally uses the word 'solemn' in describing the judgments of the Church, he gives no reason for thinking that he has in mind any kind of external solemnity (e.g. of language or circumstance) as necessarily characterizing such judgments, nor does he distinguish between solemn and non-solemn judgments: the term is used in a descriptive rather than a quali-fying sense (that is, the judgments of the Church are solemn in and of them-selves). The same could be said of his use of the term 'formal' as descriptive of the judgments of the Church and of the term 'extraordinary'. The way Kleutgen uses these terms, there are no ordinary or non-formal judgments of the Church; rather, all the judgments of the Church are of themselves solemn, formal, and extraordinary.

The ordinary magisterium is identified with the living tradition of the Church, the constant and perpetual process of handing down the faith received from the apostles. This teaching office *(Lehramt)* of the Church is described as the 'ordinary and perpetual' *(ordentlich und immerwährend)*, the 'constant and ordinary' *(beständig und ordentlich)*, and the 'usual' *(gewöhnlich)* magisterium of the Church, or in Latin the 'common magisterium' *(magisterium communis)* of the Church. The distinguishing feature of the ordinary magisterium, by con-trast with the extraordinary magisterium, lies in its intangibility – its teaching is something upon which one cannot directly put one's finger. The teaching of the ordinary magisterium is that teaching of the Church that is not formulated in the documents of the Church. The teaching of this father or of that father, of this bishop or that bishop, of this or that doctor, may indeed be tangible and explicit; but only through the unanimity of their teaching are we able to recognize the common teaching of the Church.

The ordinary magisterium is always exercised by the Church in her condition of being dispersed throughout the world for the simple reason that the teaching of an ecumenical council is always quite tangible and explicit. But the converse is not true: the exercise of the magisterium of the Church dispersed throughout the world need not always be ordinary. Kleutgen holds that the Church dispersed can also exercise the extraordinary magisterium. But although the ordinary magisterium is properly exercised by the bishops dispersed throughout the world, this does not mean that one looks only to their public statements in order to find what the ordinary magisterium teaches. Rather one looks to the whole living tradition of which they are the heirs and bearers: to Scripture first of all, and then to the fathers and doctors of the Church and other eminent ecclesiastical writers, to the monuments of antiquity, to the customs, laws, and liturgies of the Church, and only in the last place to the decrees of individual bishops and local councils; or, as a short and easy path, one may look immediately to the unanimous consensus of eminent Catholic theologians.

As with the definitions of the extraordinary magisterium, the teaching of the ordinary magisterium may be properly dogmatic or merely doctrinal, so that it would be heresy to reject a doctrine pertaining to faith or morals that is universally believed and taught in the Church as divinely revealed (that is, a dogma proposed by the ordinary magisterium) whereas it would not be heresy but would still be culpable error to reject a doctrine pertaining to faith or morals universally held and taught in the Church as certainly true. The key points in determining whether a doctrine is taught infallibly by the ordinary magisterium are the universality of the doctrine and the note with which it is held and taught. That is, it must be or at least have been held and taught in the whole Church, and not only in part of the Church; and it must be believed and taught precisely as a divinely revealed truth (in order to be counted as a dogma of faith) or as a truth that is absolutely certain (in which case it is not a dogma, but still a definitive doctrine of the Church).

5.2 Assessment of Kleutgen's Contribution

It would be hard to overestimate the scale of Kleutgen's achievement. As McCool notes, "Joseph Kleutgen was the most profound and original thinker among the Jesuit neo-Thomists. He was also the most influential."[103] The same judgment holds true with regard to his theology of the magisterium and its operations. The originality of his thought can be seen in his reinterpretation of the living tradition of the Church as an exercise of the magisterium; and his novel terminology of a distinction between an ordinary and an extraordinary magisterium of the Church has passed into the common vocabulary of theology.

Kleutgen's introduction of the distinction between the ordinary and extraordinary magisterium was shaped by the needs of his overarching neo-scholastic project. His ultimate goal was to show that the method of modern (specifically, German) theology led to grave theological errors whereas the scholastic method could both meet the demands of a rigorous science (conceived in the Aristotelian sense) and also remain adequate to the demands of the Catholic faith. And the first error that he chose to target as an example of this was the dogmatic minimalism represented by Hirscher – the idea that Catholics are free to follow their own opinions in any matter not explicitly determined by a formal judgment of the Church. Such an idea is indeed at odds with the traditional belief and practice of the Church, as Kleutgen was at pains to demonstrate. However, Kleutgen was also committed to the neo-scholastic view of the magisterium of the Church as the proximate rule of faith (with Scripture and

---

103 McCool, *Nineteenth-Century Scholasticism*, 167. On the impact of Kleutgen's work, he writes: "*Die Theologie der Vorzeit* and *Die Philosophie der Vorzeit* made an enormous impression not only in Germany but in other European lands. Kleutgen's prodigious erudition enabled Catholic theologians, whose own knowledge of scholasticism was often sketchy, to become acquainted with the range of scholastic literature [...] Kleutgen manifested in his volumes that, while he knew German philosophy and theology thoroughly and accurately, the German theologians did not know scholasticism at all. In a land where accusations of 'scholastic obscurantism' were frequent that point went home. Furthermore, despite their vast historical erudition, Kleutgen's works presented a clear and coherent view of the whole of nineteenth-century theology. Kleutgen had the gift of lucid and organized exposition. He surveyed the major issues in nineteenth-century Catholic theology, found their common source in the controversy over grace and nature, and traced the roots of that controversy to the confusion in method introduced into Catholic theology by modern philosophy. Kleutgen was not interested in producing a *Summa Theologiae*. He was arguing for the scholastic position in nineteenth-century theology and he never forgot his purpose for a moment. His analyses were careful, his arguments cogent, his tone confident, irenic, and serene [...] In Kleutgen's works a powerful mind was arguing with almost overwhelming reasonableness for the course of action which the Holy See would take in the last three decades of the nineteenth century" (ibid., 175-76).

Tradition constituting the remote rule of faith).[104] Kleutgen was thus wary of asserting the authority of Scripture and Tradition apart from the explicit judgments of the magisterium without linking them in some way to the magisterium. To do so would leave him open to the charge of adopting the Protestant principle of private interpretation, whereby the authority of Scripture is unmediated by the Church, in place of the principle of ecclesiastical mediation of divine revelation. Hence the reinterpretation of the living tradition of the Church, by which Scripture and the oral tradition are perpetually handed down in the Church, as an exercise of the magisterium of the Church. Since Scripture itself is handed down in the Church as the inspired word of God, then any doctrine that is clearly and unambiguously taught in Scripture is also taught by the Church even if there has been no formal judgment proclaiming it as a doctrine of the Church. Kleutgen thus introduced the terminology of an ordinary magisterium in order to allow him to tread the narrow path between dogmatic minimalism and private interpretation.

Another central aspect of Kleutgen's overarching project was his critique of the Cartesianism at the heart of modern philosophy. Philosophy after Descartes, and even more so after Kant, had a decided epistemological bent. Epistemology had effectively displaced metaphysics as the 'first philosophy', and modern epistemology is preoccupied to a great extent with the question of certitude. In the nineteenth century, philosophy and the natural sciences alike were at great pains to establish the certainty of their conclusions. And the modern theology of which Kleutgen is critical was anxious to model itself upon this pattern. Kleutgen, meanwhile, although critical of the whole project of modern philosophy, was also concerned to show that scholastic theology could answer its demand for certitude. Hence his strong emphasis on the infallibility of the Church as the ground for the certitude of a theology based on faith rather than based on methodological doubt. One of the principal criticisms that Alasdair MacIntyre levels against Kleutgen was his failure to distinguish adequately between the thought of Aquinas himself and that of his commentators, especially Francisco Suarez, the great Jesuit Thomist whom Kleutgen follows closely. For the typically modern emphasis on epistemology was already present in Suarez's brand of Thomism. "Suarez, both in his preoccupations and in his methods, was already a distinctively modern thinker, perhaps more authenti-

---

104 This view later found expression in Pope Pius XII's Encyclical Letter *Humani generis* (1950), § 18: "This sacred office of teacher *(magisterium)* in matters of faith and morals must be the proximate and universal criterion of truth for all theologians" (Denz. 3884).

cally than Descartes the founder of modern philosophy."[105] And "it was no accident," MacIntyre later remarks, "that Descartes was taught by Jesuits influences by Suarez."[106] Commenting on the encyclical letter *Aeterni Patris* (1879), MacIntyre notes:

> Epistemological questions are nowhere adverted to. Yet those who responded to *Aeterni Patris* all too often followed Kleutgen in making epistemological concerns central to their Thomism. And in so doing they doomed Thomism to the fate of all philosophies which give priority to epistemological questions: the indefinite multiplication of disagreement. There are just too many alternative ways to begin.[107]

Kleutgen's emphasis on the infallibility of the Church as the ground of theological certitude is therefore partly due to the epistemological preoccupation of modern philosophy while at the same time serving as part of his critique of modern philosophy.

A third point worth addressing here is the difficulty that arises from the intrinsically binary nature of Kleutgen's distinction between an ordinary and extraordinary magisterium. Such a division of the magisterium does not appear to leave space for any other kind of magisterial teaching. Moreover, Kleutgen regarded both the ordinary and the extraordinary magisterium as infallible modes of teaching. He does not positively exclude a 'non-definitive' exercise of the magisterium; he simply fails to address it at all. Now this is understandable in view of the polemical rather than systematic nature of his work, but it nevertheless remains that an adequately developed theology of the magisterium requires a place for formal and explicit yet 'non-definitive' acts of teaching (such as is commonly found in papal encyclical letters), and this is made more difficult by the binary nature of Kleutgen's distinction.

Another difficulty that arises out of Kleutgen's understanding of the magisterium is the tension between his typically neo-scholastic identification of the magisterium with the hierarchy and his desire to include under the operations of the ordinary magisterium many other elements in the life of the Church. On the one hand, he is reacting against a complete identification of the teaching of the Church with the explicit teaching of the hierarchy, advocating instead a broader view that sees the teaching of the Church also in the consensus of the fathers and doctors, the consensus of the faithful, the liturgical

---

105 Alasdair MacIntyre, *Three Rival Versions of Moral Enquiry: Encyclopaedia, Genealogy, and Tradition* (Notre Dame, IN: University of Notre Dame Press, 1990), 73.
106 Ibid., 75.
107 Ibid.

laws and customs of the Church, and in many other places. But on the other hand, he wants to bring all of this under the heading of an ordinary magisterium that is still exercised by the hierarchy at least insofar as the pope and bishops act as supervisors of all the daily teaching carried on within the Church.

Questions to be kept in mind as we carry our investigation forward therefore include whether and to what extent the intended meaning of the terms ordinary and extraordinary magisterium as they are used in the documents of the Church and in later theology correspond to Kleutgen's conception of the magisterium; how to integrate an understanding of 'non-definitive' magisterial teaching within or alongside the now established distinction between the ordinary and extraordinary magisterium; and how to describe the relationship between the hierarchical and non-hierarchical aspects of the ordinary magisterium.

PART II.

POPE PIUS IX AND VATICAN I: THE INITIAL ADOPTION OF KLEUTGEN'S TERMINOLOGY IN THE DOCUMENTS OF THE CHURCH

The aim of this part of the work is to examine the meaning and use of the terminology of ordinary and extraordinary magisterium in the foundational texts of the magisterium that first take up this distinction in order to see how far the original conception of Kleutgen is either confirmed or modified therein. The texts treated in this part of the work are the apostolic letter *Tuas libenter* (1863) of Pope Pius IX, which laid the foundation for the adoption of Kleutgen's terminology into the official language of the Church, followed by the documents of the First Vatican Council: the dogmatic constitutions *Dei Filius* (1870) and *Pastor Aeternus* (1870).

Key questions to be considered include the proper context of the distinction; the intended target of the distinction; the subject of the ordinary magisterium; the act of the extraordinary magisterium; the extension of both to the secondary object of the magisterium; and the question of whether or not the exercise of the extraordinary magisterium is restricted to the settling of legitimate controversies. In all of these questions, these three texts show clear and consistent agreement with Kleutgen's understanding of the meaning and use of the terms 'ordinary magisterium' and 'extraordinary magisterium', from which I conclude that there is a strong argument in favor of understanding this terminology today in light of Kleutgen's original conception.

1. The Apostolic Letter *Tuas libenter* (1863)

In 1863, ten years after Kleutgen published the first edition of his treatise on the rule of faith, the term 'ordinary magisterium' appeared for the first time in a public document of the Church: the apostolic letter *Tuas libenter* of Pope Pius IX to the Archbishop of Munich-Freising. This letter was occasioned by the Munich Congress of 1863 and it shows, both in substance and in terminology, a remarkable agreement with Kleutgen's treatise, especially with regard to the two principal points urged therein: (1) that divine faith is due not only to explicitly defined dogmas but also to the dogmas taught by the ordinary magisterium of the Church dispersed throughout the world; and (2) that submission is due not only to divinely revealed truths but also to Catholic doctrine in matters connected with divine revelation.[1]

1.1 The Munich Congress of 1863

The Munich Congress of 1863 was a gathering of German Catholic scholars organized by Ignaz von Döllinger,[2] among others, which caused concern in some quarters due to its having been organized without the knowledge or approval of any bishop and on account of the views held by some of the theologians involved on the nature of the relationship between ecclesiastical authority and the necessary independence of scientific research. John Boyle's research into the Vatican archives has uncovered the correspondence and notes on the subject from Archbishop Gonella (the papal nuncio in Munich), Cardinal Antonelli (the Secretary of State in Rome), and Cardinal von Reisach (a curial prefect who had formerly been Archbishop of Munich), in which they were discussing the need for a papal intervention in response to this event before it even happened. The event did eventually receive the approbation of the Archbishop of Munich, Gregor von Scherr, who even celebrated the opening Mass at the congress. And the position of the congress on the question of the relationship between Church authority and science was summed up in three propositions that respectfully expressed the subordination of scientific inquiry to the magisterium. These propositions appear in the published proceedings of the congress as follows:

> 1. An inner attachment to the revealed truth that is taught in the Catholic Church is an important and indispensable condition for the progressive development of a true and comprehensive speculation, both in general and for overcoming the prevalent errors of the day in particular.[3]

---

1 For a detailed study of the historical context and causes leading up to *Tuas libenter*, see Boyle, *Church Teaching Authority*, 10–29.

2 Johann Joseph Ignaz von Döllinger (1799–1890) was a priest and professor of theology at the University of Munich known for his liberal views. When the infallibility of the pope was defined at the First Vatican Council, Döllinger issued a public rejection of the dogma, for which he was excommunicated. Although he never formally joined the 'Old-Catholic Church', which broke away from Rome on account of the definition of papal infallibility, he was an influential contributor to its growth and development.

3 Pius Gams, ed., *Verhandlungen der Versammlung katholischer Gelehrten in München vom 28. September bis 1. Oktober 1863* (Regensburg: Manz, 1863), 97: "Der innige Anschluß an die geoffenbarte Wahrheit, welche in der katholischen Kirche gelehrt wird, ist eine wichtige und unerläßliche Bedingung für die fortschreitende Entwicklung einer wahren und umfassenden Speculation überhaupt und für die Ueberwindung der gegenwärtig herrschenden Irrthümer insbesondere."

2. He who takes his stand upon the Catholic faith is bound in conscience to submit himself in all his scientific investigations to the dogmatic pronouncements of the infallible authority of the Church. This submission to authority does not contradict the nature of science and its necessary freedom.[4]

3. This assembly by no means misjudges the progress which the modern age offers in all the branches of science; but at the same time, she believes that nothing could be more conducive to the speculative research of the present than an unprejudiced study of the great tradition of Christian philosophy, which has taken up into itself and furthered the results of ancient thought.[5]

Although clearly expressing respect for and willing subordination toward the authority of the Church, the dogmatic minimalism implied in the second proposition became the principal target of the papal response to the entire episode.[6]

This dogmatic minimalism, which acknowledges the need for submission only to the dogmatic pronouncements of the Church, is exactly what Kleutgen found objectionable in the writings of Hirscher. And it was precisely as a response to this problem that he first introduced the term 'ordinary magisterium'. Ten years later, when faced with the same problem, Pius IX adopted the same solution and so introduced the term 'ordinary magisterium' into the official vocabulary of the Church. And even if the influence of Kleutgen's thought on the papal letter were not sufficiently evident from their striking similarity, John Boyle has also traced the historical lines of connection from Kleutgen to Cardinal von Reisach and from Cardinal von Reisach to Pope Pius IX and the composition of the letter *Tuas libenter*.[7]

---

4 Ibid., 97–98: "Für Jeden, der auf dem Standpunkt des katholischen Glaubens steht, ist es Gewissenspflicht, in allen seinen wissenschaftlichen Untersuchung sich den dogmatischen Aussprüchen der unfehlbaren Auctorität der Kirche zu unterwerfen. Diese Unterwerfung unter die Auctorität steht mit der der Wissenschaft naturgemäßen und nothwendigen Freiheit in keinem Widerspruch."

5 Ibid., 98: "Die Versammlung mißkennt keineswegs die Fortschritte, welche die neuere Zeit in allen Zweigen der Wissenschaft darbietet; aber sie glaubt zugleich, daß der speculativen Forschung der Gegenwart Richts förderlicher sein könne, als ein unbefangenes Studium der großen Tradition christlicher Philosophie, welche die Resultate des antiken Denkens in sich aufgenommen und weitergeführt hat."

6 Gaillardetz notes that this resolution "reflects a dogmatic minimalism present in the theology of Döllinger and many of the other congress participants" (Gaillardetz, *Witnesses*, 24), which echoes the remark of Kleutgen to the effect that the dogmatic minimalism present in Hirscher's work was an error spread abroad by modern theologians, especially in Germany (Kleutgen, *Die Theologie*, 1st ed., 40).

7 Boyle, *Church Teaching Authority*, 10–42. Cf. Gaillardetz, *Witnesses*, 25–26: "John Boyle has

1.2 The Ordinary and Extraordinary Teaching of the Church

The problem with the propositions of the Munich Congress lies not in what is said in them, but in what is left unsaid. That is, while it is praiseworthy that they acknowledge the obligation in conscience of Catholics toward the dogmatic pronouncements of the Church, it is potentially problematic, from the viewpoint of Pius IX, that they do not acknowledge any obligation toward any other form of Church teaching (though neither do they deny it explicitly). Hence, in order to clear up any doubts regarding the truth of the matter, while at the same time giving the authors the benefit of the doubt as to their intentions, the pope expresses himself as wishing to believe that they did not mean to imply that Catholics are absolutely bound only by the defined dogmas of the Church. He writes:

> We readily wish to accept that they did not wish to restrict the obligation by which Catholic teachers and authors are absolutely bound only to what the infallible judgment of the Church sets forth as dogmas of the faith to be believed by all.[8]

Pius IX clearly alludes here to the second proposition of the Munich Congress and rejects the dogmatic minimalism potentially implied therein.

The pope then repeats the same point with reference to the first proposition of the Munich Congress, which had acknowledged that the true progress of the sciences depends upon adherence to Catholic dogma:

> And We are likewise persuaded that they did not wish to declare that this perfect adherence to revealed truths, which they recognized as absolutely necessary to attain true progress in the sciences and to refute errors, could be obtained if faith and obedience were given only to dogmas expressly defined by the Church.[9]

---

demonstrated the influence of Cardinal Reisach on the substance of *Tuas libenter*, further showing that Reisach himself was indebted to the thought of the prominent Jesuit neo-scholastic Joseph Kleutgen (1811–83). Many of the theological formulations found in Reisach's memorandum have their source in Kleutgen's *Die Theologie der Vorzeit* and ultimately found their way into *Tuas libenter*."

8   Pius IX, *Tuas libenter*: "Persuadere Nobis volumus, noluisse obligationem, qua catholici magistri ac scriptores omnino adstringuntur, coarctare in iis tantum, quae ab infallibili Ecclesiae iudicio veluti fidei dogmata ab omnibus credenda proponuntur" (Denz. 2879). The *Syllabus of Errors* (8 Dec. 1864) also condemns the proposition that states: "The obligation by which Catholic teachers and writers are absolutely bound is restricted to those matters only that are proposed by the infallible judgment of the Church to be believed by all as dogmas of faith" (Denz. 2922).

9   Pius IX, *Tuas libenter*: "Atque etiam Nobis persuademus, ipsos noluisse declarare, perfectam illam

Twice, then, Pius IX reiterates the point that Catholics are bound to submit to more than just the expressly defined dogmas of the Church. To what else, then, are they bound? In the first place, to undefined as well as defined dogmas (that is, to the dogmatic teaching of the ordinary as well as the extraordinary magisterium); and secondly, to the merely doctrinal (non-dogmatic) teaching of the Church. To the first point, the letter continues:

> For even if it were a matter of that submission which must be manifested by an act of divine faith, nevertheless, this would not have to be limited to those matters that have been defined by explicit decrees of ecumenical councils or by the Roman pontiffs and by this Apostolic See, but would also have to be extended to those matters transmitted as divinely revealed by the ordinary Magisterium of the whole Church dispersed throughout the world and, for that reason, held by the universal and constant consensus of Catholic theologians as belonging to the faith.[10]

The focus here is only on properly dogmatic teaching; that is, on those truths proposed by the Church as divinely revealed and thus requiring the assent of divine and Catholic faith. And such an act of faith, the pope insists, must be given to the dogmas taught by the ordinary magisterium (here we have the first magisterial use of the term) as well as to those defined by explicit decrees.

Although the term 'extraordinary magisterium' is not used, it is clear by implication that it would refer to those things against which the teaching of the ordinary magisterium is contrasted. The proposition of the Munich Congress which stands in the background of this papal statement speaks of "the dogmatic pronouncements" *(den dogmatischen Aussprüchen)* of the infallible authority of the Church; Pius IX refers first to matters that are proposed "by the infallible judgment of the Church" *(ab infallibili Ecclesiae iudicio)* as dogmas of faith to be believed by all; and then again, to the dogmas "explicitly defined by the Church" *(ab Ecclesia expresse definitis);* and then finally, to those matters which "have been defined by explicit decrees of ecumenical councils or of Roman pontiffs and of this Apostolic See" *(expressis oecumenicorum Conciliorum aut*

---

erga revelatas veritates adhaesionem, quam agnoverunt necessariam omnino esse ad verum scientiarum progressum assequendum et ad errores confutandos, obtineri posse, si dumtaxat dogmatibus ab Ecclesia expresse definitis fides et obsequium adhibeatur" (Denz. 2879).

10 Ibid.: "Namque etiam ageretur de illa subiectione, quae fidei divinae actu est praestanda, limitanda tamen non esset ad ea, quae expressis oecumenicorum Conciliorum aut Romanorum Pontificum huiusque Apostolicae Sedis decretis definita sunt, sed ad ea quoque extendenda, quae ordinario totius Ecclesiae per orbem dispersae magisterio tanquam divinitus revelata traduntur ideoque universali et constanti consensu a catholicis theologis ad fidem pertinere retinentur" (Denz. 2879).

Romanorum Pontificum huiusque Sedis decretis definita sunt). The terms 'judgment' and 'definition' and the insistence on their explicit character correspond precisely to Kleutgen's writings on the extraordinary magisterium.

The subject of these infallible judgments or definitions is at first identified simply as 'the Church' before it is made clear that this power of the extraordinary magisterium of the Church is able to be exercised by ecumenical councils and by the Roman pontiffs. In this Pius IX goes a step beyond Kleutgen, who had affirmed this power unequivocally only of the whole college of bishops (whether gathered in council or not). Writing a few years prior to the definition of papal infallibility, Kleutgen hesitated to identify papal judgments as judgments of the Church without qualification. Pius IX does not hesitate to do so, and even mentions the decrees of the Holy See apparently in addition to those of the Roman pontiff, which could be taken to imply that even the Roman Congregations, contrary to what is now usually assumed,[11] can participate in the infallible power of the extraordinary magisterium of the pope.

With regard to the ordinary magisterium, what is expressed in the papal letter is entirely consistent with Kleutgen's writings: by contrast with the explicit definitions of the extraordinary magisterium, it appears as somehow implicit or intangible; and it is said to be exercised by the Church dispersed throughout the world. From Kleutgen's point of view, this would not be because the teaching of the Church dispersed throughout the world is as such the teaching of the ordinary magisterium (recall that he allowed for an exercise of the extraordinary magisterium by the Church dispersed throughout the world as well), but rather because the teaching of a pope or an ecumenical council cannot help being explicitly documented teaching of the Church. Pius IX also speaks in terms of doctrines being 'transmitted' *(traduntur)* by the

---

11   See, for example, Ladislas Örsy, *The Church: Learning and Teaching* (Wilmington: Glazier, 1987), 52, n. 8: "I do not know of any thorough study from a theological point of view of the power of the Roman curia. In general it is said that it is the arm of the pope in governing the church, which is of course true. An ambivalence that would deserve serious study is in the situation that the pope cannot hand over to anyone his charism of infallibility (fidelity to the message) but he can let others participate in his power to govern (jurisdiction)." Or similarly: Gaillardetz, *Teaching with Authority*, 287: "While canon law envisions the participation of the Roman curia in papal governance of the Church, there is reason to question whether the curia can similarly participate in the doctrinal teaching authority of the pope. This authority cannot be delegated because it is his by virtue of his episcopal office as bishop of Rome." To this line of argument, one could reply that the pope also governs the Church in virtue of his episcopal office as bishop of Rome. And thus if the pope can exercise his jurisdictional powers through the curia, why not his magisterial powers as well, including even his infallibility?

ordinary magisterium, which recalls Kleutgen's identification of the ordinary magisterium with the living tradition of the Church; he agrees with Kleutgen in stressing the equally binding authority of the ordinary magisterium, although he does not refer to its infallibility; and he mentions the consensus of Catholic theologians in connection with the teaching of the ordinary magisterium.

1.3 The Consensus of Theologians

There are two points that need to be addressed in connection with the teaching of *Tuas libenter* on the relationship of the consensus of theologians to the ordinary magisterium. Firstly, according to Boyle's reading of *Tuas libenter* and of Kleutgen, the consensus of theologians would appear as a third mode of teaching or a third source of certainty alongside the ordinary and extraordinary magisterium. He writes:

> There is yet another source of doctrinal certainty, however, and that is the unanimous opinion of theologians that a doctrine is revealed [...] There is no need to illustrate the argument further. What is of interest is that *Tuas libenter* has taken over in brief and schematic form the three sources of dogmatic teaching Kleutgen has presented.[12]

Gaillardetz – apparently relying on Boyle – interprets Kleutgen in the same manner but sees additional significance in the connection made between the ordinary magisterium and the consensus of theologians in the papal letter. He writes: "While Kleutgen presumed that the unanimous consensus of the approved theologians was another source of doctrinal certitude, *Tuas libenter*, significantly, appeared to connect the exercise of the ordinary magisterium with the consensus of theologians."[13] It seems to me, however, that this is based on a misunderstanding of the place Kleutgen assigned to the consensus of theologians within his treatise on the rule of faith. I do not think that he ever intended it to be understood as a third source of doctrinal certainty alongside the ordinary and the extraordinary magisterium, but merely one way – *'einen kurzen und sicheren Weg'*[14] – of recognizing the teaching of the ordinary magisterium.

---

12 Boyle, *Church Teaching Authority*, 35–36.
13 Gaillardetz, *Witnesses*, 28.
14 Kleutgen, *Die Theologie*, 1st ed., 57–58: "so wollen wir doch hier noch auf einen kurzen und sicheren Weg, auch in schwierigen Fällen zu erkennen, ob etwas zum allgemeinen Glauben der Kirche gehöre, aufmerksam machen. Es ist dies aber kein anderer, als jener, auf welchem man auch ermittelt, ob eine Lehre von der Kirche ausdrücklich entschieden sei, oder nicht. Wenn nämlich die angesehnsten Theologen über die Aechtheit und den Sinn einer Entscheidung immer übereingestimmt haben; so sieht man, und gewiß mit vollem Rechte, die Sache als ausgemacht

There has also been no little discussion recently as to whether, according to the teaching of *Tuas libenter*, a consensus of theologians is to be regarded as a necessary or merely as a sufficient condition for recognizing the teaching of the ordinary magisterium. Gaillardetz, for example – following the interpretation pioneered by Sullivan – writes:

> In fact, based on the wording of the papal brief, it would seem legitimate to conclude that where there is no universal and constant consensus of Catholic theologians the infallibility of a teaching of the ordinary magisterium might itself be called into question. Curiously, this reference to the universal consensus of theologians will be absent from all later ecclesiastical articulations of the ordinary magisterium.[15]

The wording to which Gaillardetz refers in support of this position is especially the use of '*ideoque*' (and therefore) in connecting the teaching of the ordinary magisterium and the consensus of theologians. The papal letter teaches that divine faith is owed to "those matters transmitted as divinely revealed by the ordinary Magisterium" and therefore *(ideoque)* "held by the universal and constant consensus of Catholic theologians as belonging to the faith."[16] The use of 'therefore' implies that the consensus of theologians is a sign of, rather than constitutive of, the teaching of the ordinary magisterium: theologians are witnesses rather than judges of the faith; but the use of 'and' could be taken to imply that the single object of the demand for submission of faith is the doctrine that is *both* taught by the ordinary magisterium *and* held by the consensus of theologians. While the papal letter does seem to admit of this reading, it does not seem to require it. And, especially in light of the historical context and connections, it seems more plausible to interpret the single obscure line of the papal letter in light of the clear and comprehensive exposition of Kleutgen, according to which the consensus of theologians is a sufficient but not a necessary condition for recognizing the teaching of the ordinary magisterium. For Kleutgen, the consensus of theologians was merely a short and easy path for recognizing the teaching of the ordinary magisterium; it was by no means the only path, nor indeed the most fundamental. There is first of all

---

an. Nun aber kann man mit derselben Zuversicht sagen, was die angesehensten Theologen einstimmig für eine unzweifelhafte Glaubenslehre erklären, das ist Lehre der allgemeinen Kirche, auch wenn es nicht durch feierlichen Ausspruch entschieden ist."

15 Gaillardetz, *Witnesses*, 27–28. I would suggest that the reason this reference is absent from all later ecclesiastical articulations of the ordinary magisterium is precisely on account of its being open to such interpretations.

16 Pius IX, *Tuas libenter* (Denz. 2879).

Scripture, then the fathers and doctors of the Church, the liturgy, customs, laws, and monuments of the Church, etc. It is true that the papal letter mentions none of these; but the singling out of the consensus of theologians seems sufficiently explicable in light of the special attention that Kleutgen gives the topic (a full and separate section in each edition of his treatise), which only serves to reinforce the point that Kleutgen's work constitutes the proper historical context in light of which *Tuas libenter* should be read.

1.4 The Non-Dogmatic Teaching of the Church

The next step taken in the papal letter – again paralleling Kleutgen's work – is to insist that submission is due not only to dogma (defined and undefined) but also to the merely doctrinal or non-dogmatic teaching of the Church:

> But, since it is a matter of that subjection by which in conscience all those Catholics are bound who work in the speculative sciences, in order that they may bring new advantages to the Church by their writings, on that account, then, the men of that same convention must recognize that it is not sufficient for learned Catholics to accept and revere the aforesaid dogmas of the Church, but that it is also necessary to subject themselves to the decisions pertaining to doctrine that are issued by the Pontifical Congregations and also to those points of doctrine that are held by the common and constant consent of Catholics as theological truths and conclusions, so certain that opinions opposed to these same forms of doctrine, although they cannot be called heretical, nevertheless deserve some other theological censure.[17]

In connection with Kleutgen's exposition, we addressed two questions at this point: whether the ordinary and extraordinary magisterium are involved in this kind of teaching, and whether it is infallible. The same questions may be considered here.

To begin with, it must be admitted that neither the ordinary nor the extraordinary magisterium is explicitly mentioned in this paragraph. At the

---

17 Ibid.: "Sed cum agatur de illa subiectione, qua ex conscientia ii omnes catholici obstringuntur, qui in contemplatrices scientias incumbunt, ut novas suis scriptis Ecclesiae afferant utilitates, idcirco eiusdem conventus viri recognoscere debent, sapientibus catholicis haud satis esse, ut praefata Ecclesiae dogmata recipiant ac venerentur, verum etiam opus esse, ut se subiciant tum decisionibus, quae ad doctrinam pertinentes a Pontificiis Congregationibus proferuntur, tum iis doctrinae capitibus, quae communi et constanti Catholicorum consensu retinentur ut theologicae veritates et conclusiones ita certae, ut opiniones eisdem doctrinae capitibus adversae, quamquam haereticae dici nequeant, tamen aliam theologicam mereantur censuram" (Denz. 2880).

same time, however, it would not be too difficult to see the same distinction implied in the contrast between the doctrinal decisions of the Pontifical Congregations and the doctrines that are held by the common and constant consent of Catholics as theological truths and conclusions. Although it may be surprising to think of the doctrinal decisions of the Roman Congregations as exercises of the extraordinary magisterium, it is not entirely implausible that Pius IX would have viewed them in that light; and, as we have already seen, there was some indication of this already in his reference to the decrees of the Holy See together with the pope and ecumenical councils in the context of dogmatic definitions. As for the doctrines "held by the common and constant consensus of Catholics *(communi et constanti Catholicorum consensu retinen-tur)* as theological truths and certain conclusions," this parallels very closely the earlier reference to dogmas "held by the universal and constant consensus of Catholic theologians *(universali et constanti consensu a catholicis theologis retinentur)* as belonging to the faith." This latter reference to the consensus of Catholics (the *consensus fidelium)* is much less remarked upon than the consensus of theologians, but it seems quite likely that this text – especially given the many and clear connections between the papal letter and the work of Kleutgen – should be read as referring to the ordinary magisterium manifested in the infallibility of the whole people of God.

In any case, there can be little doubt that the teaching of Kleutgen – both in substance and in terminology, both in its main lines and in many of its details – has been taken up into the teaching of *Tuas libenter*. With regard to the mode of teaching, Catholics are bound not only by the extraordinary judgments or definitions of the Church but also by her ordinary teaching; and with regard to the object of teaching, they are bound not only by properly dogmatic teaching but also by merely doctrinal teaching.

2. The Dogmatic Constitution *Dei Filius* (1870)

In 1867, four years after the publication of *Tuas libenter*, Kleutgen's *Die Theologie der Vorzeit vertheidigt* appeared in a much-enlarged second edition. Two years after that, the First Vatican Council was convened. Two dogmatic constitutions – *Dei Filius* (on the Catholic faith) and *Pastor Aeternus* (on the Church of Christ) – were promulgated by the council before it was cut short by the onset of the Franco-Prussian War and the subsequent capture of Rome by the newly united Kingdom of Italy. The focus of *Dei Filius* is not directly ecclesiological – it is concerned with the Church's doctrine on divine revelation and the theological virtue of faith – but the term 'ordinary magisterium' is used, thus permanently enshrining this new terminology in a document of the highest authority in the Church.

Joseph Kleutgen served at the council as a theological advisor to the deputation on faith, which was responsible for revising the schema on the Catholic Faith, into which it inserted the term 'ordinary magisterium' and maintained it even against the wishes of many of the fathers of the council. The doctrine and terminology of Kleutgen and of *Tuas libenter* were thus publicly and prominently enshrined; from this point on it would be impossible for Catholic theology to ignore the terminology of an ordinary and an extra-ordinary magisterium.[18]

2.1 Initial Drafting and Revision of the Text

The first draft of the constitution on the Catholic faith was prepared prior to the opening of the First Vatican Council by Johann Baptist Franzelin (1816–1886), an Austrian Jesuit theologian. The terminology of ordinary and extraordinary magisterium did not appear in this schema, but it did distinguish between the 'definition' and the 'proposition' of the articles of faith, and the official notation made it clear that this was intended as a distinction between solemn definitions and the general profession and preaching of the faith, which corresponds in substance with Kleutgen's distinction between the ordinary and extraordinary magisterium.[19]

When the council began, the deputation for the faith judged that Franzelin's draft was too technical in style and so undertook a revision before

---

18 On the influence of Kleutgen on this text, see Gaillardetz, *Witnesses*, 29: "The understanding of the ordinary magisterium, as first articulated in Kleutgen's theology and in *Tuas libenter*, was solidified in *Dei Filius*." See also Boyle, *Church Teaching Authority*, 40: "What entered into an official papal document in *Tuas libenter* was further pushed into the mainstream of Catholic theology by the Constitution on the Catholic Faith *Dei Filius* of the First Vatican Council [...] Thus did the language of Kleutgen's book pass into the conciliar constitution and on into the theology of the twentieth century."

19 See Gaillardetz, *Witnesses*, 29. Cf. Marc Caudron, "Magistère ordinaire et infaillibilité pontificale d'après la constitution *Dei Filius*," *Ephemerides Theologicae Lovanienses* 36 (1960): 398. Caudron's work remains a standard point of reference for the study of *Dei Filius*. Other important studies on *Dei Filius* include Jean-Michel-Alfred Vacant, *Etudes théologiques sur les Constitutions du Concile du Vatican d'après les Actes du Concile* (Paris: Delhomme et Briguet, 1895); Roger Aubert, *Le Problème de l'Acte de Foi* (Louvain: Wainy, 1945), 131–91; Jean-Pierre Torrell, *La théologie de l'épiscopat au premier concile du Vatican* (Paris: Cerf, 1961); Hermann J. Pottmeyer, *Der Glaube vor dem Anspruch der Wissenschaft: Die Konstitution über den katholischen Glauben "Dei Filius" des 1. Vatikanischen Konzils und die unveröffentlichten theologischen Voten der vorbereitenden Kommission* (Freiburg: Herder, 1968).

submitting it to the general assembly for discussion. Bishop Martin of Paderborn, assisted by Joseph Kleutgen, oversaw this initial revision of the text. In a
meeting of the deputation, Bishop Senestréy of Regensburg suggested that it
should be made more clear that, in addition to solemn definitions, there is
another form of teaching in the Church that is equally authoritative.[20] His
suggestion was to express this other form of teaching in terms of the 'ordinary
and perpetual magisterium' of the Church, which directly echoes Kleutgen's
'ordentliche und immerwährende Lehramt'.[21] What eventually appeared in the
revised schema was this:

> Further, all those things are to be believed by divine and Catholic faith which
> are contained in the word of God, written or handed down, and proposed by
> the Church to be believed either by a solemn judgment (solemni iudicio) or by
> the ordinary magisterium (ordinario magisterio).[22]

In the thirtieth general congregation (18 March 1870), Archbishop Simor, the
Primate of Hungary, introduced the revised schema on behalf of the deputation
for the faith. Regarding the paragraph in question he remarked that, "it is
directed against those who say that only what has been defined by a council
needs to be believed, and not also that which the dispersed teaching Church
preaches and teaches with unanimous consensus as divinely revealed."[23] The
discussion that followed this introduction unfolded in two distinct stages.

2.2 First Stage of Conciliar Discussion

The conciliar discussion of the third chapter of the draft began in the thirty-
seventh general congregation (30 Mar. 1870). Several bishops commented on
the paragraph beginning 'Porro fide divina'. Bishop Rivet of Dijon remarked
that this teaching would seem to belong to the schema on the Church rather
than that on the Catholic faith, but requested in any case that the phrase 'sive
solemni iudicio sive ordinario magisterio' should be deleted entirely, arguing:

> If one attends to the rigor of theological words it is not able to be said that all
> those things proposed by the ordinary magisterium are to be believed with

---

20 See Gaillardetz, Witnesses, 29.
21 See Boyle, Church Teaching Authority, 40.
22 Mansi 51:35: "Porro fide divina et catholica ea omnia credenda sunt quae in verbo Dei scripto vel
    tradito continentur, et ab ecclesia sive solemni iudicio sive ordinario magisterio credenda
    proponuntur."
23 Mansi 51:47: "Quae sequitur paragraphus: Porro fide divina, dirigitur contra illos, qui dicunt illud
    solum credendum esse quod concilium definivit, et non etiam illud quod ecclesia docens dispersa
    unanimi consensu tamquam divinitus revelatum praedicat ac docet."

Catholic faith; because only those things that have been defined are to be believed with Catholic faith. Therefore, in order to remove all ambiguity, the words '*sive solemni iudicio sive ordinario magisterio*' should be suppressed.[24]

Here is at least one bishop who apparently shared the minimalist view against which the teaching of the text is specifically directed. Then Bishop Gignoux of Beauvais, speaking, he notes, on behalf of many fathers, also requested the suppression of these words on the grounds that they are "obscure and open to other interpretations.".[25] The variety of interpretations and the confusion surrounding the term 'ordinary magisterium' in the subsequent history of theology has largely borne out this judgment. The disputed phrase found a supporter in Bishop Martinez of Saint Christopher of Havana, who instead of deletion suggested an addition that would make clear that the term 'ordinary magisterium' was to be understood (as he supposed) as a reference to the magisterium of the pope.[26]

The next day, in the thirty-eighth general congregation, Archbishop Errington of Trebizond urged two reasons against the inclusion of the phrase. First, like Bishop Rivet, he argued that a statement about the different modes of operation of the magisterium belonged more properly to the schema on the Church rather than to the schema on faith.[27] And secondly, he objected that the

---

24 Mansi 51:207: "In phrasi qui incipit 'porro fide divina et catholica', si attenditur ad theologicum verborum rigorem, dici non potest ea omnia fide catholica credenda esse, quae ordinario magisterio proponuntur; quandoquidem ea tantum fide catholica credenda sint, quae definita fuerunt. Ideo, ut omnis tollatur ambiguitas, supprimantur verba: *sive solemni iudicio sive ordinario magisterio.*" Cf. Mansi 51:304, emendatio proposita 48c.

25 Mansi 51:208: "Plures episcopi, quorum sum interpres, in phrasi quae sic se habet 'Porro fide divina et catholica ea omnia credenda sunt, quae in verbo Dei scripto vel tradito continentur, et ab ecclesia sive solemni iudicio sive ordinario magisterio credenda proponuntur', incisum illus, 'sive solemni iudicio, sive ordinario magisterio' supprimendum censuerunt, tanquam subobscurum et alienis interpretationibus ansam praebens." Cf. Mansi 51:304, emendatio proposita 48b.

26 Mansi 51:216: "Venerable fathers, what is this ordinary magisterium of the Church, if not the magisterium of the Roman pontiff, the head of the Church, the vicar of our Lord Jesus Christ, who after eighteen centuries teaches and has taught the Church infallibly and will teach infallibly unto the consummation of the world? Therefore it should be said more clearly: all those things which are taught by the solemn judgment of the Church or by the ordinary magisterium of the Roman pontiff, the venerable head of this Church, are to be believed and held by faith." Cf. Mansi 51:304, emendatio proposita 49.

27 Mansi 51:222: "This explanation of the Church does not pertain, strictly speaking, to this place. Here we are speaking of faith and of the Church only as the rule of faith: but the modes in which she exercises her magisterium pertains to another schema, in particular to the schema on the Church." Cf. Mansi 51:304, emendatio proposita 48a.

phrase would be a source of confusion, as proof of which he noted that even among the bishops and theologians gathered there, the term 'ordinary magisterium' was understood in entirely different ways. Bishop Martinez, for example, understood the distinction as one between conciliar and papal teaching; whereas he and others understood it as distinguishing between "definitions of the articles of faith," on the one hand, and "the doctrine of the Church drawn from the deposit of faith and given by the shepherds to their flock before some of these things were instituted as articles of faith," on the other.[28] Errington also objected to Martinez's proposed amendation on the grounds that it introduced the infallibility of the Roman pontiff (at that point as yet undefined), and would thus prejudice without adequate discussion the principal question of the council.[29]

At this point, Bishop Martin of Paderborn, who had overseen the revision of this schema, intervened in order to clarify several points about the intended meaning of this text. The reaction thus far had been far from positive – all but one who had spoken on the subject had requested the deletion of the text. One complaint was that the doctrine was simply false; another was that a distinction between modes of operation of the magisterium was out of place in the

---

28 Mansi 51:222–23: "These words seem to be insufficiently precise. For there are none of the words that are usually employed in explaining this idea. And it suffices to prove the truth of this opinion, that even in this gathering of bishops and theologians entirely different significations are attributed to these words. For we heard yesterday the bishop of Saint Christopher of Havana, who by these two phrases (namely, "solemn judgment" and "ordinary magisterium") understood on the one side (namely, by "solemn judgment") the decrees of councils, and on the other side (namely, by "ordinary magisterium") the decrees of the Roman pontiffs. But it seems to me and to others whom I heard speaking about this matter, that by these two phrases it is to be understood simply thus: the 'solemn judgment' is what is usually referred to as definitions of the articles of faith, and the 'ordinary magisterium' is the doctrine of the Church drawn from the deposit of faith and given by the shepherds to their flock before some of these things were instituted as articles of faith."

29 Mansi 51:222: "But before I proceed to another observation, let me add two words about the amendment proposed yesterday by the illustrious bishop of Saint Christopher; this amendation seems to me to be beyond the bounds of what has been proposed to us, and so should not be able to be proposed. For that most eloquent bishop wants not only, that the ordinary magisterium should be understood as referring to the documents, constitutions, and other such things published by the Roman pontiffs: he also desires in this amendation that this assembly should profess faith in the infallibility of their decisions. Since, however, this question is entirely extraneous, and has its place in another schema, surely it is not fitting that this amendation should be accepted, since the principal question of the whole council would thus be treated and defined covertly and without discussion."

constitution on faith, belonging rather to the constitution on the Church; a third, and the most common, was that the term 'ordinary magisterium' was obscure and ambiguous; a fourth was that a clarification of the term along the lines proposed by Martinez would be prejudicial to the forthcoming discussion of papal infallibility.

Martin's speech attempted to address each of these concerns. First of all, he declared that, "it was in no way the intention of the deputation to touch, either directly or indirectly, on the question of the infallibility of the supreme Pontiff."[30] Rather, the intention of the deputation was merely to describe the material object of faith after having describing the formal object of faith in the chapter on faith – thus addressing also the objections concerning proper context.[31] In response to the dogmatic minimalism voiced by Rivet, Martin reiterated that this was precisely the error that the deputation wished to condemn: "the deputation wanted to direct this paragraph against those theologians who say that only those things that have been openly defined by ecumenical councils are to be believed by divine faith."[32] Then, in response to the charge of obscurity and ambiguity, Martin appealed to the text of *Tuas libenter* as the source of the terminology,[33] and explained its meaning by reference to one of the primary

---

30 Mansi 51:224: "Reverendissimis patribus equidem declaro, quod intentio deputationis quoad hanc tertiam paragraphum 'porro fide divina' vobis exhibitam, intentio, inquam, deputationis pro fide nullatenus ea fuit, ut vel directe vel indirecte attingeret quaestionem de infallibilitate summi Pontificis."

31 Mansi 51:224: "The deputation wanted to explain what is the material object of faith, after it had explained, in the first paragraph those things which seemed to them to concern the formal object of faith. Therefore it only wanted to express those things which are to be believed with respect to the material object of faith." It is worth noting that the original context of the distinction in Kleutgen's works is also dogma and the rule of faith – as it is here in *Dei Filius* – rather than the modes of exercise of the magisterium, where Rivet and Errington expected to see it. This difficulty about the proper context of the distinction points ahead to some of the issues that will later arise when it is transposed from one context to the other.

32 Mansi 51:224: "Et voluit dirigere hanc paragraphum contra eos theologos qui dicerent tantummodo ea fide divina credenda esse, quae ab oecumenicis conciliis aperte definita essent."

33 Mansi 51:224–25: "But the reason, which it had, the deputation for the faith took from the apostolic letter of the supreme pontiff Pius IX sent to the archbishop of Munich and Freising in the year 1863, where it is written (at the end of the apostolic letter): 'For even if it concerns that subjection which is to be shown by an act of divine faith, it must not be limited to those things which have been expressly defined in the decrees of ecumenical councils, or of Roman pontiffs and of this Apostolic See, but must also be extended to those things which are handed down as divinely revealed by the ordinary magisterium of the whole Church dispersed throughout the world.' The deputation for the faith looked, therefore, to these words, when it defined what is the material object of faith."

examples also utilized by Kleutgen – the Church's faith in the divinity of Christ prior to its solemn definition at the Council of Nicaea:

> All of you, most reverend fathers, know that before the Council of Nicaea all the Catholic bishops believed in the divinity of our Lord Jesus Christ: yet before the Council of Nicaea this dogma was not openly defined and openly declared. Therefore, at the time before the Council of Nicaea this dogma was taught by the ordinary magisterium.[34]

Thus he concludes: "This therefore was the only intention of the deputation for the faith. Let these words suffice for the right understanding of our intention."[35]

2.3 Second Stage of Conciliar Discussion

Following this clarification, the remaining fathers to speak publicly on the text of '*Porro fide divina*' voiced their support for its inclusion, but proposed important additions for the sake of greater clarity. Benvenuto Monzon y Martins, the Archbishop of Granada, requested an addition that would clarify that not everything proposed by the ordinary magisterium is to be believed as a dogma of faith, but only those things proposed to all the faithful precisely as divinely revealed truths. As an example, he cited the Church's teaching on the Immaculate Conception of the Blessed Virgin Mary. This doctrine was proposed, he says, prior to its solemn definition, by the ordinary magisterium of the Church as a truth to be believed by all the faithful. But it was not proposed as a dogma to be believed with divine faith until its solemn definition. Likewise, he continued, the doctrine of the blessed Virgin's bodily Assumption was already proposed by the ordinary magisterium of the Church as a truth to be believed; but it was not yet (in 1870) proposed as a dogma to be believed by divine faith.[36] His point is not that nothing proposed by the ordinary magisterium can be

---

34 Mansi 51:225: "Omnes vos, reverendissimi patres, scitis ante concilium Nicaenum omnes catholicos episcopos credidisse in divinitatem Domini nostri Iesu Christi: neque tamen hoc dogma ante concilium Nicaenum erat aperte definitum et aperte declaratum. Igitur tunc temporis ante hoc concilium Nicaenum per ordinarium magisterium hoc dogma docebatur."

35 Mansi 51:225: "Haec igitur solummodo erat intentio deputationis pro fide. Haec satis sint, ut recte intelligatur intentio nostra."

36 Mansi 51:225: "Before the dogmatic definition of the Immaculate Conception of the blessed virgin Mary, this doctrine was proposed to the faithful to be believed through the ordinary magisterium [...] And nevertheless it was not to be believed by divine faith until the definition of the Roman pontiff. The Church now proposes to the faithful through the ordinary magisterium [...] that it should be believed that the blessed virgin Mary was assumed into heaven in body and soul; and nevertheless this is not to be believed as of divine faith."

proposed as a dogma of divine faith, but rather that some things proposed by the ordinary magisterium are not thus proposed; and therefore only those things proposed to all the faithful specifically 'as of divine faith' *(tanquam de fide divina)* are material objects of divine and Catholic faith. Thus he suggested that the words *'omnibus fidelibus tanquam de fide divina'* should be added to the text in order to clarify this point.[37]

Felix Dupanloup, Bishop of Orléans, shared the same concern that not every doctrine proposed by the Church is to be believed with divine faith, but only those that are proposed specifically as divinely revealed truths. He refers here to theological conclusions (drawn partly from revelation and partly from reason) and the condemnation of erroneous (as opposed to heretical) propositions. These things, he argues, are not proper objects of divine and Catholic faith.[38] And so the phrase *'tanquam divinitus revelata de fide'* should be inserted prior to the words *'credenda proponuntur'*.[39]

Monzon y Martins and Dupanloup also expressed their understanding of the concept of the ordinary magisterium in ways that correspond to the understanding of Kleutgen. According to Monzon y Martins, the ordinary magisterium refers to the "daily preaching, liturgical prayers, method of conducting and defining business in the episcopal courts, and especially in the congregations of the holy Roman Church, the mother and teacher of all churches."[40] "The Church," he says, "is not only infallible when speaking through councils

---

37 Mansi 51:225–26: "Therefore, so that no doubt should appear in these words (for it seems to me that there is obscurity in the words, although not in the intention of the deputation) it seems to me that these words should be reformulated in this way: *Further, all those things are to be believed by divine and Catholic faith which are contained in the word of God, written or handed down, and proposed by the Church, either by solemn judgment or by the ordinary magisterium, to all the faithful as to be believed by divine faith.*" Cf. Mansi 51:304, emendatio proposita 52. Monzon y Martins also requested that a canon containing an anathema be added: *"If anyone should say that all those things are not to be believed by divine and Catholic faith which are contained in the word of God, written or handed down, and proposed by the Church, either by solemn judgment or by the ordinary magisterium, to all the faithful as to be believed by divine faith, let him be anathema"* (Mansi 51:226; cf. Mansi 51:311, emendatio proposita 121).

38 Mansi 51:229: "Therefore this paragraph as it is so indeterminately worked out is rightly rebuked, as it seems from the words of the paragraph that many propositions should be *de fide catholica*, which are by no means truths of faith, but only theological conclusions; and indeed they certainly pertain to the faith and are to be believed on account of the judgment of the Church, but nevertheless not with divine and Catholic faith."

39 Mansi 51:230; cf. Mansi 51:304, emendatio proposita 51.

40 Mansi 51:225: "Quid intelligitur per ordinarium magisterium ecclesiae? Absque dubio praedicatio quotidiana, oratio liturgica, ratio expediendi et definiendi negotia in curiis episcopalibus, et praesertim in congregationibus sacrae Romanae ecclesiae, magistrae et matris omnium ecclesiarum."

and when speaking through her head the Roman pontiff; but is also infallible in the ordinary and universal magisterium of her pastors and in the understanding of all the faithful."[41] For Dupanloup, "The ordinary magisterium is exercised in the Catholic Church under the authority of the universal supreme pontiff through the pastors and teachers, through the bishops and parish priests, through the words of the divine preachers, through the orthodox theologians, through the approved books, but mostly indeed through the liturgical books and catechisms."[42]

The last of the council fathers to speak on the paragraph was Leo Meurin, titular bishop of Ascalon, who proposed that the words 'public and universal' be added to the term 'ordinary magisterium', in order to indicate more clearly its intended meaning.[43] Then he proceeds to expound the nature of the distinction between the ordinary and extraordinary magisterium in a manner that follows Kleutgen's exposition almost verbatim. He begins:

> This refutes the error enunciated more than once, that only those things can and should be believed, which the Church, in solemn definitions, or in dogmatic decrees, or under anathema, proposes to all as to be believed: while that faith by which one believes things that have not been proposed by the Church in this way is not divine faith but human faith.[44]

Following Kleutgen and Bishop Martin, he gives the example of Christ's divinity prior to the Council of Nicaea, which, he says, "could have been and should have been believed by divine and Catholic faith even though it was not defined as of Catholic faith."[45] Then he continues:

---

41 Mansi 51:225: "Expungenda igitur sunt haec verba 'magisterio ordinario?' Nullatenus, quia ecclesia non solum infallibilis est coadunata, sed etiam dispersa. Ecclesia non solum infallibilis est, dum loquitur conciliariter et dum loquitur per suum caput Romanum pontificem; sed etiam infallibilis est in magisterio universali et ordinario pastorum et in omnium fidelium intelligentia."

42 Mansi 51:229–30: "Magisterium quo fideles edocentur, magisterium ordinarium exercetur in ecclesia catholica sub universali summi pontificis auctoritate per pastores et doctores, per episcopos et parochos, per verbi divini praedicatores, per theologos orthodoxos, per probatos libros, maxime vero per libros liturgicos et catecheticos."

43 Mansi 51:234: "I propose that to the words "sive ordinario magisterio" there should be added: *publico et universale*, in order to more clearly indicate the magisterium referred to." Cf. Mansi 51:304, emendatio proposita 50.

44 Mansi 51:234: "Refellitur hic error non semel enuntiatus, illud tantum credi posse et debere, quod ecclesia in definitionibus solemnibus, vel in dogmaticis decretis, vel sub anathemate omnibus ut credendum proponit: fidem vero, qua creditur illud, quod ab ecclesia non est tali modo propositum, non esse fidem divinam, sed humanam."

45 Mansi 51:234: "Optimum est illud exemplum, quod modo reverendissimus episcopus Paderbornensis attulit: divinitas Christi ante concilium Nicaenum fide divina et catholica credi potuit et

There is in the Church a double proposition and a double magisterium: one is
a solemn judgment, which is rarely exercised, and is therefore also called by
many an extraordinary judgment; but the other is the perpetual magisterium,
by which the faithful are instructed under the vigilance of their pastors, and
which is therefore called ordinary. For there are many truths (e.g. concerning
the love of one's enemies) that are objects of faith and yet have never been
defined as articles of faith, neither by councils nor by the pope: they are *de fide
catholica non definita*. Thus also facts of the greatest importance in the life of
Christ (e.g., the flight of Christ into Egypt) or in the Acts of the Apostles that
are not defined by the Church are nevertheless *de fide catholica*.[46]

In content, in the mode of expression, and even in the particular examples
chosen, Meurin could almost be reading his speech from the pages of
Kleutgen's *Die Theologie der Vorzeit*. He considers the common objection that
one may not defend as a dogma what has not been defined by the Church, and
explains (as Kleutgen also does) that this applies only to matters of legitimate
controversy among faithful children of the Church, but not at all to matters in
which all faithful Catholics are in agreement since these things are proposed as
divinely revealed by the public and universal ordinary magisterium.[47]

Meurin next cites the relevant portion of *Tuas libenter*, and then concludes
by proposing that a canon excluding dogmatic minimalism should also be
included in the text. He argues that it is good to condemn errors when they can
be foreseen and feared, even more urgent to do so when they have begun to
grow, but absolutely necessary when they have already been widely scattered
abroad, as this error has been, he says, since the end of the eighteenth century.[48]

---

debuit, quamvis non fuerit de fide catholica definita."

46 Mansi 51:234: "Datur in ecclesia duplex propositio et duplex magisterium; alteram est solemne
iudicium, quod raro exercetur, et ideo a multis dicitur extraordinarium iudicium; alteram vero
est perpetuum magisterium, quo fideles sub vigilantia pastorum instruuntur, et quod ideo vocatur
ordinarium. Multae enim sunt veritates, verbi gratia de dilectione inimicorum, quae sunt
obiectum fidei, et tamen non sunt definitae ut articuli fidei neque a conciliis, neque a papa: sunt
de fide catholica non definita. Sic etiam facta maximi momenti in vita Christi, verbi gratia fuga
Christi in Aegyptum, vel in actis apostolorum, quae non sunt definita ab ecclesia, sunt tamen de
fide catholica."

47 Mansi 51:234: "It is commonly asserted, it is true, that if something has not yet been defined by
the Church, it may perhaps be defended as a certain opinion, but not as a dogma. But, reverend
fathers, this is true only when it concerns matters of controversy among Catholics, and not at all
when Catholics agree that something is revealed, since it is proposed as such through the public
and universal, although ordinary, magisterium."

48 Mansi 51:234–35: "Finally, although canons should not be unduly multiplied, they should be
admitted when the necessity is urgent. The time for rejecting an error against the faith is

The canon he proposes is as follows: "If anyone says, that whatever has not been defined by the Church by a solemn judgment as a dogma of faith, cannot be believed except by human faith, let him be anathema."[49] Excluding this error in a canon is all the more important, he notes, since it is akin to another error that holds that definitions are to be found only in the canons and not also in the chapters of the ecumenical councils: "Unless, therefore, this error is excluded in a canon, it will not be efficaciously or sufficiently rejected."[50]

Following the conclusion of the general discussion in the conciliar hall, the deputation for the faith considered the various amendations proposed by the fathers of the council, and decided to accept two of them as the basis for a revision of the paragraph. Bishop Martin delivered the official *relatio* on behalf of the deputation in which he presented the newly revised text and explained the changes. The first change was the insertion of the term 'universal', as suggested by Meurin, so that the revised text read 'ordinary and universal magisterium' in place of 'ordinary magisterium'. The intention, according to Martin's *relatio*, was in order to make it clear that the text spoke of the magisterium exercised by the whole Church dispersed throughout the world and not of the magisterium of the Roman pontiff.[51] The second change was the insertion of the phrase 'as divinely revealed', as suggested by Monzon y Martins

---

opportune when the error is feared or foreseen: when an error has already begun to grow, the time is even more opportune; but the condemnation of the error is necessary when it is seen to be already widely dispersed. And this error began to be taught already from the end of the last century, unless I am mistaken, by Muratori and it grows greater roots in these days."

49 Mansi 51:235: "Ideo propono humiliter ut etiam in canone peculiari sequenti modo notetur: *Si quis dixerit, quidquid ab ecclesia solemni iudicio tanquam fidei dogma definitum non sit, credi non posse nisi fide humana, anathema sit.*" Cf. Mansi 51:311, emendatio proposita 122.

50 Mansi 51:235: "Praecipua ratio proponendi canonem est haec: error notatus affinis est errori, qui dicit solum ea de fide definita esse, quae in canonibus exprimuntur, non vero etiam ea, quae in capitulis conciliorum; nisi ergo hic error canone excludatur, non erit efficaciter vel sufficienter reiectus."

51 Mansi 51:322: "For the reason why we wish that this word *universal* should be placed with the word 'magisterium' in our text is this, namely so that no one would think that we speak in this place about the infallible magisterium of the holy Apostolic See, as opposed to the infallible magisterium of general councils. For I had recently the honor of declaring to you that it was in no way the intention of the Deputation to touch either directly or indirectly upon this question of the infallibility of the supreme pontiff; and therefore this word *universal* signifies nearly the same thing as that which the holy father referred to in his apostolic letter, namely the magisterium of the whole Church dispersed throughout the world. Therefore, for the removal of this false opinion we thought it opportune to take this word *universal* from the 50th proposed amendation and to insert it into our text." Cf. the amendation proposed by Leo Muerin (Mansi 51:304).

and Dupanloup. The intention here was to make clear that the text is concerned only with doctrine specifically proposed as dogmas of divine faith and not with the opinions of the schools or other doctrines of lesser theological note.[52] The complete amended text, therefore, was presented as follows: "Further, all those things are to be believed by divine and Catholic faith, which are contained in the word of God, written or handed down, and proposed by the Church, whether by solemn judgment or by the ordinary and universal magisterium, as to be believed as divinely revealed."[53] This remained the form in which the paragraph was finally promulgated in the dogmatic constitution *Dei Filius*.

2.4 *Dei Filius* on the Ordinary Magisterium

The main conclusion that can be drawn about the meaning and use of the term 'ordinary magisterium' in the text of *Dei Filius* is that it largely confirms the doctrine of Kleutgen. Despite some opposition from those who thought such a distinction between modes of operation of the magisterium should be moved to the treatise on the Church, the distinction between an ordinary and an extra-ordinary magisterium was introduced (as it was for Kleutgen) in the context of the rule of faith as a description of the material object of faith. The teaching of this text is directed (as it was for Kleutgen) against the dogmatic minimalism of those who would say that Catholics are bound to believe with divine faith only those things that have been defined by the Church as dogmas of faith. Against this, the council agrees with Kleutgen in proclaiming that everything universally believed and taught as a divinely revealed truth, even if it has not been defined as such, is to be accepted with divine and Catholic faith as a dogma proposed by the ordinary magisterium. The paradigmatic example referenced by Martin in his official explanation and by several fathers in their speeches is

---

52 Mansi 51:322: "And then, the words of our holy father taken from the apostolic letter sent to the Archbishop of Munich in the year 1863, namely 'tamquam divinitus revelata' were inserted after the word 'magisterium' [...] For this modification, or rather the addition of both parts, namely 'universal' and these words which the holy father uses, in the first place satisfies the desire of many reverend fathers who have spoken about this phrase, namely that the opinions of the schools, which are handed down by Catholic scholars, even if certain, are not assimilated to the doctrine of faith; for if it is said that the Church teaches something as divinely revealed, it is not possible for it to be merely an opinion of the schools. According to this modification the whole material object of divine faith is more precisely determined, and the errors of our time obviated."

53 Mansi 51:322: "Porro fide divina et catholica ea omnia credenda sunt, quae in verbo Dei scripto vel tradito continentur, et ab ecclesia sive solemni iudicio, sive ordinario et universali magisterio tamquam divinitus revelata credenda proponuntur." The entire third chapter of the revised draft appears in Mansi 51:336–38. For the document as finally promulgated, see Mansi 51:429–37.

the same as that used by Kleutgen, the doctrine of the divinity of Christ prior to its definition at the Council of Nicaea. Just as it was necessary for Catholics then to believe this dogma with divine and Catholic faith prior to its solemn definition, so it remains necessary for Catholics today to believe with divine and Catholic faith the still undefined dogmas that are universally believed and taught in the Church as divinely revealed truths (such as, perhaps, the moral obligation of Christians to love their enemies).

Following *Tuas libenter*, the council also connects the ordinary magisterium to the Church dispersed throughout the world by the addition of the word 'universal'. But the ordinary and universal magisterium is not something other than the ordinary magisterium. The term 'universal' was not added in order to distinguish a 'universal' ordinary magisterium from a 'non-universal' ordinary magisterium, but in order to describe more clearly the nature of the ordinary magisterium as such. The ordinary magisterium is not one thing when exercised by the bishops dispersed throughout the world and another thing when exercised by the bishops gathered in council or by the pope. The ordinary magisterium just is the magisterium exercised by the whole Church dispersed throughout the world.[54] From this point of view, to speak of an 'ordinary papal magisterium' or an 'ordinary conciliar magisterium' seems completely foreign to the intended meaning of the text of *Dei Filius*, just as it would have been completely foreign to Kleutgen.

Furthermore, although the ordinary magisterium is carried out under the vigilance of the bishops dispersed throughout the world, it does not seem to be the case that its exercise was meant to be limited to the direct and explicit statements of the bishops. The speeches of several of the fathers of the council refer to the teaching of the ordinary magisterium evident in the common liturgical prayers of the Church, in the actions of episcopal courts and the Roman congregations, in the consensus of all the faithful, in the unanimity of orthodox theologians, and in the approved books of doctrine and catechisms.

---

54 An indication of this complete identity between the ordinary magisterium and the ordinary and universal magisterium can be seen in the first version of the post-Vatican II profession of faith promulgated by the CDF in 1967: "Firmiter quoque amplector et retineo omnia et singula quae circa doctrinam de fide et moribus ab Ecclesia, sive solemni iudicio definita sive ordinario magisterio adserta ac declarata sunt, prout ab ipsa proponuntur, praesertim ea quae respiciunt mysterium sanctae Ecclesiae Christi, eiusque Sacramenta et Missae Sacrificium atque Primatum Romani Pontificis" (AAS 59 [1967]: 1058). The assumption that the terms meant something different, however, led to some confusion and the term 'ordinary and universal magisterium' was substituted in the revised version of 1988.

When one considers the development of the '*Porro fide divine*' paragraph
from the earliest drafts, through the conciliar discussions, to the revision and
final promulgation of the text, it is hard to overestimate the influence exerted
by the thought of Kleutgen. The terminology is taken from his works; the
context of the distinction is the same; the target is the same; the authority and
mode of exercise of the ordinary magisterium are the same. It would seem,
therefore, hard to avoid the conclusion that the key to interpreting the distinction between the ordinary and the extraordinary magisterium as it is enshrined
in *Dei Filius* is to read it in light of Joseph Kleutgen's treatise on the rule of faith
together with the text of *Tuas libenter*, which is itself also indebted to Kleutgen.

However, while the teaching of *Dei Filius* largely confirms the doctrine of
Kleutgen with regard to the ordinary magisterium, the conciliar discussions
also reveal the problematic ambiguity inherent in his choice of terminology. In
the context of a description of the rule of faith, where only the infallible
teaching of the Church is under consideration, the terminology applies clearly
enough to the distinction between defined and undefined doctrines. But in the
context of the hierarchical magisterium of the Church as such, it will be impossible to avoid the question of a 'non-definitive' exercise of the magisterium,
and in that context it will be hard to avoid the temptation of extending the term
'ordinary magisterium' to the non-solemn teaching of popes and ecumenical
councils (whether that be taken to refer to their 'non-definitive' teaching or
their infallible teaching that merely lacks the use of solemn formulae). And as
we have seen, several fathers of the council complained that the distinction
would belong more properly to the treatise on the Church, showing that the
terminology was already being applied in another context in the minds of
some.[55] The first signs of greater confusion to come could already be seen here,

---

55 Gaillardetz, who relies here on Caudron, concludes that the fathers of the council understood the
import of the term 'solemn judgment' much more precisely than the term 'ordinary magisterium',
which was defined in the text only negatively in opposition to solemn judgments: "Given the two
modes of teaching, the fathers understood quite clearly the first form, that of a solemn definition.
Here the emphasis was on that of judgment or decision. The ordinary magisterium was essentially
defined in opposition to this form of teaching. Yet apart from this negative definition of the
ordinary magisterium (a teaching which does not issue from a solemn judgment), the fathers
seemed quite imprecise. One must presume that the bishops were aware of the ancient conviction
that the universal agreement of the episcopate was a sure sign of the authenticity of a teaching.
Evidence from the acta suggests that they were less comfortable with its more recent formulation
in both *Tuas libenter* and *Dei Filius*. Caudron finds the use of such terms as *propositio, professio
et praedicatio, doctrina*, and *praedicat et docet* to describe the ordinary magisterium. In sum, one
must conclude that the fathers generally had little understanding of the precise meaning of the

as perhaps they saw who argued against the use of this terminology on the grounds that it was obscure and open to alternate interpretations and that it would be a source of confusion.

3. The Dogmatic Constitution *Pastor Aeternus* (1870)

Unlike *Dei Filius*, the dogmatic constitution *Pastor Aeternus* is directly ecclesiological, but it deals only with the question of the papal primacy and papal infallibility. The original schema for a constitution on the Church had been much broader in scope, but due to the controversial nature of the question of papal infallibility it was decided to treat this separately in a first constitution on the Church, which was to have been followed and completed by a second constitution on the Church. This, however, was prevented when the council was suspended indefinitely. No use is made in *Pastor Aeternus* of the terminology of an ordinary and an extraordinary magisterium, but the definition of papal infallibility does shed important light on our understanding of the extraordinary magisterium inasmuch as the act of definition described therein is identified with the solemn judgments that characterize the extraordinary magisterium.[56]

Our first task, therefore, must be to establish this identity between the act of definition and the exercise of the extraordinary magisterium, after which we shall proceed to a careful consideration of the official explanation of the definition of papal infallibility, with two questions principally in mind: first, whether the act of definition, and therefore the exercise of the extraordinary magisterium, is limited to properly dogmatic definitions *(de fide credenda)* or whether it extends to merely doctrinal definitions *(de fide tenenda)*; and secondly,

---

expression *magisterium ordinarium*" (Gaillardetz, *Witnesses*, 31; cf. Caudron, 426–28).

56 The definition of papal infallibility reads as follows: "And so, faithfully keeping to the tradition received from the beginning of the Christian faith, for the glory of God our Savior, for the exaltation of the Catholic religion, and for the salvation of Christian peoples, We, with the approval of the sacred council, teach and define that it is a dogma revealed by God: That the Roman pontiff, when he speaks *ex cathedra*, that is, when, acting in the office of shepherd and teacher of all Christians, he defines, by virtue of his supreme apostolic authority, a doctrine concerning faith or morals to be held by the universal Church, possesses through the divine assistance promised to him in blessed Peter the infallibility with which the Divine Redeemer willed his Church to be endowed in defining the doctrine concerning faith or morals; and that such definitions of the Roman pontiff are therefore irreformable of themselves, not because of the consent of the Church. But if anyone – God forbid – presumes to contradict this Our definition, let him be anathema" (Denz. 3074).

whether the act of definition, and therefore the exercise of the extraordinary magisterium, is limited to settling legitimately disputed questions or whether it extends to matters already definitively held and taught by the Church.

3.1 Definition as the Act of the Extraordinary Magisterium

The term 'extraordinary magisterium' is not used in either of the documents of the First Vatican Council, but from the immediate context and the broader discussion examined above it is safe to conclude that the 'solemn judgment' spoken of in *Dei Filius* is to be understood as the characteristic exercise of the extraordinary magisterium and that these solemn judgments are equivalent to the 'infallible judgments' and 'express definitions' spoken of in *Tuas libenter*. Other terms used equivalently by the council fathers in their discussion of *Dei Filius*, by way of contrast with the ordinary magisterium, include 'definition', 'dogmatic definition', 'solemn definition', 'dogmatic decree', and 'extraordinary judgment'. Such varied usage corresponds to that of Kleutgen, whose preferred term is 'judgment', but who also uses terms such as 'definition', 'decision', and 'declaration' interchangeably when speaking of the extraordinary magisterium. Already from the context of *Dei Filius*, therefore, it appears that the extraordinary magisterium is exercised in the issuing of a solemn judgment, which is the same as the act of defining doctrine.

Further evidence may also be found in the final *relatio* on the fourth chapter of *Pastor Aeternus* (containing the definition of papal infallibility) delivered by Vincent Gasser, Prince-Bishop of Brixen in the Austrian Tyrol, on behalf of the deputation for the faith. This official explanation, on the basis of which the final vote was taken at the council and the definition of papal infallibility passed, is perhaps the single most important source for understanding the intended sense of the definition of papal infallibility.[57] In his *relatio*, Bishop Gasser describes the infallible pontifical definitions under consideration in the text of *Pastor Aeternus* in many ways: 'definitive decisions',

---

57 The entire text of Gasser's *relatio* of 11 Jun. 1870 appears in Mansi 52:1204–30; it has been translated into English with commentary by James T. O'Connor in *The Gift of Infallibility* (San Francisco: Ignatius Press, 2008), 19–91. In the words of Dom Cuthbert Butler, Gasser "stands out as the most prominent theologian of the Council." See Cuthbert Butler, *The Vatican Council: The Story Told from Inside in Bishop Ullathorne's Letters*, vol. 2 (New York: Longmans, Green and Co., 1930), 134; Butler devotes an entire chapter of his history to Gasser's influential speech (ibid., 134–48), as does Theodor Granderath, *Geschichte des Vatikanischen Konzils: von seiner ersten Ankündigung bis zu seiner Vertagung: nach den authentischen Dokumenten*, vol. 3, ed. Konrad Kirch (Freiburg: Herder, 1906), 455–77.

'definitions', 'dogmatic definitions', 'solemn definitions', 'solemn dogmatic definitions', 'judgments', 'infallible judgments', 'dogmatic judgments', and 'solemn judgments' (the same term used in *Dei Filius* by way of contrast with the ordinary magisterium). This variety of terms used equivalently (no attempt is made at distinguishing between them), which corresponds to that seen in the discussion of *Dei Filius*, is further evidence of an identity in meaning between the 'solemn judgment' of *Dei Filius* and the 'definition' of *Pastor Aeternus*. And in one place Gasser even explicitly equates them: "The Pope is only infallible when, by a solemn judgment, he defines a matter of faith and morals for the universal Church."[58] On the basis of such evidence it seems safe to conclude that every act of teaching by a pope that qualifies as a 'definition' in the sense intended by the First Vatican Council also qualifies as a 'solemn judgment' in the sense intended by the same council, and therefore as an exercise of the extraordinary magisterium.[59]

3.2 Properly Dogmatic and Merely Doctrinal Definitions

We have seen that Avery Dulles and Umberto Betti refrain from attributing the Second Vatican Council's teaching on the sacramentality of the episcopate to the extraordinary magisterium on the grounds that it is "not a dogmatic definition in the strict sense" or not a definition "in the technical sense of the word" because to reject it would not be heresy. To reason from the premise that an act of teaching is not dogmatic in the sense that its rejection would not be heretical, to the conclusion that it is not an act of the extraordinary magisterium at all logically implies the assumption that the scope of the extraordinary magisterium is limited to the primary object of the magisterium; that is, that only properly dogmatic definitions *(de fide credenda)* are to be counted as solemn judgments or as definitions in the technical sense, which implies a denial of the possibility of merely doctrinal definitions *(de fide tenenda)* of the extraordinary magisterium. Now there would appear to be a basis for this supposition if the papal definitions spoken of in *Pastor Aeternus* were to be strictly identified only with dogmatic definitions, and in very many places – by far the majority – Gasser does use the terms 'dogmatic definition' and 'dogmatic judgment' in referring to the infallible papal definitions under

---

58   O'Connor, *The Gift of Infallibility*, 46; Mansi 52:1213: "papa solummodo sit infallibilis quando solemni iudicio pro universa ecclesia res fidei et morum definit."

59   This conclusion would exclude Fenton's opinion that there can be a non-solemn but still infallible *ex cathedra* definition that is an act of the ordinary papal magisterium.

discussion.[60] However, on closer examination, it can be seen quite clearly that the term 'definition' as it is used in the final text of *Pastor Aeternus*, is specifically intended to include merely doctrinal definitions in addition to properly dogmatic definitions.

The drafting of the definition of the infallibility of the papal magisterium took place in several stages. A first draft was prepared by the theological commission prior to the council in case the question should arise. When it was introduced at the request of the bishops, this text was distributed and the bishops were invited to submit their written observations on it to the deputation for the faith, which was entrusted with the drafting of the definition. The deputation then prepared a revised draft to serve as the basis of discussion in the council hall. After the closure of the conciliar debate, the draft returned to the deputation for further revision. Among some fifty proposals for an amended formula, one was selected by the deputation, and then a third draft was presented to the bishops, voted upon again, and finally promulgated on July 18, 1870.

The most important changes which can be noted from one draft to the next concern the extension of the object of papal infallibility. The initial draft of the theological commission describes the object of infallible papal definitions as: "What in things of faith and morals is to be held by the universal Church" *(quid in rebus fidei et morum ab universa Ecclesia tenendum sit).*[61] The second draft, prepared by the deputation, inserted an additional qualification: "What in things of faith and morals is to be held by the universal Church by divine faith or to be rejected as contrary to the (same) faith" *(quid in rebus fidei et morum ab universa Ecclesia fide divina tenendum vel tamquam [eidem] fidei contrarium reiiciendum sit).*[62]

---

60 O'Connor, *The Gift of Infallibility,* 33, 34, 41, 42, 51, 52, 53, 54, 56, 58, 62, 64, 68.

61 The Latin text of the draft is provided by Granderath, *Geschichte des Vatikanischen Konzils,* vol. 3, 123: "Definimus per divinam assistentiam fieri, ut Romanus Pontifex [...] cum supremi omnium Christianorum doctoris munere fungens pro auctoritate definit, quid in rebus fidei et morum ab universa Ecclesia tenendum sit, errare non possit; et hanc Romani Pontificis inerrantiae seu infallibilitatis praerogativam ad idem obiectum porrigi, ad quod infallibilitatis Ecclesiae extenditur."

62 Ibid., 125: "Declaramus Romanum Pontificem [...] vi divinae promissionis et assistentiae Spiritus Sancti errare non posse, cum supremi omnium Christianorum doctoris munere fungens pro Apostolica sua auctoritate definit, quid in rebus fidei et morum ab universa Ecclesia *fide divina* tenendum vel tamquam *(eidem) fidei* contrarium reiiciendum sit [...] Porro cum una eademque sit Ecclesiae infallibilitas, sive spectetur in capite Ecclesiae sive in universa Ecclesia docente cum capite unita, *hanc (unam) infallibilitatem etiam ad unum idemque obiectum sese extendere docemus.*"

A note from the diary of Ignatius von Senestréy, the Bishop of Regensburg and a member of the deputation for the faith, explains the significance of this change, and how it came about. He notes that Cardinal Luigi Bilio, the president of the deputation, criticized the first draft at a meeting on May 5, 1870, arguing that:

> No more can be defined concerning the infallibility of the pope than has been defined concerning the infallibility of the Church; but of the Church this only is of faith, that she is infallible in dogmatic definitions strictly taken; therefore the question arises whether in the proposed formula the infallibility of the pope be not too widely extended.[63]

The problem concerned the precise theological note or qualification to be assigned to distinct propositions. The practice of theological notation involves two basic considerations: divine revelation and ecclesiastical proposition. With regard to divine revelation, there are first of all doctrines of faith or morals which are immediately revealed by God, which are at least materially dogmas of divine faith *(de fide divina)*. This constitutes the primary object of the magisterium. Secondly, there are truths which are connected with divine revelation in such a way that their denial would undermine the deposit of faith. The truth of these doctrines, which belong to the secondary object of the magisterium, is guaranteed by their close connection with divine revelation, on account of which they are called theologically certain.

To this consideration of divine revelation may then be added that of ecclesiastical proposition. In order to be a dogma in the strict sense it is necessary not only that a truth be divinely revealed, but that it also be proposed precisely as a divinely revealed truth by the Church. This is the same issue that was raised in the discussion of *Dei Filius* and finally resolved by the addition of the phrase *'tanquam divinitus revelata'* in order to restrict the scope of that teaching to the primary object of the magisterium. But the Church may also propose teachings on matters of faith or morals as truths that are definitively to be held *(definitive tenenda)* on account of being at least intimately connected with divine revelation. Such teachings are not dogmas, but are often called truths of Catholic doctrine, or simply Catholic doctrines.

To return, then, to the problem posed by Cardinal Bilio in the meeting of the deputation for the faith, it was clear to all present that the infallibility of the Church in defining dogmas was itself a dogma to be held by divine and Catholic faith. That the Church was likewise infallible in her merely doctrinal (non-

---

63 The entry from Senestréy's diary is recorded in Mansi 53:276–86. The English translation is provided by Butler, *The Vatican Council*, vol. 2, 123.

dogmatic) definitions was held to be certainly true and at least intimately connected with divine revelation, but it had never been settled whether this was immediately revealed by God (primary object) or merely theologically certain (secondary object). Cardinal Bilio's point was that the solution of this question should not be pre-empted by the definition of papal infallibility; therefore the infallibility of the pope should be defined only as extending to truths of divine revelation.

For Bilio, at least, it was clear that the formulation of the object of papal infallibility as 'things of faith and morals to be held by the universal Church' would include secondary truths of Catholic doctrine; therefore he insisted on the addition of the words 'by divine faith' *(fide divina)* which excludes them, for only divinely revealed dogmas are held by divine faith: secondary truths of Catholic doctrine are held by Catholic or ecclesiastical faith.[64] The counter-argument reported by Senestréy was that Bilio's formula would be widely misinterpreted as not only a non-affirmation of papal infallibility with regard to the secondary object of the magisterium, but rather as a positive denial of it. And taken together with the clause equating the infallibility of the pope with that of the Church, this would then be taken to mean that the Church herself had been positively declared fallible in such matters. Cardinal Bilio's arguments prevailed in the deputation, however, and the revised draft with the restricted object was distributed to the bishops.

Nevertheless, in the final draft, which was ultimately approved and promulgated by the council, the crucial qualification 'by divine faith' *(fide divina)* was removed. The object was again said to be simply "doctrine of faith or morals to be held by the universal Church" *(doctrinam de fide vel moribus ab universa Ecclesia tenendam)*.[65] Although this formulation once again includes the secondary object within the scope of infallibility, it must be noted that the definition does not simply declare that the pope's merely doctrinal (non-

---

64 This neo-scholastic distinction between divine faith and ecclesiastical faith should not be misunderstood as implying that the two are mutually exclusive. For faith in the Church's teaching (ecclesiastical faith) is ultimately grounded in the belief that God constituted the Church as an authoritative teacher (divine faith).

65 Granderath, *Geschichte des Vatikanischen Konzils*, vol. 3, 474: "Romanum Pontificem, cum ex cathedra loquitur, id est, cum omnium Christianorum pastoris et doctoris munere fungens, pro suprema sua Apostolica auctoritate doctrinam de fide vel moribus ab universa Ecclesia tenendam definit, per assistentiam divinam, ipsi in beato Petro promissam, ea infallibilitate pollere, qua divinus Redemptor Ecclesiam suam in definienda doctrina de fide vel moribus instructam esse voluit, ideoque eiusmodi Romani Pontificis definitiones esse ex sese irreformabilis." The three drafts are also presented together in English translation by Butler, *The Vatican Council*, vol. 2, 133.

dogmatic) definitions are infallible, but rather that he enjoys the same infallibility which the Church enjoys in defining doctrine of faith and morals. It was for Gasser to explain how this final formulation could satisfy the objections of those like Cardinal Bilio who feared to define too much and of those like Senestréy who feared to define too little. When he comes in the course of his *relatio* to the object of papal infallibility he makes three points about the way in which infallibility pertains to different classes of doctrine. First of all, he says:

> It is certain that the infallibility promised by God completely includes the same extent of truths whether that infallibility resides in the whole Church teaching, when it defines truths in council, or in the supreme pontiff considered in himself. This is so since the purpose of infallibility is the same in whichever mode it is exercised.[66]

His second point is that there can be no doubt that the divinely revealed promise of infallibility (whether exercised by the pope alone or by the bishops together) includes the fact that it extends at least to divinely revealed truths:

> Hence it clearly is believed and must be believed as a matter of faith by all the children of holy Mother Church that the Church is infallible in proposing and defining dogmas of faith. Now in the same manner, the infallibility of the head of the Church is not able to be revealed and defined unless, by that very fact, it is revealed and defined that the pontiff is infallible in defining dogmas of faith.[67]

Gasser's third point then addresses those truths that fall under the secondary object of the magisterium: "Together with revealed truths, there are," he says, "other truths more or less strictly connected. These truths, although they are not revealed *in se*, are nevertheless required in order to guard fully, explain properly and define efficaciously the very deposit of faith."[68]

---

66   O'Connor, *The Gift of Infallibility*, 78; Mansi 52:1226: "Iam [...] certum est, infallibilitatem a Deo promissam, sive in tota ecclesia docente, cum in concilia veritates definit, sive in ipso summo pontifice [...] ad eundem omnino ambitum veritatum extendi; cum idem sit finis infallibilitatis, utrovie modo ea consideretur."

67   Ibid., 79; Mansi 52:1226: "Hinc sane de fide creditur et credendum est ab omnibus filiis matris ecclesiae, ecclesiam in proponendis ac definiendis dogmatibus fidei infallibilem esse. Eodem autem modo infallibilitas capitis ecclesiae revelata esse et definiri non poterit, quin eo ipso revelatum sit ac definiatur pontificem esse infallibilem in definiendis fidei dogmatibus."

68   Ibid., 79; Mansi 52:1226: "At vero cum dogmatibus revelatis, ut [...] ante dixi, veritates alias magis vel minus stricte cohaerent, quae licit in se revelatae non sint, requiruntur tamen ad ipsum depositum revelationis integre custodiendum, rite explicandum et efficaciter definiendum."

Gasser proceeds to explain the same problem already raised by Cardinal Bilio:

> All Catholic theologians completely agree that the Church, in her authentic proposal and definition of truths of this sort, is infallible, such that to deny this infallibility would be a very grave error. A diversity of opinion turns only on the question of the degree of certitude, i.e., on whether the infallibility in proposing these truths – and therefore in proscribing errors through censures inferior to the note of heresy – should be considered a dogma of faith, so that to deny this infallibility to the Church would be heretical, or whether it is a truth not revealed in itself but one deduced from revealed dogma and as such is only theologically certain.[69]

Since the same must be said of the infallibility of the pope as of the infallibility of the whole Church, the problem arises as to how to define the extension of the papal infallibility with the proper theological note. It is agreed that the pope is infallible in dogmatic definitions, and that this is divinely revealed; it is agreed that the pope is also infallible in merely doctrinal (non-dogmatic) definitions, but it is unclear whether this is divinely revealed or merely theologically certain. Having decided that it would be better not to settle this latter question, but to leave theologians free to discuss it, the deputation proposed a solution which would define the truth of papal infallibility generically, while leaving open the question of which theological note should be applied in the specific case. Gasser explains:

> Thus, the present definition about the object of infallibility contains two parts which are intimately connected. The first part enunciates the object of infallibility only generically, namely that it is doctrine of faith and morals. The second part of the definition distinctly sets forth this object of infallibility, not indeed by individual considerations, but by circumscribing and determining it by comparing it with the infallibility of the Church in defining, so that the very same thing must be confessed about the object of infallibility when the pope is defining as must be confessed about the object of infallibility when the Church is defining.[70]

---

69   Ibid., 79–80; Mansi 52:1226: "Hinc omnes omnino catholici theologi consentiunt, ecclesiam in huiusmodi veritatum authentica propositione ac definitione esse infallibilem, ita ut hanc infallibilitatem negare gravissimus esset error. Sed opinionum diversitas versatur unice circa gradum certitudinis, utrum scilicet infallibilitas in hisce veritatibus proponendis, ac proinde in erroribus per censuras nota haereseos inferiores proscribendis debeat conseri dogma fidei, ut hanc infallibilitatem ecclesiae negans esset haereticus; an solum sit veritas in se non revelata, sed ex revelata dogmata deducta, ac proinde solum theologice certa."

70   Ibid., 80–81; Mansi 52:1226–27: "Hinc praesens definitio de obiecto infallibilitatis duas continet

The force of Gasser's explanation of this carefully formulated definition of the object of papal infallibility can be summarized in three points: (1) the infallibility of the pope extends generically to all matters of faith and morals; (2) the extension of papal infallibility to divinely revealed truths is itself divinely revealed; (3) the extension of papal infallibility to secondary truths of Catholic doctrine is at least theologically certain. The definition of papal infallibility, as explained by Gasser, is intended to expresses each of these three truths in a single succinct formulation.

The question that usually arises here is how to understand the precise doctrinal status of the doctrine of the Church's infallibility with regards to the secondary object of the magisterium. It is clearly not defined as a dogma; it could perhaps be argued that it is implicitly defined as a truth of Catholic doctrine; it could also be argued that it remained the same undefined theological certainty that it was before the council; in any case it has since been taught more clearly by Vatican II such that it is at least authentic Catholic doctrine requiring the religious submission of will and intellect.[71] However, this question of the doctrinal status of the infallibility of the merely doctrinal definitions of the pope is distinct from the question of whether they are definitions at all, and thus whether they belong to the extraordinary magisterium.

After Gasser's lengthy introduction to the new formulation of the definition, a vote was taken two days later, which allowed the bishops to vote *placet* (it pleases), *non placet* (it does not please), or *placet iuxta modum* (it pleases with reservations). Those who voted *placet iuxta modum* were required to submit their reservations or suggestions for alterations in writing to the

---

partes inter se intime nexas. Pars prior obiectum infallibilitatis solum generice enunciat, illud nempe esse doctrinam de fide et moribus; pars vero altera noc obiectum non quidem per singula distincto declarat, sed illud circumscribit ac determinat per comparationem cum infallibilitate in definitionibus ecclesiae, adeo ut omnino idem profitendum sit de obiecto infallibilitatis in definitionibus editis a pontifice, quod profitendum est de obiecto infallibilitatis in definitionibus ecclesiae."

71 Vatican II, *Lumen gentium*, § 25: "And this infallibility with which the Divine Redeemer willed his Church to be endowed in defining doctrine of faith and morals extends as far as the deposit of revelation extends, which must be religiously guarded and faithfully expounded (Denz. 4149). The official explanation of this text given by the Theological Commission to the fathers of the council prior to their final vote makes it clear that the last phrase is intended to be understood of the secondary object of the magisterium: "The object of the infallibility of the Church thus explained, has the same extension as the revealed deposit; hence it extends to all those things, and only to those, which either directly pertain to the revealed deposit itself, or are required in order that the same deposit may be religiously safeguarded and faithfully expounded" (AS, III/1, 251; translation taken from Sullivan, *Magisterium*, 132).

deputation *de fide*. Then, on July 16, Bishop Gasser again took to the floor in order to explain why some of these proposed amendations had been rejected by the deputation while others were accepted. It was at this point that the title of the fourth chapter of the constitution was changed from "on the infallibility of the pope" to "on the infallible magisterium of the pope" in order to preclude the misconception that the pope was being declared impeccable. The final clause rejecting the necessity of the consent of the Church as a condition of the irreformability of papal definitions was also added against the Gallican doctrine. And Gasser again had to clarify the import of the definition on the object of papal infallibility, this time in connection with the word 'defines' *(definit)*.

Some of the council fathers were afraid that the word 'defines' would be construed as limiting papal infallibility to properly dogmatic definitions. Hence alternative words such as 'decree' were proposed instead. In response to this Gasser explains:

> Indeed, the Deputation *de fide* is not of the mind that this word should be understood in a juridical sense (Lat. *in sensu forensi*) so that it only signifies putting an end to controversy which has arisen in respect to heresy and doctrine which is properly speaking *de fide*. Rather, the word 'defines' signifies that the pope directly and conclusively pronounces his sentence about a doctrine which concerns matters of faith or morals and does so in such a way that each one of the faithful can be certain of the mind of the Apostolic See, of the mind of the Roman pontiff; in such a way, indeed, that he or she knows for certain that such and such a doctrine is held to be heretical, proximate to heresy, certain or erroneous, etc., by the Roman pontiff.[72]

The main point here again is that, like the formulation "doctrine of faith or morals to be held *(tenendam)* by the whole Church," the word 'defines' is intended to be understood generically as embracing not only divinely revealed truths and condemnations of heresy, but also secondary truths of Catholic doctrine which correspond to censures less than heresy. Following these final changes and explanations, the text of *Pastor Aeternus* was passed and promulgated two days later on July 18, 1870. In light of Gasser's detailed explanations,

---

72 O'Connor, *The Gift of Infallibility*, 74; Mansi 52:1316: "Utique Deputatio de fide non in ea mente est, quod verbum istud debeat sumi in sensu forensi, ut solummodo significet finem impositum controversiae, quae de haeresi et de doctrina quae proprie est de fide, agitata fuit; sed vox *definit* significat, quod papa suam sententiam circa doctrinam, quae est de rebus fidei et morum, directe et terminative proferat, ita ut iam unusquisque fidelium certus esse possit de mente sedis apostolicae, de mente Romani pontificis; ita quidem ut certo sciat a Romano pontifice hanc vel illam doctrinam haberi haereticam, haeresi proximam, certam vel erroneam, etc."

especially this last one, it is hard to see how one could maintain that papal or conciliar definitions must be properly dogmatic in order to qualify as solemn definitions of the extraordinary magisterium.

3.3 Definition as the Act of Judging Disputed Questions of Faith

Another question regarding the exercise of the extraordinary magisterium is whether it is limited to judging legitimately disputed questions in matters of faith or morals such that it would be impossible for the Church to define by the extraordinary magisterium a doctrine already infallibly taught by the ordinary magisterium. Ratzinger and Bertone, as we have seen, argue from the premise that the doctrine declared in *Ordinatio sacerdotalis* had already been taught infallibly by the ordinary and universal magisterium to the conclusion that this declaration is not an act of the extraordinary magisterium. This logically implies the assumption that the activity of the extraordinary magisterium is limited to settling legitimately disputed questions (or at least questions that have not been infallibly settled). That is, it implies that a doctrine already infallibly taught cannot later be infallibly defined. Once again there would appear to be some grounds for this in the connection commonly drawn between papal infallibility and the office of judging disputes about the faith. Gasser even says at one point in his *relatio* that the pope is only infallible "when he really and actually exercises his duty as supreme judge and universal teacher of the Church in disputes about the faith."[73] It would require a further step, however, to argue that he is only infallible when judging *legitimate* disputes about faith, for there are innumerable examples of doctrines that have continued to be disputed even after having been infallibly taught by the Church.

But Gasser later notes that, "Dogmatic judgments of the Roman pontiff are especially concerned with controversies about the faith in which recourse has been had to the Holy See,"[74] which appears to leave some room for dogmatic judgments that are not concerned with controversies about the faith. But even more substantial evidence that the prior state of a doctrine is irrelevant to its definability can be seen in Gasser's description of the quality and condition of the act of infallible papal definitions. This is the act of speaking *ex cathedra*, which means two things: first, that he speaks not merely as a private teacher,

---

73 Ibid., 46; Mansi 52:1213: "sed assistentia divina ipsi promissa, qua fit, ut errare non possit, solummodo tunc gaudet, cum munere supremi iudicis in controversiis fidei et universalis ecclesiae doctoris reipsa et actu fungitur."

74 Ibid., 56; Mansi 52:1217: "iudicia dogmatica pontificis Romani vel maxime versentur circa controversias fidei, in quibus fit recursus ad sacram sedem."

nor only as a local bishop, but precisely as the universal shepherd and teacher of the whole Church; and secondly, "not just any manner of proposing doctrine is sufficient even when he is exercising his office as supreme pastor and teacher."[75] Then Gasser continues:

> Rather, there is required the manifest intention of defining doctrine, either of putting an end to a doubt about a certain doctrine or of defining a thing, giving a definitive judgment and proposing that doctrine as one which must be held by the universal Church. This last point is indeed something intrinsic to every dogmatic definition of faith or morals that is taught by the supreme pastor and teacher of the universal Church and which is to be held by the universal Church. Indeed this very property and note of a definition, properly so-called, should be expressed, at least in some way, since he is defining doctrine to be held by the universal Church.[76]

The note of definition properly so-called – that by which an act of definition can be recognized as such – is the manifest intention of defining doctrine, which may be seen, according to Gasser's explanation, *either* in the intention of putting an end to doubt about a doctrine (that is, settling a controversy) *or* of giving a definitive judgment and proposing a doctrine as one that must be held by the universal Church. According to this formulation of the note of definition, the exercise of the extraordinary magisterium indeed appears in the settling of doctrinal controversies, but it does not appear to be limited to this; that is, the exercise of the extraordinary magisterium does not appear to be limited even to the settling of matters of dispute, much less matters of legitimate dispute. On the contrary, it can also be seen in any definitive doctrinal judgment issued for the whole Church by the supreme authority in the Church.[77] In order to determine whether a particular act of teaching is to be

---

75 Ibid., 77; Mansi 52:1225: "Secundo non sufficit quivis modus proponendi doctrinam, etiam dum pontifex fungitur munere supremi pastoris et doctoris."

76 Ibid., 77–78; Mansi 52:1225: "[S]ed requiritur intentio manifestata definiendi doctrinam, seu fluctuationi finem imponendi circa doctrinam quamdam seu rem definiendam, dando definitivam sententiam, et doctrinam illam proponendo tenendam ab ecclesia universali. Hoc ultimum est quidem aliquid intrinsecum omni definitioni dogmaticae de fide vel moribus, quae docentur a supremo pastore et doctore ecclesiae universalis et ab universa ecclesia tenenda: verum hanc proprietatem ipsam et notam definitionis proprie dictae aliquatenus saltem etiam debet exprimere, cum doctrinam ab universali ecclesia tenendam definit."

77 Much the same can be inferred from Gasser's later and more detailed explanation of the intended meaning of the term 'defines', already referenced above: "The word 'defines' signifies that the pope directly and conclusively pronounces his sentence about a doctrine which concerns matters of faith or morals and does so in such a way that each one of the faithful can be certain of the mind

counted as a definition of the extraordinary magisterium, it seems from these texts that the relevant question is not whether it was necessary in order to settle a dispute but only whether it was sufficient to do so.

Perhaps most conclusively of all, however, Gasser explains that one of the proposals of the council fathers for an amendment to the text of the definition can not be permitted because "the reverend Father appears to restrict pontifical infallibility only to controversies of faith, whereas the pontiff is also infallible as universal teacher and as supreme witness of tradition, the deposit of faith."[78] Here an interpretation that would limit the scope of the pope's extraordinary judgments to the settling of controversies is specifically rejected in favor of an interpretation that is also open to infallible definitions that witness to the received tradition without settling controversies of faith.

3.4 *Pastor Aeternus* on the Extraordinary Magisterium

If the act of definition spoken of in *Pastor Aeternus* is the same as the act of solemn judgment spoken of in *Dei Filius*, and therefore the act of the extraordinary magisterium, then we are in a position to draw several conclusions about the nature of the extraordinary magisterium from Gasser's official explanation of the intended sense of the definition of papal infallibility.

In the first place, regardless of how one interprets the First Vatican Council's teaching on the extension of infallibility to the secondary object of the magisterium, there can be little question that the act of definition itself extends to the secondary object. When *Dei Filius* speaks of solemn judgments, it indeed has in view only properly dogmatic definitions because it is speaking of the material object of divine and Catholic faith. *Pastor Aeternus*, however, has in view (among other things) the act of definition as such and this includes merely doctrinal definitions. Indeed, this is the principal point of Gasser's final words on the meaning of the term 'defines'.

Secondly, the distinguishing note of the act of definition is set forth as the manifest intention on the part of the supreme teacher to issue a definitive judgment on a doctrine as one that must be held by the whole Church. An act

---

of the Apostolic See, of the mind of the Roman pontiff; in such a way, indeed, that he or she knows for certain that such and such a doctrine is held to be heretical, proximate to heresy, certain or erroneous, etc., by the Roman pontiff" (O'Connor, *The Gift of Infallibility*, 74).

78 Ibid., 74; Mansi 52:1224: "Emendatio 47ᵃ etiam non potest admitti, sed alia ex causa, non propter conditiones appositas, sed quia reverendissimus emendator infallibilitatem pontificiam videtur coarctare ad solas controversias fidei, cum tamen pontifex etiam sit infallibilis qua doctor universalis, qua supremus testis traditionis, depositi fidei."

of teaching need not be a *new* definition (intended to settle a matter of legitimate dispute) any more than it needs to be a *dogmatic* definition in order to be recognized as a definition in the relevant sense, and thus as an act of the extraordinary magisterium.

In both of these points, the official explanation of the teaching of *Pastor Aeternus* coheres closely with Joseph Kleutgen's original conception of the distinction between the ordinary and the extraordinary magisterium.

4.   Concluding Observations

Considering the historical connections between *Tuas libenter* and Cardinal von Reisach, between von Reisach and Joseph Kleutgen, and between Kleutgen and the texts of the First Vatican Council at which he served as a *peritus*, the extent to which Kleutgen's thought is reflected in these documents can come as no surprise. Motivated by opposition to the dogmatic minimalism that was gaining traction especially in Germany (frequently from the laudable intention of aiding the work of ecumenism), Pius IX and the First Vatican Council adopted the strategy prepared by Kleutgen for the same purpose: an emphasis on the authority of the ordinary magisterium of the whole Church dispersed throughout the world alongside of and equal to the authority of the comparatively extraordinary solemn judgments of popes and ecumenical councils.

From these three documents of the magisterium, read carefully in light of their historical background and textual development with reference to the official explanations of the intended sense of the conciliar texts, the following general picture of the nature and operations of the ordinary and extraordinary magisterium can be drawn. The extraordinary magisterium is exercised in the act of judgment *(Dei Filius)* which is the same as the act of definition *(Pastor Aeternus)*. Such definitions are by their own nature solemn and extraordinary. It can be exercised by ecumenical councils *(Tuas libenter)* and by the pope *(Tuas libenter; Pastor Aeternus)*. And it can be properly dogmatic *(Tuas libenter; Dei Filius; Pastor Aeternus)* or merely doctrinal *(Tuas libenter; Pastor Aeternus)*. The characteristic note of definition is the manifest intention of pronouncing a definitive judgment on a doctrine as one that must be held by the whole Church (Gasser on *Pastor Aeternus);* and the exercise of the extraordinary magisterium is not limited to settling controversies of faith since the pope is not only supreme judge but also supreme teacher and witness of tradition (Gasser on *Pastor Aeternus).* Judging disputed questions in matters of faith may be the paradigmatic exercise of the extraordinary magisterium, but it need not be the exclusive exercise.

The authority of the ordinary magisterium is equal to that of the extraordinary magisterium *(Tuas libenter; Dei Filius)*. It consists in the daily preaching and teaching of the faith (Martin on *Dei Filius)*. It is exercised by the whole Church dispersed throughout the world *(Tuas libenter; Dei Filius)* and not by the pope alone (Martin on *Dei Filius)*. It can be properly dogmatic *(Tuas libenter; Dei Filius)* or merely doctrinal *(Tuas libenter)*. And its teaching can be recognized in the consensus of theologians or the consensus of the faithful *(Tuas libenter)*.

All of this constitutes a strong argument for interpreting the Church's use of the terminology of an ordinary and an extraordinary magisterium along the lines laid down by Kleutgen. However, this should not be taken to mean that every detail of Kleutgen's system has been or needs to be adopted into the official teaching of the Church. Kleutgen's idea of an exercise of the extraordinary magisterium by the Church dispersed throughout the world, for example, seems to have been abandoned completely. And even the reference in *Tuas libenter* to the consensus of theologians as a sign of the teaching of the ordinary magisterium has disappeared from later magisterial statements on the subject.

Furthermore, some of the shortcomings that we encountered in the works of Kleutgen reappear in the documents of the magisterium. In none of these documents is there anything approaching an adequate treatment of the non-infallible teaching of the Church. The possibility is not positively excluded, but as with Kleutgen, it is nowhere sufficiently developed or integrated into a broader understanding of the magisterium.[79] The terminology of ordinary and extraordinary, moreover, which seems to imply an exhaustive division of the modes of operation of the magisterium, compounds the difficulty inasmuch as both are treated as equally infallible. Terminologically, it would have been easier to develop an account of the 'non-definitive' teaching of the magisterium as a third kind of teaching alongside of the 'definitions of the Church' and the 'living tradition of the Church' since these latter names do not imply an exhaustive division. Instead, however, the tendency has been to force the non-infallible teaching of the magisterium into the category of the ordinary magiste-

---

79 The only apparent reference to such teaching is in the *monitum* at the conclusion of *Dei Filius*, which has usually been interpreted in this sense: "It is, however, not enough to avoid the wickedness of heresy unless those errors that lead close to it are also carefully avoided. We therefore remind all of their duty to observe also the constitutions and decrees by which such perverse opinions, which are not explicitly enumerated here, are proscribed by this Holy See" (Denz. 3045).

rium. Hence the later development of referring to the 'non-definitive' teaching of popes or ecumenical councils as exercises of an 'ordinary papal magisterium' or an 'ordinary conciliar magisterium'.

Further compounding the difficulty is the ambiguity over the proper context of the distinction. For Kleutgen, the distinction originated in the context of a discussion of the rule of faith rather than in a treatise on the Church as such, and this is where it remained in *Tuas libenter* and in *Dei Filius*, the constitution on the Catholic Faith; *Pastor Aeternus*, the constitution on the Church, makes no reference to the terms. However, the applicability of the distinction to the latter context is clear and many bishops urged that the council's treatment of the distinction should be relocated to the treatise on the Church. In the context of the rule of faith, which addresses only doctrine that is binding on the consciences of the faithful, the problem of 'non-definitive' teaching does not arise, which may explain why it is not addressed by Kleutgen or by Pius IX or Vatican I; but in the context of a treatise on the Church, which addresses modes of Church teaching directly, the question of 'non-definitive' teaching must be treated; the difficulty is how to do so using a terminology developed in another context to solve a different problem without essentially altering the meaning of the terms being used.

PART III.

FROM VATICAN I TO VATICAN II:
THEOLOGICAL DEVELOPMENTS AND DEPARTURES

Following our examination of the initial adoption of the terminology of ordinary and extraordinary magisterium in the documents of the Church by Pope Pius IX and the First Vatican Council, we turn next to consider some of the principal lines of interpretation that developed after Vatican I together with the major documents of the magisterium that touch upon the distinction, up to and including the teaching of the Second Vatican Council in its dogmatic constitution *Lumen gentium* (1964).

The first line of interpretation to be considered is the tradition of speculation that developed regarding a distinctly papal exercise of the ordinary magisterium. At the origin of this tradition stands Jean-Michel-Alfred Vacant (1852–1901), a professor of fundamental and dogmatic theology at the seminary in Nancy, France, and the primary editor of the monumental French *Dictionnaire de théologie catholique*. In 1887 he published "what appears to be the first theological monograph to focus exclusively on the ordinary magisterium of the Church, *Le Magistere ordinaire de l'eglise et ses organs*."[1] This landmark treatise, which would exercise a strong influence on the theological interpretation of the ordinary magisterium for many decades to come, contains several noteworthy contributions, including his original argument for an infallible ordinary papal magisterium. The encyclical letter *Humani generis* (1950) of Pope Pius XII eventually took up this idea of a papal exercise of the ordinary magisterium, but without attributing to it infallibility.

The second line of thought that I propose to trace is the interpretation that views the extraordinary magisterium as the instrument of doctrinal innovation; that is, the view that sees the extraordinary magisterium at work only in the creation of new doctrinal obligations – the settling of questions previously open to legitimate dispute. Louis Billot (1846–1931) appears to stand in some way at the origins of this view, though his own position on the question is not entirely clear. Billot was a French Jesuit priest and theologian who was made a Cardinal in 1911 but resigned from the office in 1927 apparently due to disagreements with Pope Pius XI over the French Catholic political movement Action Française. Author of a widely read and highly regarded treatise on the Church,

---

1   Gaillardetz, *Witnesses to the Faith*, 81.

entitled *Tractatus de Ecclesia Christi (sive continuatio theologiae de verbo incarnato)*, his contributions to ecclesiology exercised a powerful and lasting influence due to his position as a professor of dogmatic theology at the Gregorian University in Rome and his pre-eminence as a theologian and a leading figure of the neo-Thomistic revival. In this section we will also look at the teaching of the encyclical letter *Mortalium animos* (1928) of Pope Pius XI and the apostolic constitution *Munificentissimus Deus* (1950) of Pope Pius XII to see what light they shed on this question.

Thirdly, and finally, we will then undertake a thorough treatment of the Second Vatican Council's teaching on the magisterium through an examination of paragraph 25 of *Lumen gentium*. Our focus will be on the understanding presented therein of the (merely) authentic magisterium, the ordinary and universal magisterium, and the extraordinary magisterium.

1. The Ordinary Magisterium and the Pope

The object of our consideration in this chapter is the notion, developed in the period between Vatican I and Vatican II, of a papal exercise of the ordinary magisterium. We will confine our examination to the introduction of this idea in the writings of J.-M.-A. Vacant and then to its eventual adoption in the encyclical letter *Humani generis* of Pope Pius XII.

1.1 J.-M.-A. Vacant on the Ordinary Magisterium

Vacant's work, *Le Magistere ordinaire de l'eglise et ses organs*, is divided into six chapters, which treat of (1) the general idea of the ordinary and universal magisterium; (2) the ministers who serve as organs and instruments of the ordinary magisterium; (3) the modes of expression of the ordinary magisterium; (4) the obligations imposed by the ordinary magisterium in matters of doctrine; (5) the doctrinal authority of the majority of the bishops dispersed throughout the world; and (6) the part played personally by the pope in the exercise of the ordinary magisterium.

There are several noteworthy points within this treatise. In the first place, it contains a much more fully developed account of the daily teaching activity of the ordinary magisterium and the ways in which the hierarchy and the lay faithful alike are called to participate in its exercise. Whereas Kleutgen had highlighted the role of theologians in bearing witness to the teaching of the ordinary magisterium, Vacant expands upon the many organs and instruments of the ordinary magisterium. Only the bishops exercise the ordinary magisterium directly by divine right, but they are able to exercise their authority through the instrumentality of many other members of the Church, as the soul is able to act through the various organs of the body (Vacant's interpretation of the Pauline doctrine of the Church as the Mystical Body of Christ views the hierarchy – rather than the Holy Spirit – as the soul of the Church). Instruments of the ordinary magisterium of the Church thus include all those who are authorized to teach the faith in any capacity: pastors and other priests and clergy in teaching the flock entrusted to their care; Roman congregations in their function as instruments of the Holy See; Catholic Universities in forming their students in the study of the faith; theologians in their work and their writings; teachers of Christian education in schools; and even parents teaching the faith to their own children. Vacant compares the ordinary magisterium to the roar of the sea: a vast multitude of individual voices coming together in a harmonious living transmission of the faith.[2] In order to know the teaching of the ordinary magisterium, however, it is not necessary to listen to every voice. It is enough to consult the universal and constant teaching of the fathers and doctors of the Church, or even more simply, he says, to consult the Creeds and Catechisms of the Church.

This leads us to another interesting feature of Vacant's exposition: his division of the modes of expression of the ordinary magisterium into explicit, implicit, and tacit acts of teaching. The explicit teaching of the ordinary magisterium is that explicitly doctrinal proposition of the faith by the bishops, fathers, doctors, and all the rest. This explicit ordinary teaching is found most conveniently in the Creeds and Catechisms of the Church. The implicit teaching of the ordinary magisterium refers to the doctrinal truths implied in the discipline and worship of the Church or in the moral conduct of pastors and faithful. The officially sanctioned practice of eucharistic adoration, for example, implies the doctrine of the Real Presence of Christ in the Eucharist. Finally, the tacit teaching of the ordinary magisterium refers to the silent

---

2   Vacant, *Le Magistere ordinaire*, § 2: "Le magistère ordinaire et universel de l'Église, encore qu'il soit tout entier sous l'action du corps épiscopal, est donc formé par le concert d'un nombre infini de voix qui s'élèvent sans cesse d'un bout à l'autre de l'univers. C'est comme le bruit du vaste océan, où le murmure des moindres flots se mêle au fracas des grandes vagues. Mais, tandis qu'il ne sort du sein de la mer que des mugissements confus, toutes les voix que nous entendons dans l'Église se font les instruments du magistère de l'épiscopat: ce sont comme des échos vivants ou, suivant la belle comparaison de saint Ignace, martyr *(ad Ephes.)*, comme les cordes d'une lyre qui s'harmonisent sans cesse avec la voix du Souverain Pontife et des évêques; car un organe n'exerce aucune fonction que sous l'influence du principe vital et un instrument n'agit que sous l'impulsion de celui qui l'emploie."

transmission of Scripture and the monuments of tradition. A doctrine clearly contained in Scripture, for example, or a solemn judgment contained in the decrees of an ancient ecumenical council, are tacitly taught by the ordinary magisterium today, whether or not the current members of the hierarchy explicitly advert to them.

This threefold division of the exercise of the ordinary magisterium seems to be original to Vacant. Kleutgen made no such distinction, nor is there any hint of it in the documents of the Church reviewed above. Yet it appears to be a development substantially consistent with Kleutgen's conception of the ordinary magisterium. And it has been taken up in various forms (usually reduced to a twofold division between explicit and implicit teaching) by other influential authors through the years, including Ratzinger and Bertone in their doctrinal commentary on the concluding formula of the profession of faith.[3]

At the same time, however, it must be acknowledged that Vacant's addition of these distinctions within the exercise of the ordinary magisterium lends itself to confusion over the nature of the more basic distinction between the ordinary and extraordinary magisterium inasmuch as it too is based, at least for Kleutgen, on the distinction between explicit (documented) and implicit (undocumented) teaching of the Church. According to Kleutgen, the explicit definitions of the Church belong to the extraordinary magisterium, while the teaching of the ordinary magisterium is by contrast implicit. Now Vacant introduces the idea that some of this ordinary (implicit) teaching of the Church is explicit, some is implicit, and some is tacit. The danger of confusion here would be hard to overstate.

In the fourth chapter of his work, Vacant discusses the obligation imposed by the ordinary magisterium in matters of doctrine by posing two questions: whether the teaching of the ordinary magisterium is sufficient to impose obligatory adherence to a doctrine; and whether the ordinary magisterium is able to make obligatory a point of doctrine that had previously been a matter of free opinion.[4] The first question is resolved in the affirmative with reference

---

3   Ratzinger and Bertone, *Doctrinal Commentary*, § 9, n. 1: "It should be noted that the infallible teaching of the ordinary and universal Magisterium is not only set forth with an explicit declaration of a doctrine to be believed or held definitively, but it is also expressed by a doctrine implicitly contained in a practice of the Church's faith, derived from revelation, or, in any case, necessary for eternal salvation, and attested to by the uninterrupted tradition" (Denz. 5072).

4   Vacant, *Le Magistere ordinaire*, § 4: "On peut se demander en effet: 1° si la proposition du magistère ordinaire suffit pour qu'une doctrine s'impose à notre adhésion; 2° si cette proposition a la force de rendre obligatoire même un point librement controversé jusque-là. Ces deux questions méritent d'être examinées séparément."

to the texts of *Dei Filius* and *Tuas libenter*, which make it clear that the teaching of the ordinary magisterium is just as binding as the solemn judgments of the Church. The second question is more difficult. Some doctrines have been explicitly believed and taught from the beginning (such as, for example, the divinity of Christ). Others were long matters of free opinion before being settled by a solemn judgment of the Church (such as, for example, the Immaculate Conception of Mary). In teaching these doctrines the ordinary magisterium only affirms an existing obligation. But can the ordinary magisterium, by its own strength, create a new obligation where there had not been one previously? Vacant's answer, drawn from several examples of the historical practice of the Church, is that by the ordinary magisterium alone a doctrine can be removed from the field of free opinion and become a certain and infallible doctrine of the Church; but it cannot be made a dogma of faith binding under pain of heresy without the intervention of the extraordinary magisterium. In order to create new dogmas a solemn judgment seems to be necessary.

Now Gaillardetz appears to conclude from this that Vacant denies entirely the possibility of attaching the note of heresy to the denial of a dogma taught only by the ordinary magisterium.[5] As far as I can see, however, Vacant defends only the more limited claim that the ordinary magisterium cannot impose any *new* dogma; he does not deny – in fact, he seems to affirm – the existence of dogmas imposed "under pain of heresy"[6] that have always been taught by the ordinary magisterium from the beginning. He concludes thus: "The ordinary magisterium is therefore infallible in all its assertions; but it has not so far proposed and it would be hard to propose dogmas of Catholic faith other than those that have been such from the time of the Apostles or have become such

---

5 Gaillardetz, *Witnesses of the Faith*, 87: "The note of heresy could only be attached to a teaching which rejected defined dogma, and not to undefined dogma taught by the ordinary universal magisterium. The French theologian maintained that for the assignment of such a negative note (heresy) it was necessary that the given dogma be taught with the clarity which could be offered only in a solemn definition." Ibid., 90: "Vacant's claim that the ordinary magisterium could not declare a teaching heretical reflected a cautious respect for the lack of clarity found in the teaching of the ordinary magisterium; while it possessed the same authority as solemn judgments, only a solemn judgment could define a teaching and only a solemn judgment could determine that a teaching was actually heretical."

6 Vacant, *Le Magistere ordinaire*, § 4: "Nous avons établi que les symboles et les professions de foi employés par l'Eglise universelle sont l'expression infaillible de son enseignement quotidien; il suffit d'ajouter que tous les points qui y sont affirmés s'imposent, comme de foi catholique, et, par conséquent, sous peine d'hérésie. Tel est, en effet, le sentiment des pasteurs et des fidèles."

in virtue of a solemn judgment."[7] The focus here is on the narrower question of whether the ordinary magisterium by itself can raise the status of a doctrine to the level of dogma; not whether it can teach dogma at all. Strictly speaking, restricting the creation of new dogmas to the extraordinary magisterium does not logically imply a restriction of the extraordinary magisterium to the creation of new dogmas (since universal affirmative propositions are not convertible); but historically, this may well represent the first step on the road to the 'new dogmatization' thesis of Ratzinger and Bertone.

The last two chapters of Vacant's work are devoted to the parts played by the bishops and by the pope, respectively, in the exercise of the ordinary magisterium. In considering the doctrinal authority of the bishops dispersed throughout the world, he raises the question of whether a majority of bishops teaching the same doctrine is sufficient for the exercise of the ordinary magisterium. He notes that there are good authorities on both sides, but he defends the sufficiency of a majority of bishops, at least among those who exercise legitimate jurisdiction in the Church, to teach a doctrine infallibly by the ordinary magisterium; complete unanimity is not required since God would not allow even the majority of the Church to fall into error.[8]

And then, in the final chapter, Vacant introduces the concept of a distinct papal exercise of the ordinary magisterium and defends its infallibility. The pope, says Vacant, is infallible in his solemn judgments of faith and in the ordinary magisterium that he exercises together with the bishops dispersed throughout the world. "But can we distinguish the ordinary magisterium of the bishops united to the pope and the personal ordinary magisterium of the supreme pontiff, as we distinguish the solemn decisions of councils and those of popes? I believe so."[9] Vacant is well aware that in proposing this he is breaking new ground theologically. He writes:

---

7   Ibid.: "Le magistère ordinaire est donc infaillible dans toutes ses affirmations; mais il n'a proposé jusqu'ici et il ne peut guère proposer d'autres dogmes de foi catholique que ceux qui sont tels depuis le temps des apôtres ou qui le sont devenus en vertu d'un jugement solennel."

8   Ibid., § 5: "Toute doctrine enseignée comme obligatoire par la majorité, et surtout par l'unanimité des évêques catholiques, est donc obligatoire pour toute l'Église dans la mesure où ils l'affirment; car on peut être assuré qu'ils la proposent à la croyance des fidèles, en union avec le Souverain Pontife, et que, par conséquent, cette doctrine est enseignée infailliblement par le corps épiscopal tout entier, c'est-à-dire par le Pape et les évêques unis au Pape."

9   Ibid., § 6: "Mais ne peut-on distinguer le magistère ordinaire de l'épiscopat uni au Pape et le magistère ordinaire personnel du Souverain Pontife, comme on distingue les jugements solennels des conciles et ceux des Papes? Je le crois."

So I will put forward a proposal that I have not read so far, in explicit terms, in any work, but which seems to me consistent with the teaching of all the authors who supported the infallibility of the pope, namely that the pope personally exercises his infallibility not only through solemn judgments but also through an ordinary magisterium that extends perpetually to all the truths required for the whole Church.[10]

The first step for Vacant is to try to demonstrate that the pope does personally exercise the ordinary magisterium in all its forms – explicit, implicit, and tacit. He takes as typical of the extraordinary magisterium solemn judgments such as the definition of the Immaculate Conception, which are "clothed in all the forms proper to express clearly that it is the intention of the pope to impose the truth being taught on the faith or consent of the whole Church."[11] Every kind of papal teaching that falls short of these external forms is then attributed to the ordinary magisterium. As examples, Vacant cites the interviews of the pope with bishops on their official visits *ad limina* and the recitals of previous solemn definitions. It would be impossible, he says, to draw an exact line between the ordinary magisterium of the pope and his solemn judgments, but it is certain that many acts of papal teaching do not meet all the external conditions and forms that typically characterize solemn definitions.[12]

---

10 Ibid.: "Aussi vais-je avancer une proposition que je n'ai lue jusqu'ici, en termes exprès, dans aucun ouvrage, mais qui me paraît conforme à la doctrine de tous les auteurs qui ont soutenu l'infailli-bilité du Pape, savoir que le Pape exerce personnellement son magistère infaillible non seulement par des jugements solennels, mais encore par un magistère ordinaire qui s'étend à toutes les vérités obligatoires pour toute l'Eglise."

11 Ibid., § 6: "On peut considérer, comme types des jugements solennels, les définitions revêtues de toutes les formes propres à exprimer nettement soit la vérité qui en fait l'objet, soit l'intention que le Pape a de l'imposer à la foi ou à l'assentiment de toute l'Eglise. Telle fut, par exemple, la définition de l'Immaculée Conception."

12 Ibid.: "Or, il est une foule d'actes pontificaux qui se rapprochent plus ou moins, les uns des jugements solennels, les autres de l'enseignement quotidien, et, si l'on en dressait une liste complète, il serait impossible de marquer, dans cette liste, le point où le magistère ordinaire commence et celui où cessent les jugements solennels. En effet, comme les caractères de ces jugements sont multiples, beaucoup d'actes pontificaux ne sont revêtus que d'une partie de ces caractères. Faut-il, par exemple, ranger parmi les jugements solennels ou parmi les actes du magistère quotidien les diverses lettres apostoliques qui ne sont pas adressées à tous les évêques du monde, les allocutions consistoriales et celles que le Souverain Pontife prononce dans certaines audiences publiques? Je n'essayerai pas de le déterminer. Ce qui est certain, c'est que ces actes ne remplissent pas toutes les conditions extérieures et, si je puis ainsi dire, de forme qui caractérisent les définitions solennelles que j'ai prises pour type."

As a test case, Vacant takes up the *Syllabus of Errors* published by Pope Pius IX in 1864. This, he argues, is a clear example of ordinary papal teaching. He notes that there is a recognized consensus that it does not meet the conditions required by canonists for authentic laws.[13] The individual condemnations contained in the *Syllabus* are drawn from consistorial speeches, encyclicals and other apostolic letters, which he takes as clearly belonging to the pope's ordinary magisterium. But instead of promulgating this collection of condemned errors in a solemn definition, the pope simply sent it as it is to all the bishops together with his encyclical letter *Quanta cura* (1864). Is the *Syllabus of Errors* therefore infallible? Vacant argues that it is on the grounds that the condemnations contained in it are imposed on the faith or consent of all Catholics in virtue of the supreme papal authority, which is always infallible regardless of the external form in which the act is clothed.[14] Many theologians, as Vacant remarks, rank the *Syllabus of Errors* as a papal definition *ex cathedra*, which he thinks can be justified if we introduce a distinction between solemn and ordinary *ex cathedra* definitions:

> If we apply the name 'definition *ex cathedra*' to all acts of the supreme pontiff which fulfill the conditions under which the Vatican Council declares that the successor of St. Peter is infallible, then we must place the acts of which we have been talking among these definitions; but, in this case, it is necessary to distinguish two kinds of *ex cathedra* definition: those brought by solemn decrees and those brought by the daily magisterium of the supreme pontiff.[15]

---

13 Ibid.: "N'oublions pas non plus que Pie IX a fait publier un document célèbre qui, on s'accorde à le reconnaître, n'est pas revêtu des conditions exigées par les canonistes pour les lois authentiques."

14 Ibid., § 6: "Mais, demandera-t-on, ces actes du magistère quotidien du Pape peuvent-ils être infaillibles? Oui; car nous y trouvons des doctrines que le magistère ordinaire impose, par ces actes mêmes, à la foi ou à l'assentiment de tous les catholiques. C'est ce que Pie IX a déclaré, en affirmant qu'il avait condamné les principales erreurs de notre époque, dans plusieurs encycliques, aussi bien que dans des allocutions consistoriales et d'autres lettres apostoliques qui avaient été publiées; car condamner une erreur, c'est défendre d'y adhérer, et, quand le Pape porte une telle défense en vertu de sa suprême autorité, il le fait infailliblement, de quelque forme que son acte soif revêtu."

15 Ibid.: "Si l'on applique, en effet, le nom de définition *ex cathedra* à tous les actes du Souverain Pontife qui remplissent les conditions dans lesquelles le Concile du Vatican déclare que le successeur de saint Pierre est infaillible, il faut placer les actes dont nous venons de parler parmi ces définitions; mais, en ce cas, il y a lieu de distinguer deux sortes de définitions *ex cathedra*: celles qui sont portées par des décrets solennels et celles qui sont portées par le magistère quotidien du Souverain Pontife."

Thus Vacant does not regard solemn papal judgments as identical with infallible papal definitions *ex cathedra*. In fact, he says, it is the failure to distinguish between these categories that has led very respectable authors to deny the infallibility of the *Syllabus*. According to Vacant, a papal act is ranked as a solemn judgment only if it meets the more stringent canonical criteria for promulgation of law; but it is an infallible definition *ex cathedra* if it meets the conditions imposed by the Vatican Council.[16] The *Syllabus*, Vacant argues, does not meet the conditions for a solemn judgment, but it does meet the conditions for an *ex cathedra* definition.

Now if the encyclical letters, speeches, and other such things are explicit exercises of the ordinary magisterium, the pope also exercises the ordinary magisterium implicitly and tacitly. The implicit teaching of the ordinary magisterium is seen above all in the discipline and worship of the Church, which are legislated mostly by the pope; and as regards the tacit preservation of the monuments of the faith, "this role of silent guardian of doctrine still belongs, more than anyone, to the successor of St. Peter, who confirms his brethren in the faith."[17] Vacant admits that the Vatican definition of papal infallibility concerns only the explicit teaching of the pope, and so the infallibility of these modes of exercise of the ordinary magisterium by the pope can be established only as a theological conclusion. "But nothing," he says, "prevents the conditions for an *ex cathedra* definition being realized in some express teachings of the ordinary magisterium. So it would be wrong to think that the fathers of the Vatican wanted to speak only of the solemn judgments of the supreme pontiff."[18]

---

16 Ibid.: "C'est, entre autres motifs, pour avoir confondu les décrets solennels, portés suivant les règles que le droit Canon exige pour une loi, avec les définitions *ex cathedra*, où les conditions posées par le Concile du Vatican sont remplies, que des auteurs très respectables ont nié l'infaillibilité du *Syllabus*." Here Vacant adds a lengthy footnote: "Le cardinal Mazzella dit de ceux qui soutiennent ce sentiment, qu'ils sont '*viros aliquot, paucos tamen haud mediocris ingenii*' (*de Ecclesia*, p. 822). Il fait allusion à Mgr Fessier qu'il nomme. J'ignore s'il a en vue d'autres personnages distingués par leur science; mais j'ai sous les yeux des notes prises à Rome, en 1883–84, aux conférences d'un canoniste célèbre, et où l'on soutient que le Syllabus n'est pas une définition infaillible, parce que c'est une collection privée, semblable au décret de Gratien et qui n'a pas été promulguée par le Pape lui-même, suivant les règles du droit. Je ne sais si la doctrine du conférencier a été bien rendue par l'étudiant qui rédigeait ces notes; mais les notes ont le tort de supposer que, pour être infaillibles, les enseignements pontificaux doivent être tous édités dans la forme exigée pour l'authenticité des lois."

17 Ibid., § 6: "Or, ce rôle de gardien muet de la doctrine appartient encore, plus qu'à personne, au successeur de saint Pierre, chargé de confirmer ses frères dans la foi."

18 Ibid.: "Mais rien n'empêche les conditions d'une définition *ex cathedra* de se réaliser dans certains

Summing up the extent of Vacant's influence on the theological reception of the Church's teaching on the ordinary and extraordinary magisterium is no simple matter. On the one hand, his work represents a substantial development of Kleutgen's original doctrine and of the official teaching of the Church on the question, going beyond them while remaining for the most part faithful to them. This can be seen especially in his more detailed working out of the various modes of participation in the ordinary magisterium of all the members of the Church – bishops, priests, theologians, catechists, parents; and in his theological grounding of this in the Pauline image of the Church as the Mystical Body of Christ. It can also be seen in his extensive working out of the various modes of exercise of the ordinary magisterium itself with his introduction of new distinctions between explicit, implicit, and tacit modes of ordinary teaching.

In some ways, however, Vacant's work also represents a departure from or even distortion of the meaning of the distinction between the ordinary and the extraordinary magisterium. For Kleutgen, this was a distinction between the definitive teaching of the Church that comes to us directly from the supreme authority in the Church – the pope or the bishops gathered in council (extraordinary); and the definitive teaching of the Church that comes to us indirectly via the evidence gathered from the sources of revelation (ordinary). For Vacant, it appears instead to be a distinction between the teaching presented in the externally solemn form (extraordinary) that meets the more stringent requirements of the canonists for the enactment of doctrine as law; and the teaching presented without these solemn external forms, and therefore without meeting these more stringent requirements, but still potentially meeting the requirements of the First Vatican Council for infallible definitions.

This altered conception of the nature of the distinction appears to follow primarily from the introduction of a distinct papal exercise of the ordinary magisterium. For if the pope can exercise the same ordinary magisterium that is infallible when exercised by the college of bishops, then it should also be infallible when exercised by the pope; and if the pope has an infallible ordinary magisterium, then what distinguishes it from his extraordinary magisterium? Both are equally explicit and definitive. So the distinction was interpreted in terms of external solemnity. Although novel, it was perhaps almost inevitable that this step should be taken. An apparently exhaustive division of the modes of exercise of the magisterium had been established with only two categories:

enseignements exprès du magistère ordinaire. On se tromperait donc, en pensant que les Pères du Vatican n'ont voulu parler que des jugements solennels du Souverain Pontife."

ordinary and extraordinary. Much of the teaching activity of the pope clearly did not fit in the category of extraordinary solemn judgment. What could be more natural than describing this daily teaching of the pope as a papal exercise of the ordinary magisterium? And yet, as Gaillardetz comments, "It is remarkable, coming from a theologian who wrote a major work on Vatican I's *Dei Filius*, that he completely ignored the significance of the council's explicit addition of the word *universale* to the ordinary magisterium, an act intended to make it clear that the council fathers were referring to the college of the bishops and not to any ordinary papal magisterium."[19] It seems that the addition of this word and the reference to *Tuas libenter* may not have been enough to remove the obscurity and ambiguity that many of the council fathers feared.

1.2 The Encyclical Letter *Humani generis* (1950)

Pope Pius XII's encyclical letter *Humani generis*, in which he undertook to correct "some false opinions threatening to undermine the foundations of Catholic doctrine,"[20] generated a massive response in the theological literature of the time, largely due to the fact that it was directed against certain trends in theology itself.[21] The background of the document is the whole complex of currents in mid-twentieth century theology centered around the tension between the neo-scholastic method of theology, on the one hand, which its opponents characterized as "a theology occupied with erecting a static skeleton of Christian dogma whose members were rigidly connected, one with the other, by logical terms functioning exclusively with the forces of Aristotelian dialectic,"[22] and the method of the so-called "new theologians" who were looking for a more dynamic approach to theology.[23]

---

19 Gaillardetz, *Witnesses to the Faith*, 91.
20 Pope Pius XII, Encyclical Letter concerning Some False Opinions Threatening to Undermine the Foundations of Catholic Doctrine *Humani generis* (12 Aug. 1950).
21 A good indication of this can be seen in the bibliography of commentaries compiled by Gustave Weigel in "Gleanings from the Commentaries on *Humani generis*," *Theological Studies* 12 (1951): 520–49. Published only eighteen months after *Humani generis*, it already contained some eighty entries in nine languages.
22 Gustave Weigel, "The Historical Background of the Encyclical *Humani generis*," *Theological Studies* 12.2 (1951): 213.
23 Weigel highlights the French Jesuit theologians Henri de Lubac, Jean Daniélou, and Henri Bouillard, and the French Dominicans Marie Dominique Chenu, Yves Congar, and André Marie Dubarle (Weigel, "Historical Background," 217).

By the time of *Humani generis* the initial step taken by Vacant in applying the distinction between the ordinary and extraordinary magisterium of the Church to the magisterium of the pope had led to a sometimes bewildering diversity of positions in the theological literature and manuals, compounded by an inconsistent terminology. As Edmond Benard noted, Vacant and Dublanchy held that the pope could teach infallibly through his ordinary magisterium, whereas Dieckmann (and apparently Benard himself) equated the ordinary magisterium of the pope with his 'non-definitive' teaching. Again, authors such as Billot and Tanquerey held that the pope could teach infallibly without speaking *ex cathedra*, while Zapelena, Diekamp, d'Herbigny, Schultes, Pesch, and Bainvel held that every infallible papal pronouncement is necessarily also an *ex cathedra* pronouncement.[24] Fenton likewise noted (apparently with surprise) that authors such as Briere, Heris, Manzoni, Felder, Lercher, Benard, Chevasse, Salaverri, and Billot identify every *ex cathedra* definition as necessarily solemn and extraordinary, whereas Fenton follows Vacant in distinguishing between ordinary and solemn *ex cathedra* definitions.[25]

Humani generis did not directly touch the question of infallibility, but it did make use of the term 'ordinary magisterium' with reference to the general teaching of the papal encyclical letters, which marks a real departure from Kleutgen's original conception of the ordinary magisterium as an intangible or non-documentary means of transmitting the faith, as opposed to the explicitly documented teaching of the Church. The relevant passage of the encyclical letter reads as follows:

> Nor must it be thought that what is expounded in encyclical letters does not of itself demand consent, since in writing such letters the popes do not exercise the supreme power of their Teaching Authority. For these matters are taught with the ordinary teaching authority, of which it is true to say: "He who hears you hears me" [*Lk 10:16*], and generally what is expounded and inculcated in encyclical letters already for other reasons appertains to Catholic doctrine. But if the supreme pontiffs in their official documents purposely pass judgment on a matter up to that time under dispute, it is obvious that that matter, according to the mind and will of the pontiffs, cannot be any longer considered a question open to discussion among theologians.[26]

---

24 Benard, "Doctrinal Value," 78–79.
25 Fenton, "Infallibility in the Encyclicals," 181–82.
26 Pius XII, *Humani generis*, § 20: "Neque putandum est, ea quae in Encyclicis Litteris proponuntur, assensum per se non postulare, cum in iis Pontifices supremam sui Magisterii potestatem non exerceant. Magisterio enim ordinario haec docentur, de quo illud etiam valet: 'Qui vos audit, me audit' [*Lc 10:16*]; ac plerumque quae in Encyclicis Litteris proponuntur et inculcantur, iam

The main point here seems to be that the teaching expounded in papal encyclical letters cannot simply be ignored or dismissed but requires consent. Because the assent required is not said to be an assent of faith, it is generally understood to be the religious submission of mind and will such as is due to the authoritative but 'non-definitive' teaching of the magisterium.[27] While this does not completely rule out an infallible exercise of the ordinary papal magisterium, as Fenton ingeniously argues,[28] it does appear to fit more easily with the view that equates the ordinary magisterium of the pope with his 'non-definitive' magisterium.[29]

There can be no doubt that *Humani generis* marks an important stage in the history of the Church's teaching on the modes of exercise of the magisterium. As Fenton remarks, "the declaration of the *Humani generis* to the effect that teaching presented authoritatively [...] in the papal encyclicals comes to us by way of the *magisterium ordinarium* is definitely a contribution to modern theological thought."[30] But the difficulty is how to understand this ordinary magisterium of the pope in relation to the ordinary and universal magisterium of the bishops dispersed throughout the world. For they differ in several important respects: first of all, the ordinary magisterium of *Humani generis* is exercised by the pope alone, whereas *Dei Filius* specifically intended a non-papal exercise of the magisterium of the whole Church dispersed throughout the world; secondly, the teaching found in the encyclical letters is explicitly documented teaching of the Church, whereas the teaching of the ordinary and universal magisterium was originally conceived of as non-explicit and undocumented; thirdly, the ordinary and universal magisterium is presented in *Dei Filius* as an organ of infallible teaching, whereas the ordinary papal magisterium presented in *Humani generis* appears to be an organ of 'non-definitive' teaching.

On the basis of such marked differences, I would suggest that *Humani generis* is best understood as using the term 'ordinary magisterium' in a sense almost entirely different from that intended by *Tuas libenter* and *Dei Filius*. If

---

aliunde ad doctrinam catholicam pertinent. Quodsi Summi Pontifices in actis suis de re hactenus controversa data opera sententiam ferunt, omnibus patet rem illam, secundum mentem ac voluntatem eorumdem Pontificum, quaestionem liberae inter theologos disceptationis iam haberi non posse" (Denz. 3385).

27 See, for example, Francis J. Connell, "Theological Content of *Humani generis*," *American Ecclesiastical Review* 123 (1950): 324; Fenton, "The *Humani generis*," 54; Benard, "Doctrinal Value," 92.

28 Fenton, "Infallibility in the Encyclicals," 183–85.

29 Benard, "Doctrinal Value," 84–85.

30 Fenton, "The *Humani generis*," 57.

the extraordinary magisterium of the Church is characterized as the organ of Church teaching that is at once both explicit and definitive, then two very different kinds of teaching can be contrasted against it, and both will appear to be ordinary by comparison. One is the teaching of the Church that is definitive but not explicit, and this is what Kleutgen had in mind, and what was intended by the term 'ordinary magisterium' as it was used by Pius IX and by the term 'ordinary and universal magisterium' as it was used at Vatican I. The other is the teaching of the Church that is explicit but not definitive, and this appears to be what Pius XII has in mind when he calls for an assent, such as is due to 'non-definitive' teaching, to the explicit teaching contained in papal encyclical letters. The former 'ordinary magisterium' is the living tradition itself; the latter 'ordinary magisterium' is the 'non-definitive' magisterium of the pope and bishops. These are completely distinct forms of teaching, sharing in common only the fact that neither is a third thing, namely the extraordinary magisterium. Calling these two things by the same name would be very much like calling angels and apes by the same name simply because neither are men.

The tables below attempt to illustrate the double meaning of the term 'ordinary magisterium' that developed out of the transposition of the distinction between ordinary and extraordinary magisterium from its original context within the treatise on the rule of faith to the context of the magisterium within the treatise on the Church.

Original Conception Context: The Rule of Faith	
	(Infallible)
Explicit	Extraordinary Magisterium (defined dogmas)
Non-Explicit	Ordinary Magisterium (undefined dogmas)

Inter-Conciliar Development Context: The Magisterium of the Church		
	Definitive	*Non-Definitive*
(Explicit)	Extraordinary Magisterium	Ordinary Magisterium

Combined View		
	Definitive	*Non-Definitive*
Explicit	Extraordinary Magisterium	Ordinary Magisterium (of popes and ecumenical councils)
Non-Explicit	Ordinary Magisterium (of the Church dispersed throughout the world)	

2. The Extraordinary Magisterium and Doctrinal Innovation

Our object in this chapter is to take up a second line of thought that developed in the period between Vatican I and Vatican II relating to the distinction between the ordinary and the extraordinary magisterium. And this is the attribution of all confirmation or reaffirmation of existing doctrine to the ordinary magisterium and the corresponding restriction of the extraordinary magisterium to the creation of new doctrinal obligations (the settling of questions previously open to legitimate dispute). As in the previous chapter, we will confine our attention primarily to the initial introduction of this idea and to the official documents of the Church that touch upon this question. Thus we will look first at the writings of Louis Billot and then at the encyclical letter *Mortalium animos* and the apostolic constitution *Munificentissimus Deus*.

2.1 Louis Billot on the Extraordinary Magisterium

The Jesuit theologian Louis Billot was one of the foremost ecclesiologists of the early twentieth century. His two volume *Tractatus de Ecclesia Christi* is an outstanding representative of the genre of theological manuals in common use in the century prior to Vatican II. First published in 1898, it was reprinted many times and was widely used in seminaries up until the eve of the Second Vatican Council.

Billot's treatment of the distinction between the ordinary and the extraordinary magisterium occurs within his general consideration of the Church's magisterium. It does not recur in his later treatment of the papal magisterium nor in the sections devoted to the bishops and to general councils. His treatment of the ordinary magisterium contains little that is new; perhaps the most noteworthy feature is how undeveloped it remains. Here he contents himself with a brief defense of its existence and authority and notes that the constant and unanimous consensus of Catholic theologians is a certain and unequivocal sign of its teaching.[31] Regarding the solemn definitions characteristic of the extraordinary magisterium, Billot offers five distinguishing marks or notes by which a solemn definition can be recognized. From the examples he gives, it appears that he has in mind chiefly, though not exclusively, the solemn definitions of ecumenical councils. Infallible papal definitions are the subject of a separate consideration further on. The first mark of a solemn definition is when a doctrine is explicitly proposed in the terms themselves as revealed by God; a second mark is the condemnation of a contradictory assertion as heresy; thirdly, one can recognize a solemn definition where it is said to be about a truth of faith; a fourth note appears where the faith of the Church is declared in the form of a Creed or Symbol; the fifth and final mark of a solemn definition adduced by Billot is the use of the words '*anathema sit*'.[32]

Much more extensively developed is Billot's treatment of the infallibility of papal definitions *ex cathedra*, and it is here that his influence on the understanding of the extraordinary magisterium in particular is felt more keenly, albeit indirectly inasmuch as he makes no use of that terminology in this part of his work. The question *De successore Petri Romano Pontifice* contains a lengthy section on papal infallibility, in the course of which he makes several remarks pertinent to the nature and exercise of the extraordinary magisterium.[33] Billot begins his consideration of the First Vatican Council's teaching

---

31 See Billot, *De Ecclesia*, vol. 1, 420–22.

32 Ibid., 422: "Prima, et ea quidem manifesta, si ipsis terminis proponatur doctrina tanquam a Deo revelata, uti factum est in duabus ultimis definitionibus de immaculata Deiparae conceptione et de Romani Pontificis infallibilitate: *Definimus doctrinam quae tenet beatissimam Virginem Mariam in primo instanti suae conceptionis fuisse ab omni originalis culpae labe praeservatam immunem, esse a Deo revelatam,* etc. Docemus et divinitus revelatum dogma esse definimus: *Romanum Pontificem, cum ex cathedra loquitur,* etc. Altera, si contrarium asserentes pro haereticis iudicentur. Cuius rei exempla habes ex Concilio Lateranensi IV, cap. Damnamus, de Summa Trinitate: *Si quis igitur doctrinam praefati Ioachim in hac parte defendere vel approbare praesumpserit, tanquam haereticus ab omnibus habeatur.* Tertia, si definitio fieri dicatur de fidei veritate, ut in Concilio Florentino: *In nomine Sanctae Trinitatis [...] diffinimus ut haec fidei veritas ab omnibus christianis credatur.* Quarta, si non secus ac in Symbolo, Ecclesiae fides declaretur, sicut in Lateranensi IV, cap. Firmiter: *Credimus et simpliciter confitemur quod unus solus est verus Deus,* etc., et in Vaticano: *Sancta Catholica Apostolica Romana Ecclesia credit et confitetur unum esse Deum verum,* etc. Quinta, cum in hanc formam decretum praescribitur: *Si quis hoc vel illud senserit, anathema sit,* locutione desumpta ab Apostolo, Gal. I-8, contra eos qui haeretica pravitate evangelium Christi subvertere volebant."

33 Billot's chapter on the hierarchy is distinctly monarchical. The question *De successoribus aposto-*

by asking what it means for the pope to define doctrine. His answer: "For a definition there must be a judgment and it must be ultimate and definitive."[34] In support of this he cites Gasser's *relatio*: "The word *definit* signifies that the pope directly and conclusively *(directe et terminative)* proffers his sentence concerning doctrine that is about things of faith or morals."[35] Billot thus reasons that a papal statement can fall short of being a definition in two ways: either by not containing a dogmatic judgment, or by containing a judgment that is not ultimate and conclusive. As examples of judgments that are not conclusive, he mentions the decree of Pope Stephen against the rebaptism of heretics, the approval and confirmation of the doctrinal decisions of the Roman Congregations, and constitutions in which certain things are established more as matters of housekeeping than as definitive judgments. Then as examples of statements that do not contain judgments at all, he refers to the many encyclical letters of recent pontiffs, in which, he says:

> [T]hey indeed, by their apostolic office, expound Catholic doctrine, but not through the mode of defining, that is not bringing in a new doctrinal judgment, but more by instructing the faithful about those things which are in the preaching of the Church, the pillar and foundation of truth. And although there seems to be no doubt that the popes are infallible in documents of this kind sent to the universal Church (certainly with regard to those things proposed in them directly and *per se*, as has been said elsewhere), yet there is not there that locution *ex cathedra* according to the Vatican canon.[36]

---

lorum episcopis takes up only 8 pages; the question *De conciliis* is given only 6 pages. Even taken together these are mere footnotes in comparison to the 117 pages devoted to the question on the pope. Moreover, neither the question on bishops nor that on councils considers the episcopal exercise of the magisterium, either ordinary or extraordinary. The question on bishops is dominated by questions of jurisdiction in relation to the papacy; the question on councils is largely preoccupied with concerns over the role of the pope in convoking, presiding over, and confirming general councils.

34 Billot, *De Ecclesia*, vol. 1, 640: "Ad definitionem autem oportet esse iudicium, illudque ultimatum ac definitivum."

35 Ibid.: "Vox *definit* significat quod Papa suam sententiam circa doctrinam quae est de rebus fidei et morum, directe et terminative proferat." For the source text see Mansi 52:1316.

36 Ibid., 640–41: "Prioris vero casus exempla sunt in permultis encyclicis recentiorum Pontificum, ubi pro munere suo apostolico doctrinam quidem catholicam exponunt, at non per modum definientium, id est non interponendo novum doctrinale iudicium, sed magis instruendo fideles de his quae sunt in praedicatione Ecclesiae columnae ac firmamenti veritatis. Et quamvis nullatenus dubitandum videatur quin in documentis huiusmodi ad universalem Ecclesiam missis infallibiles sint Pontifices (utique quantum ad ea quae directe et per se in eis proponuntur, ut alias in simili dictum est), non tamen ibi ea locutio ex cathedra est, quam attendit canon Vaticanus."

Billot is usually counted among the supporters of an infallible ordinary papal magisterium on the basis of this text inasmuch as he attributes infallibility to the things taught directly and *per se* in the papal encyclicals while also denying that these constitute *ex cathedra* definitions. Though it is interesting to note that he does not use the language of 'ordinary magisterium'. Even more interesting, however, is his apparent reason for denying that this kind of teaching constitutes an act of definition. He contrasts the 'new doctrinal judgment' *(novum doctrinale iudicium)*, which he attributes to the mode of definition, with the instruction of the faithful regarding things already within the preaching of the Church. This seems very much like a restriction of the act of definition to the introduction of new doctrines along the lines of the 'new dogmatization' thesis of Ratzinger and Bertone. In the encyclicals the popes do not present new doctrinal judgments but only confirm and explain existing doctrine; therefore they are not to be counted as *ex cathedra* definitions. Fenton, a great admirer of Billot,[37] carried forward this line of thinking into the middle of the twentieth century. Commenting on the definition of Vatican I, Fenton writes: "What is required for the issuance of an *ex cathedra* judgment is a pontifical definition, an absolutely definitive and irrevocable decision on some point which had hitherto been subject to free discussion among Catholic theologians."[38] To say that a doctrine was open to free discussion is the same as saying that it had not been definitively taught by the ordinary magisterium or previously defined by the extraordinary magisterium. To make this a require-ment for an extraordinary definition effectively excludes the possibility of solemn definitions of truths already defined or already infallibly taught by the ordinary magisterium.

Yet for all that Billot's statement appears to lay the foundation of what has become, through his own considerable influence and now also through that of Ratzinger and Bertone, a widely accepted basis of distinction between the ordi-nary and extraordinary magisterium, there is much within Billot's own writing that tends strongly in the opposite direction. The question is this: Is the act of definition limited to judgments concerning new doctrines? Or can it include judgments confirming or reaffirming existing doctrine? The text cited above certainly appears to support the former position. But when Billot comes to an

---

37 See, for example, Fenton, "Infallibility in the Encyclicals," 177: "Cardinal Louis Billot was certainly one of the greatest ecclesiologists of the generation just past. There are many who consider him the ablest writer on the treatise *de ecclesia* since the time of the Vatican Council."

38 Ibid., 189.

explicit consideration of the meaning of the term 'defines' as it is used in the definition of papal infallibility, he writes:

> This is to be taken indiscriminately, whether about a thing never before defined, or about a thing already previously contained explicitly in the rule of the ecclesiastical magisterium, confirmed again by a new sentence and a new judgment of the pope, just as we see practiced in the ecumenical councils for the apparition of new errors or the return of old ones.[39]

Here Billot seems quite clearly to envisage the possibility of an act of definition that introduces no new content into the teaching of the Church but merely confirms what had already been part of the Church's explicit teaching. He still refers to such acts of confirmation as new sentences and new judgments, but the only thing new about them is the new repetition the same doctrine. And he refers to the example of the ecumenical councils, in the long history of which the same doctrines have sometimes been defined more than once. Billot himself cites the Creeds of Lateran IV and Vatican I as examples of solemn definitions of the doctrine that there is only one true God.[40] The fact that this doctrine had already been defined at Lateran IV (and in fact many times over back to the Council of Nicaea) in no way precluded its being defined again at Vatican I. From this it appears that Billot would perhaps include judgments confirming or reaffirming existing doctrine as solemn definitions after all.

From the act of definition, Billot turns next to consider the object of papal infallibility. Taking his point of departure from the text of the Vatican definition, *doctrinam de fide vel moribus ab Ecclesia tenendam*, Billot argues that the object of an *ex cathedra* definition includes not only truths directly revealed by God but also those connected to divine revelation and thus said to belong to the secondary object of the magisterium. An *ex cathedra* definition does not appear therefore only in cases where the pope defines something as to be believed by divine faith, to reject which would be heresy; rather, "The locution *ex cathedra* is every definition by which some truth is defined as to be held in some way,

---

39 Billot, *De Ecclesia*, vol. 1, 641: "Quod indiscriminatim accipiendum est, sive de re nusquam antea definita, sive de re quae iam pridem in regula ecclesiastici magisterii explicite contenta, nova iterum sententia novoque iudicio a Pontifice firmatur, non secus ac in Conciliis etiam oecumenicis pro grassantium errorum nova apparitione vel recrudescentia factitatum videmus."

40 Ibid., 422: "Quarta, si non secus ac in Symbolo, Ecclesiae fides declaretur, sicut in Lateranensi IV, cap. Firmiter: *Credimus et simpliciter confitemur quod unus solus est verus Deus*, etc., et in Vaticano: *Sancta Catholica Apostolica Romana Ecclesia credit et confitetur unum esse Deum verum*, etc."

and this locution has for its object everything that pertains to revealed doctrine of faith and morals, whether as constitutive of it or only as connected to it."[41]

And then, finally, the subject of a pontifical definition is the pope exercising his supreme office of universal pastor and teacher, that is, acting precisely as head of the whole Church and not merely as a private person. This much is uncontroversial with respect to the text of the Vatican definition, *omnium christianorum Pastoris et Doctoris munere fungens*. But Billot also argues that, "It is not necessary for a pontifical document to be directed materially to all the faithful or bishops; it is enough that it has to do with something pertaining to the deposit of faith and that there is present the manifest intention of putting an end to fluctuation through a definitive sentence not subject to further determination."[42] As an example of this he cites the tome of Pope Leo the Great condemning the heresy of Eutyches. Billot's argument here is essentially that the exercise of the pope's supreme apostolic authority is necessarily implied in the act of defining doctrine such that any case wherein it is manifestly the intention of the pope to give a definitive judgment on a doctrinal question is *ipso facto* a case of the pope acting as universal pastor and teacher of the Church. Since doctrine pertains to the whole Church (in a way that disciplinary rules do not since these can vary in different places and for different persons), such acts of doctrinal definition pertain formally to the whole Church even if directed materially only to a certain part of the Church.

Billot's approach to determining whether any given papal statement is an infallible definition *ex cathedra* can be reduced in the end to the sole question of whether the act manifests the intention of defining doctrine. If a doctrine is defined, then it is to be held in some way as connected with divine revelation and therefore it must fall within the object of infallibility; likewise if a doctrine is defined, then it must have been by an exercise of the pope's supreme apostolic authority over the whole Church. What is crucial is that there should be a manifest intention of giving an ultimate and conclusive judgment on a question of doctrine. Although in many respects quite clearly a maximalist when it comes to the question of papal infallibility, Billot does recognize that

---

41 Ibid., vol. 1, 641: "Sed a primo ad ultimum dicendum restat, locutionem ex cathedra esse omnem definitionem qua aliqua veritas definitur quolibet modo tenenda, et hanc locutionem in suo obiecto habere quidquid vel constitutive vel solum connexive pertinet ad revelatam fidei et morum doctrinam."

42 Ibid., 642: "Quanquam non oporteat ut pontificium documentum ad omnes ubilibet fideles vel episcopos materialiter dirigatur, sed sat est ut agatur de re ad depositum fidei attinente, et adsit intentio manifestata fluctuationi finem imponendi per sententiam definitivam, non subiacentem ulteriori determinationi."

this requisite intention to define doctrine might not always be clear, that there will be cases where it can be legitimately disputed whether something should be counted as a definition, and that in such cases the rule applies: "a doubtful obligation is no obligation."[43]

In summary, Louis Billot was a papal monarchist and a maximalist in his interpretation of papal infallibility. In his treatise on the Church he had little to say about the ordinary magisterium of the whole Church; but he had much to say about the teaching authority of the pope. Billot's influence on the theological interpretation of the distinction between the ordinary and extraordinary magisterium was exercised above all through his treatment of the act of definition. His comment that the teaching proposed directly and *per se* in a papal encyclical letter is infallible despite not being an *ex cathedra* definition reinforced and further disseminated Vacant's thesis that the pope exercises an infallible ordinary magisterium. Billot does not himself describe this kind of teaching as an exercise of the ordinary magisterium, but this is usually taken as implied from the fact that he distinguishes it from the solemn definitions of the pope.

Moreover, whereas Vacant apparently distinguished between the ordinary and extraordinary teaching of the pope on the basis of external solemnity, Billot appeared to introduce a distinction based on tradition versus innovation. By equating the 'mode of definition' with the introduction of 'new doctrinal judgments' and by denying that the encyclicals contain such definitions, but rather instruct the faithful about existing Catholic doctrine, he quite clearly gives the impression that the ordinary magisterium is essentially traditional, in the sense of handing on what has always and everywhere been believed, while the extraordinary magisterium is essentially innovative, in the sense of imposing new doctrinal obligations by resolving questions that had previously been open to legitimate dispute. Thus he appears to restrict the extraordinary magisterium to the settling of legitimate matters of controversy, much like Ratzinger and Bertone in their attribution of *Ordinatio sacerdotalis* to the ordinary magisterium. At the same time, we also saw elsewhere that Billot explicitly allows for solemn definitions of doctrines already contained explicitly in the teaching of the Church. Such doctrines, he says, can be confirmed again by a new judgment of the pope where the only thing new is the new repetition of the same doctrine.

---

43   Ibid., vol. 1, 645: "obligatio dubia, obligatio nulla, utique in eo ordine et intra eos limites in quibus est dubia."

2.2 The Encyclical Letter *Mortalium animos (1928)*

The importance of Pope Pius XI's encyclical letter *Mortalium animos* for our question lies in the fact that it is the only major document of the magisterium to make use of the term 'extraordinary magisterium'. And though brief in itself, its discussion of the nature and purpose of the extraordinary magisterium is the most expansive to be found in the documents of the Church.

This encyclical letter, which is on the topic of religious unity, was issued against the backdrop of the early stages of the modern ecumenical movement, which is often dated to the World Missionary Conference held at Edinburgh in 1910. From there, preparations were launched for the first World Conference on Faith and Order, which was finally held in 1927 at Lausanne. The goal of the Faith and Order Movement was to discuss matters of doctrine and ecclesiastical organization in the context of the search for Christian unity. Shortly before this, in 1925, the first World Conference of Life and Work was held in Stockholm in order to promote cooperation among Christians of different denominations in matters of practical action and social order. In 1948 these two movements merged together to form the World Council of Churches.

Pope Pius IX issued his encyclical letter on religious unity early in 1928, less than a year after the Faith and Order conference of 1927. Against the backdrop of growing international conversation aimed at fostering unity among all Christians, the pope wanted to explain why the Catholic Church felt herself unable to participate in these ecumenical gatherings and to set forth the main principles by which Catholics should be guided in their thinking about undertakings aimed at restoring unity among all Christians. At the heart of the pope's teaching is the idea that the only acceptable means of achieving real unity among all Christians is for those Christian bodies who have been separated from the Catholic Church to return to her.[44] The encyclical is thus a prime example of what has come to be called an 'ecumenism of return'.[45]

The pope invokes the distinction between the ordinary and the extraordinary magisterium in the course of arguing against those who would try to bring about unity by means of a distinction between fundamental doctrines (e.g. the Trinity, the Incarnation), which must be accepted by all, and doctrines

---

44 Pope Pius XI, Encyclical Letter on Religious Unity *Mortalium animos* (6 Jan. 1928), § 10: "christianorum enim coniunctionem haud aliter foveri licet, quam fovendo dissidentium ad unam veram Christi Ecclesiam reditu" (AAS 20 [1928]: 14).

45 See, for example, Jeffrey Thomas VanderWilt, *Communion with Non-Catholic Christians: Risks, Challenges, and Opportunities* (Collegeville, MN: Liturgical Press, 2003), 16, who contrasts this approach with an 'ecumenism of convergence, mutual reconciliation, and dialogue'.

that are not fundamental (e.g. the Marian dogmas and papal primacy), which could be left to the free opinion of each community or individual. This is very much like Hirscher's distinction between essential and unessential points of faith, to which Kleutgen responded that the maxim is *'libertas in dubiis'*, not *'libertas in parvis'*. Unlike Kleutgen, however, who was anxious to defend the importance of the ordinary magisterium against those who would exalt the authority of the extraordinary magisterium, Pius XI is concerned rather to defend the equal authority of the extraordinary magisterium, with its later definitions of less fundamental doctrines, against those who would prioritize the ordinary magisterium, with its constant and universal teaching of the more fundamental doctrines of the faith. He writes:

> For the teaching authority of the Church, which in the divine wisdom was constituted on earth in order that revealed doctrines might remain intact forever and that they might be brought with ease and security to the knowledge of men and which is daily exercised through the Roman pontiff and the bishops who are in communion with him, has also the office of defining, when it sees fit, any truth with solemn rites and decrees, whenever this is necessary either to oppose the errors or the attacks of heretics or more clearly and in greater detail to stamp the minds of the faithful with the articles of sacred doctrine that have been explained.[46]

One point worth noting is that here too there is an exercise of the ordinary magisterium attributed to the Roman pontiff, though this is placed in conjunction with the bishops in communion with him, and therefore it is not clear that Pius XI has in mind a distinct exercise of the ordinary magisterium by the pope.

More instructive for our present question is the statement of a double purpose of the extraordinary magisterium: a solemn definition may be used either "to oppose the errors and the attacks of heretics" or "more clearly and in greater detail to stamp the minds of the faithful with the articles of sacred doctrine that have been explained." Paradigmatic examples of the former would probably include the definitions of Nicaea against Arius and of Ephesus against Nestorius; the definitions of the Immaculate Conception and the Assumption

---

46 Pius XI, *Mortalium animos*, § 9: "Etenim Ecclesiae magisterium – quod divino consilio in terris constitutum est, ut revelatae doctrinae cum incolumes ad perpetuitatem consisterent tum ad cognitionem hominum facile tutoque traducerentur – quamquam per Romanum Pontificem et episcopos cum eo communionem habentes cotidie exercetur, id tamen complectitur muneris, ut, si quando aut haereticorum erroribus atque oppugnationibus obsisti efficacius aut clarius subtiliusque explicata sacrae doctrinae capita in fidelium mentibus imprimi oporteat, ad aliquid tum sollemnibus ritibus decretisque definiendum opportune procedat" (Denz. 3683).

of Mary are likely examples of the latter. The pope then proceeds to make the point that nothing substantially new is introduced into the deposit of faith even through the use of the extraordinary magisterium:

> But in the use of this extraordinary teaching authority no newly invented matter is brought in, nor is anything new added to the number of those truths that are at least implicitly contained in the deposit of revelation, divinely handed down to the Church: rather, either what perhaps might until then have seemed obscure to many is clarified or what some have previously called into question is determined to be of faith.[47]

Here too a double reason is given for the exercise of the extraordinary magisterium: either something obscure to many may be clarified or something called into question may be determined to be of faith. Neither part of this text limits the use of the extraordinary magisterium to the settling of legitimate doctrinal controversies or the imposition of new doctrinal obligations. And although the question is not raised directly, this presentation of the various uses of the extraordinary magisterium seems very much open to a solemn judgment that confirms or reaffirms an already existing truth of Catholic doctrine, for it can easily happen that infallibly taught truths of faith can still be obscure to many or can still be called into question by some.

2.3 The Apostolic Constitution *Munificentissimus Deus* (1950)

The apostolic constitution *Munificentissimus Deus*, solemnly defining the dogma of the bodily Assumption of the blessed Virgin Mary, was promulgated by Pope Pius XII in 1950. The definition itself is a pre-eminent example of the exercise of the extraordinary magisterium.[48] But in addition to this, there is in the text of the constitution prior to the definition an illuminating discussion of

---

47 Ibid., § 9: "Quo quidem extraordinario magisterii usu nullum sane inventum inducitur nec quidquam additur novi ad earum summam veritatum, quae in deposito revelationis, Ecclesiae divinitus traditio, saltem implicite continentur, verum aut ea declarantur, quae forte adhuc obscura compluribus videri possint aut ea tenenda de fide statuuntur, quae a nonnullis ante in controversiam vocabantur" (Denz. 3683).

48 Pope Pius XII, Apostolic Constitution *Munificentissimus Deus* (1 Nov. 1950), § 44: "For this reason [...] to the glory of Almighty God, who has lavished his special affection upon the Virgin Mary, for the honor of her Son, the immortal King of the Ages and the Victor over sin and death, for the increase of the glory of that same august Mother, and for the joy and exultation of the entire Church; by the authority of our Lord Jesus Christ, of the blessed apostles Peter and Paul, and by Our (own authority), We pronounce, declare, and define it to be a divinely revealed dogma: that the Immaculate Mother of God, the ever Virgin Mary, having completed the course of her earthly life, was assumed body and soul into heavenly glory" (Denz. 3903).

the interplay between the extraordinary magisterium and the ordinary and universal magisterium. Pius XII refers to the letter he sent to all the bishops asking them whether they judged that the doctrine could be defined and whether they with their clergy and people desired its definition. The response was almost unanimously affirmative on both points, which he takes as evidence that the doctrine had already been proposed as a dogma of faith through the ordinary and universal magisterium of the Church:

> This "outstanding agreement of the Catholic prelates and the faithful," affirming that the bodily Assumption of God's Mother into heaven can be defined as a dogma of faith, since it shows us the concordant teaching of the Church's ordinary doctrinal authority and the concordant faith of the Christian people which the same doctrinal authority sustains and directs, thus by itself and in an entirely certain and infallible way, manifests this privilege as a truth revealed by God and contained in that divine deposit which Christ has delivered to his Spouse to be guarded faithfully and to be taught infallibly.[49]

He makes the same point further on, when he concludes:

> Thus, from the universal agreement of the Church's ordinary teaching authority we have a certain and firm proof, demonstrating that the Blessed Virgin Mary's bodily Assumption into heaven [...] is a truth that has been revealed by God and consequently something that must be firmly and faithfully believed by all children of the Church. For, as the Vatican Council asserts, "all those things are to be believed by divine and Catholic faith which are contained in the written Word of God or in Tradition, and which are proposed by the Church, either in solemn judgment or in its ordinary and universal teaching office, as divinely revealed truths which must be believed."[50]

---

49   Ibid., § 12: "Haec 'singularis catholicorum Antistitum et fidelium conspiratio', qui Dei Matris autumant corpoream in Caelum Assumptionem ut fidei dogma definiri posse, cum concordem Nobis praebeat ordinarii Ecclesiae Magisterii doctrinam concordemque christiani populi fidem – quam idem Magisterium sustinet ac dirigit – idcirco per semet ipsam ac ratione omnino certa ab omnibusque erroribus immuni manifestat eiusmodi privilegium veritatem esse a Deo revelatam in eoque contentam divino deposito, quod Christus tradidit Sponsae suae fideliter custodiendum et infallibiliter declarandum" (AAS 42 [1950]: 756).

50   Ibid.: "Itaque ex ordinarii Ecclesiae Magisterii universali consensu certum ac firmum sumitur argumentum, quo comprobatur corpoream Beatae Mariae Virginis in Caelum Assumptionem [...] veritatem esse a Deo revelatam, ideoque ab omnibus Ecclesiae filiis firmiter fideliterque credendam. Nam, ut idem Concilium Vaticanum asseverat: 'Fide divina et catholica ea omnia credenda sunt, quae in verbo Dei scripto vel tradito continentur, et ab Ecclesia sive sollemni iudicio, sive ordinario et universali Magisterio tamquam divinitus revelata credenda proponuntur'" (AAS 42 [1950]: 757).

Of course, these paragraphs do not belong to the definition itself; yet they clearly show that, at least according to the mind of Pope Pius XII, the bodily Assumption of the blessed Virgin Mary was already infallibly taught as a dogma of the faith by the ordinary and universal magisterium prior to his definition of it. And by proceeding to define it as a dogma of faith, he shows that there is nothing to prevent a doctrine already infallibly taught by the ordinary and universal magisterium being afterwards defined by the extraordinary magisterium, contrary to the new dogmatization thesis implied by Billot and taken up by Ratzinger and Bertone.

Far from rendering a doctrine undefinable, the fact that a doctrine has already been infallibly taught by the ordinary and universal magisterium is taken by Pius XII as a clear sign of its definability. And in fact, the same conclusion was reached by the theological commission established by Pope Pius IX to study the definability of the Immaculate Conception prior to its solemn definition in 1854. Among the marks judged as sufficient was this: "A proposition may be defined as Catholic dogma if it is preached as a part of divine public revelation in the concordant teaching of the actual episcopate."[51] Apparently there was no concern here that defining a doctrine already taught by the ordinary and universal magisterium would diminish in any sense the respect due to the infallibility of the ordinary and universal magisterium.

3. The Dogmatic Constitution *Lumen gentium* (1964)

Following our review of some of the major lines of interpretation that developed in the period between Vatican I and Vatican II, we turn now to a more detailed account of the teaching of the Second Vatican Council itself. The dogmatic constitution on the Church *Lumen gentium* treats of the *munus docendi* of the bishops in paragraph 25. Following the ordering of the paragraph, we will consider in turn its treatment of the merely authentic magisterium, the ordinary and universal magisterium, and the extraordinary magisterium.

3.1 The (Merely) Authentic Magisterium

The teaching of *Lumen gentium* on the (merely) authentic, that is, the authoritative but 'non-definitive', teaching of the bishops and the pope is expressed as follows:

---

51 Cited in Joseph C. Fenton, "The Requisites for an Infallible Pontifical Definition according to the Commission of Pope Pius IX," *American Ecclesiastical Review* 115 (1946): 381.

Bishops, teaching in communion with the Roman pontiff, are to be respected by all as witnesses to divine and Catholic truth. In matters of faith and morals, the bishops speak in the name of Christ, and the faithful are to accept their teaching and adhere to it with a religious assent. This religious submission of mind and will must be shown in a special way to the authentic Magisterium of the Roman pontiff, even when he is not speaking *ex cathedra*; that is, it must be shown in such a way that his supreme Magisterium is acknowledged with reverence and that the judgments made by him are sincerely adhered to, according to his manifest mind and will. His mind and will in the matter may be principally known either from the character of the documents, from his frequent repetition of the same doctrine, or from his manner of speaking.[52]

This text teaches that a religious submission of will and intellect is due to the authoritative teaching *(act)* of the bishops and the pope *(subject)* in matters of faith and morals *(object)*. An examination of the textual history of this text reveals three significant points: first, the authentic magisterium of the pope is deliberately placed within the context of the magisterium of the other bishops; secondly, the authentic magisterium spoken of here is intended to refer to non-infallible teaching; and thirdly, the term 'ordinary magisterium' is not used.

In the first draft of the text, prepared by the doctrinal commission prior to the council but discarded at the beginning of the council, the authentic magisterium of pope and bishops were treated separately. The "interior religious assent of the mind" due to the (merely) authentic magisterium of the bishops was mentioned only briefly at the end of the paragraph.[53] The (merely) authentic magisterium of the pope was given a much lengthier discussion immediately after the treatment of papal infallibility. Here the first draft began by setting forth the "religious submission of will and intellect" due to the authoritative

---

52 Vatican II, *Lumen gentium*, § 25: "Episcopi in communione cum Romano Pontifice docentes ab omnibus tamquam divinae et catholicae veritatis testes venerandi sunt; fideles autem in sui Episcopi sententiam de fide et moribus nomine Christi prolatam concurrere, eique religioso animi obsequio adhaerere debent. Hoc vero religiosum voluntatis et intellectus obsequium singulari ratione praestandum est Romani Pontificis authentico magisterio etiam cum non ex cathedra loquitur; ita nempe ut magisterium eius supremum reverenter agnoscatur, et sententiis ab eo prolatis sincere adhaereatur, iuxta mentem et voluntatem manifestatam ipsius, quae se prodit praecipue sive indole documentorum, sive ex frequenti propositione eiusdem doctrinae, sive ex dicendi ratione" (Denz. 4149).

53 AS I/4, 51: "Singulorum vero Episcoporum de rebus fidei et morum authenticum magisterium, dum in communione cum Apostolica Sede ceterisque catholicae Ecclesiae Episcopis suum munus exercent, a subditis interiore religiosoque animi assensu est accipiendum, et ab omnibus christifidelibus tamquam divinae et catholicae veritatis testimonium est venerandum."

teaching of the pope "even when he is not speaking *ex cathedra*."⁵⁴ Following *Humani generis*, however, it then expands upon this by placing a great emphasis on the authority of the papal magisterium exercised in "certain Apostolic Constitutions, Encyclical Letters, and more solemn Allocutions," which it refers to as "documents of the ordinary magisterium of the Church," before closing with a long and nearly verbatim quotation from the text of *Humani generis*.⁵⁵

The second draft, introduced as the basis for discussion in the council, made drastic changes. The material was reordered to give priority to the magisterium of the bishops, turning only afterwards to the magisterium of the pope. The religious submission due to the authentic magisterium of the pope was mentioned only briefly at the end of the paragraph (where the first draft had placed its teaching on the authentic magisterium of the bishops).⁵⁶ But the most drastic change was the elimination of the term 'ordinary magisterium' and every other reference to *Humani generis* from the discussion of the authentic papal magisterium.

The third draft, amended on the basis of the conciliar discussion, reorganized the material again. The treatment of the authentic papal magisterium was brought forward from the end of the paragraph to be incorporated into the opening treatment of the authentic magisterium of the bishops.⁵⁷ As the official

54 AS I/4, 49: "Romani Pontificis authentico magisterio, etiam cum non ex cathedra loquitur, religiosum voluntatis et intellectus obsequium praestandum est, quo nempe magisterium eius supremum reverenter agnoscatur, et sententiae ab eo propositae sincere adhaereatur, idque iuxta mentem et voluntatem manifestatam ipsius, quae se prodit praecipue vel ex indole documentorum, vel ex frequenti propositione eiusdem doctrinae, vel ex dicendi ratione."

55 AS I/4, 49–50: "Mens autem et voluntas Romanorum Pontificum manifestatur praesertim per acta doctrinalia universam Ecclesiam respicientia, ut sunt quaedam Constitutiones Apostolicae vel Encyclicae Litterae vel sollemniores Allocutiones: haec sunt enim praecipuum ordinarii Ecclesiae magisterii documenta, ad illudque declarandum vel efformandum imprimis conferunt, et quae ibi docentur et inculcantur plerumque iam aliunde ad catholicam doctrinam pertinent. Quodsi Summi Pontifices in his actis suis de re hactenus controversa data opera sententiam ferunt, omnibus patere debet rem illam, secundum mentem et voluntatem eorumdem Pontificum, quaestionem publicae inter theologos disceptationis iam haberi non posse."

56 AS II/1, 238–39: "Romani Pontificis authentico magisterio, etiam cum non ex cathedra loquitur, religiosum voluntatis et intellectus obsequium praestandum est, quo nempe magisterium eius supremum reverenter agnoscatur, et sententiae ab eo propositae sincere adhaereatur, idque iuxta mentem et voluntatem manifestatam ipsius, quae se prodit praecipue vel ex indole documentorum, vel ex frequenti propositione doctrinae, vel ex dicendi ratione."

57 AS III/1, 220: "*Episcopi in communione cum Romano Pontifice docentes ab omnibus tamquam divinae et catholicae veritatis testes venerandi sunt* (D); fideles *autem in sui* Episcopi sententiam *de huiusmodi rebus nomine* (E) Christi prolatam concurrere, eique *religioso animi obsequio*

relatio explains, this was because "it seemed better to treat of the non-infallible magisterium of the Roman pontiff *in the context of the magisterium of the whole episcopal body*, which is the object of this paragraph."[58] In this statement we can also see that the authentic magisterium spoken of here is explicitly intended to refer to non-infallible ('non-definitive') teaching.[59]

One more change occurred in the final version of this text, but it is relatively insignificant.[60] What stands out as most significant for our purposes, in the council's final promulgated teaching on the non-infallible magisterium of the bishops and the pope, is the fact that it chooses to use the term 'authentic magisterium' rather than 'ordinary magisterium', deliberately leaving behind the language of *Humani generis*.

3.2 The Ordinary and Universal Magisterium

The final text of *Lumen gentium* proceeds next to a statement of the infallibility exercised by the college of bishops even in their state of dispersion throughout the world:

> Although the individual bishops do not enjoy the prerogative of infallibility, they nevertheless proclaim Christ's doctrine infallibly whenever, even though dispersed throughout the world, but still maintaining the bond of communion among themselves and with the successor of Peter, and authentically teaching matters of faith and morals, they are in agreement on one position as definitively to be held.[61]

---

adhaerere debent (F). *Hoc vero religiosum voluntatis et intellectus obsequium singulari ratione praestandum est Romani Pontifice authentico magisterio etiam cum non ex cathedra loquitur; ita* nempe ut magisterium eius supremum reverenter agnoscatur, et sententiis ab eo *prolatis* sincere adhaereatur, iuxta mentem et voluntatem manifestam ipsius, quae se prodit praecipue *sive* indole documentorum *sive* ex frequenti propositione eiusdem doctrinae, *sive* ex dicendi ratione (G)." Italics in the original.

58 AS III/1, 250: "(G) Transferuntur ad hunc locum verba T. P. p. 69, l. 3-12, paucis inductis immutationibus ipsa transpositione requisitis, ut melius pateat de magisterio Romani Pontificis non-infallibili agi *in contextu magisterii totius corporis episcopalis*, quod est obiectum huius paragraphi." Italics in the original.

59 The same point appears in the official commentary on the same part of the second draft: "Ulterius determinatur quinam assensus Magisterio authentico citra gradum infallibilitatis docenti debeatur" (AS II/1, 255).

60 The phrase 'de fide et moribus' was substituted in place of the phrase 'de huiusmodi rebus' in the second line of the text: "158 – Pag. 67, linn. 40-41: Proponunt duo Patres ut loco: 'de huiusmodi rebus', dicatur: 'de fide et moribus', quia non bene videtur quid significet illud 'huiusmodi'. R. – Admittitur propositio" (AS III/8, 88).

61 Vatican II, *Lumen gentium*, § 25: "Licet singuli praesules infallibilitatis praerogativa non polleant,

Although the term 'ordinary and universal magisterium' is not used here, it is clear from the citation of *Dei Filius* and *Tuas libenter* in the notes that this is what is intended. And once again, there are several important insights into the meaning of this text that can be gained from an examination of the textual history.

The first draft contains a statement similar to that which remained in the final text,[62] but then followed this up with a lengthier explanation that referred to this infallible teaching of the bishops dispersed throughout the world as an exercise of the ordinary magisterium, contrasted it against solemn definitions, and made it clear that it extended beyond the primary object of the magisterium: "matters of faith and morals held and taught by the ordinary magisterium of all the bishops in every place together with the Roman pontiff, even those that have not been solemnly defined, are to be held as irrevocably true in the sense in which they are taught; and if they are proposed as divinely revealed they are to be believed with divine and Catholic faith."[63]

The second draft makes several changes to the first sentence and deletes the second sentence entirely, once again eliminating the term 'ordinary magisterium' from the text.[64] But while the text is reduced, the footnotes are expanded. After the original citation of *Dei Filius*, there is added a reference to a note attached to the First Vatican Council's first schema on the Church, which is taken from St. Robert Bellarmine. This note reads:

> And when we say that the Church is not able to err, we understand this just as much of all the faithful as of all the bishops, such that this should be the meaning of the proposition 'The Church is not able to err', that is, that which

---

quando tamen, etiam per orbem dispersi, sed communionis nexum inter se et cum Successore Petri servantes, authentice res fidei et morum docentes in unam sententiam tamquam definitive tenendam conveniunt, doctrinam Christi infallibiliter enuntiant" (Denz. 4149).

62 AS I/4, 50: "Corpus legitimorum Ecclesiae pastorum et doctorum infallibilitatis praerogativa gaudet non tantum cum sollemni iudicio in Oecumenico Concilio potestatem docendi collegialiter exercet, verum etiam cum singuli in sua quisque dioecesi authentice docentes, una cum Romano Pontifice ut testes fidei in revelata doctrina tradenda in unam sententiam conveniunt."

63 AS I/4, 50–51: "Quaecumque igitur in rebus fidei et morum ubique locorum ab universis Episcopis, una cum ipso Summo Pontifice, tenentur et ordinario magisterio docentur, ea etiam citra sollemnem definitionem tamquam irrevocabiliter vera eo sensu quo docentur tenenda sunt, et si tamquam divinitus revelata proponuntur fide divina et catholica sunt credenda."

64 All that remains is this: "Imo, licet singuli praesules infallibilitatis praerogativa non polleant, quando tamen, etiam per orbem dispersi, sed collegialem nexum servantes, authentice docentes una cum Romano Pontifice ut testes fidei in revelata fide tradenda in unam sententiam conveniunt, doctrinam Christi infallibili oraculo enunciant" (AS II/1, 238).

all the faithful hold as of faith is necessarily true and of faith; and similarly that which all the bishops teach as pertaining to faith is necessarily true and of faith.[65]

Then follows a reference to Joseph Kleutgen's commentary, as official *relator*, on the First Vatican Council's schema for a second constitution on the Church, a document that was never promulgated. The comment cited is as follows:

> Now this exceptional gift, by which '*The Church of the living God is the pillar and foundation of truth*' (1 Tim. 3:15), we define to be such that neither all the faithful in believing, nor all those who are endowed with the power of teaching the whole Church, when exercising this office, are able to fall into error. Therefore whatever in matters of faith and morals is held or handed down as undoubted in every place under the bishops adhering to the Apostolic See, and also whatever is defined by the same bishops, with the confirmation of the Roman pontiff, or by the Roman pontiff himself speaking *ex cathedra* as to be held and handed down by all, is to be considered as infallibly true.[66]

Another note is then added referencing further commentary on the same constitution, which "clearly distinguishes a double subject of infallibility [...] namely the episcopacy united to the Roman pontiff and the Roman pontiff alone speaking *ex cathedra*."[67] This last note, with its reference to a double subject of infallibility, would eventually be eliminated. But the references to Bellarmine and Kleutgen remain in the final promulgated text of *Lumen gentium*, though without the full text of the citations.[68]

---

65   AS II/1, 249: "Cf. notam primo schemati de Ecclesia adiecta, et ex Bellarmino desumptam: MANSI 51, 579 C: 'Et cum dicimus Ecclesiam non posse errare, id intelligimus tam de universitate fidelium, quam de universitate Episcoporum, ita ut sensus sit eius propositionis '*Ecclesia non potest errare*', id est, id quod tenent omnes fideles tanquam de fide, necessario est verum et de fide; et similiter id quod docent omnes Episcopi tanquam ad fidem pertinens, necessaria est verum et de fide'."

66   AS II/1, 249–50: "Commentarius KLEUTGEN: MANSI 53, 313 AB: 'Iamvero praecelsum hoc donum, quo '*Ecclesia Dei vivi columna et firmamentum veritatis* est' (1 Tim. 3, 15), in eo positum esse definimus, ut neque fideles universi credendo, nec ii qui potestate docendi totam Ecclesiam praediti sunt, cum hoc munere funguntur, in errorem labi possint. Quaecumque igitur in rebus fidei et morum ubique locorum sub Episcopis Apostolicae Sedi adhaerentibus tanquam indubitata tenentur vel traduntur, necnon quae sive ab iisdem Episcopis, accedente Romani Pontificis confirmatione, sive ab ipso Romano Pontifice ex cathedra loquente ab omnibus tenenda et tradenda definiuntur, ea pro infalliibiter veris habenda sunt'."

67   AS II/1, 250: "In Commentario ad Const. II de Ecclesia, clare distinguit duplex subiectum infallibilitatis: MANSI 53, 325 A: 'Episcopatus scilicet una cum Romano Pontifice, et Romanus Pontifex solus e cathedra loquens'."

68   What remains in the final version of the note is this: "Cf. CONC. VAT. I, Const. dogm. *Dei Filius*,

One conclusion that can be drawn from this is that Kleutgen remains, also after Vatican II, an important point of reference for the right understanding of the ordinary and universal magisterium. Even more important, however, is the more balanced perspective given through these notes on the exercise of the ordinary and universal magisterium. Read in isolation, the final text of *Lumen gentium* can easily give the impression that the exercise of the ordinary and universal magisterium is restricted to the direct activity of the bishops. Certainly the bishops can exercise the ordinary and universal magisterium directly, but the notes allow that it can also be exercised by the whole people of God under the supervision of the bishops. This intimate connection between the infallibility of the people of God and the ordinary and universal magisterium opens up space for an understanding of the latter that is not narrowly focused only on the explicit statements of the hierarchy.

The third draft made several further refinements to the text.[69] Firstly, the phrase "but preserving the collegial bond" *(sed collegialem nexum servantes)* was replaced by the phrase "preserving the bond of communion" *(communionis nexum servantes)*, according to the *relatio* of the Theological Commission, "in order to avoid the disputed question as to whether a strictly collegial act should be verified in the ordinary and universal magisterium, as in an ecumenical council."[70] Although this does not settle the question one way or the other, it is at least a clear indication that it would be going beyond the teaching of Vatican II to insist on a strictly collegial act in order to recognize an exercise of the ordinary and universal magisterium.

3: Denz. 1792 (3011). Cf. nota adiecta ad Schema I *De Eccl.* (desumpta ex S. ROB. BELLARMINO): MANSI 51, 579C; necnon Schema reformatum Const. II *De Ecclesia Christi*, cum commentario KLEUTGEN: MANSI 53, 313 AB. PIUS IX, Epist. *Tuas libenter*: Denz. 1683 (2879)."

69 AS III/1, 220–21: "Licet singuli praesules infallibilitatis praerogativa non polleant, quando tamen, etiam per orbem dispersi, sed *communionis* nexum *inter se et cum Successore Petri* servantes (H), authentice *res fidei et morum* (I) docentes in unam sententiam *tamquam definitive tenendam* conveniunt, doctrinam Christi infallibiliter (J) enunciant (40). Quod adhuc manifestius habetur quando, in Concilio Oecumenico coadunati, pro universa Ecclesia fidei et morum doctores et iudices sunt, quorum definitionibus *fidei obsequio est adhaerendum* (41) (K)."

70 AS III/1, 250–51: "(H) Loco 'sed collegialem nexum servantes' (T. P., p. 67, l. 39 s.), ponitur 'communionis nexum servantes', ad vitandam quaestionem disputatam utrum in magisterio ordinario et universali verificetur actus stricte collegialis, prouti in Concilio Oecumenico habetur." This point is repeated in a later response of the Theological Commission to a suggested amendation of the text: "Textus approbatus, ut iam in Resp. ad Modum 59 dictum est, nullo modo suggerit hunc actum esse *stricte 'collegialem'*. In hanc quaestionem Concilium non intrat; solum *factum* infallibilitatis hic enunciat, de quo omnes concordant" (AS III/8, 89).

A second important clarification made in the third draft regards the object of the infallible teaching of the ordinary and universal magisterium. Whereas it had been clear in the first draft that this was meant to extend to the secondary object of the magisterium, the second draft had eliminated every reference to the object of teaching except the phrase "in handing down revealed faith" *(in revelata fide tradenda)*. This was replaced with the phrase "teaching matters of faith and morals" *(res fidei et morum docentes)*, according to the *relatio* of the Theological Commission, "lest it seem that the infallibility of the episcopal body should be restricted only to those things which are proposed by them as to be believed as divinely revealed."[71]

A third noteworthy change in the third draft is the addition of the phrase "as definitively to be held" *(tamquam definitive tenendam)*. Where the first two drafts had said only "coming together in one judgment," the third draft said "coming together in one judgment as definitively to be held *(definitive tenendam conveniunt)*."[72] On the one hand, this is further confirmation of the fact that this text intends to extend the infallibility of the ordinary and universal magisterium to the secondary object of the magisterium inasmuch as it chooses the more generic "to be held" *(tenendam)* over the more restrictive "to be believed" *(credendam)*. Just as importantly, however, it specifies the note of conclusiveness required for infallible teaching. Not just any kind of unanimous teaching in matters of faith and morals suffices for infallibility, but only teaching unanimously propounded as definitively to be held. If all the bishops of the Church were to agree in teaching some doctrine as true, this would not suffice for an infallible exercise of the ordinary and universal magisterium; it is further required that they agree in presenting a doctrine with the note of absolute and definitive certainty.

The conditions for the infallibility of the bishops dispersed throughout the world are thus brought into agreement with the conditions required for the infallible definitions of a pope or a council. They differ only as regards the subject of teaching, though even here they come together in requiring that the subject be one that exercises supreme authority over the whole Church: either the pope acting as supreme pastor and teacher of all the faithful, or the college of bishops maintaining the bond of communion among themselves and with

71 AS III/1, 251: "(I) Pro verbis: 'in revelata fide tradenda' (T. P., pp. 67-68, l. 41-1), ponuntur verba '*res fidei et morum* docentes', ne videatur infallibilitas corporis episcopalis coarctari tantum ad ea quae ab eodem ut divinitus revelata credenda proponuntur."

72 AS III/1, 251: "Additur tamen quod agitur de casu quo proponunt sententiam *tamquam definitive tenendam*."

the successor of Peter. But the object of infallibility is the same in all three modes: matters of faith or morals belonging to the primary or secondary object of the magisterium. And the note required for infallibility is the same: the proposition of a doctrine as definitively to be held *(tamquam definitive tenendam)*. According to *Lumen gentium*, the bishops are infallible, more manifestly when gathered in council, but also when dispersed throughout the world, "when they come together in one judgment *(sententia)* as definitively to be held *(tamquam definitive tenendam)*."[73] Similarly, according to Vatican I, the pope is infallible when he defines *(definit)* a doctrine to be held *(tenendam)* by the whole Church,[74] which Gasser explains as the giving of a definitive judgment *(definitivam sententiam)* proposing a doctrine to be held *(tenendam)* by the universal Church.[75] By this addition of the phrase *'tamquam definitive tenendam'*, the text of *Lumen gentium* thus avoids giving the impression that may have otherwise been given, namely that the conditions placed upon the exercise of infallibility by the bishops dispersed throughout the world are less strict than those placed upon the exercise of infallibility by the pope or by the bishops gathered in council, which would then have reinforced the semi-Gallican and anti-conciliarist tendencies noted in the introduction.

No further changes were made to this part of the text prior to its final promulgation. So we can summarize the Second Vatican Council's teaching on the ordinary and universal magisterium as follows: its subject is the college of bishops dispersed throughout the world but maintaining communion with each other and with the pope; it can be exercised directly through their own teaching activity or indirectly through their oversight of the infallible faith of the whole people of God; its object is matters of faith and morals extending to the secondary object of the magisterium; and the note that characterizes its infallible operation is the note of conclusiveness, the proposition of a doctrine as definitively to be held. However, it should also be remembered that the text avoids using the term 'ordinary magisterium' and links this text on the infallibility of the bishops dispersed throughout the world with the following text on the infallibility of the bishops gathered in ecumenical council, so that the primary division of the whole paragraph appears to be between the (merely) authentic

---

73 Vatican II, *Lumen gentium*, § 25: "quando [...] authentice res fidei et morum docentes in unam sententiam tamquam definitive tenendam conveniunt" (Denz. 4149).

74 Vatican I, *Pastor Aeternus*, cap. 4: "cum [...] doctrinam de fide vel moribus ab universa Ecclesia tenendam definit" (Denz. 3074).

75 Mansi 52:1225: "sed requiritur intentio manifestata definiendi doctrinam, seu fluctuationi finem imponendi circa doctrinam quamdam seu rem definiendam, dando definitivam sententiam, et doctrinam illam proponendo tenendam ab ecclesia universali."

magisterium and the infallible magisterium rather than between the ordinary and the extraordinary magisterium. This latter, were the terms used, would appear instead as a subdivision of the treatment of the infallible magisterium.[76]

3.3 The Extraordinary Magisterium

The remainder of paragraph 25 deals with the infallible definitions of the bishops gathered in ecumenical council and of the popes speaking *ex cathedra*. Once again, the term 'extraordinary magisterium' is not used, though it seems clear that the definitions spoken of here are identical to the solemn judgments mentioned by Vatican I.

The first draft contained a lengthy statement on the infallibility of papal definitions *ex cathedra*,[77] the most remarkable feature of which was the addition of a statement intended to teach that no solemn definition could be inopportune.[78] The definitions of the college of bishops gathered in ecumenical council were treated more briefly, and were explained chiefly by comparison to papal definitions *ex cathedra*.[79]

---

76   See the diagram on p. 158, below.

77   AS I/4, 49: "Est igitur Romanus Pontifex pro universa Ecclesia catholica veritatis supremus magister, illique praecipue officium et ius competit integre custodiendi, defendendi et infallibiliter proponendi doctrinam salutis pro christifidelibus universis. Quod cum facit, cum nempe pro suprema sua apostolica auctoritate nomine Iesu Christi ex cathedra in rebus fidei et morum loquitur, ipsius sententia ex sese, utpote nomine Christi prolata, non autem ex consensu fidelium vel aliorum Episcoporum, infallibilis ideoque etiam irreformabilis est, atque divina operante Providentia fidem Ecclesiae saltem implicitam exprimit vel tuetur eiusque bonum promovet. Tunc autem Romanus Pontifex, etsi propria auctoritate doceat, non tamen ut persona privata suam sententiam proponit, sed tamquam universalis Ecclesiae Pastor et Doctor et Collegii Episcoporum Caput divinam exponit vel tuetur veritatem, quae, scripta vel tradita, per legitimam Episcoporum successionem et imprimis ipsius Apostolicae Sedis studio integra transmittitur, et praelucente Spiritu veritatis in Ecclesia fideliter servatur; ad quam cognoscendam media apta a divina Providentia Romano Pontifici suppeditantur. Quare cum doctrinam de fide vel moribus ab universa Ecclesia tenendam definit, eo ipso certum est hanc in deposito revelato contineri vel cum eodem necessario cohaerere."

78   A note on the words, "atque divina operante Providentia fidem Ecclesiae saltem implicitam exprimit vel tuetur eiusque bonum promovet," reads as follows: "CONCILIUM VATICANUM explicite quidem definivit tantum factum infallibilitatis definitionis Romani Pontificis ex cathedra loquentis; at, ex principio certissimo supernaturalis Providentiae qua vita Ecclesiae a Suo Capite caelesti dirigitur et a sua anima, Sancto scilicet Spiritu, praesenti ope adiuvatur, iure deducitur actus tam vitales pro Ecclesia, ut sunt definitiones ex cathedra, non posse inopportune evenire et non prodesse aedificationi Ecclesiae in fide et caritate. Quae conclusio theologica confirmatur declarationibus ipsius magisterii de opportunitate definitionis sollemnis" (AS I/4, 58).

79   AS I/4, 50: "cum vero in Oecumenico Concilio collegium episcopale adunatur una cum capite suo,

The ordering of the parts of the final draft is much different: it introduces its discussion of infallible definitions with the definitions of ecumenical councils; it turns next to a statement of the object of the infallibility of the Church; only then are papal definitions *ex cathedra* taken up; these are then related back to the definitions of the bishops gathered in council and to the faith of the whole Church; and then it closes by emphasizing that the magisterium of the Church is exercised always in subordination to divine revelation.

In the final text, the infallible definitions of ecumenical councils are introduced in close connection to the infallible teaching of the bishops dispersed throughout the world. Referring back to the infallibility of that teaching, the text reads: "This is even more clearly verified when, gathered together in an ecumenical council, they are teachers and judges of faith and morals for the universal Church, whose definitions must be adhered to with the submission of faith."[80] Two changes occurred in this text between the second and third drafts. The words *'una cum Romano Pontifice'*, were dropped.[81] And instead of saying that the definitions of the Church "ought to be received by all with a sincere mind" *(ab omnibus sincero animo accipi debent)*, it is said instead that they "are to be adhered to with the submission of faith" *(fidei obsequio est adhaerendum)*. The explanation given by the Theological Commission is that this phrase better expresses the kind of response due to conciliar definitions, and it specifies that the more generic phrase *'fidei obsequio'* is deliberately chosen rather than *'fidei divinae obsequio'* because "the submission of faith admits of diverse grades according to the greater or lesser relation of the defined truth with divine revelation."[82] Here, then, is further evidence that the

---

Romano Pontifice, numquam autem sine eo eique non subordinatum, Episcopi synodaliter congregati fiunt pro universa Ecclesia fidei et morum doctores et iudices, et una cum ipso supremam exercent docendi potestatem, Synodique ipsius definitiones eadem infallibilitate gaudent qua Romani Pontificis definitiones ex cathedra."

80　Vatican II, *Lumen gentium*, § 25: "Quod adhuc manifestius habetur quando, in Concilio Oecumenico coadunati, pro universa Ecclesia fidei et morum doctores et iudices sunt, quorum definitionibus fidei obsequio est adhaerendum" (Denz. 4149).

81　The second draft reads: "Quod adhuc manifestius habetur, quando in Concilio Oecumenico adunati, una cum Romano Pontifice, sunt pro universa Ecclesia fidei et morum doctores et iudices, quorum definitiones ab omnibus sincero animo accipi debent" (AS II/1, 238). The third draft is identical here to the final text. The explanation for the change is given in the relatio: "Loco locutionis bis repetitae 'una cum Romano Pontifice', ponitur semel in initio sententiae: 'communionis *inter se et cum successore Petri*'" (AS III/1, 251).

82　AS III/1, 251: "(K) Loco antiquioris formulae (T. P., p. 68, l. 7): 'sincero animo accipi debent' haec ponitur, quo melius urgeatur adhaesio definitionibus Concilii debita. Quae talis est, ut *sinceram animi adhaesionem superet,* quippe quae, ubi de definitionibus agitur, obsequium fidei penitus

definitions of the Church are to be understood as extending to the secondary object of the magisterium; that is, truths having a "lesser relation" with divine revelation can still be defined by the extraordinary magisterium.

The next part of the final text explicitly takes up this question of the object of the Church's infallibility: "And this infallibility with which the Divine Redeemer willed his Church to be endowed in defining doctrine of faith and morals extends as far as the deposit of faith extends, which must be religiously guarded and faithfully expounded."[83] Here too several changes were made between the second and third drafts,[84] in order to clearly affirm two things: first, that "the infallibility with which Christ willed his Church to be endowed is entirely identified with the infallibility of the Church teaching; and indeed: whether the episcopate as a whole or the Roman pontiff individually."[85] And secondly, that "the object of the infallibility of the Church, thus explained, has the same extension as the revealed deposit; and therefore it extends to all those things, and only to those things, which either pertain directly to the revealed deposit itself, or which are required for the same deposit to be religiously guarded and faithfully expounded."[86] Here again is yet more evidence that the infallibility of the Church in defining doctrine extends to the secondary object of the magisterium, and thus also that the exercise of the extraordinary magisterium extends to the secondary object of the magisterium.

---

attingat: quod quidem fidei obsequium gradus diversos admittit iuxta maiorem vel minorem relationem veritatis definitae cum divina Revelatione. Ad hunc disparem adhaesionis gradum, adhibetur formula generica '*fidei obsequio*', non autem: 'fidei *divinae* obsequio'."

83 Vatican II, *Lumen gentium*, § 25: "Haec autem infallibilitas, qua Divinus Redemptor Ecclesiam suam in definienda doctrina de fide vel moribus instructam esse voluit, tantum patet quantum divinae Revelationis patet depositum, sancte custodiendum et fideliter exponendum" (Denz. 4149).

84 The second draft reads: "In definitionibus suis Concilium ea infallibilitate pollet qua Divinus Redemptor Ecclesiam suam in definiendo doctrinam de fide et moribus instructam esse voluit" (AS II/1, 238). The third draft is identical here to the final text.

85 AS III/1, 251: "(L) 'In definitionibus suis [...] esse voluit' (T. P., lin. 8–11) aliter ordinantur et notabiliter *complentur*, ut haec duo indubitanter affirmentur: *a)* Infallibilitas qua Christus Ecclesiam instructam esse voluit prorsus *identificatur* cum infallibilitate Ecclesiae docentis; et quidem: sive totius Episcopatus, sive singulariter Romani Pontificis."

86 AS III/1, 251: "*b) Obiectum infallibilitatis* Ecclesiae, ita explicatae, eamdem habet extensionem ac depositum revelatum; ideoque extenditur ad ea omnia, et ad ea tantum, quae vel directe ad ipsum depositum revelatum spectant, vel quae ad idem depositum sancte custodiendum et fideliter exponendum requiruntur, ut habetur in CONC. VAT. I: Denz. 1836 (3070), ubi de infallibilitate Romani Pontificis."

Only at this point does the final text of *Lumen gentium* 25 take up the First Vatican Council's teaching on papal infallibility. It begins with a reformulation of the conditions required for an *ex cathedra* definition: "And this is the infallibility that the Roman pontiff, the head of the college of bishops, enjoys in virtue of his office, when, as the supreme shepherd and teacher of all the faithful, who confirms his brethren in their faith [*cf. Lk 22:32*], by a definitive act he proclaims a doctrine of faith or morals."[87] The same three essential conditions of infallibility appear both here and in the text of Vatican I: (1) the subject of teaching must be the pope acting as supreme head of the whole Church; (2) the object of teaching must be doctrine concerning faith or morals; and (3) the act of teaching must be definitive.

This is followed by an explanation of the intended sense of the '*ex sese*' clause in the text of the First Vatican Council:

> And therefore his definitions, of themselves, and not from the consent of the Church, are justly styled irreformable, since they are pronounced with the assistance of the Holy Spirit, promised to him in blessed Peter, and therefore they need no approval of others, nor do they allow an appeal to any other judgment. For then the Roman pontiff is not pronouncing judgment as a private person; but rather, as the supreme teacher of the universal Church, in whom the charism of infallibility of the Church herself is individually present, he is expounding or defending a doctrine of Catholic faith.[88]

This text was added, according to the Theological Commission, because the '*ex sese*' clause was "not rightly understood by many non-Catholics. Therefore this

---

87 Vatican II, *Lumen gentium*, § 25: "Qua quidem infallibilitate Romanus Pontifex, Collegii Episcoporum Caput vi muneris sui gaudet, quando, ut supremus omnium christifidelium pastor et doctor, qui fratres suos in fide confirmat [*cf. Lc 22:32*], doctrinam de fide vel moribus definitivo actu proclamat" (Denz. 4149). The *relatio* of the Theological Commission makes two points here: first, the phrase 'head of the college of bishops' is retained, despite the suggestions of some of the fathers, because it is not a restrictive clause and because it explains why the magisterium of the pope is treated in a paragraph whose object is the *munus docendi* of the college of bishops; and secondly, the term '*christifidelium*' is chosen instead of '*christianorum*' because Protestants and Orthodox call themselves 'Christians', whereas they do not generally use the former term (see AS III/1, 251–52).

88 Vatican II, *Lumen gentium*, § 25: "Quare definitiones eius ex sese, et non ex consensu Ecclesiae, irreformabiles merito dicuntur, quippe quae sub assistentia Spiritus Sancti, ipsi in beato Petro promissa, prolatae sint, ideoque nulla indigeant aliorum approbatione, nec ullam ad aliud iudicium appellationem patiantur. Tunc enim Romanus Pontifex non ut persona privata sententiam profert, sed ut universalis Ecclesiae magister supremus, in quo charisma infallibilitatis ipsius Ecclesiae singulariter inest, doctrinam fidei catholicae exponit vel tuetur" (Denz. 4149).

explanation has an ecumenical intention."[89] The explanation then proceeds to give the formal *ratio* of the irreformability of the such definitions, followed by two consequences of their irreformability, and then the reason for the pope's infallibility when he speaks *ex cathedra*.[90]

After this, the infallibility of the pope in defining doctrine is related back to the magisterium of the bishops, which is the principal object of the whole paragraph: "The infallibility promised to the Church resides also in the body of bishops when that body exercises the supreme Magisterium with the successor of Peter."[91] This is then followed by a clause that bears almost no superficial resemblance to the '*ex sese*' clause of Vatican I, yet which serves a similar purpose with respect to conciliar definitions as that had served with respect to papal definitions: "To these definitions the assent of the Church can never be wanting, on account of the activity of that same Holy Spirit, by which the whole flock of Christ is preserved and progresses in unity of faith."[92] The purpose of this text is to deny that the definitions of the bishops are subject to the approval of the people, just as the definitions of the pope are not subject to the approval of the bishops or faithful.[93]

---

89 AS III/1, 252: "*a)* de infallibilitate Romani Pontificis, de qua iam Conc. Vat. I claram definitionem dogmaticam protulit, hic agitur tantummodo ex iusta praeoccupatione dandi de eadem *congruam explicationem*, praesertim quod attinet ad verba quibus dicitur huiusmodi definitiones Romani Pontificis irreformabiles esse *ex sese, et non ex consensu Ecclesiae;* quae verba a pluribus acatholicis non recte intelliguntur. Explicatio igitur intentionem oecumenicam habet."

90 AS III/1, 252: "*b)* Haec autem congrua explicatio gradatim exhibetur: primo dicitur quaenam sit *ratio formalis irreformabilitatis* huiusmodi definitionum, videlicet assistentia Spiritus Sancti singulariter Romano Pontifici in beato Petro promissa; secundo, indicantur *duae consequentiae,* non adaequate distinctae, illius irreformabilitatis, quibus fit ut dictae definitiones nulla aliorum approbatione indigeant, nec ullam ad aliud iudicium (ne quidem ad aliud iudicium ipsius Romani Pontificis) appellationem patiantur. *c)* Infallibilitas autem ex eo evenit quod Romanus Pontifex, quando ex cathedra loquitur, *non ut persona privata* sententiam profert, sed tanquam *magister supremus Ecclesiae* docet; in quo actu charisma infallibilitatis ipsius Ecclesiae ei singulariter inest, et ipse totam Ecclesiam repraesentat."

91 Vatican II, *Lumen gentium,* § 25: "Infallibilitas Ecciesiae promissa in corpore Episcoporum quoque inest, quando supremum magisterium cum Petri Successore exercet" (Denz. 4149). The Theological Commission explains: "*d)* Eadem infallibilitas agnoscitur quoque *Corpori Episcoporum,* quando *simul cum Romano Pontifice* definitionem profert. Quod ad obiectum praecipuum et directum huius paragraphi pertinet" (AS III/1, 252).

92 Vatican II, *Lumen gentium,* § 25: "Istis autem definitionibus assensus Ecclesiae numquam deesse potest propter actionem eiusdem Spiritus Sancti, qua universus Christi grex in unitate fidei servatur et proficit."

93 AS III/1, 252–53: "*e) Assensus autem Ecclesiae* ad huiusmodi definitiones nunquam deesse potest propter *Spiritum Sanctum,* cuius assistentia definitiones ab errore immunes sunt, et cuius actione

Finally, *Lumen gentium* 25 concludes with an important reminder that the magisterium of the Church is always subordinate to divine revelation:

> But when either the Roman pontiff or the body of bishops together with him defines a judgment, they pronounce it in accordance with revelation itself, which all are obliged to abide by and be in conformity with, that is, the revelation that as written or orally handed down is transmitted in its entirety through the legitimate succession of bishops and especially in care of the Roman pontiff himself, and which under the guiding light of the Spirit of truth is religiously preserved and faithfully expounded in the Church. The Roman pontiff and the bishops, in view of their office and the importance of the matter, by fitting means diligently strive to inquire properly into that revelation and to give apt expression to its contents; but a new public revelation they do not accept as pertaining to the divine deposit of faith.[94]

An interesting change occurred in this text between the third draft and the final promulgation. Where it now refers to the judgments defined by "the Roman pontiff or the body of bishops together with him," it had previously read more simply "the Roman pontiff or a council."[95] Three fathers of the council requested this change because, they argued, "the assertion does not necessarily require the form of a council." The Theological Commission accepted the change, provided

---

totus grex Christi eis adhaeret et in fide etiam *proficit.* Hoc autem valet de definitionibus, sive a Romano Pontifice, sive a Corpore Episcoporum cum eo prolatis, ita ut etiam definitiones Concilii *ex sese* irreformabiles sint et approbatione populi non indigeant, ut erronee plures in Oriente tenent, sed consensum totius communitatis secum ferant et exprimant."

94 Vatican II, *Lumen gentium*, § 25: "Cum autem sive Romanus Pontifex sive Corpus Episcoporum cum eo sententiam definiunt, eam proferunt secundum ipsam Revelationem, cui omnes stare et conformari tenentur et quae scripta vel tradita per legitimam Episcoporum successionem et imprimis ipsius Romani Pontificis cura integre transmittitur, atque praelucente Spiritu veritatis in Ecclesia sancte servatur et fideliter exponitur. Ad quam rite indagandam et apte enuntiandam, Romanus Pontifex et Episcopi, pro officio suo et rei gravitate, per media apta, sedulo operam navant; novam vero revelationem publicam tamquam ad divinum fidei depositum pertinentem non accipiunt" (Denz. 4149). The Theological Commission explains: "In hac alinea affirmatur quod definitiones praedictae *cum Revelatione necessario concordant;* quod Romanus Pontifex et Episcopi definientes verbo Dei scripto et tradito conformari tenentur, ut explicat GASSER in CONC. VAT. 1: MANSI 1216 D: '*eosdem fontes* habent quales habet Ecclesia'; et denique quod Magisterium *media apta investigationis* adhibere debet. Commissioni non placuit hic consultationem 'theologorum et exegetarum' vel *peritorum* explicite nominari, sed simpliciter media apta indicari" (AS III/1, 253).

95 The third draft reads: "Cum autem sive Romanus Pontifex sive Concilium sententiam definiunt, eam proferunt secundum ipsam Revelationem" (AS III/1, 222).

that it should still be understood of what are properly called 'definitions'.[96] Thus this would appear to leave the door open for an exercise of the extraordinary magisterium by the college of bishops outside of an ecumenical council.

The schema below attempts to diagram the operations of the magisterium as outlined in *Lumen gentium*. That which is given explicitly in the text of *Lumen gentium* is indicated in standard type; that which is implied through the *relationes* and footnotes is placed in *italics*.

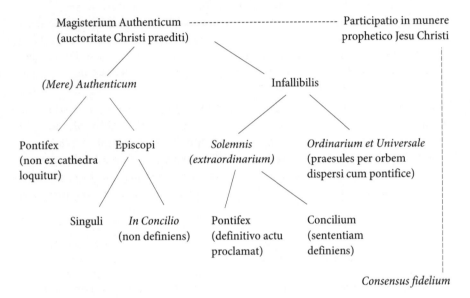

4.   Concluding Observations

Much of the confusion concerning the meaning and use of the terms 'ordinary magisterium' and 'extraordinary magisterium' appears to stem from the application of this terminology to the teaching activity of the popes in the years following the First Vatican Council. That this would be the case was even foreshadowed in Bishop Martinez's misapprehension of the intended meaning of the term 'ordinary magisterium' in the text of *Dei Filius*, when he took it to refer to the papal magisterium, and in the warnings of Archbishop Errington

---

96   AS III/8, 92: "176 – Pag. 69, lin. 15: Proponunt 3 Patres ut mutetur vox 'Concilium', in: '*Corpus Episcoporum cum Ipso* sententiam definiunt', quia assertio non necessario formam *Concilii* exigit. R – Admittitur, dummodo agatur de proprie dicta 'definitione'."

and others that the term was obscure, open to differing interpretations, and would be a source of confusion.

The terms 'ordinary magisterium' and 'extraordinary magisterium' appear to imply an exhaustive division of the magisterium. After Vatican I, the pope was clearly understood to exercise the extraordinary magisterium in his solemn definitions; but many of the magisterial acts of the popes clearly fell short of being solemn definitions; thus they were attributed to an ordinary magisterium exercised by the pope. This had several effects. One was a distortion in the meaning of the term 'ordinary magisterium'. Since the 'ordinary' teaching of the popes was quite explicit and documented, Kleutgen's emphasis on the ordinary magisterium as a means of transmitting the faith apart from the documents of the hierarchy faded from view. The concept of an ordinary magisterium, which had been intended to move beyond a narrow focus on the doctrinal statements of the hierarchy toward a broader view of the rule of faith grounded in Scripture, tradition, the liturgy, the *sensus fidelium*, etc., was reinterpreted as just another kind of statement emanating from the ecclesiastical hierarchy, thus reinforcing instead of challenging the notion that the hierarchy is the only source of doctrinal certitude.

A second effect was a distortion in the meaning of the term 'extraordinary magisterium'. If the pope exercised an ordinary magisterium; and if the pope possessed the same infallibility as the Church; and if the Church was infallible in its exercise of the ordinary magisterium; then the pope must be able to exercise the ordinary magisterium infallibly. So reasoned Vacant and many who followed him. But if the pope is infallible both in his ordinary and in his extraordinary magisterium, then what is the difference between them? Following Vacant, one could say that both forms may meet the criteria of Vatican I for an infallible definition, but that only the extrinsically solemn are to be counted as extraordinary; or following Billot, one could say that all those that meet the criteria of Vatican I are solemn and extraordinary, but that some teaching falling short of that may still be infallible. The latter view attributes infallibility beyond what was established at Vatican I; but the former view separates the extraordinary magisterium from the infallible definitions of the Church, exaggerating both the solemnity and the rarity of the extraordinary magisterium. That is, it makes the extraordinary magisterium even more rare and more solemn than the infallible definitions of popes and ecumenical councils.

Those who reject both horns of this dilemma; that is, those who maintain the identity of *ex cathedra* definitions with the extraordinary magisterium, but who refuse to extend the infallibility of the pope beyond *ex cathedra* definitions, can only conclude that the ordinary magisterium of the pope is not infallible.

But this causes the infallibility of the pope to appear to be more restricted than the infallibility of the bishops who are able to teach infallibly through the ordinary magisterium. And *Humani generis*, by referring to the papal encyclicals as exercises of the ordinary magisterium, but without addressing any of the questions about its infallibility or its relation to the ordinary and universal magisterium of the bishops, merely reinforces this problem without offering a solution.

A third effect of the application of the distinction between an ordinary and an extraordinary magisterium to the magisterium of the pope was a distortion in the understanding of the precise nature of this distinction. Since the ordinary teaching of the pope is quite explicit, Kleutgen's distinction could not be maintained; since the bishops can teach definitively and infallibly through both modes, neither can the distinction be based on these things. What remains? It would seem that a definition would have to be more than just definitive. Following Vacant, one could say that it must be extrinsically solemn in addition to being a definitive judgment; or following Billot (at least apparently), one could say that it must be a new in addition to being a definitive judgment. This latter option, however, is at least open to serious question on the basis of *Mortalium animos* and it is implicitly denied in *Munificentissimus Deus*.

The first draft of a constitution on the Church prepared prior to Vatican II would have reinforced these difficulties since it followed closely the language of *Humani generis* in referring to the 'non-definitive' teaching of the pope as an exercise of the ordinary magisterium while also referring to the infallible teaching of the bishops dispersed throughout the world as an exercise of the ordinary magisterium. More than anything else this would have reinforced the apparent inequality between papal and episcopal infallibility. As it happened, however, this first draft was discarded and the final text of *Lumen gentium* reveals an unmistakable shift in terminology and a significant reorganization of the material. The terms 'ordinary magisterium' and 'extraordinary magisterium' appear nowhere in the text. And instead of dividing its treatment of the magisterium based on the subject of the magisterium, as the first draft had done (first the pope and then the bishops), or on the distinction between an ordinary and an extraordinary magisterium, it was divided on the basis of the distinction between the (merely) authoritative magisterium and the infallible magisterium. The 'non-definitive' teaching of the bishops and of the pope are treated together; then the infallible teaching of the bishops, whether dispersed throughout the world or gathered in council; and then the infallible teaching of the pope. The distinction between ordinary and extraordinary is latent (through the footnotes) in the distinction between the bishops dispersed throughout the world and gathered in council, but these terms are not used.

Several other significant contributions of *Lumen gentium* to our understanding of the modes of operation of the magisterium are worth noting more briefly. Kleutgen and Gasser are cited as authorities for the right understanding of the ordinary and universal magisterium and of papal infallibility, respectively. The notion of an infallible ordinary papal magisterium is implicitly denied inasmuch as every act of papal teaching short of an *ex cathedra* definition is treated as requiring only a religious submission of will and intellect rather than the submission of faith. The link between the ordinary magisterium and the bishops dispersed throughout the world is maintained (via the footnotes). The connection between the ordinary magisterium of the bishops in teaching and the infallibility of the people of God in believing is hinted at (again, via the footnotes). Both the ordinary and extraordinary modes of teaching are extended to the secondary object of the magisterium. And the note of infallibility in every mode of teaching lies in the definitiveness of its proposition.

CONCLUSION

From the outset of this work, the primary aim has been to shed some light on the nature of the distinction between the ordinary and the extraordinary magisterium. Is it essentially a distinction between the teaching of the Church gathered in council and that of the Church dispersed throughout the world? Or is it rather essentially a distinction between externally solemn teaching and teaching that lacks such external solemnity? Or again, is it essentially a matter of teaching that defines doctrine and teaching that does not define? Or finally, is it a distinction between traditional and innovative teaching? All of these positions can be found in the theological literature of the twentieth century. And the lack of a clear and consistent usage of the terms 'ordinary magisterium' and 'extraordinary magisterium' among theologians causes further difficulties in many already complex controversies surrounding the degree of authority of various magisterial teachings.

Hoping that a clearer conception of these terms would serve a more consistent usage, I set out to examine the nineteenth century origins of this terminology in the works of Joseph Kleutgen, its subsequent adoption by Pope Pius IX and the First Vatican Council, and its later development up through the Second Vatican Council.

In the neo-scholastic ecclesiological framework of Joseph Kleutgen, the concept of an ordinary magisterium served a very specific purpose: it allowed him to tread the narrow path between dogmatic minimalism and the principle of private interpretation. On the one hand, he was determined to oppose the idea that Catholics are free to follow their own opinions in any matter not explicitly determined by a formal judgment of the Church; on the other hand, he was also committed to the neo-scholastic view of the magisterium as the proximate rule of faith. Reacting against a modern tendency to focus exclusively on positive Church teaching, such as is found in the documents of popes and ecumenical councils, Kleutgen wanted to re-emphasize the basic and primary authority of Scripture and Tradition. But how could he do so without laying himself open to the charge of endorsing the Protestant principle of private interpretation? His solution was to take the ancient concept of the 'living tradition of the Church' and re-christen it as the 'the ordinary magisterium of the Church'. The ordinary magisterium is the living tradition of the Church understood as the ongoing and perpetual process of handing on the faith from one generation to the next outside of the more rare and extraordinary solemn pronouncements of the Church. The teachings of the ordinary magisterium can be verified from all the sources of theology, beginning with Scripture, but most easily (according to Kleutgen) from the consensus of theologians. The distinction between the ordinary and the extraordinary magisterium, in its origins, is a distinction within the infallible magisterium of the Church. It is a distinction between the explicitly documented definitions of the Church and her undocumented but equally definitive teaching.

Kleutgen's terminology made its way quickly into the documents of the Church. It was first adopted by Pius IX in his apostolic letter *Tuas libenter* and was then enshrined in the dogmatic constitution *Dei Filius* of Vatican I. A detailed examination reveals that the intended sense of the term 'ordinary magisterium' in both of these documents is substantially identical with the original meaning and usage of Kleutgen. This is no surprise when one considers how influential he was in Rome at the time and how closely involved he was in the drafting of *Dei Filius*. In every case the context is the same: the rule of faith; and the target is the same: dogmatic minimalism. *Tuas libenter* explicitly conects the ordinary magisterium to the teaching activity of the Church dispersed throughout the world, which *Dei Filius* confirms by addition of the term 'universal' (so that now we speak of an 'ordinary and universal magisterium'). A review of the definition of papal infallibility in *Pastor Aeternus* also reveals substantial agreement between Kleutgen and the council with respect to the extraordinary magisterium. Already at Vatican I, however, many of the council fathers warned that the term 'ordinary magisterium' was inherently ambiguous and open to different interpretations.

The reception of this teaching in the decades that followed Vatican I proved this warning true as the term was indeed understood and applied differently by different theologians. The first shift of meaning appeared in the work of J.-M.-A. Vacant, who applied the term 'ordinary magisterium' to certain forms of explicit papal teaching that fell short of his criteria for solemn and extraordinary definitions. Interestingly enough, however, Vacant still believed that this ordinary papal magisterium was infallible. This initiated several decades of controversy regarding the authority of the ordinary papal magisterium. But whether the term 'ordinary magisterium' should ever have been applied to the papal magisterium at all was mostly passed over without question. In *Humani generis*, Pius XII adopted Vacant's application of the term 'ordinary magisterium' to papal teaching (though without addressing the question of infallibility). But such an application of the term to documents such as papal encyclicals constitutes a real shift inasmuch as the 'ordinary magisterium' of the pope cannot be understood as an essentially non-documentary form of magisterial teaching. This new distinction between solemn and non-solemn forms of explicit teaching was thus superimposed upon the original distinction between documented and undocumented forms of Church teaching.

This leads to what is perhaps the most important conclusion of the present study on the nature of the distinction between the ordinary and the extraordinary magisterium: that this terminology covers not one distinction but two. One use of the terminology of ordinary and extraordinary magisterium refers to the distinction between defined (extraordinary) and 'non-definitive' (ordinary) doctrines taught infallibly by the Church; another use of the same terminology refers to the distinction between infallible (extraordinary) and merely authentic (ordinary) acts of teaching by the ecclesiastical hierarchy. And whereas the meaning of the term 'extraordinary' converges in both uses, the meanings of 'ordinary' diverge. One 'ordinary magisterium' is ordinary in its lack of explicit formulation; the other 'ordinary magisterium' is ordinary in its lack of definitiveness. The later history of theology has therefore vindicated those council fathers who opposed the use of the term 'ordinary magisterium' on the grounds that it is inherently ambiguous, open to different interpretations, and therefore a source of confusion rather than clarity.

This account of the ambiguity of the term 'ordinary magisterium' also reveals the fallacy hidden in the typical neo-scholastic arguments for the infallibility of the ordinary papal magisterium. As outlined in the introduction, that argument can be summarized as follows: the Church is infallible in her ordinary magisterium; the pope possesses the same infallibility as the Church; therefore, the pope is infallible in his ordinary magisterium. In the first premise, the term 'ordinary magisterium' refers to the definitive teaching of the Church dispersed throughout the world; in the conclusion, the same term refers to the 'non-definitive' teaching of the pope. The ambiguously used term vitiates the argument. The conclusion does not follow because the infallibility of the bishops dispersed throughout the world follows upon the definitiveness of that teaching, which is precisely what the 'non-definitive' teaching of the pope lacks. There is no infallible 'ordinary magisterium' of the pope, just as there is no infallible 'ordinary magisterium' of an ecumenical council because the term 'ordinary' in these contexts simply means 'non-definitive'. Nor does this imply that there is any greater power of infallible teaching attributed to the bishops than to the pope, or to the bishops dispersed throughout the world than to the bishops gathered in council. For the infallible teaching of the ordinary magisterium of the bishops dispersed throughout the world, *Lumen gentium* requires the proposition of a judgment in matters of faith or morals as one that is 'definitively to be held' *(definitive tenendam)*. Any act of teaching, however, by which a pope or an ecumenical council proposes a judgment in matters of faith or morals as one that is 'definitively to be held', is by that very fact a definition of the extraordinary magisterium. The unique mode of infallibility exercised by the bishops in their state of dispersion throughout the world is not, therefore, due to a greater gift of infallibility; it is due rather to the unique nature of that dispersion itself, which results in an implicit or non-documentary mode of teaching. And this mode of infallible teaching is not shared by popes or by ecumenical councils simply because their definitive teaching is quite explicit and documentary. When the term 'ordinary magisterium' is understood as a reference to the non-documentary infallible teaching characteristic of the Church in its state of dispersion throughout the world, it becomes clear why ecumenical councils and popes do not exercise an infallible ordinary magisterium.

Practical Applications for Ecclesiology Today

If the conclusions reached above are correct, they would have at least three practical and immediate applications for contemporary theological discussion. The first regards terminology. In order to facilitate clarity of thought and avoid unnecessary misunderstandings in theological discussions of these matters, I would propose that theologians follow the lead of the Second Vatican Council in avoiding the use of the terms 'ordinary magisterium' and 'extraordinary magisterium' as often as these can be replaced by terms that convey a clearer sense of their meaning. Terms such as 'solemn judgment' or 'definition' are usually adequate without recourse to the notion of an 'extraordinary magisterium'. The term 'authentic magisterium' should be used in place of 'ordinary magisterium' whenever it is a question of 'non-definitive' teaching of the pope or bishops.

Secondly, it will be important to be more attentive to context when applying these distinctions. When it is a question of evaluating the doctrinal weight of a formal and explicit magisterial teaching document, the terminology of ordinary and extraordinary magisterium is out of place and that between infallible and 'non-definitive' magisterium should be used instead. The distinction between ordinary and extraordinary magisterium serves its purpose when it is a question of classification of doctrine, which is the *object* of teaching. In other words, it belongs more properly to the treatise on the faith than to the treatise on the Church. It is significant that *Dei Filius* (on the faith) makes use of the distinction between the ordinary and the extraordinary magisterium, whereas *Pastor Aeternus* (on the Church) does not; and that *Lumen gentium* (on the Church) utilizes the terminology of infallible and authentic magisterium rather than ordinary and extraordinary magisterium.

A third application of the conclusions reached above regards the need for a re-evaluation of the doctrinal status of several declarations of Vatican II and of Pope John Paul II in particular. The present study has revealed no firm basis in the documents of the Church for a restriction of the extraordinary magisterium either to the primary object of the magisterium or to the creation of new doctrinal obligations (the settling of matters previously open to legitimate dispute); in fact, there is strong evidence to the contrary on both points. The official explanations of Bishop Gasser at Vatican I and of the Theological Commission at Vatican II make clear that the secondary object of the magisterium is intended to be understood within the scope of infallible definitions. And Pope Pius XI in *Mortalium animos* at least implies what Pope Pius XII brings out more clearly in *Munificentissimus Deus*, namely that the extraordinary magisterium can be used to define a doctrine that has already been taught infallibly by the ordinary and universal magisterium.

But if it is true that a doctrine already taught infallibly by the ordinary and universal magisterium of the Church can afterwards be defined by the extraordinary magisterium, then Ratzinger's reason for attributing the declaration contained in *Ordinatio sacerdotalis* to the ordinary papal magisterium does not hold, and hence his conclusion regarding its *per se* non-infallibility is undermined. Of course, even if it is the case that there is a flaw in Ratzinger's argumentation, that would not prove the opposite conclusion to be true – it would not prove that *Ordinatio sacerdotalis* contains an infallible definition. But insofar as much of the consensus against its infallibility appears either to depend upon Ratzinger's authority or to share his presuppositions regarding the ordinary and extraordinary magisterium, the question at least deserves serious reconsideration.

The same could be said regarding several of the doctrinal declarations of the Second Vatican Council. It is often heard and repeated that Vatican II avoided using the extraordinary magisterium or that it avoided teaching anything with the note of infallibility attached to it. But this does not quite accurately convey what Paul VI said in his famous remarks about the theological qualification of the teaching of the Second Vatican Council. In his concluding address at the closing session of the council, he says that the council did not wish to issue "extraordinary dogmatic pronouncements."[1] And again, a few weeks later in a general audience, he remarked that the council "avoided pronouncing in an extraordinary way dogmas endowed with the note of

---

1   Pope Paul VI, *Address during the Last General Meeting of the Second Vatican Council* (7 Dec. 1965). Taken from the website of the Holy See (www.vatican.va).

infallibility."[2] In both cases, Paul VI denies that Vatican II issued solemn dogmatic definitions. But this is at least open to the interpretation that he was denying the use of the extraordinary magisterium only with regard to the primary object of the magisterium. Even if Vatican II did not issue any solemn definitions of truths to be believed as divinely revealed, it may have issued solemn definitions of truths to be held definitively. The denial of all dogmatic definitions is not necessarily a denial of all solemn definitions absolutely speaking.

Let us take the example of the council's declaration regarding the sacramentality of the episcopate.[3] If it is true that the extraordinary magisterium extends to the secondary object of the magisterium, then it follows that the extraordinary magisterium can define a doctrine without making it such that its denial would constitute heresy. But in this case, the reason adduced by Congar and Betti for denying that this teaching of Vatican II is a definition "in the strict sense" does not hold; and if this is a solemn definition, then the assertion that Vatican II taught nothing infallibly (or even that it taught nothing new infallibly) would be undermined. Here again, insofar as much of the consensus against the infallibility of Vatican II appears either to depend upon the authority of authors such as Congar and Betti or at least to share their presuppositions regarding the scope of the extraordinary magisterium, this question too deserves serious reconsideration.

And what of the explicitly solemn declaration contained in *Orientalium Ecclesiarum*:

> [*The sacred council*] solemnly declares *(sollemniter declarat)* that the Churches of the East, as much as those of the West, have a full right and are in duty bound to rule themselves, each in accordance with her own established disciplines, since all these are praiseworthy by reason of their venerable antiquity, more harmonious with the character of their faithful, and more suited to the promotion of the good of souls.[4]

---

2   Pope Paul VI, *General Audience* (12 Jan. 1966): "dato il carattere pastorale del Concilio, esso ha evitato di pronunciare in modo straordinario dogmi dotati della nota di infallibilità." Taken from the website of the Holy See (www.vatican.va).

3   Vatican II, *Lumen gentium*, § 21: "And the sacred council teaches that by episcopal consecration the fullness of the sacrament of orders is conferred, that fullness of power, namely, which both in the Church's liturgical practice and in the language of the Fathers of the Church is called the high priesthood, the supreme power of the sacred ministry" (Denz. 4145).

4   Vatican Council II, Session V, Decree on the Catholic Churches of the Eastern Rite *Orientalium Ecclesiarum* (21 Nov. 1964), § 5: "[*Sancta Synodus*] sollemniter declarat, Ecclesias Orientis sicut et Occidentis iure pollere et officio teneri se secundum proprias disciplinas peculiares regendi,

The same declaration is emphatically repeated in *Unitatis redintegratio:*

> To remove, then, all shadow of doubt *(ad omne dubium tollendum)*, this holy council declares *(Sacra Synodus declarat)* that the Churches of the East, while remembering the necessary unity of the whole Church, have the power to govern themselves according to the disciplines proper to them, since these are better suited to the character of their faithful and more for the good of their souls.[5]

Formulas such as these, while indeed falling short of being dogmatic definitions in the strict sense of being imposed under pain of heresy, nevertheless appear to bear all the characteristic marks of merely doctrinal solemn definitions, that is, definitions of doctrine to be held *(tenendam)* by the whole Church even if not definitions of doctrine to be believed *(credendam)* by the whole Church. Once again, insofar as the arguments against regarding these declarations as infallible definitions of the extraordinary magisterium hinge upon the fact that they are not imposed under pain of heresy, they also deserve serious reconsideration in light of the conclusions reached in the present study.

Indications of a Way Forward

The investigation undertaken in this work concludes with the teaching of the Second Vatican Council. At the Second Vatican Council, decisive steps were taken in the drafting of the text of *Lumen gentium* that serve to open up some not yet fully realized possibilities for carrying forward the development of our understanding of the nature and operation of the magisterium within the broader life of the Church. To be sure, there are certain limitations in the text of *Lumen gentium* 25, but there are also indications of a positive way forward. Firstly, we can see in *Lumen gentium* a renewed emphasis on the proclamation of the Gospel as the primary task of the bishop in the exercise of his *munus docendi*. This emphasis, however, is not carried through the whole of *Lumen gentium* 25. As Hünermann notes, "The four sections reveal a remarkable narrowing of view. After a short characterization of the preaching of the Gospel in the first section, the following sections treat of the question of the infallibility

---

utpote quae veneranda antiquitate commendentur, moribus suorum fidelium magis sint congruae atque ad bonum animarum consulendum aptiores videantur" (Denz. 4180).

5   Vatican Council II, Session V, Decree on Ecumenism *Unitatis redintegratio* (21 Nov. 1964), § 16: "Sacra Synodus, ad omne dubium tollendum, declarat Ecclesias Orientis, memores necessariae unitatis totius Ecclesiae, facultatem habere se secundum proprias disciplinas regendi, utpote indoli suorum fidelium magis congruas atque bono animorum consulendo aptiores" (Denz. 4193).

of the Church."[6] Hünermann is disappointed that the majority of *Lumen gentium* 25 still deals with the formal and infallible teaching of the Church and not with "the various forms of service to the Word – preaching and homilies, catechesis, religious education, theology, religious publication," nor does it mention "the duty of the bishop to demand, order, or supervise these various forms of proclamation."[7] Even the reference to the ordinary magisterium, which could include all these missing elements, is expressed in *Lumen gentium* in a way that makes it appear very much like merely another formal and juridical mode of teaching emanating from the hierarchy.

Despite the initial emphasis on the daily proclamation of the Gospel, there is a decided preoccupation, both in *Lumen gentium* 25 and in the wider culture of the Church, with the formal statements of the magisterium.[8] A more highly developed understanding of the ordinary magisterium could serve as a corrective to an approach that concentrates too much on teaching in the form of solemn pronouncements and formal documents; it could serve to draw out the vital importance of that more common form of general preaching. In an age of ever increasing access to information combined with an ever increasing emanation of documentation from the Vatican,[9] a renewed appreciation for the primary importance of the ordinary magisterium can serve as a salutary reminder that the main task of the Church is not simply to issue more and more

6   Peter Hünermann, "Theologischer Kommentar zur dogmatischen Konstitution über die Kirche *Lumen gentium*," in *Herders Theologischer Kommentar zum Zweiten Vatikanischen Konzil*, vol. 2, ed. Bernd Hilberath and Peter Hünermann, 263–582 (Freiburg; Basel; Vienna: Herder, 2009), 434: "LG 25 behandelt den Verkündigungsauftrag der Bischöfe. Die vier Abschnitte verraten eine merkwürdige Blickverengung. Nach einer kurzen Charakterisierung der Verkündigung des Evangeliums im 1. Abschnitt behandeln die folgenden Abschnitte die Frage der Unfehlbarkeit der Lehre."

7   Ibid.: "Es ist weder von den verschiedenen Formen des Dienstes am Wort – der Predigt und Homilie, der Katechese, dem Religionsunterricht, der Theologie, der religiösen Publizistik – die Rede, noch von der Aufgabe des Bischofs, diese mannigfachen Formen des Verkündigungsdienstes zu fördern, zu ordnen, zu überwachen."

8   Cf. Ibid., 443: "Überblickt man die Ausführungen von Artikel 25, dessen Thema die Verkündigung des Evangeliums durch die Bischöfe ist, so verwundert, wie stark die Aufmerksamkeit das ‚sententialiter definire', die lehrsatzmäßige Entscheidung und zwar besonders in der Form der definitiven, infalliblen Entscheidung konzentriert ist."

9   Cf. Ibid., 435: "Die pausenlose Produktion von bischöflichen und päpstlichen Lehrschreiben, die weit in wissenschaftliche Fachdiskussionen hineinführen, stellt somit eine gewisse Verkennung des eigentlichen bischöflichen Auftrages und damit auch eine gewisse Kompetenzüberschreitung dar. Die Verheißung des Geistesbeistandes bezieht sich auf jene Momente, die für den bischöflichen Dienst wesentlich sind."

documents, but most fundamentally to preach the same Gospel ever anew. That Christians have a moral duty to love their enemies, that blessed are the poor in spirit; that the meek shall inherit the earth; these are the kinds of things taught by the ordinary magisterium in the primary and fundamental work of preaching the Gospel. Such a view of the ordinary magisterium could also impact our understanding of dogma, opening up a wider notion of dogma as divinely revealed truth and not just as defined formulas. The work of the magisterium of the Church is not only to define formulas of faith but to preach truths of faith that are not only correct statements but also invitations to a living encounter with a person, Jesus Christ, who is the way, the truth, and the life.

A second point is this: the prevailing understanding of the ordinary and universal magisterium is tightly bound to the direct action of the hierarchy. And it must be admitted that this is reinforced in *Lumen gentium* by the reference to the ordinary and universal magisterium as a form of infallible teaching exercised by the bishops dispersed throughout the world. But at the same time there is also a renewed connection forged (though subtly and only through the footnotes) between the ordinary magisterium and the infallibility of the whole people of God exercised via the *consensus fidelium*.[10] This connection is rich with possibilities for a way of understanding the necessary distinction between hierarchy and laity in the context of a broader and more fundamental communion with shared responsibilities for preserving and transmitting the faith received from the apostles.

Even more than this, however, a more highly developed conception of the ordinary magisterium would include not only the passive agreement of the faithful in believing, but also the active teaching and transmitting of the faith that occurs within the whole Church under the supervision of the hierarchy. In light of the renewed emphasis of the Second Vatican Council on the active participation of the lay faithful in the life of the Church and in the threefold ministry of Christ as priest, prophet, and king,[11] there is promising work to be done here in further developing an understanding of not only bishops, but also priests, professors, teachers, and even parents as instruments of the ordinary

---

10   Thus Cardinal Dulles is able to refer to the consensus of the faithful as a means of their "participation in the hierarchical magisterium" (Dulles, *Magisterium*, 39, 44–46).

11   Vatican II, *Lumen gentium*, § 31: "These faithful are by baptism made one body with Christ and are constituted among the people of God; they are in their own way made sharers in the priestly, prophetical, and kingly functions of Christ; and they carry out for their own part the mission of the whole Christian people in the Church and in the world" (Denz. 4157).

magisterium whenever they are engaged in proclaiming and transmitting the truth of Gospel.

All of this, however, raises further questions. If, as suggested above, non-hierarchical members of the Church are able to participate in the teaching activity of the ordinary magisterium, how are we to describe the subject of the ordinary magisterium? From Kleutgen to Vatican II the exercise of the ordinary magisterium has been consistently attributed to the bishops of the Church. If we accept a broader understanding, according to which the subject of the ordinary magisterium is the Church as such, which is not simply identified with the hierarchy, how does this affect our understanding of the theological criteria for recognizing the binding character of doctrines taught by the ordinary magisterium? Such questions deserve further study, which may perhaps also contribute to the development of a broader understanding of the magisterium itself as something that goes beyond the expression of faith in sentences transmitted by formal teaching to embrace every authentic witness to the truth of the Gospel.

JOSEPH KLEUTGEN'S TREATISE ON THE RULE OF FAITH:
FROM THE FIRST EDITION OF *DIE THEOLOGIE DER VORZEIT*

Die Theologie der Vorzeit vertheidigt
von Joseph Kleutgen, Priester der Gesellschaft Jesu.
Erster Band. Münster 1853.
Erster Theil. Von der Lehre der Vorzeit.
Erste Abhandlung. Von der Glaubensnorm.

Unter Glaubensnorm versteht man den höchsten Grundsatz, nach welchem zu entscheiden ist, was zum Glauben der Kirche gehöre, und folglich von allen Katholiken als geoffenbarte Wahrheit angenommen und bekannt werden müsse. Es scheint also zweckmäßig, daß wir die Untersuchung jener Lehren der Theologen, welche man für irrige und willkürliche erklärt, mit einer Verständigung über die Glaubensnorm beginnen; um so mehr als Hirscher und zum Theile auch Hermes Ansichten aussprechen, die mit der richtigen Erklärung der katholischen Glaubensregel nicht in Einklang gebracht werden können.

I. Wesentliche und unwesentliche Glaubenspunkte.

Hirscher redet von dem Gegenstand, den wir hier behandeln, am ausführlichsten in der „*Erörterung* über die *Einheit* der Lehre und des Glaubens in der Kirche[2]." Er beantwortet daselbst zunächst die Frage: „Wie weit die Einheit der Ueberzeugung gehen müsse, um zur Gemeinschaft einer Kirche zu gehören;" also: „Ich glaube, daß man keinen Lehrsatz haben dürfe, welcher dem gemeinsamen Lehrbegriff der Kirche in einem wesentlichen Punkte widerspricht. Ein unentwickelter Glaube, ein einseitiger Glaube, ein in Außerwesentlichem irrender Glaube ist wohl ein Mangel, und das unvermeidliche Loos der menschlichen Schwachheit, aber kein Gegensatz gegen den gemeinsamen religiösen Glauben, und kein Abfall von demselben."

---

1   [Deviations from today's spelling (e.g. "nöthig" instead of "nötig") and irrelevant spelling variations ("Papst" oder "Pabst") are maintained. Stoppages in the original text are represented by italic print; author's note].
2   Erörterungen. 14 Erört. S. 163 u. ss.

Diese Antwort nun können wir, wenigstens wenn von der katholischen Kirche die Rede ist, durchaus nicht gelten lassen, ohne das, was Hirscher vom Wesentlichen und Außerwesentlichen sagt, zu streichen. Allerdings ist die Einheit der Kirche im Glauben nicht nothwendig eine materiale; das heißt, damit die Kirche im Glauben einig sei, wird nicht erfordert, daß ihre Bekenner in allen und jeden religiösen Fragen dasselbe denken und sagen; aber sie ist nothwendig eine *formale,* das ist: alle, die zu ihr gehören, müssen das Princip der Einheit, ihr unfehlbares Lehramt anerkennen. Wer von diesem Prinzip abfällt, der fällt auch von der Gemeinschaft der Gläubigen ab. Nun aber gibt man doch offenbar dieses Princip ebenso wohl auf, wenn man in einem außerwesentlichen, als wenn man in einem wesentlichen Punkte dem kirchlichen Lehrbegriff widerspricht. Und eben deßhalb heißt es nicht in *parvis,* sondern in *dubiis libertas.* Wohl darf auch der Katholik zwischen wesentlichen und nicht wesentlichen (ich würde lieber sagen zwischen wichtigen und minder wichtigen) Glaubenslehren insofern unterscheiden, als einige Glaubenswahrheiten ihrem Inhalte nach von größerer Bedeutung sind, als andere; aber nicht in jenem Sinne, daß man zur Annahme der einen verpflichtet, der Glaube an die andere aber frei gegeben sei. Dies würde ja geradezu auf die protestantische Lehre von den Fundamentalartikeln führen. –

Wir klagen Hirscher deßhalb nicht an, daß er diese vorzutragen beabsichtigt habe, und wollen gern hierin nichts anders, als ein Versehen finden. – Vielleicht hat er auch, da er vom unvermeidlichen Loose der menschlichen Schwäche redet, an einen aus bloßer Unwissenheit Irrenden gedacht. Aber dann hat er erstlich die Frage: wie weit die Einheit der Ueberzeugung gehen müsse, um zur Gemeinschaft der Kirche zu gehören, in einem Sinne gefaßt, den sie weder ihrem Wortlaute, noch dem Zwecke der ganzen Abhandlung nach haben kann; und überdies in ihrer Beantwortung zu viel gefordert. Denn ein unschuldig Irrender fällt von der Einheit der Kirche nicht ab, wenn er gleich in einem wesentlichen d. h. höchst wichtigen Punkt irrt.

II. Das alte Testament.

Um nun den Lehrbegriff der Kirche, dem ein Katholik nicht widersprechen darf, näher zu bestimmen; läßt Hirscher eine Beweisführung des in der Kirche fortdauernden Apostolats oder unfehlbaren Lehramtes folgen, und zieht daraus den Schluß, daß die *Gemeinpredigt* des Apostolates und der *Gemeinglaube* der Christenheit die Norm unseres Glaubens sei. Hierauf aber folgt die Frage: wo diese einstimmige Predigt des Apostolats zu finden sei? und nach einer Darstellung des Entstehens der apostolischen Schriften und ihres Verhältnisses zum „mündlichen Lehrwort" der Kirche, wird uns die Antwort gegeben: „Die einstimmige Lehre des Apostolats ist zu finden *in den Schriften des neuen Testaments, beglaubigt, erhalten, erklärt und ergänzt von der Gesammtkirche.* " Gern erkenne ich an, daß Hirscher an dieser Stelle die katholische Lehre von der mündlichen Ueberlieferung eben so lichtvoll, als, so viel ich urtheilen kann, richtig dargestellt hat. Auf wenigen Seiten scheint er mir mit den triftigsten Gründen dargethan zu haben, wie nothwendig es war, daß die h. Schrift durch die mündliche Lehre der Kirche als ächt anerkannt, unverfälscht bewahrt, richtig ausgelegt, und zur vollständigen Offenbarungslehre ergänzt wurde. Aber eben so wenig kann ich das Befremden bergen, daß er sowohl im Laufe der Abhandlung nur von den Büchern des neuen Bundes redet, als auch in der eben mitgetheilten Antwort, die das Ergebniß seiner Untersuchung enthält, diese allein als Quelle der christlichen Offenbarung angibt. Es läßt sich dies nicht dadurch rechtfertigen, daß es von der Predigt der Apostel handelt. Denn die Apostel haben ebenso wohl das alte, als das neue Testament gepredigt, was ja, auch wenn die Natur der Sache es nicht lehrte, alle ihre Briefe an die verschiedenen christlichen Gemeinden offenbar beweisen. Und überdieß versteht er unter dieser Predigt der Apostel nichts anders, als die göttlichen Offenbarungen, welche wir glauben. Nun werden wir zwar später, wenn von dem Verhältnisse des alten Bundes zum neuen ausführlicher die Rede sein wird, manchen Behauptungen Hirscher's widersprechen müssen; aber wie er dieselben immer mag verstanden haben, sie werden ihn doch nicht dahin geführt haben, anzunehmen, daß wir Christen nicht nur entbunden seien, das Cermonial- und Civil-Gesetz der Juden zu beobachten, sondern auch die Lehre des alten Testamentes und zwar ganz, wie sie da liegt, zu glauben. Wahrscheinlich wird er dies nur mit gewissen Beschränkungen, die sich aus dem, was er in der Moral lehrt[3], entnehmen lassen, zugeben, und, um in der mehr populären Schrift gelehrte und weitläufige Erklärungen zu vermeiden, vorgezogen haben, nur des neuen Testamentes zu erwähnen. Aber billiger Weise sollte dies allein großes Mißtrauen zu Ansichten einflößen, die es nicht zulassen, zu reden, wie alle Christgläubigen reden, und immer geredet haben. Denn hier handelt es sich doch gewiß nicht um eine mehr oder minder bestimmte Schulsprache, sondern um den einfachen Ausdruck eines der höchsten Glaubenssätze. Der Kirchenrath von Trient wollte, wie er selber sagt, allen kund machen, welcher Beweisquellen und Hülfsmittel er sich bedienen werde, um in der Kirche den Glauben zu befestigen und die Sitten zu verbessern, und zu diesem Zwecke hat er über dieselbe Frage, die Hirscher untersucht, wo nämlich die Predigt des Apostolates zu finden sei, sich feierlich erklärt. Denn er sagt: Weil jene Heilswahrheit und

---

3   Erster Band. S 6.

Sittenlehre, die unser Herr Jesus Christus zuerst selbst verkündigt, und dann seinen Aposteln in der ganzen Welt zu predigen befohlen habe, in Büchern und mündlichen Ueberlieferungen enthalten seien; so nehme die heilige Synode, dem Beispiele der rechtgläubigen Väter folgend, alle Bücher sowohl des alten als des neuen Testamentes, da der eine selbe *Gott beider Urheber* sei, wie auch die Ueberlieferungen, mögen sie den Glauben oder die Sitten betreffen, [...] mit gleicher frommen Ergebung und Ehrfurcht an[4].

Die Bücher, von welchen die Synode im Nachsatze erklärt, daß sie dieselben als Gottes Wort mit gleicher Ehrfurcht annehme, sind doch eben jene, von welchen sie im Vordersatze gesagt hatte, daß sie, verbunden mit der Tradition, die von Jesus Christus und auf seinen Befehl von den Aposteln verkündigte Lehre enthalten. Gerade nach diesen Büchern aber fragte Hirscher; er mußte also auch, wie das Concilium, antworten. Und gewiß so wenig als ein Rechtgläubiger, wenn er gefragt wird, wo die Predigt Jesu und der Apostel zu finden sei, mit Uebergehung der Tradition nur der Schrift erwähnen darf; eben so wenig darf er statt der gesammten Schrift das bloße neue Testament nennen. Was immer nun Hirscher zu jener Sonderbarkeit, (denn wir mögen nichts anders darin sehen), verleitet haben mag; wir müssen hier, wo es sich um die genaue Bestimmung der Norm handelt, nach der wir später, ob dies oder jenes zum Glauben gehöre, urtheilen sollen, wir müssen, sage ich, darauf dringen, daß keine andere, als die von der Kirche bestimmte Norm angenommen werde:

> *Zum Glauben gehört alles, was in den Schriften des neuen und alten Bundes und in den göttlichen Ueberlieferungen enthalten ist.*

III. Entscheidungen der Kirche.

Hiermit ist nun aber der kirchliche Glaube noch nicht hinreichend bestimmt. Denn es fragt sich eben, wie Hirscher richtig bemerkt, was in dem geschriebenen und nicht geschriebenen Worte Gottes enthalten sei. Wenn er also hier auf

---

4   Sess. IV. Sacrosancta [...] synodus [...] hoc sibi perpetua ante oculos proponens, ut sublatis erroribus puritas ipsa evangelii in ecclesia conservetur, quod promissum ante per Prophetas in scripturis sanctis Dominus noster Jesus Christus, Dei Filius, proprio ore primum promulgavit, deinde per suos Apostolos tanquam fontem omnis et salutaris veritatis et morum disciplinae, omni creaturae praedicare jussit, perspiciensque hanc veritatem et disciplinam contineri in libris scriptis et sine scripto traditionibus quae ab ipsius Christi ore ab Apostolis acceptae aut ab ipsis Apostolis Spiritu sancto dictante, quasi per manus traditae ad nos usque pervenerunt: orthodoxorum Patrum exempla secuta, omnes libros tam veteris quam novi testamenti, cum utriusque unus Deus sit auctor; necnon traditiones ipsas tum ad fidem tum ad mores pertinentes, tanquam vel oretenus a Christo vel a Spiritu sancto dictatas et continu a successione in ecclesia catholica conservatas, pari pietatis affectu ac reverentia suscipit et veneratur.

die Bekenntnisse hinweist, in welchen die Kirche ihren Glauben anfangs nur kurz, in der Folge aber der Irrlehrer wegen in manchen Stücken ausführlicher ausgesprochen habe; so ist dagegen nichts einzuwenden, in sofern nur die Rede ist von einem „gedrängten Ausdrucke" des Inhalts der göttlichen Offenbarung, nicht aber von dem vollständigen Lehrbegriff, das heißt, von dem Ausdruck alles dessen, was die Kirche glaubt und lehrt. Denn die Glaubensbekenntnisse sind von der Kirche verfaßt, weil das ausdrückliche Bekenntniß der wichtigsten und der zur Zeit am meisten bekämpften Lehren zu mehr als einem Zwecke nothwendig und heilsam ist; nicht aber um uns eine concrete d. h. materiell vollständige Glaubensnorm zu geben, so daß, was in ihr nicht ausgesprochen wäre, als unentschieden betrachtet, und ohne Sünde geläugnet werden könnte. Aber dies hat Hirscher auch gewiß nicht sagen wollen. Denn er weiß ja, daß die Kirche sowohl auf eben den Concilien, welche die Glaubensbekenntnisse verfaßten, als auch bei vielen andern Gelegenheiten gar manche Dogmen festgesetzt hat, die in jenen Bekenntnissen nicht ausgedrückt sind.

Aber dies behauptet er ausdrücklich, daß eine solche *Entscheidung* der Kirche nothwendig sei, um unsere Meinungsfreiheit in Glaubenssachen zu beschränken.

„Jeder, sagt er[5], darf, ohne im geringsten aufzuhören, ein glaubenstreuer Katholik zu sein, in allen Fragen, über welche der Lehrbegriff nicht kirchlich fixirt ist, jener Ansicht folgen, welche ihm nun eben die richtige zu sein scheint. Das steht theoretisch fest, in der Wirklichkeit aber möchte man nicht selten ob einer Ketzerei mildere Beurtheilung erfahren, als ob einer Abweichung von gangbaren, vielleich eben gerade im Zenith stehenden theologischen Meinungen." Daß er unter dieser kirchlichen Fixirung die Entscheidungen, d. h. die Urtheile, welche die Kirche als höchste Richterin in Glaubenssachen erläßt, verstehe, geht aus dem gleich Folgenden hervor. „Unsere Dogmatiker sind daran, das System ihrer Wissenschaft (wie sie sagen) auszubauen, und was in den *kirchlichen Entscheidungen* noch nicht *fixirt* ist, vollends definitiv festzustellen." Und in der Moral lesen wir: „Wenn als Abweichung von der Einheit des Lehrbegriffs bezeichnet wird, worüber von der Kirche *gar nicht entschieden ist*; so ist das Verketzerungssucht, und nicht gut[6]."

Doch mit welcher Zuversicht auch Hirscher diese Behauptung ausspricht, wir können darin nichts anders, als einen Irrthum sehen, den einige Theologen der neuesten Zeit, besonders in Deutschland, verbreitet haben. Jedoch ehe wir uns in diese Untersuchung einlassen, müssen wir zuvor noch zur näheren

---

5   Kirchliche Zustände S. 68.
6   4. Aufl. Bd. 3. S. 237.

Bestimmung dessen, was unter Entscheidung der Kirche zu verstehen sei, einiges bemerken. Manche neuere Schriftsteller nämlich reden so, als wäre nur das ein entschiedener Glaubenssatz, was die Kirche als solchen anzunehmen unter dem Anathem befohlen hat. Entscheidungen der Kirche sind ihnen nur die *Canones* der allgemeinen Concilien. Aber diese Beschränkung ist eine rein willkürliche. Denn wenn der Glaube sich so weit ausdehnt, als die Lehre der Kirche, wie sollte denn das nicht zum Glauben gehören, was die Kirche selbst in authentischen Actenstücken als ihre Lehre ausgesprochen hat? Was immer also in den Decreten der Concilien so vorgetragen wird, daß die Absicht der Väter, was Lehre der Kirche sei, vor der ganzen Christenheit zu erklären, unverkennbar ist; das muß man gewiß als katholische Glaubenswahrheit annehmen; obwohl deßhalb nicht auch alles, was zur Begründung oder Beleuchtung derselben zuweilen hinzugefügt wird.

Andere wollen wenigstens nur in den Concilienbeschlüssen Entscheidungen der Kirche in Glaubenssachen anerkennen. Aber können sie behaupten, daß die Vollmacht in Glaubensstreitigkeiten zu richten, der Kirche unter der Bedingung einer bestimmten Form des Gerichtes, ertheilt sei? oder ohne vom katholicismus abzufallen, läugnen, daß die *Ecclesia per orbem dispersa* eben so unfehlbar ist, als die *Ecclesia in concilio congregata*? Wir verstehen hier unter Kirche den Lehrkörper, dem alle Gläubigen unterworfen sind, also die Bischöfe in Vereinigung mit ihrem Haupte, dem Papste. Auf doppelte Weise übt dieser Lehrkörper, auch wenn er nicht versammelt ist, sein höchstes Richteramt in Glaubenssachen erstlich durch Annahme von Partikular-Concilien; – auf diese Weise haben unter andern die gegen die Pelagianer gehaltenen Provinzial-Synoden das Ansehen allgemeiner Kirchenversammlungen bekommen; – zweitens durch die päpstlichen Entscheidungen ertheilte Zustimmung. Diese Zustimmung kann zum voraus ertheilt werden; wenn nämlich die Bischöfe vom h. Stuhle, bevor derselbe eine Entscheidung erläßt, befragt werden, wie dies in dem bekannten Streit über die drei Kapitel geschah, und in diesen unsern Tagen in Betreff einer andern Glaubensfrage geschieht. Aber es ist klar, daß eine solche Zustimmung eben sowohl nachher, durch die Annahme, nämlich der päpstlichen Erlasse, stattfinden kann, und dieses ist es, worauf wir hier besonders aufmerksam machen müssen. Daß der Papst, wenn er von jener Lehrvollmacht, die ihm, wie das Concilium von Florenz sagt, über die ganze Kirche von Christus dem Herrn gegeben ist[7], Gebrauch machend eine Glau-

---

7   Definimus [...] *Pontificem Romanum* [...] totius ecclesiae caput et *omnium Christianorum* patrem
     ac *doctorem* existere; et ipsi in B. Petro *pascendi* (d. h. in der Kirchensprache docendi) regendi et
     gubernandi *universalem ecclesiam* a Domino nostro Jesu Christo *plenam potestatem* traditam esse.
     Decret Unionis.

bensfrage entscheidet, nicht irren könne; glaubte *Melchior Canus* durch Gründe darthun zu können, die stärker und klarer seien, als jene, womit wir manche Lehren, die ohne Zweifel eigentliche Glaubenspunkte sind, zu beweisen pflegen. Er würde deßhalb, fügt er hinzu, gar kein Bedenken tragen, die entgegengesetzte Meinung für häretisch zu erklären, wenn er sich nicht scheute, dem Urtheile der Kirche zuvor zu kommen[8]. Ebenso reden *Bellarmin, Suarez* und so viele der größten Theologen. Nur weil die entgegenstehende Lehre in *Gerson* und andern Gallikanern Vertheidiger, denen man ein gewisses Ansehen nicht absprechen kann, gefunden, und die Kirche sich bis jetzt nicht ausdrücklich erklärt habe; nicht aber weil die Beweise aus Schrift und Tradition nicht stark und entscheidend genug seien, geben sie zu, daß die Unfehlbarkeit des Papstes kein Glaubensartikel ist. Auf dieses Zugeständniß pflegen sich nun aber manche neuere Theologen zu stützen, um ohne weiters zu behaupten, die päpstlichen Erlasse in Glaubenssachen gehörten nicht zu jenen Entscheidungen, durch welche man die Lehre der Kirche mit dogmatischer Gewißheit erkenne. Namentlich glaube ich hier der *Regula fidei Catholicae* des *Veronius* erwähnen zu müssen. Dieses Werk, auf das man sich in neuester Zeit sehr oft und mit großer Zuversicht beruft, hat in der Kirche nicht geringen Widerspruch gefunden; und zwar darum, weil es dem Wunsche Hirscher's, „den Kreis freier Bewegung und Ansicht so weit als möglich zu ziehen[9]," über Gebühr nachzukommen schien. Einem wahrhaft gläubigen Gemüth, scheint mir, sollte ein solcher Wunsch fremd sein: nicht nur weil ihm die Unterwerfung des Verstandes unter Gottes Wort, wie jede Pflichterfüllung, süß ist; sondern weil eben, wo der Kreise freier Bewegung beginnt, auch das Gebiet der Ungewißheit beginnt. Ist es denn als ein hartes Loos zu betrachten, wenn wir statt hin und her zu schwanken, oder doch nur auf unser menschliches Dafürhalten uns zu stützen, in mehr und mehr Stücken durch das untrügliche Licht des Glaubens geleitet werden? Nichts destoweniger darf man jene Wunsch mit Rücksicht auf die menschliche Schwäche hegen; und wirklich hat auch diese Rücksicht *Veronius* in der Verfassung jenes Werkes geleitet. Um den Protestanten die Annahme des katholischen Bekenntnisses zu erleichtern; soll man, sagt er, so wenig als möglich von ihnen fordern. Auch Hirscher erinnert hieran an mehr als einer Stelle. Aber gewiß muß man sich dabei doch hüten, irgend einen Theil der katholischen Wahrheit zu verrathen, oder diejenigen, welche an die Rückkehr zur wahren Kirche denken, zu täuschen. Dieses thut man aber, wenn man mit Veronius so ohne alle Unterscheidung daraus, daß die Unfehlbarkeit des Papstes kein

---

8   De locis theol. I. VI. c. 7.
9   Kirchl. Zustände. S. 69.

Glaubensartikel sei, folgert, päpstliche Erlasse seien keine dogmatische Entscheidungen; oder wenn man mit eben demselben so redet, als könne man jede Lehre, welche nicht erwiesen häretisch ist, nach Gutdünken annehmen oder verwerfen. Ueber dieses letztere später; hier nur einige Bemerkungen über die päpstlichen Entscheidungen.

Wenn man zugibt, daß die Lehre von der Unfehlbarkeit des Papstes kein Dogma sei, so folgt daraus nichts anders, als daß die Erlasse des h. Stuhles in Glaubensfragen nicht ohne weiters und an sich als Urtheile der unfehlbaren Kirche anzusehen seien; daß man sie aber als solche betrachten müsse, sobald sie vom Episkopat angenommen sind, geben auch die hartnäckigsten Gallikaner zu, und müssen alle zugeben, welche nicht die erste Grundlehre der katholischen Kirche läugnen wollen. Nach solcher Annahme sind nämlich jene Erlasse offenbar Beschlüsse der über den Erdkreis zerstreuten Kirche. – Nun räumen zwar die Gallikaner selber ein, daß zu einer solchen Annahme, eben weil es sich um den Glauben handle, nach allen Grundsätzen des Kirchenrechts das bloße Stillschweigen der Bischöfe genüge. Aber möge man auch mehr, nämlich irgend eine öffentliche Handlung, durch welche die Bischöfe ihre Zustimmung erklären, fordern, so bleibt immer wahr, daß, wenn nicht alle, gewiß die meisten päpstlichen Entscheidungen, die wir haben, durch diesen Beitritt der Mehrheit der Bischöfe zu Beschlüssen der allgemeinen Kirche erhoben worden sind. Denn noch keiner ist von andern, als von dem kleinen Haufen jener, deren Irrthümer verdammt wurden, widersprochen worden, und von den meisten läßt es sich nachweisen, daß sie fast von sämmtlichen Hirten der Kirche mit Ehrfurcht aufgenommen, in ihren Sprengeln verkündigt und dem amtlichen Verfahren zu Grunde gelegt worden sind.

Weil wir von jenen Bullen, welche die Lehre des *Bajus* und der *Jansenisten* verdammen, oft Gebrauch machen müssen, so wird hier die Bemerkung nicht überflüssig sein, daß von diesen wenigstens, was wir eben von den meisten päpstlichen Entscheidungen sagten, ganz gewiß ist. Die Irrthümer des Bajus wurden in den aus seinen Schriften ausgehobenen Lehrsätzen von Pius V., und wiederum von Gregor XIII. und nochmals von Urban VIII. verdammt. Dieser selbe Papst erließ die erste Bulle gegen den *„Augustinus"* des Jansenius, weil in demselben Bajus Irrlehren zum großen Theil von neuem vorgetragen wurden. Nicht lange nachher verdammte Innocens X. auf das ausdrückliche Verlangen einer großen Anzahl von Bischöfen die fünf Sätze, auf welche sich die meisten Irrlehren der Jansenisten zurückführen lassen. Mehrere der nachfolgenden Päpste bestätigten dieses Verdammungsurtheil, bis endlich die Bulle Clemens XI. *Vineam Domini* dem Streite über Jansenius Schrift ein Ende machte. In dieser Bulle, welche nicht bloß von dem Gallikanischen Clerus, sondern auch

von der ganzen Kirche öffentlich und ausdrücklich angenommen wurde,
erklärt der Papst, daß alle Schriftgläubigen verpflichtet seien, sich nicht bloß
durch äußeres Stillschweigen, sondern auch durch inneren Gehorsam den
wider Jansenius erlassenen Entscheidungen der Kirche zu unterwerfen, und die
Lehre desselben mit Herz und Mund als ketzerisch zu verdammen. – Nun
wurde aber bekanntlich die ganze Lehre des Bajus und Jansenius mit vielen
Zuthaten von *Quesnell* erneuert. Gegen ihm erließ der selbe Papst Clemens XI.
die berühmte Bulle *Unigenitus*. Auch diese wurde zuerst durch Innocenz XIII.
und dann von Benedict XIII. an der Spitze einer in Rom versammelten Synode
bestätigt. Um aber den neuen Jansenisten jede Ausflucht zu benehmen, ward
sie nicht bloß von den Provinzial-Synoden in Avignon und Embrun und dem
gallikanischen Clerus, sondern auch fast von allen Metropolitanen des ganzen
Erdkreises im Namen ihrer Suffragane durch authentische Erklärungen, und
zwar als ein dogmatisches und unwiderrufliches Urtheil der allgemeinen Kirche
angenommen[10]. – Endlich sind dieselben Irrthümer mit manchen andern in der
Bulle *Auctorem fidei*, welche Pius VI. gegen die *Synode zu Pistoja* erließ, nochmals feierlich verurtheilt worden. – Wenn nun *Bossuet* selber zugibt, daß die
dogmatische Entscheidung eines Papstes, wenn sie von einem zweiten oder
dritten Papste ausdrücklich bestätigt werde, bereits das Ansehen eines Ausspruchs der allgemeinen Kirche erhalte; was müssen wir von einer Lehre sagen,
welche während zwei voller Jahrhunderte von einer ganzen Reihenfolge von
Päpsten mit ausdrücklicher Zustimmung des gesammten Episkopates verworfen worden ist?

IV. Nicht in den Entscheidungen der Kirche allein ist ihr Lehrbegriff zu suchen.

Wir kommen nun auf die oben erwähnte Behauptung neuerer Theologen, es
gehöre nichts anders zum katholischen Glauben, als was von der Kirche ausdrücklich entschieden sei, zurück. Dieselbe beruht auf einem Mißverständniß,
das hier näher zu erörtern ist. – Redet man vom religiösen Glauben im Allgemeinen, so kann man als Gegenstand desselben schlechthin bezeichnen: alles,
was von Gott geoffenbart ist. Wenn aber von dem religiösen Glauben, den die
Gemeinschaft der Schriften bekennt, die Sprache ist; so versteht man unter der
göttlichen Offenbarung nicht jedwede, sondern nur jene, welche die Apostel auf
Befehl Jesu Christi verkündigt haben. Mag es gleich Gott gefallen haben, auch

---

10　Diese Actenstücke befinden sich in der königlichen Bibliothek zu Paris; wurden aber zur Zeit vom
　　Kardinal-Erzbischof von Mecheln durch den Druck veröffentlicht. Temoignages de l'Eglise
　　universelle en faveur de la Bulle Unigenitus.

in späteren Zeiten manche Seelen noch besonderer Offenbarungen zu würdigen; so kann doch durch diese der allgemeine schriftliche Glaube keinen Zuwachs erhalten. Auch die Kirche empfängt keine neue Offenbarungen; wohl aber ist sie von Gott bestellt, um sein, durch die Apostel gepredigtes Wort unverfälscht zu bewahren, zu verkündigen und zu erklären. Nur das also nehmen wir als eine von Gott geoffenbarte Wahrheit an, was die Kirche als eine solche lehrt. Hierin besteht das eigenthümliche katholische Prinzip. Um also die Norm des katholischen Glaubens auszudrücken, fügen wir den Worten:

> *Alles das (und nur das) gehört zum Glauben, was Gott geoffenbart hat, (d. h. was in dem geschriebenen und mündlich überlieferten Worte Gottes enthalten ist),*

diese andern hinzu:

> *und als solches von der Kirche allen zu glauben vorgelegt wird.*

Nun nehmen aber einige neuere Theologen ohne weiters an, daß die Kirche nur dann etwas zu glauben vorlege, wenn sie eine Glaubensstreitigkeit als höchste Richterin feierlich entscheide, und dies ist das Mißverständniß, dessen wir erwähnten. Es übt nämlich die Kirche ein doppeltes Lehramt aus. Das eine ist das ordentliche und immerwährende, und besteht in eben jenen fortdaurenden Apostolate, von dem Hirscher an der angeführten Stelle redet. Das andere ist außerordentlich, wird nur zu besonderen Zeiten, wenn nämlich Irrlehrer die Kirche beunruhigen, geübt, und ist nicht schlichtweg Lehramt, sondern zugleich Richteramt. In diesem wehrt die Kirche nur die feindseligen Angriffe auf das Heiligthum, das sie bewahrt, ab; in jenem öffnet sie ihren Kindern den reichen Schatz, der bei ihr hinterlegt ist.

Wenn man also die Lehre der Kirche, durch welche wir, was geöffenbart ist, mit gewißheit erkennen, auf jene Sätze beschränken will, durch welche sie Irrlehren verworfen hat; so stellt man dadurch erstlich eine bis auf unsere Zeiten unerhörte Behauptung auf. Veronius stellt an die Spitze seines Werkes den Satz, der ihm unter Katholiken keines Beweises zu bedürfen schien:

> *Illud omne et solum est de fide catholica, quod est revelatum in verbo Dei, et propositum omnibus ab ecclesia catholica, fide divina credendum. Neque refert, an illa propositio emanet ex concilio aliquo universali, ex eius decreto et definitione, an ex sensu fidelium omnium.*

Ein anderes, allgemein als classisch anerkanntes Werk, ist jenes des Cardinals *Lugo De virtute fidei divinae.* Auch in ihm wird dieser Grundsatz überall als ausgemacht vorausgesetzt[11]. Wir könnten uns nun ebenso auf viele, ja auf alle

---

11   Vergl. besonders Disp. 1. s. 12. und Disp. 20.

anderen ausgezeichneten Theologen berufen; wenn es nicht gerade diese wären, deren Vertheidigung wir unternommen haben. Gehen wir also bis in die ersten Jahrhunderte der Kirche zurück. Die h. Väter weisen fast immer auf die in der Kirche allgemeine Lehre, als auf die sicherste Glaubensnorm hin. Wenn sie nun aber der Meinung gewesen wären, was allgemeine Lehre der Kirche sei, lasse sich nur aus den Entscheidungen der Kirche erkennen: wie hätte sie dann so manche Neuerer, als den *Marcion*, den *Arius*, den *Nestorius* ausdrücklich und öffentlich der Ketzerei beschuldigen, wie hätten auch die Hirten einzelner Sprengel sie aus demselben Grunde mit dem Bannfluche belegen können, ehe die Kirche über jene Irrlehrer irgend eine Entscheidung erlassen hatte? Und doch sind das Thatsachen, die um so weniger eines Beweises bedürfen, als sie im Laufe der folgenden Jahrhunderte sich oft wiederholt haben.

Wohl begegnet man, sowohl in den Schriften der hh. Väter, als der späteren Theologen Aeußerungen, die jenen, welche wir bekämpfen, ähnlich lauten: man müsse, bevor man Andersdenkende der Ketzerei bezüchtige, das Urtheil der Kirche abwarten. Aber sie reden dann von einzelnen Fragen, über welche auch unter den treuen und erleuchteten Kindern der Kirche Streit obwaltete; nie aber haben sie den allgemeinen Satz ausgestellt, jeder dürfe in allen Stücken, über welche die Kirche nicht entscheiden habe, der Ansicht folgen, die ihm nun eben die richtigste zu sein scheine.

Es könnte ferner auf das, was so eben von dem Irrlehrern der ersten Jahrhunderte gesagt wurde, entgegnet werden, daß man nichtsdestoweniger ihretwegen die Entscheidungen der Concilien noch für nöthig gehalten habe. Aber um nichts davon zu sagen, daß jene Zusammenkünfte der Hirten der Kirche oft nicht sowohl die Ermittelung, als die feierlichere Verkündigung der Glaubenslehre, wie auch manches andere Gute zum Zwecke hatten; so konnte die Lehre der Neuerer der Hauptsache nach mit sicherheit als irrig erkannt werden, und doch zur Feststellung mancher einzelnen Punkte die Berathung der Väter erwünschlich sein. Ja, es kann etwas in der Kirche als geoffenbarte Wahrheit allgemein gelehrt und geglaubt, und deßhalb der ihr entgegenstehende Irrthum mit Zuversicht als Ketzerei verworfen, und dennoch über eben diesen Gegenstand eine kirchliche Entscheidung nothwendig werden. Wenn es nämlich den Neuerern gelingt, einen Anhang zu gewinnen, und wohl gar einzelne Vorsteher der Kirche oder andere Männer von großem Ansehen zu verführen, so wird es, besonders für die Menge der Gläubigen, leicht zweifelhaft, auf welcher Seite die Wahrheit sei. Und im Grunde ist ja dies die wahre Geschichte aller Ketzereien. Wir läugnen also nicht, daß, um die Glaubenslehre mit gewißheit zu erkennen, die ausdrückliche Entscheidung der Kirche in manchen Fragen und in manchen Zeiten nöthig ist; wir läugnen nur, daß sie es in allen Fragen und immer sei.

Um aber dies nun nicht bloß durch das Ansehen des Alterthums zu bekräftigen, sondern auch aus dem Prinzip des Katholicismus zu beweisen; so gehört diesem zufolge alles zum katholischen Glauben, wovon wir durch das Ansehen der Kirche gewiß sind, daß es geoffenbart ist. – Nun fragt es sich also, ob wir nur durch die ausdrücklichen Entscheidungen der Kirche zu dieser Gewißheit gelangen können. – Die Kirche hat, anfangs durch jenes ihr beständiges und ordentliches Lehramt, in der Folge auch durch ausdrückliche Concilienbeschlüsse, die h. Schrift, wie wir sie jetzt haben, für das ächte und unverfälschte Wort Gottes erklärt. Sie hat uns also auch den ganzen Inhalt derselben als Offenbarung Gottes zu glauben vorgelegt. Sobald wir demnach nicht zweifeln können, daß etwas in der Schrift enthalten ist; so sind wir auch gewiß, daß dies von der Kirche als geoffenbarte Wahrheit gelehrt wird. Wie groß nun aber auch die Dunkelheit sehr vieler Stellen der h. Schrift sein mag; so ist doch hinwiederum ihr Sinn auch oft so klar, daß er keinen Zweifel zuläßt. Sollte man dennoch fürchten, daß hiermit der eigenmächtigen Deutung des göttlichen Wortes zu viel eingeräumt werde, und daran erinnern, daß der wahre Sinn der heiligen Bücher, auch wo er dem unbefangenen Gemüthe vollkommen klar zu sein scheint, durch gewaltsame und grübelnde Deutelei oft verdunkelt worden ist; so können wir dagegen behaupten, daß man nichtsdestoweniger von jeher die meisten Thatsachen der h. Geschichte und gar viele Lehren über Gott, Tugend and Laster, ohne eine ausdrückliche Entscheidung der Kirche abzuwarten, auf die Worte der Schrift gestützt, als Glaubenswahrheiten vorgetragen hat. Und tragen wir etwa Bedenken eben diese Thatsachen und Lehren, den Deutungen, die man sich in unserm Zeitalter erlaubt hat, gegenüber als geoffenbarte Wahrheiten festzuhalten? – Es wurde hiedurch keineswegs jene eigenmächtige Auslegung des göttlichen Wortes, die unsere Kirche verwirft, geübt, auch wenn man sich dabei nur auf den natürlichen Sinn des h. Textes beriefe. Denn wenn gewisse Worte und Ausdrucksweisen nicht mehr durch sich selbst hinreichend klar sein sollen; so gibt es am Ende also gar kein Mittel mehr, sich durch die Sprache zu verständigen; und es würden dann auch wieder die Entscheidungen der Kirche selbst, ehe man sie für Glaubenssätze ausgeben dürfte, durch authentische Erklärungen der Kirche erläutert werden müssen, und so des Zweifels kein Ende sein. Aber wir können nun überdies behaupten, daß sich der Katholik, auch bei Erklärung dieser einzelnen Stellen, auf das Ansehen seiner Kirche, nämlich auf ihre auch ohne ausdrückliche Entscheidung hinlänglich bekannte Lehre stützt. Oder bedarf es etwa vieler Nachforschung, um mit voller Gewißheit behaupten zu können, daß z.B. das Opfer Abraham's, die Verschlingung Jonas vom Wallfisch und ähnliches, als historische Thatsache, und nicht als allegorische Dichtung; daß die Wunder

Jesu und der Apostel als wahre Wunder immer von der ganzen Kirche betrachtet und vorgestellt worden sind? Und dürfen wir etwa anstehen die entgegengesetzten Deutungen nicht nur für unvernünftig, sondern auch für ketzerisch zu erklären? Ebenso bedarf es gewiß keines Beweises, daß die ganze Kirche von jeher in der Schrift gelesen hat, es müsse in der menschlichen Gesellschaft das Eigenthum und die Ehe heilig gehalten werden; und daß folglich die Lehre des Sozialismus ebensowohl der Offenbarung als der gesunden Vernunft widerstreitet. –

Aber auch für jene Stellen der göttlichen Bücher, deren Auslegung größeren Schwierigkeiten unterworfen ist, verweist uns die Kirche selbst nicht gerade auf ihre in förmlichen Beschlüssen niedergelegte Erklärung, sondern nur überhaupt auf „den Sinn, den unsere Mutter, die h. Kirche, festgehalten hat, und festhält," und auf die einstimmige Auslegung der hh. Väter[12]. – Dies nun führt uns auf die andere Quelle der Offenbarungslehre, die Tradition. Hirscher faßt dieselbe, wie schon bemerkt worden ist, als jenes mündliche Lehrwort, als jenes Apostolat auf, durch das die Kirche gegründet wurde, und das, durch den Beistand des h. Geistes unfehlbar, in ihr fortdauert, die h. Schrift als Gottes Wort beglaubigend, unverfälscht bewahrend, erklärend und ergänzend. So wäre sie dasselbe, was wir oben das beständige und ordentliche Lehramt der Kirche nannten. Obschon man nun oft unter Tradition nur jene mündlich überlieferten Lehren versteht, die in der Schrift gar nicht oder nur unvollständig erhalten sind; so ist doch diese umfassendere Erklärung viel geeigneter, den wahren Begriff und somit auch die hohe Bedeutung der mündlichen Ueberlieferung in ihrem Verhältnisse zum geschriebenen Worte Gottes auszudrücken. Es wird hiermit auch einem nicht seltnem Mißverständnisse vorgebeugt. Man erklärt sich nämlich oft die Tradition auf diese Weise: die Apostel hätten neben der h. Schrift, in welcher sie die wichtigeren Glaubenspunkte aufgezeichnet, einige minder wichtige Lehren mündlich hinzugefügt, welche dann später von den hh. Vätern aufgeschrieben worden seien. Demzufolge sucht man denn auch die Tradition nur in den Schriften der Väter. Aber die Apostel haben die ganze Heilslehre mündlich verkündigt, und in ihren schriftlichen Aufsätzen nur das widerholt, was für den jedesmaligen besonderen Zweck nothwendig war. Diese mündliche, die ganze Offenbarung umfassende Unterweisung dauert aber in der Kirche bis ans Ende der Zeiten fort. Ist nun dies die Tradition, so hat man sie nicht ausschließlich in den Schriften der hh. Väter zu suchen. Nicht bloß aus diesen, sondern auch aus den übrigen in der Kirche geschätzten Schriftstellern, ferner aus den Denkmalen des christlichen Alterthums, den Gräbern mit ihren

12 Trid. s. IV.

Inschriften und symbolischen Verzierungen, den Kirchen mit ihren Altären und ihren Gemälden, vor allen aber aus der Handlungsweise der Kirche, ihrem Verfahren in der Leitung der Gläubigen ihren Gebräuchen beim Gottesdienst, ihren liturgischen Büchern, und endlich aus den öffentlichen Erlassen ihrer Hirten, besonders wenn dieselben in Partikular-Synoden versammelt waren, läßt sich ohne Zweifel erkennen, was in der Kirche allgemein gelehrt und geglaubt werde. Nun aber fragen wir auch hier, ob man aus solchen Quellen nicht vor jeder ausdrücklichen Entscheidung der Kirche zur vollen Gewißheit gelangen könne, was die katholische Kirche, wie über viele andere Wahrheiten, so besonders über jene Punkte, die mit dem christlichen und kirchlichen Leben in nächster Beziehung stehen, lehre; z.B. über das Fegfeuer und die Fürbitte für die Verstorbenen, über die Anrufung und Verehrung der Heiligen, über sämmtliche Sakramente, über die geistliche Gewalt des Papstes und der Bischöfe. Wenn nicht, nun so hat man auch, bevor die Concilien oder die Päbste über alle diese Punkte in späteren Jahrhunderten dogmatische Beschlüsse erließen, jene so tief und so mannigfaltig in das Leben eingreifenden Wahrheiten nicht mit voller Beruhigung glauben können. Und dieses ist es, was wir der Ansicht, die wir bestreiten, im Allgemeinen entgegensetzen. Wenn nichts zum Glauben gehört, als was die Kirche durch ausdrückliche Entscheidung festgesetzt hat; so konnte man in der Kirche viele Jahrhunderte lang über die wichtigsten Geheimnisse und Sittenlehren der Religion keinen Glaubensact erwecken, und jeder der Ansicht folgen, die ihm nun eben die richtigste zu sein schien. Wird man die neumodige Theorie von „dem sich allmälig entwickelnden Bewußtsein der Kirche" soweit ausdehnen? Uebrigens scheinen jene, die derlei Grundsätze vertheidigen, nicht zu erwägen, daß sie durch dieselben das Recht in Glaubenssachen etwas mit Bestimmtheit zu behaupten, in eben dem Maaße beschränken, als sie das Recht zu läugnen oder zu zweifeln ausdehnen. Wird es Hirscher etwa auf sich nehmen, für alle Lehren, die er in seiner Moral und im Katechismus mit großer Zuversicht als geoffenbarte Wahrheiten vorträgt, Entscheidungen der Kirche vorzubringen?

Indessen möchte man doch wider das bisher Gesagte einwenden, auf solche Weise werde die Bestimmung des Glaubens auch in der katholischen Kirche von dem Resultat der Forschung eines jeden abhängig gemacht, und mithin das Prinzip des Protestantismus angenommen. Nämlich auch die Frage nach der Lehre der allgemeinen Kirche kann ihre Schwierigkeiten haben, und daher von dem einen so, von dem andern anders gelöst werden; so wäre denn zuletzt der ganze Unterschied, daß der Protestant glaubt, was nach seiner subjectiven Ueberzeugung in der Bibel steht, und der Katholik, was nach seiner subjectiven Ueberzeugung die allgemeine Kirche lehrt. – Ein scheinbar sehr starker Einwurf: aber man bedenke, daß man demselben dadurch nicht ausweicht, daß man die Entscheidungen der Kirche für die einzige Richtschnur des Glaubens ausgiebt. Oder ist es in allen Fällen so leicht, die Aechtheit und den wahren und vollen Sinn dieser Entscheidung zu erkennen? und sind nicht auch hierüber viele und bedeutende Streitfragen entstanden? Nicht darin besteht also der Unterschied des katholischen und protestantischen Prinzips, daß der Katholik eine Glaubensnorm habe, nach der er alle religiösen Fragen ohne Schwierigkeit entscheiden könne, sondern darin, daß er für alle – einen lebendigen Lehrer und Schiedsrichter anerkennt. Zwar unterwirft sich auch der Protestant dem Ansehen des göttlichen Wortes, aber um zu wissen, was das Wort Gottes rede, ist er in allen Fällen einzig auf seine subjective Ansicht hingewiesen. Um das, was andere in der Bibel finden, hat er sich nicht zu kümmern; die todte Schrift selbst aber steht ihm nicht Rede. Der Katholik fragt, was die Kirche als geoffenbarte Lehre verkünde, und diese Frage ist in sehr vielen Fällen, wie gesagt, eben so leicht zu beantworten, als jene, was die allgemeine Kirche ausdrücklich entschieden habe; kann sie aber nicht mit Bestimmtheit gelöst werden, so fragt er weiter nach jenen ausdrücklichen Entscheidungen; sind auch diese nicht vorhanden, oder waltet über ihre Aechtheit und ihren Inhalt Zweifel ob, so entscheidet er nicht mit Zuversicht, was Glaubenslehre sei, sondern erwartet dafür eine bestimmtere Erklärung seiner Kirche. Und aus diesem Grunde haben wir schon oben zwische materialer und formaler Einheit der Kirche unterschieden.

V. Begriff und Eintheilung der Dogmen.

Wir haben bisher gegen einige Behauptungen Hirscher's geredet; um aber das Gesagte noch schärfer zu bestimmen, wird es gut sein, wenn wir auch, was Hermes über die Bedeutung des Wortes Dogma lehrt, näher betrachten. Gewöhnlich, sagt er, verstehe man unter Dogma „jede besondere theologische Lehre, welche erweislicher Maßen oder nach dem allgemeinen Dafürhalten von Gott übernatürlich geoffenbart sei;" von einigen Theologen jedoch werde außerdem noch eine ausdrückliche Erklärung der Kirche gefordert. Da nun aber ein vollendeter Beweis und der allgemeine Glaube *(traditio universalis)*, daß eine besondere Lehre geoffenbart sei, nach katholischen Grundsätzen ihre Offenbarung eben sowohl, als die ausdrückliche Lehre der Kirche verbürgen; so schlage er vor, statt Dogma in jenem ersteren Sinne *dogma revelatum*, *Offenbarungslehre,* und statt Dogma in dem zweiten Sinne *dogma declaratum v. definitum, erklärte Offenbarungslehre* zu sagen. Dieses stimme auch mit dem theologischen Sprachgebrauch überein; indem man unter *„dogma fidei"* oder es ist „de fide," verstehe: *dogma fidei (declaratae)* und *de fide (declarata).* Dann fügt er noch die Anmerkung hinzu: „Wer wissentlich einem *dogma declaratum* widerspricht, sagt sich von der Gemeinschaft der Kirche los, nicht so, wer dem *dogma revelatum* widerspricht, weil die *Allgemeinheit* der Annahme desselben gewöhnlich unbekannt ist.“

Wenn Hermes hier lehrt, ein vollendeter Beweis oder der allgemeine Glaube, daß eine Lehre geoffenbart sei, verbürge die Offenbarung derselben eben so gut, als eine ausdrückliche Erklärung der Kirche, so scheint das mit dem, was wir von der richtigen Auffassung der katholischen Glaubensnorm eben gesagt haben, übereinzustimmen. Dennoch können wir das nur zugeben, wofern er erstlich unter dem vollendeten Beweis einen solchen versteht, der entweder auf ganz klaren und unzweideutigen Stellen der Schrift, oder auf der einstimmigen Erklärung der Väter beruht; und der folglich auch in der katholischen Kirche keinen Widerspruch von Bedeutung findet; und wofern er zweitens in einem solchen Beweis oder jenem allgemeinen Glauben darum die gesagte Bürgschaft findet, weil so bewiesene oder so angenommene Lehren zu jenen gehören, die durch das öffentliche Lehramt der Kirche zu glauben vorgelegt werden. Denn dies ist durchaus fest zu halten, daß keine anderen geoffenbarten Lehren als jene, die uns als solche durch das Ansehen der Kirche verbürgt werden, zum katholischen Glauben gehören. Und eben deßhalb ist die erste Erklärung des Wortes Dogma, die Hermes als die gewöhnliche anführt, viel zu unbestimmt. Das *eigenthümlich* katholische Prinzip ist in ihr nicht ausgesprochen. – Daß Hermes in der That dieses hier wenigstens nicht scharf in's Auge gefaßt hat, ersieht man noch deutlicher aus der Eintheilung der Dogmen, die er vorschlägt, in Offenbarungslehren, *(dogmata revelata)* und erklärte Offenbarungslehren, *(dogmata definita.)* So viel nämlich ist gewiß, daß wir alle unter Dogma eine Glaubenslehre im strengen Sinne des Wortes verstehen. Wie also eine katholische Glaubenslehre, so setzt auch ein katholisches Dogma zwei Thatsachen, die *Offenbarung* nämlich, und die *Vorlegung*, oder *Verkündigung durch die Kirche (revelatio et Ecclesiae propositio)* voraus. Es läßt sich nun zwar nicht läugnen, daß man von der Wahrheit einer göttlichen Offenbarung auch auf anderm Wege, als durch die Lehre der Kirche Gewißheit erhalten kann; was nicht nur von den schon oben erwähnten Offenbarungen, die einzelnen Gläubigen zu Theil werden, sondern auch von der allgemeinen christlichen Offenbarung gilt. Denn durch Forschung in den Quellen derselben kann jemand zur klaren Erkenntniß gelangen, daß eine Wahrheit geoffenbart sei, welche als solche in der Kirche nicht allgemein angenommen wird; wie dies z.B. *Melchior Canus* und andere von sich in Betreff der Unfehlbarkeit des Papstes bezeugen. Aber wenn gleich deßhalb ältere und ausgezeichnete Theologen lehren, daß so erkannte Offenbarungslehren Gegenstand des übernatürlichen d. h. durch die göttliche Gnade verliehenen Glaubens sein können; so räumen sie doch ein, oder dringen vielmehr darauf, daß dieselben nicht zu den christkatholischen Glaubenslehren gehören, und unterschieden deßhalb zwischen *fides divina* und *fides divina catholica*. Für jenen Glauben genügt es, von der Thatsache, daß eine Wahrheit geoffenbart sei, eine subjective Gewißheit zu haben, für diesen ist es nothwendig, daß wir davon durch das öffentliche Lehramt der Kirche versichert werden. Kann ich also nur nachweisen, daß eine Lehre in der Offenbarung enthalten ist, aber nicht zugleich, daß sie als solche von der Kirche allen zu glauben vorgelegt wird; so kann ich sie auch nicht für ein katholisches Dogma ausgeben. Hiermit streitet nicht, was oben gesagt wurde, nämlich die Erklärung der Kirche, daß die Schrift Gottes Wort sei, genüge, um auch einzelne in ihr enthaltene Lehren als solche zu betrachten, die uns von ihr als geoffenbarte zu glauben vorgelegt werden. Denn dies wurde nur behauptet und kann nur behauptet werden, wenn entweder die Worte der Schrift so bestimmt und klar sind, daß über ihren Sinn kein Zweifel sein kann; oder wenn die gelehrte Erklärung derselben, durch die jemand zu einer subjectiven Ueberzeugung kommt, in der allgemeinen Annahme ihre Bestätigung findet. – Hieraus folgt denn nun, daß man die Dogmen nicht, wie Hermes vorschlägt, in Offenbarungslehren und erklärte Offenbarungslehren *(dogmata revelata et dogmata definita)* eintheilen kann, sondern, wenn man nun ja eine derartige Eintheilung will, in Offenbarungslehren, die als solche durch das gewöhnliche Lehramt der Kirche, und in Offenbarungslehren, die durch ausdrückliche Entscheidung der Kirche zu glauben vorgelegt werden. (*Dogmata communi Ecclesiae magisterio et dogmata definitione Ecclesiae proposita.*)

Was nun die andere, von Hermes angeführte Definition, welche nichts als Dogma anerkennt, als was von der Kirche ausdrücklich entschieden ist, betrifft; so mußte sie durchaus als irrthümlich bezeichnet werden. Denn mag immer die etymologische Bedeutung des griechischen δόγμα mit einer solchen Erklärung, wie Hermes richtig bemerkt, noch besser übereinstimmen, so handelt es sich doch hier nicht um eine bloße Worterklärung. Denn jene Theologen wollen ja nicht sagen, einige Glaubenslehren seien von der Kirche ausdrücklich entschieden, andere aber nicht, und nur jene nenne man Dogmen; sondern weil sie nur das als Glaubenslehre gelten lassen wollen, was von der Kirche entschieden ist, darum beschränken sie hierauf auch den Namen Dogma. – Ebenso irrt Hermes, wenn er glaubt, die Ausdrücke *dogma fidei* und *est de fide* würden von den Theologen nur gebraucht, um die durch die Entscheidung der Kirche festgestellten Glaubenssätze zu bezeichnen. Man wird keinen älteren Theologen namhaft machen können, der sich hierüber nicht wie Veronius und Lugo erklärte. – Noch viel weniger kann man zugeben, daß nur derjenige sich von

der Gemeinschaft der Kirche lossage, der einer feierlich entschiedenen Glaubenslehre widerspreche. Wer z.B. die Verklärung des Herrn auf Thabor, oder
die Reise des Apostels Paulus nach Rom läugnen wollte; würde eben so gut von
dem Glauben der Kirche sich lossagen, als jener, der die Menschwerdung des
Sohnes Gottes anstritte; und dies, wie oben erklärt wurde, aus demselben
Grunde, weßhalb Arius auch vor dem nicenischen und Nestorius vor dem
ephesinischen Kirchenrath von den Bischöfen mit vollem Recht als Ketzer
bezeichnet und von der Gemeinschaft der Gläubigen ausgestoßen wurden[13].
Aber sonderbar ist der Grund, den Hermes für diese seine Behauptung angibt:
„Weil, sagt er, die Allgemeinheit der Annahme desselben gewöhnlich unbekannt ist." Denn entweder setzt er voraus, daß ein vollendeter Beweis auch
ohne die allgemeine Annahme hinreiche, etwas für Dogma zu erklären, und
dann gilt jener Grund wenigstens für die so bewiesenen *dogmata revelata* nicht;
oder er hält, neben dem Beweise, die allgemeine Annahme für nöthig, was
allein katholisch ist, und dann kann doch diese, so lange sie unbekannt ist, auch
keine Bürgschaft geben, und somit wäre denn die Lehre, um die es sich handel-
te, gar kein Dogma, und Hermes hätte durch diesen Zusatz selbst die Un-
richtigkeit der von ihm vorgeschlagenen Eintheilung dargethan. – Zum wenigs-
ten also muß man gestehen, daß es dieser Stelle eben an dem, was in ihr vor
allem nothwendig war, an Bestimmtheit nämlich und Genauigkeit gebricht.

VI. Was die Theologen einstimmig für ein Dogma erklären, ist als ein solches
zu betrachten.

Das Letzte jedoch, was wir gegen Hermes sagten, leitet auf eine Frage hin, die
wir nicht unberührt lassen können. Man hört nämlich oftmals sagen, es sei
freilich wahr, daß alles, was die ganze Kirche als geoffenbarte Wahrheit glaube,
zum eigentlichen Dogma gehöre; aber ohne eine ausdrückliche Entscheidung
der Kirche könne man in den meisten Fällen diesen ihren allgemeinen Glauben
nicht mit Gewißheit erkennen. Obgleich aus dem oben Gesagten sich schon
ergibt, daß dies wenigstens nicht in der Ausdehnung, in welcher man es behauptet, wahr ist; so wollen wir doch hier noch auf einen kurzen und sicheren
Weg, auch in schwierigen Fällen zu erkennen, ob etwas zum allgemeinen
Glauben der Kirche gehöre, aufmerksam machen. Es ist dies aber kein anderer,
als jener, auf welchem man auch ermittelt, ob eine Lehre von der Kirche
ausdrücklich entschieden sei, oder nicht. Wenn nämlich die angesehnsten
Theologen über die Aechtheit und den Sinn einer Entscheidung immer über-

---

13 Vergleiche Lugo: De virtute fidei divinae. Disp. 3. s. 1. n. 4. 5.

eingestimmt haben; so sieht man, und gewiß mit vollem Rechte, die Sache als
ausgemacht an. Nun aber kann man mit derselben Zuversicht sagen, was die
angesehensten Theologen einstimmig für eine unzweifelhafte Glaubenslehre
erklären, das ist Lehre der allgemeinen Kirche, auch wenn es nicht durch
feierlichen Ausspruch entschieden ist. Man wolle nicht sagen, daß auf solche
Weise die Unfehlbarkeit der Kirche auf die Theologen übertragen werde. Denn
wir reden nicht von dem Falle, wenn die Theologen, sei es auch in Glaubenssachen, eine Meinung, die sie für gegründet halten, vertheidigen; sondern von
jenem Falle, wenn sie etwas ausdrücklich und mit Zuversicht als einen Glaubenssatz vortragen. Indem sie dies thuen, behaupten sie, daß der Satz, von dem
die Rede ist, von der ganzen Kirche als geoffenbarte Wahrheit gelehrt und
geglaubt werde. Sie treten also als Zeugen dieser Thatsache auf, und es muß ihr
Zeugniß, wenn es so ausdrücklich und einstimmig ist, als unverwerflich gelten.
Angesehene Theologen nennen wir, die zu großem Rufe gelangt sind, und
deren Rechtgläubigkeit unbestritten ist. Diese Männer lebten in verschiedenen
Jahrhunderten und in verschiedenen Theilen der Kirche; sie folgten in ihrer
Wissenschaft, so weit als es erlaubt war, verschiedenen Richtungen, und sind
deßhalb in sehr vielen Fragen nicht derselben Ansicht. Ihre Uebereinstimmung
also, wenn sie dies oder jenes für eine Lehre der allgemeinen Kirche erklären,
läßt sich nur aus der Evidenz der Thatsache, die sie bezeugen, erklären. Mangel
an Kenntniß, an Aufrichtigkeit oder Ernst in der Untersuchung dieser Thatsache, läßt sich höchstens bei einzelnen, und auch bei diesen, nur in wenigen
Fällen, voraussetzen. –

Aber mehr noch. Was die angesehenen Theologen einstimmig als Glaubenslehre vortragen, das wird auch factisch in der ganzen Kirche gelehrt. Denn
wenn wir jenes in der Kirche fortdaurende Apostolat nicht bloß in der Abstraction, sondern in der Wirklichkeit betrachten; so ist es doch nichts anders,
als die Unterweisung, welche von den Lehrern, den Theologen, den Predigern,
den geistlichen Vätern, den Katecheten, kurz von allen Dienern der Kirche
unter der Aufsicht der Bischöfe und der Oberaufsicht des Papstes den Gläubigen ertheilt wird. Nun ist es aber gewiß, daß alles, was die Theologen einstimmig für eine Lehre des Glaubens erklären, in diese ganze Unterweisung
übergeht, und als solche fast von allen diesen Dienern der lehrenden Kirche
wiederholt wird. Die Hirten können aus gewissen Rücksichten die öffentliche
Rüge einer Abweichung vom kirchlichen Lehrbegriffe zuweilen unterlassen;
aber können sie dies auch, wenn Jahrhunderte lang in fast allen Theilen der
Kirche von vielen Tausenden ihrer Diener ein Irrthum verbreitet wird. Man
muß also in solchem Falle ihr Stillschweigen als Gutheißung erklären. Wir
sehen aber auch, daß die Hirten der Kirche, ohne Zweifel aus dem eben angege-

benen Grunde, mit ganz besonderer Sorgfalt, die Lehre, welche Theologen, die zu einigem Rufe gelangt sind, in Büchern oder durch mündlichen Vortrag verbreiten, überwachen; und fast alle Entscheidungen der Kirche sind das Ergebniß dieser Wachsamkeit. – Endlich scheint es auch hinlänglich klar zu sein, daß die Hirten der Kirche den Grundsatz, von dem wir reden, selbst anerkennen. Denn nicht nur wurde derselbe bis auf unsere Tage gelehrt, und auf besagte Weise in Anwendung gebracht; sondern es wurde und wird auch nach ihm in den geistlichen Gerichten über die Unschuld oder Schuld derer, welche der Ketzerei angeklagt werden, entschieden. Wer bestreitet, was sämmtliche Theologen als eine Glaubenslehre vortragen, wird für schuldig erklärt. Wie könnten nun Päpste und Bischöfe ein solches Verfahren dulden, wenn nicht auch sie in jener einmüthigen Lehre der Theologen eine sichere Regel, die Lehre der Kirche zu ermitteln, anerkännten? Damit man nun aber nicht etwa sage, es komme dies daher, weil eben die Theologen nichts für eine Glaubenslehre erklären, was nicht von der Kirche feierlich entschieden sei; so müssen wir nochmals wiederholen, daß, wie Veronius und Lugo, so die übrigen das gerade Gegentheil ausdrücklich behaupten. –

VII. Die Denk- und Lehrfreiheit ist nicht bloß durch das Dogma beschränkt.

Aber darf nun wenigstens jeder, „ohne im geringsten aufzuhören ein glaubenstreuer Katholik zu sein," in allen Stücken, von welchen man weder durch die Ueberstimmung der Theologen, noch auch auf anderm Wege nachweisen kann, daß sie zur Glaubenslehre der Kirche im strengen Sinne gehören, „der Ansicht folgen, die ihm nun eben die richtige zu sein scheint?" Auch das können wir Hirscher durchaus nicht zugeben. Ein solcher Katholik würde sich dann der Sünde der Häresie allerdings nicht schuldig machen; aber es folgt nicht, daß er allen andern Pflichten, die sich auf die Reinheit des Glaubens beziehen, getreu bleibe. Oder thut er dies, a) wenn er zwar nicht die Lehre der Kirche selbst, wohl aber die strengen Folgerungen aus derselben läugnet; b) wenn er an das Gebiet der Häresie so nahe anstreift, daß er lehrt, was zwar nicht allen, aber sehr vielen bewährten Theologen mit der Häresie eins und dasselbe zu sein scheint; c) wenn er Dinge vorbringt, welche mit der Irrlehre in mehr oder weniger enger Verbindung stehen, und deßhalb gegründete Furcht erwecken, daß er derselben ergeben sei; d) wenn er von dem kirchlichen Sprachgebrauche abweichend, der Ausdrucksweise der Sektirer sich nähert; e) wenn er über Glaubenslehren, oder auch über Gebräuche und Einrichtungen der Kirche, auf eine Weise redet, welche leicht die Frömmigkeit und die Ehrfurcht der Gläubigen vermindert; f) wenn er lehrt, was eine Verirrung anderer vom wahren Glauben zu veranlassen geeignet ist; g) wenn er Ansichten vertheidigt, welche die Gläubigen in ihrer Unterwürfigkeit gegen die lehrende Kirche wankend machen würden; h) wenn er zwar nicht in Glaubensfragen, aber doch in solchen, die mit jenen auf irgend eine Weise zusammenhängen, der einstimmigen Lehre der bewährtesten Schriftsteller der Kirche widerspricht?

Es sind dies verschiedene Abstufungen, in welchen die Kirche selbst auch solche Lehrsätze, die der ausdrücklich geoffenbarten Wahrheit nicht entgegengesetzt sind, einer öffentlichen Rüge werth findet, und zu lehren verbietet: sie bezeichnet sie als *sententias* a) *erroneas* b) *haeresi proximas*, c) *de haeresi suspectas, haeresin sapientes*, d) *male sonantes*; e) *piarum aurium offensivas*; f) *scandalosas* g) *seditiosas* h) *temerarias.* Solcher Censuren haben sich bekanntlich die Väter des Conciliums von Constanz gegen Wiklef und Huß[14], und später die Päpste in mehreren ihrer Erlase bedient. Die Kirche erkennt also jene Freiheit, die man in Anspruch nimmt, alles, was nicht häretisch ist, lehren zu dürfen, durchaus nicht an, und rechtfertigt durch jene ihre Urtheile die Unterscheidung, welche die Theologen zwischen Lehre der Kirche im strengen und im weitern Sinne des Wortes machen. Zur Lehre der Kirche im strengeren Sinne gehört, was von der Kirche als ausdrücklich geoffenbarte Wahrheit geglaubt und bekannt wird; zur Lehre der Kirche im weiteren Sinne aber auch das, was obgleich nicht ausdrücklich geoffenbart, doch mit dem Geoffenbarten in Verbindung steht, und in der Kirche mit großer Uebereinstimmung für wahr gehalten und gelehrt wird. Es ist also nicht sogleich falscher Eifer oder Verketzerungssucht, wenn Ansichten, von denen es sich nicht nachweisen läßt, daß sie häretisch sind, dennoch für unkirchlich erklärt werden.

Hieraus erkennt man nun auch die Täuschung, welche dem Werke des Veronius und so manchen ähnlichen zu Grunde liegt. Um nämlich das Ioch des Gehorsams gegen die lehrende Kirche so viel als möglich zu erleichtern, bemühen sich die Verfasser zu zeigen, daß gar manches, was von Katholiken gewöhnlich angenommen und gelehrt wird, doch nicht zum eigentlichen Dogma gehöre. Aber wie viel haben sie gewonnen, wenn sie dann (was sie freilich gewöhnlich unterlassen), hinzusetzen müssen, es hänge dieses jedoch mit dem Dogma so innig zusammen, daß die entgegengesetzte Lehre mit einer oder mehreren von jenen Censuren, die oben angeführt wurden, belegt sei? Dies ist aber in solchen Fragen fast immer der Fall. Der ganze Trost, den sie einem Protestanten, der sich bekehren, oder einem Katholiken, der so frei als möglich denken möchte, bieten können, wäre also dieser: „Die Kirche verpflichte ihn nicht, diesen oder jenen Satz als eine geoffenbarte Wahrheit, sondern nur als

---

14 Sess. VIII. § XV.

eine durch ihre Verbindung mit dem Geoffenbarten bewährte und allein richtige und heilsame Lehre festzuhalten; wenn er dieses nun nicht thue, so mache er sich zwar einer schweren Sünde schuldig, sei aber noch nicht aus der Gemeinschaft der Gläubigen ausgeschlossen; und werde von der Kirche nicht für einen Ketzer, sondern nur für einen verwegenen, ärgerlichen, aufrührerischen, dem Irrthum anhängenden Menschen erklärt. –

Wir tadeln gewiß nicht, daß man sich mit jener Untersuchung beschäftigt, und das Gebiet des eigentlichen Dogmas so genau als möglich zu bestimmen sucht; nur soll man nicht so reden, als wenn, wo dieses Gebiet aufhöre, auch ohne weiters das Gebiet der freien Ansicht beginne, und was nicht Glaubenssatz ist, sofort als Schulmeinung betrachtet werden dürfte. Auch Hermes verleitet zu diesem Irrthum, wenn er an der oben angeführten Stelle fortfährt und sagt: „man müsse das Dogma von *Propositio sive Sententia theologica* (Schulmeinung) sorgfältig unterscheiden." Diese letztere nämlich sei eine Behauptung der Theologen, welche sie zwar durch die Offenbarung bewähren wollten, die aber die allgemeine Meinung nicht als eine Offenbarungslehre annehme. – Durch die Art, in der sich Hermes ausdrückt, scheint er auch hier die Theologen beschuldigen zu wollen, daß sie bemüht gewesen, ihre Meinungen für geoffenbarte Wahrheiten auszugeben. Doch bleiben wir, hievon absehend, bei der Frage, die uns jetzt beschäftigt. Wenn man alle Lehren, die keine Glaubenssätze sind, Lehren der Theologen nennen will, so muß man durchaus unter diesen unterscheiden. Manche nämlich werden von den bewährtesten Theologen mit Uebereinstimmung als zuverläßliche Wahrheiten vorgetragen, und sind, wie wir gesehen haben, oft von der Kirche selbst als solche durch die Verwerfung der entgegengesetzten Meinungen anerkannt: über andere aber sind die Theologen selbst verschiedener Ansicht, und keine kirchlichen Entscheidungen vorhanden. Nur diese letzteren sind es, die man Schulmeinungen *(opiniones scholasticae)* nennt, und nur sie sind der freien Ansicht hingegeben. –

Es bleibt uns jedoch nun noch eine Schwierigkeit zu lösen übrig. Aus dem Gesagten folgt nämlich, daß der Gehorsam, den wir der lehrenden Kirche schuldig sind, sich weiter als das Gebiet des eigentlichen Glaubens, und folglich auch die Lehrvollmacht der Kirche über den Inhalt der Offenbarung hinaus erstreckt. Dies scheint nun aber mit dem Grundsatz zu streiten, daß die Kirche keine neuen Offenbarungen empfängt, sondern nur die einmal durch die Apostel gegebne bewahrt und verkündigt. – Wir könnten uns, um hierauf zu antworten, einfach hin darauf berufen, daß die Kirche jenes Recht ausübt, um daraus zu schließen, daß sie es auch besitzt. Jedoch wird es nicht schwer sein, auch aus der Natur der Sache den Grund dieser Ausdehnung ihrer Lehrgewalt nachzuweisen. Der Zweck der Offenbarung nämlich wird dadurch noch nicht erreicht, daß wir die Wahrheiten, die sie ausdrücklich lehrt, mit frommen Glauben annehmen; sie soll auch, wie unser Handeln und Wirken, so unser Denken und Dafürhalten, wenigstens insofern es sich auf die Religion einigermaßen bezieht, ordnen, soll unser ganzes innere und äußere Leben mit der göttlichen Wahrheit durchdringen. Dies kann aber nicht geschehen, ohne bald die geoffenbarten Lehren näher zu bestimmen, bald ihren Inhalt zu entwicklen, bald aus ihnen zu folgern, und viele andere Gegenstände nach ihnen zu beurtheilen. Ist nun die Kirche kraft ihres Hirtenamtes bestellt, das göttliche Licht, so weit als es der Zweck der Offenbarung erfordert, zu verbreiten; so sind wir auch bei dieser näheren Bestimmung, Entwicklung und Anwendung oder Benutzung der geoffenbarten Wahrheiten für die Wissenschaften und das Leben auf sie als unsere Lehrerin hingewiesen. Und weil sie in eben der Sphäre, in welcher sie die Wahrheit verbreiten soll, auch den Irrthum abwehren muß; so hat sie die Gewalt, nicht nur jene Lehren zu verbieten, welche der geoffenbarten Wahrheit unmittelbar widerstreiten, sondern auch diejenigen, welche im Lichte der Offenbarung als irrig, gottlos, verführerisch und schädlich erkannt werden. –

Joseph Kleutgen's Chapter on the Teaching of the Church:
From the Second Edition of *Die Theologie der Vorzeit*

Die Theologie der Vorzeit vertheidigt
von Joseph Kleutgen, Priester der Gesellschaft Jesu.
Erster Band. Zweite verbesserte und sehr vermehrte Auflage. Münster, 1867.
Erster Theil. Von der Lehre der Vorzeit.
Erste Abhandlung. Von der Glaubensnorm.
Zweites Hauptstück. Von der Lehre der Kirche.

I. Von den Bekenntnissen und Beschlüssen der Kirche.

50. Daß alles das und nur das Gegenstand des christlichen Glaubens ist, was die Kirche als von Gott geoffenbarte Wahrheit lehrt, wird allgemein als das eigenthümlich katholische Prinzip anerkannt. Wenn wir nun weiter fragen, wo die Lehre der Kirche zu finden sei, so kann ebenso wenig ein Zweifel sein, daß zunächst in ihren *Bekenntnissen und Beschlüssen.* Denn in jenen hat sie selbst den Inhalt der göttlichen Offenbarung seinen wichtigsten Punkten nach zusammengefaßt, und in diesen sich über einzelne derselben näher ausgesprochen. Aber nicht mit gleicher Uebereinstimmung erklärt man sich in neuerer Zeit darüber, was als ein Beschluß der Kirche in Glaubenssachen anzuerkennen sei: dies also ist die erste Frage, die wir hier zu behandeln haben.

Manche Schriftsteller reden so, als wäre nur das von der Kirche als Glaubenslehre festgestellt, dessen Gegentheil sie zu behaupten unter dem Anathem verboten hat: Entscheidungen der Kirche sind ihnen nur die Canones der allgemeinen Concilien. Aber diese Beschränkung ist ganz gewiß rein willkürlich, und wird sowohl durch die Weise, in welcher die Beschlüsse der Kirche abgefaßt sind, als auch durch diesen beigefügte Erklärungen ganz offenbar widerlegt. Zwar hat die Kirche nicht selten ihre Lehre nur durch Verwerfung der entgegengesetzten Irrthümer ausgesprochen, und einer solchen Verwerfung pflegt das Anathem beigefügt zu werden. Der tridentinische Kirchenrath verfuhr also in der fünften Sitzung von der Erbsünde, und wiederum in der siebenten von den Sakramenten handelnd; und in derselben Weise wurde die Lehre der Kirche auf dem zweiten Concil zu Konstantinopel wider Origines, und auf der Synode zu Milevi und Orange wider die Pelagianer festgestellt. – Zuweilen jedoch finden wir umgekehrt die katholische Wahrheit, welche von den Sektirern geläugnet oder entstellt wurde, in positiver Weise vorgelegt und erläutert, und außerdem entweder gar keine oder nur eine allgemeine Verurtheilung der mit ihr streitenden Irrthümer. Man sehe den Brief Leo's des Großen wider Eutyches, dem der Kirchenrath zu Chalcedon feierlich beistimmte, und den Beschluß dieses Kirchenrathes selber; ferner die Entscheidung des dritten Concils zu Konstantinopel, die Beschlüsse, welche zu Florenz für die Griechen und Armenier erlassen wurden, und in der vierten Sitzung des tridentinischen Concils die Erklärung über die Schrift und Tradition, obschon diese mit einem Canon schließt, welcher die wesentlichen Punkte des vorhergehenden Bekenntnisses wiederholt. – Diese letztere Weise, welche die beiden früheren vereinigt, wurde auch vom Concilium zu Vienne und von jenem zu Florenz im Decrete wider die Jacobiten, beobachtet: den einzelnen Punkten der katholischen Lehre wird jedesmal die Verwerfung des entgegengesetzten Irrthums beigefügt. Wenn aber der Kirchenrath zu Trient in den meisten Sitzungen zuerst die rechtgläubige Lehre mehr oder weniger ausführlich vorlegt, und dann in einer Reihe von Canonen die Verwerfung der Irrthümer folgen läßt; so waren auch darin ihm ältere Concilien, z.B. das vierte lateranensische vorausgegangen. Dennoch sind es besonders die Beschlüsse des tridentinischen Kirchenrathes, welche zu der Behauptung, von der wir reden, Veranlassung gegeben haben: nur die *Canones*, nicht auch die *Capita*, sagt man, seien als dogmatische Entscheidungen zu betrachten.

51. Aber weil, wie eben gezeigt wurde, die Kirche, um ihren Glauben auszusprechen, von jeher sich bald der positiven, bald der negativen Form bedient hat; wie kann man da berechtigt sein in den Fällen, wenn sie beide vereinigt, nur was in der letzteren ausgesprochen ist, als Beschluß oder Entscheidung gelten zu lassen? Und gewiß welchem Theologen ist es vordem eingefallen, einen solchen Unterschied zwischen den beiden Hauptstücken des eben erwähnten vierten Concils im Lateran zu machen, und nur das *Caput. Damnamus*, aber nicht das *Caput. Firmiter*, als vollgültige Entscheidung der Kirche anzuerkennen? Was aber den tridentinischen Kirchenrath angeht, so finden wir in ihm erstlich jene Auseinandersetzung der katholischen Lehre und der auf sie folgenden Verwerfung der Irrthümer als zwei Abtheilungen, unter dem gemeinsamen Titel *Decretum* vereinigt. Sodann aber beginnt die Auseinandersetzung mit eben den Ausdrücken, denen sich die alten Concilien in ihren Bekenntnissen oder Entscheidungen bedienen, z.B. „die h. Synode erklärt,“ „bekennt,“ „lehrt“ – und dieselben Redeweisen werden bei manchem neuen Abschnitt wiederholt. Endlich aber erklärt der Kirchenrath am Schlusse fast eines jeden dieser Lehrvorträge, daß er in ihm „die katholische Wahrheit, welche alle glauben und festhalten müssen,“ vorgelegt habe, und giebt als

Grund, weßhalb er die *Canones* folgen lasse, nicht etwa an, damit man aus ihnen ersehe, welche Punkte der vorhergehenden Erörterung als entschiedene Glaubenssätze gelten müßten, sondern vielmehr, damit nicht bloß die Wahrheiten, die wir glauben, sondern auch die Irrthümer, die wir meiden müssen, besser erkannt werden[1]. – Wie man also bei solchen ausdrücklichen Erklärungen hat behaupten können, daß nur die *Canones* und nicht auch die *Capita* des tridentinischen Concils die Kraft kirchlicher Entscheidungen haben, ist kaum begreiflich. Was könnte denn noch als entschiedener Glaubenssatz gelten, wenn nicht einmal mehr das, was die Kirche öffentlich und feierlich als katholische Wahrheit bekennt, und als in der Schrift und Tradition enthaltene Lehre allen, die selig werden wollen, zu glauben vorlegt? – Wir dürfen demnach als allgemeinen Grundsatz aussprechen: Was immer in den Beschlüssen der Concilien so vorgetragen wird, daß die Absicht der Väter, was geoffenbarte Lehre und Glaube der Kirche sei, vor der ganzen Christenheit zu erklären, unverkennbar ist; das muß als katholische Glaubenswahrheit anerkannt werden: – obwohl deßhalb nicht auch alles, was zur Begründung oder Beleuchtung der Lehre, welche eigentlicher Gegenstand der Erklärung ist, hinzugefügt wird[2]. –

52. Selbst Veronius[3] und Chrismann[4], welche sich, wie sie sagen, alle Mühe gegeben haben, das Gebiet des Glaubens so enge als möglich zu begränzen, stimmen dennoch diesem Grundsatze bei. Der letztere jedoch bekennt sich zugleich zu einem andern, von dem ich nicht weiß, ob er vor ihm irgend Jemand in den Sinn gekommen. Damit die Entscheidungen der Concilien, sagt

---

1   Post hanc *catholicam* de justificatione *doctrinam, quam nisi quisque fideliter firmiterque receperit, justificari non potest,* placuit S. Synodo, hos canones subjungere, ut omnes sciant, non solum, quid tenere et sequi, sed etiam quid vitare et fugere debeant. Sess. XVI. Ante canones de justificatione. – Quoniam autem non est satis veritatem dicere nisi detegantur et refellantur errores; placuit S Synodo hos canones subjungere, ut omnes *jam agnita catholica doctrina,* intelligant quoque, quae ab illis haereses caveri vitarique debeant. Sess. XIII. Ante canones de Sacr. ss. Euch. – Haec sunt, quae de Poenitentiae et extremae Unctionis Sacramentis haec s. oecumenica Synodus *profitetur et docet, atque omnibus Christi fidelibus credenda et tenenda proponit.* Sequentes autem Canones inviolabiliter servandos esse tradit, et asserentes contrarium perpetuo damnat et anathematizat. Sess. XIV. Ante Canones de SS. Poenit. Sacram. – Quia vero adversus *veterem hanc* in sacrosancto *Evangelio,* Apostolorum *traditionibus* sanctorumque Patrum doctrina *fundatam fidem,* hoc tempore multi disseminati sunt errores multaque a multis docentur, atque disputantur; s. Synodus post multos gravesque his de rebus mature habitos tractatus unanimi Patrum omnium consensu, quae huic purissimae fidei sacraeque doctrinae adversantur, damnare et a S. Ecclesia eliminare per subjectos hos canones constituit. Sess. XXII. Ante Canones de Sacrif. Missae.

2   Cf. Vasquez. In Summam S. Thom. p. 1. 2ᵈᵃᵉ. disp. 200. c. 6. p. 3. disp. 181. c. 9. disp. 207. c. 3.

3   Regula fidei. c. 1. §. 4. n. 5.

4   Regula fid. cath. p. 1. sect 3. cap. 4. § 104. n. 5. 6. 7.

er, sicher und unfehlbar seien, müssen sie auf die göttliche Offenbarung gestützt sein. Nun dürfen wir zwar, wenn die Concilien, ohne irgend welche Gründe anzuführen, Glaubenssätze feststellen, nicht zweifeln, daß diese in der Schrift und Tradition gegründet sind; aber wenn sie Gründe, die nicht aus diesen Quellen der Offenbarung, sondern aus den menschlichen Wissenschaften entnommen sind, beifügen, dann hören ihre Entscheidungen auf dogmatisch zu sein, und fordern nur noch menschlichen, nicht aber göttlichen Glauben[5].

Chrismann geht, wie wir sehen, auch hier von dem Grundsatze aus, daß nichts Gegenstand des übernatürlichen Glaubens sein kann, was nicht von Gott geoffenbart ist. So wahr und anerkannt nun dieser Grundsatz ist, dürfen wir über denselben doch nie den andern vergessen, daß nur das aber auch alles das Gegenstand des Glaubens ist, was die Kirche als solchen verkündigt. Was folgt aber aus der Verbindung dieser beiden Grundsätze, wenn nicht, daß die Kirche nie etwas für Gegenstand des Glaubens erklärt, was nicht geoffenbart ist? Darum ja hatte Chrismann selbst kurz vorher gesagt, daß wir nicht zweifeln können, ob, was die Kirche als Glaubenslehre vorträgt, in der Offenbarung enthalten sei, möge sie auch ihrer Erklärung keine aus der Offenbarung entnommenen Gründe beifügen. So wird es also immer nur darauf ankommen, ob die Thatsache, daß die Kirche etwas als Gegenstand des Glaubens verkündige, außer Zweifel sei. Woraus erkennen wir aber dieses? Chrismann selbst verweist uns mit allen Theologen auf die klaren und bestimmten Erklärungen, deren sich die Kirche in ihren Entscheidungen bedient, indem sie bald allen Gläubigen vorschreibt, die Lehre, von welcher sie redet, mit festem Glauben anzunehmen, bald die entgegengesetzte Meinung als häretisch verwirft, bald ihren eigenen Glauben bekennt, bald bezeugt, daß also die Schrift oder die Ueberlieferung der Väter lehre. Von welchen kirchlichen Lehrvorträgen oder Denkschriften also redet Chrismann, wenn er behauptet, daß sie der philosophischen

---

5   Si rationes aliunde, quam ex Scriptura aut Traditione divina sint repetitae, nec ad fidem spectant, nec infallibili judicio ab Ecclesia proponuntur. Sic ubi in Conc. Lat. sub Leone X. definitur, omnem assertionem veritati illuminatae fidei contrariam omnino falsam esse, *quia verum vero minime contradicit,* ob hanc philosophicam rationem *canon iste dogmaticus non est.* – In dem ersten dieser beiden Sätze behauptet Chrismann nichts anders, als daß derlei philosophische Gründe nicht zum Glauben gehören; aber im zweiten folgert er, daß auch der Canon, in dem sie angeführt werden, deßhalb aufhöre dogmatisch zu sein, und fügt dann noch dies andere Beispiel hinzu: „Sicut anima rationalis et caro unus est homo, ita Deus et homo unus est Christus," – ad philosophiae, non fidei fundamenta pertinet; quae igitur nullo alio fundamento consistunt, quam humanis rationibus humanisque experimentis, humanam quidem, numquam tamen divinam exigere fidem neque fidei dogmatibus accenseri possunt. L. c. n. 2.

Gründe wegen, die sie enthalten, für nicht dogmatische anzusehen seien? von jenen, die derartige Erklärungen enthalten, oder von solchen, die derselben ermangeln? Wenn von den letzteren, so würden ja diese solchen Mangels wegen gar nicht als dogmatische Bestimmungen gelten können, und der Umstand, daß die Beweisgrunde nicht aus der Offenbarung entlehnt wären, uns höchstens in dem Urtheil bestärken, daß die Kirche in ihnen nicht beabsichtige eine Entscheidung zu geben. Wenn wir also den Grundsatz Chrismanns schon deßhalb, damit er nicht ganz müßig und fade sei, von jenen Erlassen verstehen müssen, in welchen die Absicht der Kirche, über eine Lehre zu entscheiden klar ausgesprochen ist; so werden wir dazu durch die Beispiele die er anführt vollends genöthigt. Das erste ist der Canon, durch den das fünfte Concilium im Lateran entscheidet, daß jede Behauptung, die mit dem Glauben streite, als falsch zu verwerfen ist. Dieser Canon also, behauptet Chrismann, ist nicht dogmatisch, weil in ihm der philosophische Grund, das Wahre könne mit dem Wahren nicht streiten, angeführt wird. Nun bedient sich aber die Kirche in diesem Canon nicht nur des so bezeichnenden Ausdrucks *Definimus*, sondern erklärt zugleich jene, welche dem entgegengesetzten Irrthume anhangen, in den allerstärksten Ausdrücken für Ketzer[6], was auch nach Chrismann eines der offenbarsten Kennzeichen ist, daß die Kirche eine Lehre als Glaubenslehre verkündige[7]. Demzufolge behauptet er durch jenen seinen Grundsatz, daß wir auch, wenn die Kirche ihre Absicht eine Entscheidung in Glaubenssachen zu geben, ausdrücklich erklärt, nichtsdestoweniger aus der Beschaffenheit der Gründe, die sie anführt, schließen dürfen, daß ihre Entscheidung keine dogmatische sei. Was heißt das aber anders, als daß wir schließen dürfen, die Kirche sei in jenen Entscheidungen von der Wahrheit abgefallen, etwas für Glaubenlehre erklärend, was nicht Glaubenslehre ist? –

53. Jedoch wie haben wir denn über die Beweisgründe, welche in den dogmatischen Beschlüssen angegeben werden, zu urtheilen? Nicht selten erklärt die Kirche mit Bestimmtheit, daß die Lehre, welche sie feststellt, in diesen oder jenen Worten der Schrift ausgesprochen, oder auch daß dieselbe der Grund sei,

---

6   Cum verum vero minime contradicat, omnem assertionem veritati illuminatae fidei contrariam, omnino falsam esse definimus: et ut aliter dogmaticare non liceat, districtius inhibeamus: omnesque hujusmodi erroris assertionibus inhaerentes veluti damnatissimas haereses seminantes, per omnia ut detestabiles et abominabiles haereticos et infideles catholicam fidem labefactantes, vitandos et puniendos fore decernimus. Conc. Lat. V. Bulla *Apostolici Regiminis*.

7   Quod jam ipsos concernit Conciliorum canones, omnes illi fidem divinam et catholicam annuntiat, quorum objectum est materia fidei divinae; id quod potissimum ex eo colligitur, [...] si contrarium asserentes pro haereticis judicentur. L. c. n. 7.

weßhalb der Ueberlieferung der Väter zufolge in der Kirche ein Gebrauch
beobachtet werde. Von dem einen und dem andern haben wir ein Beispiel in
dem Beschluß des tridentinischen Concils über die Erbsünde. Denn es wird in
demselben erklärt, daß die Kirche die Worte des Apostels über die Sündhaftig-
keit der Nachkommen Adams stets von der Sünde, in der alle, auch jene welche
von christlichen Eltern abstammen, geboren werden, verstanden, und deßhalb
auch den Unmündigen das Sakrament der Wiedergeburt ertheilt habe. In
solchen Fällen also macht die Kirche von ihrem Rechte, die Schrift und Ueberlieferung authentisch zu erklären, Gebrauch; und es kann keine Frage sein, daß
diese Erklärungen, und folglich auch die Beweise, welche durch sie geliefert
werden, dogmatisches Ansehen haben. Wo immer aber bei Anführung von
Beweisen die Absicht der Kirche, den Sinn des göttlichen Wortes zu bestimmen, nicht klar hervortritt; läßt sich nicht dasselbe behaupten. Wenn es uns
also schiene, daß die Zeugnisse der Schrift oder Tradition, auf welche in den
Beschlüssen der Kirche hingewiesen wird, keinen unumstößlichen Beweis
enthielten; dürften wir deßhalb zweifeln, ob die Lehre, welche durch jene
Beschlüsse für eine Glaubenswahrheit erklärt wird, in der That Glaubenswahrheit sei? Dies gewiß nicht: nun so muß es uns denn auch gewiß sein, daß sie,
obgleich in den angeführten Zeugnissen nicht hinlänglich ausgesprochen,
nichtsdestoweniger in der Offenbarung enthalten sei. Nicht anders aber haben
wir zu urtheilen, wenn der Grund, den die Kirche anführt, vielmehr einer
menschlichen Wissenschaft, als dem göttlichen Worte entnommen zu sein
scheint: wir dürfen nicht zweifeln, daß die Lehre, welche sie zu glauben vorschreibt, auch in diesem enthalten sei.

54. Wie mißlich es aber sei, mit zu vieler Freiheit über solche Beweise der
Kirche zu urtheilen, und auf welche Abwege überhaupt der Grundsatz Chrismanns führte; dafür liefert dieser, wie bei anderer Gelegenheit, so auch eben
hier die schlagendsten Beweise. Was entschied der lateranensische Kirchenrath?
Daß jede Behauptung, die dem Glauben zuwiderläuft, als falsch zu verwerfen
ist. Nun kann doch erstlich niemand zweifeln, ob diese *Lehre, die entschieden
wird,* im göttlichen Worte ausgesprochen sei. Oder werden wir von diesem
nicht unzählige Male aufgefordert, alle menschliche Lehre, die der göttlichen,
welche sie verkündet, widerstrebt, als Lug und Trug zu verabscheuen? Was aber
den *Grund* angeht, welchen die Kirche anführt; so ist es bekannt, wie oft die hh.
Väter, und zwar von den ältesten Apologeten angefangen, lehren, daß nichts
von dem, was die menschliche Wissenschaft Wahres enthalte, mit dem göttlichen Worte streite. Diese Lehre aber pflegen sie aus der Offenbarung selbst zu
begründen, indem sie aus ihr nachweisen, daß es derselbe Logos sei, der jeden
Menschen durch seine Vernunft erleuchte und der durch die Propheten und

Apostel geredet habe. Wie also der Kirchenrath in dem Dogma selbst, das er aufstellt: jede mit dem Glauben streitende Behauptung sei als falsch zu verwerfen, – das, was in den Warnungen und Ermahnungen der Schrift liegt, kurz zusammengefaßt hat: so hat er auch in dem Grunde, den er vorausschickte, nur die eben erwähnte Lehre der Schrift und Väter auf einen allgemeinen Grundsatz zurückgeführt. Oder was heißt denn der Satz: das Wahre widerstreite dem Wahren nicht – in dem Zusammenhang, in welchem er vorkommt, wenn nicht: was die menschliche Wissenschaft Wahres enthält, das ist mit der göttlich geoffenbarten Lehre in Einklang?

Noch viel sonderlicher aber ist das andere Beispiel, auf welches Chrismann seinen Grundsatz anwendet. In dem nach dem h. Athanasins benannten Glaubensbekenntniß heißt es: „Wie die vernünftige Seele und das Fleisch der eine Mensch, so sind Gott und der Mensch der eine Christus." Da sagt nun Chrismann frischweg, dieser Vergleich gehöre der Philosophie und nicht dem Glauben an und folgert, was also nur menschliche Vernunft und Erfahrung zur Grundlage habe, das könne auch nur menschlichen nicht göttlichen Glauben verdienen. Aber was von jenem Vergleich gehört denn zur Philosophie und nicht zum Glauben? Es wird durch ihn erklärt, nicht zwar daß in Christus Gottheit und Menschheit in jeder Hinsicht eben so wie im Menschen Seele und Leib vereinigt seien, wohl aber daß die Gottheit und Menschheit in Christus nicht bloß in irgend einen innigen Verkehr getreten, sondern wie Leib und Seele im Menschen zur Einheit des Seins und zwar des physischen und nicht bloß ethischen Seins verbunden sind. Daß es nun in Christus eine solche Einheit des Seins gebe, ist doch gewiß keine philosophische Wahrheit, sondern der innerste Kern des Dogmas, das die Kirche wider Nestorius schützte. Daß aber das menschliche Sein ein einiges ist, beweist freilich auch die Philosophie; nichtsdestoweniger ist es zugleich eine geoffenbarte Wahrheit, und als solche von der Kirche feierlich ausgesprochen. Doch gesetzten Falls es wäre dem nicht so, würde denn die Kirche schon dadurch das Gebiet der Offenbarung verlassen, daß sie, um ein Geheimniß des Glaubens zu erläutern, sich einer uns näher liegenden natürlichen Wahrheit bediente? Dann dürfte sie auch keine anderen Worte gebrauchen, als jene, mit welchen die Offenbarung selbst das Geheimniß vorträgt, und also die Vereinigung der göttlichen und menschlichen Natur in Christus, um sie von der ethischen, die zwischen Gott und den Gerechten besteht, zu unterscheiden, nicht mehr eine physische oder wesentliche, und noch viel weniger, um sie von jener zwischen Leib und Seele zu unterscheiden, eine hypostatische nennen. Denn was diese Ausdrücke bedeuten, lehrt uns nur die Philosophie. Wozu anders aber dient der Vergleich von dem wir reden, als wozu solche der Wissenschaft entlehnte Bezeichnungen dienen, den wahren

Sinn des Dogmas schärfer zu bestimmen? – Das einzige was sich sagen läßt, ist, daß die Einheit des menschlichen Wesens, wenn sie nicht anderweitig von der Kirche gelehrt würde, in Kraft dieser Stelle des athanasianischen Glaubensbekenntnisses nicht für eine dogmatisch bestimmte Wahrheit gelten könnte. Denn in ihm wird derselben nicht erwähnt, um über sie etwas zu bestimmen, sondern um, was über die Einheit Christi bestimmt wird, zu erläutern.

55. Wir haben bisher nur der Beschlüsse allgemeiner Kirchenversammlungen erwähnt: gilt aber, was wir gesagt haben nur von ihnen? Nicht wenige unserer Zeitgenossen scheinen allerdings außer diesen Beschlüssen keine Entscheidungen der Kirche in Glaubenssachen anzuerkennen. Aber können sie behaupten, daß die Vollmacht in Glaubensstreitigkeiten zu richten, der Kirche unter der Bedingung einer bestimmten Form des Gerichtes, ertheilt sei? oder ohne vom Katholizismus abzufallen, läugnen, daß die *Ecclesia per orbem dispersa* eben so unfehlbar ist, als die *Ecclesia in concilio congregata*? Wir verstehen hier unter Kirche den Lehrkörper, dem alle Gläubigen unterworfen sind, also die Bischöfe in Vereinigung mit ihrem Haupte, dem Pabste. Auf doppelte Weise übt dieser Lehrkörper, auch wenn er nicht versammelt ist, sein höchstes Richteramt in Glaubenssachen, *erstlich* durch Annahme von Particular-Concilien; – auf diese Weise haben unter andern die gegen die Pelagianer gehaltenen Provinzial-Synoden das Ansehen allgemeiner Kirchenversammlungen bekommen; – *zweitens* durch die päbstlichen Entscheidungen ertheilte Zustimmung. Diese Zustimmung kann zum voraus ertheilt werden; wenn nämlich die Bischöfe vom h. Stuhle, bevor derselbe eine Entscheidung erläßt, befragt werden, wie dies in dem bekannten Streit über die drei Kapitel geschah, und in diesen unsern Tagen in Betreff einer andern Glaubensfrage geschieht[8]. Aber es ist klar, daß eine solche Zustimmung eben sowohl nachher, durch die Annahme, nämlich der päbstlichen Erlasse, stattfinden kann, und dieses ist es, worauf wir hier besonders aufmerksam machen müssen.

Daß der Pabst, wenn er von jener Lehrvollmacht, die ihm, wie das Concilium von Florenz sagt, über die ganze Kirche von Christus dem Herrn gegeben ist[9], Gebrauch machend eine Glaubensfrage entscheidet, nicht irren könne; glaubte *Melchior Canus* durch Gründe darthun zu können, die stärker und

---

8   Als dies Werk in der ersten Auflage erschien, hatte eben der Pabst an den Episcopat über die dogmatische Entscheidung der unbefleckten Empfängniß geschrieben.

9   Definimus [...] *Pontificem Romanum* [...] totius ecclesiae caput et *omnium Christianorum* patrem ac *doctorem* existere; et ipsi B. Petro *pascendi* (d. h. in der Kirchensprache docendi) regendi et gubernandi *universalem ecclesiam* a Domino nostro Jesu Christo *plenam potestatem* traditam esse. Decret. Unionis.

klarer seien, als jene, womit wir manche Lehren, die ohne Zweifel eigentliche Glaubenspunkte sind, zu beweisen pflegen. Er würde deßhalb, fügt er hinzu, gar kein Bedenken tragen, die entgegengesetzte Meinung für häretisch zu erklären, wenn er sich nicht scheute, dem Urtheile der Kirche zuvor zu kommen[10]. Ebenso reden *Bellarmin, Suarez* und so viele der größten Theologen. Nur weil die entgegenstehende Lehre in *Gerson* und andern Gallikanern Vertheidiger, denen man ein gewisses Ansehen nicht absprechen kann, gefunden, und die Kirche sich bis jetzt nicht ausdrücklich erklärt habe; nicht aber weil die Beweise aus Schrift und Tradition nicht stark und entscheidend genug seien, geben sie zu, daß die Unfehlbarkeit des Papstes kein Glaubensartikel ist. Auf dieses Zugeständniß pflegen sich nun aber manche neuere Theologen zu stützen, um ohne weiteres zu behaupten, die päbstlichen Erlasse in Glaubenssachen gehörten nicht zu jenen Entscheidungen, durch welche man die Lehre der Kirche mit dogmatischer Gewißheit erkenne. Namentlich glaube ich auch hier der Schriften *Chrismann's* und *Veronius* erwähnen zu müssen. Beide sind verfaßt, um dem Wunsche, den auch Hirscher an den Tag legt,[11] nachzukommen, daß nämlich „der Kreis freier Bewegung und Ansicht soweit als möglich gezogen werde." Wohl durfte man sagen, daß dem wahrhaft gläubigen Gemüthe dieser Wunsch fremd sei: nicht nur weil ihm die Unterwerfung des Verstandes unter Gottes Wort, wie jede Pflichterfüllung, füß ist; sondern auch weil, wo der Kreis freier Bewegung beginnt, auch das Gebiet der Ungewißheit beginnt. Ist es denn als ein hartes Loos zu betrachten, wenn wir statt hin und her zu schwanken, oder doch nur auf unser menschliches Dafürhalten uns zu stützen, in mehr und mehr Stücken durch das untrügliche Licht des Glaubens geleitet werden? Nichts destoweniger darf man jenen Wunsch mit Rücksicht auf die menschliche Schwäche hegen; und wirklich hat auch diese Rücksicht insbesondere *Veronius* in der Verfassung seines Werkes geleitet. Um den Protestanten die Annahme des katholischen Bekenntnisses zu erleichtern; soll man, sagt er, so wenig als möglich von ihnen fordern. Auch Hirscher erinnert hieran an mehr als einer Stelle. Aber gewiß muß man doch dabei sich hüten, irgend einen Theil der katholischen Wahrheit zu verrathen, oder diejenigen, welche an die Rückkehr zur wahren Kirche denken, zu täuschen. Ist aber dies nicht zu fürchten, wenn man mit Veronius und Chrismann daraus, daß die Unfehlbarkeit des Papstes kein Glaubensartikel sei, so ohne alle Unterscheidung folgert, päbstliche Erlasse seien keine dogmatische Entscheidungen?

10　De locis theol. I. VI. c. 7.
11　Kirchliche Zustände S. 69.

Wenn die Theologen gemeiniglich einräumen, daß die Lehre von der Unfehlbarkeit des Pabstes kein Dogma sei; so folgt daraus nichts anders, als daß die Erlasse des h. Stuhles in Glaubensfragen nicht ohne weiters und an sich als Urtheile der unfehlbaren Kirche anzusehen seien: daß man sie aber als solche betrachten müsse, sobald sie vom Episkopat angenommen sind, geben auch die hartnäckigsten Gallicaner zu, und müssen alle zugeben, welche nicht die erste Grundlehre der katholischen Kirche läugnen wollen. Nach solcher Annahme sind nämlich jene Erlasse offenbar Beschlüsse der über den Erdkreis zerstreuten Kirche. – Nun räumen zwar die Gallicaner selber ein, daß zu dieser Annahme, eben weil es sich um den Glauben handle, nach allen Grundsätzen des Kirchenrechts das bloße Stillschweigen der Bischöfe genüge. Aber möge man auch mehr, nämlich irgend eine öffentliche Handlung, durch welche die Bischöfe ihre Zustimmung erklären, fordern; so bleibt immer wahr, daß, wenn nicht alle, gewiß die meisten päbstlichen Entscheidungen, die wir haben, durch diesen Beitritt der Mehrheit der Bischöfe zu Beschlüssen der allgemeinen Kirche erhoben worden sind. Denn noch keiner ist von andern, als von dem kleinen Haufen jener, deren Irrthümer verdammt wurden, widersprochen worden, und von den meisten läßt es sich nachweisen, daß sie fast von sämmtlichen Hirten der Kirche mit Ehrfurcht aufgenommen, in ihren Sprengeln verkündigt und dem amtlichen Verfahren zu Grunde gelegt worden sind. Dies also durften Veronius und Chrismann nicht mit Stillschweigen übergehen. Wenn es ihnen wichtig schien darzuthun, daß die Unfehlbarkeit des Pabstes noch immer ein Streitpunkt sei; so mußten sie jedoch nicht unterlassen aufmerksam zu machen, daß es sich in diesem Streite nur darum handle, ob eine päbstliche Entscheidung abgesehen von der Zustimmung der Bischöfe als Glaubensregel gelten müsse. Denn daraus ergiebt sich, daß, was sie von den Erlassen des h. Stuhles in sich betrachtet sagen auf jene, welche wirklich vorhanden sind, so gut als gar keine Anwendung findet, und darum denen, welchen das Joch des Glaubens eine Bürde ist, keine Erleichterung gewährt. –

56. Weil wir von jenen Bullen, welche die Lehre des *Bajus* und der *Jansenisten* verdammen, oft Gebrauch machen müssen, so wird hier die Bemerkung nicht überflüssig sein, daß von diesen wenigstens, was wir eben von den meisten päbstlichen Entscheidungen sagten, ganz gewiß ist. Die Irrthümer des Bajus wurden in den aus seinen Schriften ausgehobenen Lehrsätzen von Pius V., und wiederum von Gregor XIII. und nochmals von Urban VIII. verdammt. Dieser selbe Pabst erließ die erste Bulle gegen den „*Augustinus*" des Jansenius, weil in demselben Bajus Irrlehren zum großen Theil von neuem vorgetragen wurden. Nicht lange nachher verdammte Innocenz X. auf das ausdrückliche Verlangen einer großen Anzahl von Bischöfen die fünf Sätze, auf welche sich die meisten

Irrlehren der Jansenisten zurückführen lassen. Mehrere der nachfolgenden Päbste bestätigten dieses Verdammungsurtheil, bis endlich die Bulle Clemens XI. *Vineam Domini* dem Streite über Jansenius Schrift ein Ende machte. In dieser Bulle, welche nicht bloß von dem Gallicanischen Clerus, sondern auch von der ganzen Kirche öffentlich und ausdrücklich angenommen wurde, erklärt der Pabst, daß alle Christgläubigen verpflichtet seien, sich nicht bloß durch äußeres Stillschweigen, sondern auch durch inneren Gehorsam den wider Jansenius erlassenen Entscheidungen der Kirche zu unterwerfen, und die Lehre desselben mit Herz und Mund als ketzerisch zu verdammen. – Nun wurde aber bekanntlich die ganze Lehre des Bajus und Jansenius mit vielen Zuthaten von *Quesnel* erneuert. Gegen ihn erließ derselbe Pabst Clemens XI. die berühmte Bulle *Unigenitus*. Auch diese wurde zuerst durch Innocenz XIII. und dann von Benedict XIII. an der Spitze einer in Rom versammelten Synode bestätigt. Um aber den neuen Jansenisten jede Ausflucht zu benehmen, ward sie nicht bloß von den Provinzial-Synoden in Avignon und Embrun und dem gallikanischen Clerus, sondern auch fast von allen Metropolitanen des ganzen Erdkreises im Namen ihrer Suffragane durch authentische Erklärungen, und zwar als ein dogmatisches und unwiderrufliches Urtheil der allgemeinen Kirche angenommen[12]. – Endlich sind dieselben Irrthümer mit manchen andern in der Bulle *Auctorem fidei*, welche Pius VI. gegen die *Synode zu Pistoja* erließ, nochmals feierlich verurtheilt worden. – Wenn nun *Bossuet* selber zugiebt, daß die dogmatische Entscheidung eines Pabstes, wenn sie von einem zweiten oder dritten Pabste ausdrücklich bestätigt werde, bereits das Ansehen eines Ausspruchs der allgemeinen Kirche erhalte; was müssen wir von einer Lehre sagen, welche während zwei voller Jahrhunderte von einer ganzen Reihenfolge von Päbsten mit ausdrücklicher Zustimmung des gesammten Episkopates verworfen worden ist?

II. Von dem ordentlichen Lehramt der Kirche.

57. Nachdem wir erwogen haben, was als Entscheidung der Kirche anzuerkennen ist, stellt sich nun die Frage ein, ob wir jene Lehre der Kirche, welche uns Glaubensregel sein muß, ausschließlich in ihren Entscheidungen und Bekenntnissen zu suchen haben. Wie viele Andere, redet auch Hirscher in dieser Ueberzeugung. „Jeder," sagt er, „darf, ohne im geringsten aufzuhören ein glaubenstreuer Katholik zu sein, in allen Fragen, über welche der Lehrbegriff

---

12 Diese Actenstücke befinden sich in der königlichen Bibliothek zu Paris; wurden aber zur Zeit vom Cardinal Erzbischof von Mecheln durch den Druck veröffentlicht. *Temoignages de l'Eglise universelle en faveur de la Bulle Unigenitus.*

nicht kirchlich fixirt ist, jener Ansicht folgen, welche ihm nun eben die richtige zu sein scheint. Das steht theoretisch fest; in der Wirklichkeit aber möchte man nicht selten ob einer Ketzerei mildere Beurtheilung erfahren, als ob einer Abweichung, von gangbaren, vielleicht gerade im Zenith stehenden theologischen Meinungen."[13] Daß Hirscher unter der kirchlichen Fixirung jene, welche durch Entscheidungen der Kirche geschieht, verstehe, geht aus dem gleich Folgenden hervor: „Unsere Dogmatiker sind daran, das System ihrer Wissenschaft, wie sie sagen, auszubauen, und was in den kirchlichen Entscheidungen noch nicht fixirt ist, vollends definitiv festzustellen." Und in der Moral lesen wir: „Wenn als Abweichung von der Einheit des Lehrbegriffs bezeichnet wird, worüber von der Kirche gar nicht entschieden ist; so ist das Verketzerungssucht und nicht gut.[14] "

Doch wie zuversichtlich immer Hirscher diese Behauptung aufstellt, wir können darin nur einen Irrthum sehen, der aus einem hier zu erörternden Mißverständniß entspringt. Gemäß dem oft erwähnten Grundsatz, in dem wir alle übereinstimmen, ist nur das katholische Glaubenslehre, was die Kirche als geoffenbarte Wahrheit allen zu glauben vorlegt. Nun nimmt man aber sofort an, daß die Kirche nur dann etwas zu glauben vorlege, wenn sie eine Glaubensstreitigkeit als höchste Richterin feierlich entscheide. Es übt aber die Kirche ein doppeltes Lehramt aus. Das eine ist das *ordentliche* und immerwährende, und besteht in eben jenem fortdaurenden Apostolate, von dem Hirscher in den „Erörterungen" redet. (s. 28.) Das andere ist *außerordentlich,* wird nur zu besonderen Zeiten, wenn nämlich Irrlehrer die Kirche beunruhigen, geübt, und ist nicht schlechthin Lehramt, sondern zugleich Richteramt. In diesem wehrt die Kirche die feindseligen Angriffe auf das Heiligthum, das sie bewahrt, ab; in jenem öffnet sie ihren Kindern den reichen Schatz, der bei ihr hinterlegt ist.

58. Wenn man also die Lehre der Kirche, durch welche wir, was geoffenbart ist, mit Gewißheit erkennen, auf jene Sätze beschränken will, durch welche sie Irrlehren verworfen oder ihren Glauben urkundlich ausgesprochen hat; so stellt man dadurch erstlich eine bis auf unsere Zeiten unerhörte Behauptung auf. Nicht bloß die älteren Theologen, sondern alle, die je über die Glaubensregel geschrieben haben, Veronius, Chrismann[15] nicht ausgenommen, erklären sehr

---

13 Kirchliche Zustände. S. 68.
14 Band. 3. S. 237. (4. Auflage).
15 Veronius beginnt seine Schrift mit dem Satze: Illud omne et solum est de fide catholica, quod est revelatum in Verbo Dei, et propositum omnibus ab Ecclesia catholica fide divina credendum. – Und erklärt ihn also: Complectitur haec regula Verbum Dei: nam fides ex auditu, auditus autem per verbum Christi. Complectitur et Ecclesiam docentem, in Concilio universali expresse aliquid

bestimmt, auch das sei als von der Kirche vorgelegte Glaubenslehre zu betrachten, was in ihr allgemein als geoffenbarte Wahrheit vorgetragen und geglaubt wird. Und fanden wir nicht schon beim h. Vincenz diese selbe Lehre? Welches war die erste Regel, die er vorschrieb? Wir sollen an dem festhalten, was in allen Sprengeln rings auf dem Erdkreis gelehrt und bekannt wird, und erst, wann die Uebereinstimmung in der Gegenwart zu fehlen scheint, werden wir angewiesen zu untersuchen, ob sich die Kirche in der Vergangenheit über den fraglichen Punkt ausgesprochen habe. Ebenso mußten aber auch die übrigen Väter denken. Sie weisen stets auf die in der Kirche allgemeine Lehre, als auf die sicherste Glaubensnorm hin. Wenn sie nun aber der Meinung gewesen wären, was allgemeine Lehre der Kirche sei, lasse sich nur aus den Entscheidungen der Kirche erkennen: wie hätten sie dann so manche Neuerer, als den *Marcion*, den *Arius,* den *Nestorius* ausdrücklich und öffentlich der Ketzerei beschuldigen, wie hätten auch die Hirten einzelner Sprengel sie aus demselben Grunde mit dem Bannfluche belegen können, ehe die Kirche über jene Irrlehrer irgend eine Entscheidung erlassen hatte? Und doch sind das Thatsachen, die um so weniger eines Beweises bedürfen, als sie im Laufe der folgenden Jahrhunderte sich oft wiederholt haben.

Wohl begegnet man, sowohl in den Schriften der hh. Väter, als der späteren Theologen Aeußerungen, die jenen, welche wir bekämpfen, ähnlich lauten: man müsse, bevor man Andersdenkende der Ketzerei bezüchtige, das Urtheil der Kirche abwarten. Aber sie reden dann von Fragen, über welche auch unter den treuen und erleuchteten Kindern der Kirche Streit obwaltete; nie aber haben sie den allgemeinen Satz aufgestellt, „jeder dürfe in allen Stücken, über welche die Kirche nicht entschieden habe, der Ansicht folgen, die ihm nun eben die richtigste zu sein scheine."

Es könnte ferner auf das, was so eben von den Irrlehrern der ersten Jahrhunderte gesagt wurde, entgegnet werden, daß man nichtsdestoweniger ihretwegen die Entscheidungen der Concilien noch für nöthig gehalten habe. Aber um nichts davon zu sagen, daß jene Zusammenkünfte der Hirten der Kirche oft nicht sowohl die Ermittelung, als die feierliche Verkündigung der Glaubenslehre, wie auch manches andere Gute zum Zwecke hatten; so konnte die Lehre der Neuerer der Hauptsache nach mit Sicherheit als irrig erkannt werden, und doch zur Feststellung mancher einzelnen Punkte die Berathung der Väter erwünschlich sein. Ja, es kann etwas in der Kirche als geoffenbarte Wahrheit allgemein gelehrt und geglaubt, und deßhalb der ihr entgegenstehende Irrthum

---

definientem aut enuntiantem vel ex sensu omnium tum Pastorum tum fidelium velut practice eloquentem . . Ebenso Chrismann Reg. fidei. §. 5.

mit Zuversicht als Ketzerei verworfen, und dennoch über eben diesen Gegenstand eine kirchliche Entscheidung nothwendig werden. Wenn es nämlich den
Neuerern gelingt, einen Anhang zu gewinnen, und wohl gar einzelne Vorsteher
der Kirche oder andere Männer von großem Ansehen zu verführen; so wird es,
besonders für die Menge der Gläubigen, leicht zweifelhaft, auf welcher Seite die
Wahrheit sei. Und im Grunde ist ja dies die wahre Geschichte fast aller Ketzereien. Wir läugnen also nicht, daß, um die Glaubenslehre mit Gewißheit zu
erkennen, die ausdrückliche Entscheidung der Kirche in manchen Fragen und
in manchen Zeiten nöthig ist; wir läugnen nur, das sie es in allen Fragen und
immer sei.

59. Um aber dies nun nicht bloß durch das Ansehen des Alterthums zu bekräftigen, sondern auch aus dem Prinzip des Katholicismus zu beweisen; so gehört
diesem zufolge alles zum katholischen Glauben, wovon wir durch das Ansehen
der Kirche gewiß sind, daß es geoffenbart ist. Es fragt sich also, ob wir nur
durch ausdrückliche Entscheidungen der Kirche zu dieser Gewißheit gelangen
können. – Die Kirche hat, anfangs durch jenes ihr beständiges und ordentliches
Lehramt, in der Folge auch durch ausdrückliche Concilienbeschlüsse die h.
Schrift, wie wir sie jetzt haben, für das ächte und unverfälschte Wort Gottes
erklärt. Sie hat uns also auch den ganzen Inhalt derselben als Offenbarung
Gottes zu glauben vorgelegt. Sobald wir demnach nicht zweifeln können, daß
etwas in der Schrift enthalten ist; so sind wir auch gewiß, daß dies von der
Kirche als geoffenbarte Wahrheit gelehrt wird[16]. Wie groß nun auch die Dun-
kelheit sehr vieler Stellen der h. Schrift sein mag; so ist doch hinwiederum ihr
Sinn auch oft so klar, daß er keinen Zweifel zuläßt. –

Sollte man dennoch fürchten, daß hiermit der eigenmächtigen Deutung des
göttlichen Wortes zu viel eingeräumt werde, und daran erinnern, daß der
wahre Sinn der heiligen Bücher, auch wo er dem unbefangenen Gemüthe
vollkommen klar zu sein scheint, durch gewaltsame und grübelnde Deutelei oft
verdunkelt worden ist; so können wir dagegen behaupten, daß man nichtsdestoweniger von jeher die meisten Thatsachen der h. Geschichte und gar viele
Lehren über Gott, Tugend und Laster, ohne eine ausdrückliche Entscheidung
der Kirche abzuwarten, auf die Worte der Schrift gestützt, als Glaubenswahrheiten vorgetragen hat. Und tragen wir etwa Bedenken, eben diese Thatsachen
und Lehren, trotz der Deutungen, die man sich in unserm Zeitalter erlaubt hat,
als geoffenbarte Wahrheiten festzuhalten? – Es würde hiedurch keinesweges

---

16 Ecclesia clare et manifeste proponet credendam Scripturam et omnia et singula in ea contenta:
si ergo manifeste constat, aliquid in Scriptura contineri, aeque manifeste constare debet, id ab
Ecclesia nobis credendum proponi. Lugo. De fide. Disp. 20. sect. 2. n. 58.

jene eigenmächtige Auslegung des göttlichen Wortes, die unsere Kirche verwirft, geübt, auch wenn man sich dabei nur auf den natürlichen Sinn des h.
Textes beriefe. Denn wenn gewisse Worte und Ausdrucksweisen nicht mehr
durch sich selbst hinreichend klar sein sollen: so gibt es am Ende gar kein Mittel
mehr, sich durch die Sprache zu verständigen; und es würden dann auch
wieder die Entscheidungen der Kirche selbst, ehe man sie für Glaubenssätze
ausgeben dürfte, durch authentische Erklärungen der Kirche erläutert werden
müssen, und so des Zweifels kein Ende sein. Aber wir können überdies behaupten, daß sich der Katholik, auch bei Erklärung dieser einzelnen Stellen, auf
das Ansehen seiner Kirche, nämlich auf ihre auch ohne ausdrückliche Entscheidung hinlänglich bekannte Lehre stützt. Oder bedarf es etwa vieler Nachforschung, um mit voller Gewißheit behaupten zu können, daß z.B. das Opfer
Abraham's, die Verschlingung Jonas vom Wallfisch und ähnliches, als historische Thatsache, und nicht als allegorische Dichtung; daß die Wunder Jesu und
der Apostel als wahre Wunder immer von der ganzen Kirche betrachtet und
verkündigt worden sind? und dürfen wir etwa anstehen die entgegengesetzten
Deutungen nicht nur für unvernünftig, sondern auch für häretisch zu erklären?
Ebenso bedarf es gewiß keines Beweises, daß die ganze Kirche von jeher in der
Schrift gelesen hat, es müsse in der menschlichen Gesellschaft das Eigenthum
und die Ehe heilig gehalten werden; und daß folglich die Lehre des Sozialismus
ebensowohl der Offenbarung als der gesunden Vernunft widerstreitet. –

60. Aber auch für jene Stellen der göttlichen Bücher, deren Auslegung größeren
Schwierigkeiten unterworfen ist, verweist uns die Kirche selbst nicht gerade auf
ihre in förmlichen Beschlüssen niedergelegte Erklärung, sondern nur überhaupt auf „den Sinn, den unsere Mutter, die h. Kirche, festgehalten hat, und
festhält," und auf die einstimmige Auslegung der hh. Väter[17]. – Dies nun führt
uns auf die andere Quelle der Offenbarungslehre, die Tradition. Wir haben
dieselbe zwar vorzüglich, aber nicht ausschließlich in den Schriften der hh.
Väter zu suchen. Nicht bloß aus diesen, sondern auch aus den übrigen in der
Kirche geschätzten Schriftstellern, ferner aus den Denkmalen des christlichen
Alterthums, den Gräbern mit ihren Inschriften und symbolischen Verzierungen, den Kirchen mit ihren Altären und ihren Gemälden, vor allen aber aus der
Handlungsweise der Kirche, ihrem Verfahren in der Leitung der Gläubigen,
ihren Gebräuchen beim Gottesdienst, ihren liturgischen Büchern, und endlich
aus den öffentlichen Erlassen ihrer Hirten, besonders wenn dieselben in
Particular-Synoden versammelt waren, läßt sich ohne Zweifel erkennen, was

17 Trid. s. IV.

in der Kirche allgemein gelehrt und geglaubt werde. Nun aber fragen wir auch hier, ob man aus solchen Quellen nicht vor jeder ausdrücklichen Entscheidung der Päbste oder Concilien zur vollen Gewißheit gelangen könne, was die katholische Kirche, wie über viele andere Wahrheiten, so besonders über jene Punkte, die mit dem christlichen und kirchlichen Leben in nächster Beziehung stehen, lehre; z.B. über das Fegfeuer und die Fürbitte für die Verstorbenen, über die Anrufung und Verehrung der Heiligen, über sämmtliche Sakramente, über die geistliche Gewalt des Pabstes und der Bischöfe. Wenn nicht, nun so hat man auch, bevor die Concilien oder die Päbste über alle diese Punkte in späteren Jahrhunderten dogmatische Beschlüsse erließen, jene so tief und so mannigfaltig in das Leben eingreisenden Wahrheiten nicht mit voller Beruhigung glauben können. Und dieses ist es, was wir der Ansicht, die wir bestreiten, im Allgemeinen entgegensetzen.

Wenn nichts zum Glauben gehört, als was die Kirche durch ausdrückliche Entscheidung festgesetzt hat; so konnte man viele Jahrhunderte lang über die wichtigsten Geheimnisse und Sittenlehren der Religion keinen Glaubensact erwecken, und jeder „der Ansicht folgen, die ihm nun eben die richtigste zu sein schien." Wird man die Theorie von „dem sich allmälig entwickelnden Bewußtsein der Kirche" soweit ausdehnen? – Uebrigens scheinen jene, die derlei Grundsätze vertheidigen, nicht zu erwägen, daß sie durch dieselben das Recht in Glaubenssachen etwas mit Bestimmtheit zu behaupten, in eben dem Maaße beschränken, als sie das Recht zu läugnen oder zu zweifeln ausdehnen. Wird es Hirscher etwa auf sich nehmen, für alle Lehren, die er in seiner Moral und im Katechismus mit großer Zuversicht als geoffenbarte Wahrheiten vorträgt, Entscheidungen der Kirche vorzubringen?

61. Indessen möchte man doch wider das bisher Gesagte einwenden, auf solche Weise werde die Bestimmung des Glaubens auch in der katholischen Kirche von der Forschung eines jeden abhängig gemacht, und mithin das Prinzip des Protestantismus angenommen. Nämlich auch die Frage nach der Lehre der allgemeinen Kirche kann ihre Schwierigkeiten haben, und daher von dem einem so, von dem andern anders gelöst werden. Somit wäre denn zuletzt der ganze Unterschied dieser, daß der Protestant glaubt, was nach seiner subjektiven Ueberzeugung in der Bibel steht, und der Katholik, was nach seiner subjectiven Ueberzeugung die allgemeine Kirche lehrt. – Ein scheinbar sehr starker Einwurf: aber man bedenke, daß man demselben dadurch nicht ausweicht, daß man die Entscheidungen der Kirche für die einzige Richtschnur des Glaubens ausgiebt. Oder ist es in allen Fällen so leicht, die Aechtheit und den wahren und vollen Sinn dieser Entscheidung zu erkennen? und sind nicht auch hierüber viele und bedeutende Streitfragen entstanden? Nicht darin besteht also der

Unterschied des katholischen und protestantischen Princips, daß der Katholik eine Glaubensnorm habe, nach der er alle religiösen Fragen ohne Schwierigkeit entscheiden könne, sondern darin, daß er für alle – einen lebendigen Lehrer und Schiedsrichter anerkennt. Zwar unterwirft sich auch der Protestant dem Ansehen des göttlichen Wortes, aber um zu wissen, was das Wort Gottes rede, ist er in allen Fällen einzig auf seine eigene Ansicht hingewiesen. Um das, was andere in der Bibel finden, hat er sich nicht zu kümmern; die todte Schrift selbst aber steht ihm nicht Rede. Der Katholik fragt, was die Kirche als geoffenbarte Lehre verkünde, und diese Frage ist in sehr vielen Fällen, wie gesagt, eben so leicht zu beantworten, als jene, was die allgemeine Kirche ausdrücklich entschieden habe; kann sie aber nicht mit Bestimmtheit gelöst werden, so fragt er weiter nach jenen ausdrücklichen Entscheidungen; sind auch diese nicht vorhanden, oder waltet über ihre Aechtheit und ihren Inhalt Zweifel ob, so entscheidet er nicht mit Zuversicht, was Glaubenslehre sei, sondern erwartet dafür eine bestimmtere Erklärung seiner Kirche. Und aus diesem Grunde pflegt man zwischen materialer und formaler Einheit der Kirche zu unterscheiden.

62. Aber noch andere Einwürfe sind hier zu erwägen. „Es lasse sich, sagt man, nicht behaupten, daß außer dem erklärten Dogma noch anderes als *dogmatische* Wahrheit gelehrt und geglaubt werden müsse, *deßhalb* weil es gelehrt und geglaubt werde oder im kirchlichen Bewußtsein gegeben sei. Denn in unsern Zeiten und in der katholischen Kirche sei nicht dieses Bewußtsein die Quelle der dogmatischen Lehre, sondern die dogmatische Lehre vielmehr die Ursache und die Quelle des kirchlichen Bewußtseins. Nicht darum sei jetzt etwas Dogma, weil es allgemein geglaubt und gelehrt werde, sondern umgekehrt werde etwas allgemein geglaubt und gelehrt, weil es Dogma sei. Deßhalb also könne auch, ob etwas Dogma sei, nicht aus dem kirchlichen Bewußtsein, sondern nur durch die Aussprüche und Entscheidungen der kirchlichen Auctorität erkannt werden."[18]

In dem Grundsatz, von dem wir handeln, wird nicht bloß die allgemeine Lehre der Hirten der Kirche, sondern auch der allgemeine Glaube der katholischen Christenheit als untrügliches Kennzeichen dogmatischer Wahrheiten angegeben. Von diesem Glauben nun ist das, wovon der Einwurf anhebt, wahr und zwar ohne die Beschränkung wahr, die er beifügt. Nicht bloß jetzt und in unsern Zeiten, sondern immer und zu aller Zeit wurde etwas allgemein geglaubt, weil es Dogma war, und war nicht umgekehrt Dogma, weil es allgemein geglaubt wurde. Aber wird nun etwa auch mit Recht gefolgert, weil „dies

---

18 Frohschammer. Athenäum. Bd. 1. S. 308.

Verhältniß zwischen Dogma und Glaube stattfinde," könne aus dem allgemeinen Glauben nicht *erkannt werden*, ob etwas Dogma sei? – Auch das Holz brennt nicht, weil es raucht; sondern raucht, weil es brennt. Läßt sich aber deßhalb auch aus dem Rauche nicht erkennen, daß es brennt? Man verwechsele also den Grund der Erkenntniß nicht mit dem Grunde des Daseins, und bemerke, daß wir hier nicht untersuchen, wodurch etwas Dogma sei, sondern wodurch erkannt werde, ob etwas Dogma sei. Darum aber dürfen wir aus dem allgemeinen Glauben an eine Lehre schließen, daß dieselbe Dogma d. i. geoffenbarte und als solche überlieferte Wahrheit sei, weil die hörende Kirche ebenso wenig in ihrem Glauben, als die lehrende in ihrer Unterweisung von der Wahrheit abfallen kann.

Indessen ist es vozüglich diese Unterweisung, das Lehrwort der Kirche, worauf unser Grundsatz sich bezieht. Ist nun etwa auch diese nicht Ursache des Dogma's, so daß man mit Wahrheit sagt, nicht darum sei eine Lehre dogmatisch, weil sie in der Kirche allgemein vorgetragen werde, sondern darum werde sie allgemein vorgetragen, weil sie dogmatisch sei? Wir könnten hier wie oben antworten, daß sich nichtsdestoweniger immer aus der Allgemeinheit einer Lehre erkennen lasse, daß sie dogmatisch sei. Aber wenngleich durchaus nichts anders nothwendig ist, um den erhobenen Einwurf abzuweisen; so wird es doch zur Beleuchtung dieser ganzen Frage nicht unnütz sein, die Behauptung, daß eine Lehre nicht deßhalb dogmatisch sei, weil sie allgemein gelehrt werde, näher zu untersuchen. –

63. Auch wenn die Kirche was zu glauben sei, durch förmliche Entscheidungen feststellt, pflegt man zu sagen, daß sie nicht Dogmen mache, sondern was Dogma sei, erkläre: und demnach sagen wir hinwiederum, eine Lehre sei Dogma, weil und seitdem sie von der Kirche festgestellt worden. Um also zu sehen, wie beide Weisen zu reden gerechtfertigt werden, gehen wir auf den Begriff des Dogmas zurück.

Gegenstand des religiösen Glaubens überhaupt ist alles, was als von Gott geoffenbarte Wahrheit erkannt wird: Gegenstand des christlichen Glaubens aber kann nur das sein, was die Apostel auf Befehl Jesu Christi als von Gott geoffenbarte Wahrheit verkündigt haben. Damit nun, was an sich Gegenstand des christlichen Glaubens ist, es auch für uns sei, müssen wir es als eine so von den Aposteln verkündigte Wahrheit erkennen. Und welches Mittel ist uns dazu gegeben? Gott hat der Kirche nicht bloß für die ersten Zeiten Apostel und Evangelisten, sondern auch für alle Zeiten Hirten und Lehrer gegeben, damit sie, vom Geiste der Wahrheit geleitet, sein von den Aposteln gepredigtes Wort unverfälscht bewahren, getreu verkündigen, unfehlbar deuten. Insofern also die Kirche keine neuen Offenbarungen erhält, sondern nur die ihr von den Aposteln überlieferte Lehre bewahrt; sagt man mit Recht, daß sie keine Dogmen mache, sondern nur was Dogma, d. h. was in der von den Aposteln verkündigten, und ihr überlieferten Offenbarung enthalten ist, erkläre. Insofern wir aber oftmals ohne ihre ausdrückliche Erklärung nicht wissen können, ob eine Lehre zum Inhalt jener Offenbarung gehöre; sagen wir auch mit Wahrheit, daß diese Lehre (für uns) erst durch die Erklärung der Kirche zum Dogma wird.

Nun gilt aber dasselbe von der Allgemeinheit, womit eine Lehre in der Kirche vorgetragen wird. Diese Lehre würde nicht Dogma sein, und nicht allgemein vorgetragen werden, wenn sie nicht von den Aposteln verkündigt und als solche von den Vätern überliefert wäre; aber in manchen Fällen würden wir dies nicht erkennen, wofern es uns nicht jene Thatsache der Allgemeinheit verbürgte. Somit wird auch durch diese für uns Dogma, was es sonst zwar an sich, aber nicht für uns wäre. – Doch mehr noch. Alle Lehren, welche in der Kirche allgemein als Glaubenswahrheiten verkündigt werden, erhalten hiedurch, ganz abgesehen davon, ob wir auf anderem Wege sie als geoffenbarte und der Kirche überlieferte Lehren erkennen können oder nicht, die Eigenschaft dogmatischer Lehren. Wenn die Hirten der Kirche, sei es nun durch die Unterweisung, die sie selbst ertheilen, sei es durch jene, die in ihrem Namen und unter ihrer Aufsicht von der Geistlichkeit ertheilt wird, allgemein eine Lehre als Glaubenslehre verkündigen; so haben wir hierin ein thatsächliches Zeugniß der allgemeinen Kirche, daß diese Lehre in der ihr überlieferten Offenbarung, dem *depositum fidei*, enthalten ist, und es wäre reine Willkür dieses Zeugniß nur unter der Bedingung, daß es zugleich urkundlich von der Kirche formulirt sei, als vollgültig anerkennen wollen.

64. Aber der Einwurf läugnet auch nicht schlechthin sondern nur, daß in *unsern Zeiten* außer dem erklärten Dogma noch anderes deßhalb, weil es allgemein gelehrt werde, als dogmatische Wahrheit gelten könne. Freilich: indessen hat gerade in unsern Tagen und für unsere Tage der h. Stuhl mit allem Nachdruck eben dieses ausgesprochen. Und auf welchen Grund hin wollte man einen solchen Unterschied zwischen unsern und den früheren Zeiten behaupten? In der Natur der Sache liegt er gewiß nicht. Aus manchen leicht begreiflichen Ursachen kann es geschehen, daß eine oder die andere Wahrheit zu einer Zeit nicht allgemein vorgetragen, aber zu keiner Zeit kann es geschehen, daß allgemein als geoffenbarte Wahrheit gelehrt werde, was nicht geoffenbart ist. Denn der göttliche Stifter hat seiner Kirche verheißen, mit ihr zu sein bis an's Ende der Zeiten, und ihr den Geist der Wahrheit verliehen, damit er bei ihr bleibe ewiglich. – Doch vielleicht sucht man den Grund darin, daß es in den ersten Zeiten des Christenthums einerseits außer den kurzen Bekenntnissen keine oder nur sehr wenige Entscheidungen gab, anderseits es

aber fast dasselbe war, aus der allgemeinen Lehre der Gegenwart und aus jener des apostolischen Zeitalters, von dem man noch nicht weit getrennt war, zu schöpfen. Da dürften wir jedoch wohl fragen, zu welcher Zeit denn die Veränderung, welche man behauptet, eingetreten sei, ob erst mit dem Concil von Trient, ob schon im Mittelalter oder noch früher. Es ist wahr, daß in den ersten vier allgemeinen Concilien manche höchste wichtige Glaubenslehren festgestellt wurden. Aber wie viele Wahrheiten von hoher Bedeutung blieben eben deßhalb, weil sie allgemein gelehrt und geglaubt wurden, bis in die späteren Jahrhunderte ohne dieses Siegel eines förmlichen Urtheils der Kirche. Es genügt an die h. Eucharistie und die übrigen Sakramente, an die Vorherbestimmung, die Rechtfertigung, die Nothwendigkeit der guten Werke zu erinnern. Dieser Grund also, daß es noch an kirchlichen Entscheidungen gebrach, würde auch für spätere, und wie wir bald sehen werden, selbst für unsere gelten. – Was dann die Nähe des apostolischen Zeitalters angeht, so giebt dieselbe allerdings den Zeugnissen des Alterthums größeres Gewicht; aber schon jenes ganz besondere Ansehen, das nur die hh. Väter genießen, ist nicht darauf allein, sondern zugleich und viel mehr noch auf die Sendung gegründet, welche sie von Gott empfiengen, und welche die Kirche durch die Verehrung, die sie ihnen erweist, anerkennt. Reden wir nun erst von den Hirten der Kirche, den Päbsten und Bischöfen; so haben sie ein von der Zeit, in der sie leben, ganz unabhängiges Ansehen. Wohl müssen auch sie in der Schrift und Ueberlieferung forschen, um die geoffenbarte Wahrheit zu erkennen, und diese Forschung möchte, wenn wir nur den natürlichen Verlauf der Dinge betrachten, in späteren Zeiten größeren Schwierigkeiten unterliegen; (was wahrlich kein Grund ist, daß Gelehrte sich in der Bestimmung dessen, was geoffenbart sei, so leicht über das Alterthum erheben:) – aber der Geist Gottes, welcher den Nachfolgern der Apostel verliehen ist, und über die ganze Kirche wacht, bewirkt, daß von ihnen, wenn auch nicht immer alle und jede Wahrheit, doch nie ein Irrthum allgemein gelehrt werde. Und eben weil dies niemand läugnen kann, ohne die katholische Kirche selbst zu läugnen, muß man auch zugeben, daß eine Lehre, die zu welcher Zeit es immer sei, als eine geoffenbarte allgemein gelehrt wird, für uns bloß hiedurch und abgesehen von aller kirchlichen Entscheidung zum Dogma wird. –

65. Dem gemäß dürfen wir nun wiederholen, was wir im Anfange sagten: jene Verkündigung der Kirche *(propositio Ecclesiae)*, wodurch eine geoffenbarte Wahrheit für uns zum Dogma wird, kann in doppelter Weise stattfinden, durch die Erlassung förmlicher Entscheidungen und durch den gewöhnlichen Lehrvortrag: jedoch wie jene Erlasse nur dann dogmatische Geltung haben, wenn sie von der höchsten Lehrgewalt ausgehen, so auch dieser Lehrvortrag nur,

wenn in ihm Uebereinstimmung herrscht. – Sehr viele Wahrheiten erhalten für uns auf dem einen wie auf dem andern Wege Gewißheit; einige jedoch nur durch das ausdrückliche Urtheil, andere nur durch die übereinstimmende Lehre. Obgleich nämlich keine Wahrheit von der Kirche für dogmatisch erklärt werden kann, welche nicht in der Offenbarung enthalten ist; so folgt doch nicht, daß jedwede schon vor der Erklärung so ausdrücklich und bestimmt, als diese sie ausspricht, allgemein verkündigt und geglaubt wurde. Und darum weist man wider den Grundsatz, den wir vertheidigen, mit Unrecht auf die unbefleckte Empfängniß hin, als welche nämlich erst jetzt, da sie von der kirchlichen Auctorität für ein Dogma erklärt worden, als solches auch gelehrt werde. Denn durch jenen Grundsatz wird ja nicht behauptet, daß alle dogmatischen Wahrheiten, bevor die Kirche ihr Urtheil gesprochen, schon allgemein als solche gelehrt wurden; sondern daß jene Wahrheiten, welche also gelehrt werden, vor und abgesehen von dem richterlichen Ausspruch der Kirche, Dogmen sind. Wir haben aufmerksam gemacht, daß es deren ehemals sehr viele geben mußte. Seitdem nun im Laufe der Jahrhunderte die Kirche so oft und durch verschiedene Ursache veranlaßt worden ist, sich über ihre Lehre entscheidend auszusprechen: mögen freilich unter jenen Wahrheiten, welche man in dieser Frage, weil sie in wissenschaftlichen Werken behandelt werden, zunächst vor Augen hat, nicht viele sich finden, für welche man nicht eine Erklärung der Kirche anführen könnte; (wir werden nichtsdestoweniger später einige hervorheben): aber setzen wir den Fall, es gäbe keine mehr, so würde es doch schon deßhalb, weil es deren ehemals viele gab, für die Wissenschaft von Bedeutung sein, den Grund hievon nachzuweisen. –

66. Allein noch einen andern und sehr praktischen Werth hat diese Nachweisung. Eben dies nämlich ist gefehlt, wenn von dogmatischen Wahrheiten die Rede ist, nur an jene zu denken, welche Gegenstand wissenschaftlicher Forschung zu sein pflegen, alle übrigen aber und selbst die christliche Sittenlehre außer Acht zu lassen. Man braucht sich nur an diese zu erinnern, um sofort einzusehen, welch eine große Anzahl von Wahrheiten nicht bloß in der Moraltheologie, sondern auch im katechetischen und ascetischen Unterricht der ganzen Christenheit als unzweifelhafte Lehren der Offenbarung vorgetragen werden, für welche keine Entscheidung der Kirche aufzuweisen ist. Unsere Gegner insbesondere, welche nur die Beschlüsse allgemeiner Concilien als Entscheidungen der Kirche gelten lassen, müßten hievon überzeugt werden. Denn in diesen könnten sie gewiß kaum einige Grundwahrheiten der Moral nachweisen. Aber auch die Erlasse des h. Stuhls berühren bei weitem nicht alle Lehrpunkte derselben. Um nur ein oder das andere Beispiel anzuführen, so wüßte ich nicht, wo es jemals entschieden worden, daß die Feindesliebe Pflicht

des Christen, daß der Stolz Sünde, die Demuth Tugend ist; daß es zur Voll-
kommenheit gehört, Verfolgungen und Leiden jeder Art um Christi willen gern
zu erdulden. Ja selbst die einzelnen zehn Gebote Gottes, die Werke der leibli-
chen und geistlichen Barmherzigkeit finden sich in ihnen nur insofern, als bald
über dieses bald über jenes irgend ein spezieller Punkt festgestellt wird, und
werden somit vielmehr vorausgesetzt als entschieden. Warum dies, wenn nicht
weil es unnöthig war, was rings auf dem Erdkreis gelehrt und geglaubt, und von
den Sektirern nicht angegriffen wurde, förmlich zu entscheiden? Denn daß jene
Lehren der christlichen Moral geoffenbart sind, und es von hoher Wichtigkeit
ist, sie als geoffenbarte zu verkünden und zu bekennen, wird doch wohl niemand läugnen.

Nicht anders verhält es sich mit den Thatsachen der heiligen Geschichte,
auf welche wir schon oben hinwiesen. – Zwar sind nun wie diese Thatsachen,
so auch jene Sittenlehren meistens so klar und bestimmt in der h. Schrift
enthalten, daß sie schon deßhalb als Glaubenspunkte gelten müssen. Aber aus
diesem Grunde können sie doch nur insofern für von der Kirche entschiedene
Glaubenslehren gelten, als die Kirche entschieden hat, daß die ganze h. Schrift
Gottes Wort ist. Sodann bleibt immer wahr, daß wir sehr oft die hieher gehö-
renden Schriftstellen nur deßhalb mit voller Gewißheit ihrem natürlichen und
einfachen Sinne nach verstehen, weil wir aus dem gewöhnlichen immer fortdauernden Unterricht der Kirche erkennen, daß sie in dieser allgemein so
verstanden werden. Es giebt demnach ohne Zweifel auch jetzt noch eine Menge
Wahrheiten, welche ohne durch richterliche Aussprüche der Kirche festgestellt
zu sein, durch das ordentliche Lehramt derselben Dogmen sind.

67. Was wir eben von der h. Schrift, das haben wir oben von den Vätern der
Kirche gesagt. Wenn es außer Zweifel ist, daß dieselben mit Uebereinstimmung
eine Lehre als geoffenbarte Wahrheit vortragen; so gehört diese Lehre, auch
wenn die Kirche sich über dieselbe nicht förmlich ausgesprochen hat, zu den
dogmatischen d. h. von der Kirche uns als Glaubenssätze vorgelegten Wahrheiten.[19] Und dies aus doppelten Grunde, erstlich weil die Kirche, und zwar
schon die ältesten Concilien uns die Ueberlieferung der Väter als Norm unseres
Glaubens angeben; sodann weil, was die Väter einstimmig lehrten, zu ihrer Zeit
auch in der ganzen Kirche gelehrt und geglaubt wurde. Was immer aber, zu

---

19   Quod dictum est de re in Scriptura contenta, dicendum est cum proportione de re aliqua habita
     in Ecclesia per sufficientem traditionem. Nam sicut Ecclesia nobis proponit universam Scripturam
     et omnia in ea contenta tanquam objecta fidei, ita proponit nobis traditiones Ecclesiasticas
     tanquam sufficientes ad dogmata fidei credenda, ut constat ex Conc. Trid. Sess. 4. Lugo. De fide
     Disp. 20. sect. 2. n. 66.

welcher Zeit es sei, also gelehrt und geglaubt wurde, das ist Dogma. – Hier tritt uns nun aber von neuem Chrismann entgegen. Er bekennt sich zwar, wie wir oben bemerkten, mit allen Theologen zu dem Grundsatz, daß nicht nur was die Kirche für eine Glaubenslehre erklärt habe, sondern auch was in ihr allgemein als solche vorgetragen und geglaubt werde, zum Dogma gehört. Ferner nimmt er über das Ansehen der hh. Väter die Worte des h. Vincenz, die wir oben erwogen haben, als Grundsatz in seinen Text auf: „Was immer nicht von einem oder dem andern, sondern von allen wie mit einem Munde gelehrt wurde; das müssen auch wir ohne Wanken glauben." Aber was folgert er nun daraus? „Das übereinstimmende Zeugniß der Väter erzeuge die *höchste Gewißheit*: sei eine *moralisch gewisse Norm* des Glaubens, und daher sei jeder, der dasselbe erkenne, auch vor einer ausdrücklichen Entscheidung der Kirche, verpflichtet, das, was die Väter in solcher Weise lehren, als *moralisch gewiß* anzunehmen. Aber *Dogma* sei es darum dennoch nicht, und daher könne man die entgegengesetzte Lehre zwar verwegen *(temeraria)*, aber nicht häretisch nennen."[20]

Hätte Chrismann nichts anders gesagt, als daß es sehr bedenklich sei, eine Lehre bloß deßhalb, weil wir glauben für sie das einmüthige Zeugniß der Väter aufweisen zu können, für eine dogmatische Wahrheit, und somit die entgegengesetzte Meinung für häretisch zu erklären; so würden wir darin eine wohlbegründete Warnung sehen. Aber weßhalb? weil jenes Zeugniß, wofern es vorhanden ist, nicht genügt? Keineswegs, sondern weil es in dem Falle, von welchem wir reden, sehr schwer ist, mit hinreichender Gewißheit zu erkennen, daß es vorhanden ist. Es unterliegt keiner Schwierigkeit, für gar viele Wahrheiten und zwar gerade für die bedeutungsvollsten, das einmüthige Zeugniß der Väter darzuthun; aber diese sind dann auch wenn nicht in die Bekenntnisse und Beschlüsse, doch in die Lehre und das Leben der Kirche dermaßen übergegangen, daß sie zugleich aus andern theologischen Beweisquellen dargethan werden können.

Indeß Chrismann versteht die Sache ganz anders. Er redet in der Voraussetzung, daß die Uebereinstimmung der Väter außer Zweifel sei *(qui indubitan-*

---

20 Nach den Worten des. h. Vincenz von Lirin fährt er also fort: Consentiens itaque Patrum testimonium summam parit certitudinem: est regula fidei moraliter certa: eandemque auctoritatem sibi vindicat seu fidem illam asserant Scripturae seu traditioni inniti. Unde sequitur unumquemque fidelium, quamprimum indubitanter cognoverit, veritatem aliquam in materia fidei et morum ab omnibus Patribus tradi, consentire eamque tanquam moraliter certam amplecti debere, etiamsi nulla Ecclesiae definitio praecesserit. §. 81. 1°. Consentiens Patrum testimonium est regula fidei moraliter certa, cui proin absque nota temeritatis nemo unus contradicit. 2°. Se solo tamen spectatum istud testimonium seu ante definitionem Ecclesiae non facit dogma divinum ab omnibus fide supernaturali credendum. §. 82.

ter cognoverit), und behauptet, daß auch in diesem Falle die Lehre, welche sie bezeugen, zwar eine Art von Gewißheit, aber nicht jene der Glaubenswahrheiten habe. Da dürfen wir nun zuvörderst fragen, wie sich das mit dem Grundsatz vertrage, den er, wie gesagt, aus der Schrift des h. Vincenz entlehnt hat. Was die Väter übereinstimmend lehren, das sollen wir, heißt es in demselben, mit zweifellosem Glauben annehmen. Hätte etwa Chrismann bei diesem zweifellosem Glauben an eine feste Ueberzeugung, welche jedoch nicht jene des übernatürlichen Glaubens sei, gedacht, und nicht aus Versehen, sondern absichtlich statt *absque ulla dubitatione credendum est*, was wir beim h. Vincenz lesen, geschrieben *absque ulla dubitatione tenendum est*? Aber auch dann würde er immer noch nicht bloß mit dem Heiligen von Lirin, der offenbar von dem christlich religiösen Glauben redet, sondern auch mit sich selbst in Widerspruch sein. Oder läßt er nicht sofort die Worte folgen: „Das übereinstimmende Zeugniß der Väter erzeugt die höchste Gewißheit?" Wovon? Doch wohl davon, daß die Wahrheit, die sie als geoffenbarte lehren, wirklich geoffenbart ist. Wie soll denn also das Zeugniß, welches uns *hievon die höchste* Gewißheit giebt, nur eine *moralisch gewisse* Norm unsers Glaubens sein? So oft und aufmerksam ich auch diese ganze Stelle bei Chrismann gelesen habe, ich vermag in derselben nur Gedankenverwirrung und Mangel an Folgerichtigkeit zu finden.

68. Er führt jedoch für seine Behauptung, daß die Uebereinstimmung der Väter zwar eine moralische, aber keine dogmatische Gewißheit gewähre, in folgenden Paragraphen zwei Gründe an. Der erste ist, nicht den Vätern insbesondere, sondern der Kirche sei der göttliche Beistand verheißen; die Väter aber seien nicht die ganze Kirche[21]. – Wohl; aber hat er denn nicht mit Veronius an die Spitze seines Werkes den Grundsatz gestellt, daß die Kirche ebenso wohl in ihrem ordentlichen Lehramt als in ihren Entscheidungen vom Geiste Gottes geleitet und unfehlbar sei? Wenn also, was er an der Stelle, die wir hier betrachten, einräumt, das wahrhaft übereinstimmende Zeugniß der Väter uns volle Gewißheit giebt, daß zu ihrer Zeit eine Wahrheit als Dogma von der ganzen Kirche gelehrt und geglaubt wurde; so nöthigt uns dieses Zeugniß ebenso wohl, eine solche Wahrheit als Dogma anzuerkennen, als das Zeugniß der Geschichte, welches uns die Gewißheit giebt, daß eine allgemeine Kirchenversammlung diesen oder jenen Beschluß gefaßt habe. – Dazu kommt, daß die hh. Väter in ganz besonderer Weise von der Kirche selbst als die bewährtesten Zeugen der Ueberlieferung anerkannt sind. Wies doch Chrismann selbst, um dies zu zeigen, kurz vorher auf die Handlungsweise und Aussprüche mehrerer Conci-

---

21 Nullibi enim exstat revelatio, quae Patribus assistentiam divinam promittit, neque Patres soli constituunt ecclesiam, cui soli assistentia cognoscitur promissa. Ibid.

lien hin. Ja er führte dort sogar den Canon des Conciliums von Chalcedon an: *Si quis Patrum fidem innovet, anathema sit*; und jenen der fünfzehnten Synode von Toledo: *Quidquid contra S. S. Patres creditur, a recta fidei regula aberrare intelligitur*. Wie sollen wir nun damit seine Lehre vereinbaren, das übereinstimmende Zeugniß der Väter sei zwar eine moralisch gewisse Norm des Glaubens, aber reiche für sich allein nicht hin, um etwas mit Bestimmtheit für eine von Gott geoffenbarte Wahrheit zu erklären? Nämlich mit einem gewissen *Blau,* den er öfters anführt, behauptet er, jene allgemeine Erklärung der Kirche, daß wir den Vätern in dem, was sie übereinstimmend lehren, folgen müssen, genüge nicht; es werde überdies erfordert, daß die Kirche noch im Einzelnen bestimme, was die Väter einmüthig lehren: wie ja auch der Inhalt der h. Schrift, obgleich die Kirche ihre Göttlichkeit erklärt habe, erst Gegenstand des Glaubens werde, wenn die Kirche im Einzelnen, was dieselbe lehre, bestimme.[22]

Aber das heißt eine willkührliche Behauptung durch die andere begründen wollen. Oder worauf könnte man sich für dieselben berufen? Auf die Natur der Sache doch gewiß nicht. Wenn die Kirche uns ein Bekenntniß, daß sehr viele Bestimmungen enthält, wie z.B. das athanasianische übergiebt; läßt sich da wohl sagen, daß jene Bestimmungen erst dann als dogmatische Wahrheiten gelten können, wenn sie einzeln für solche durch Beschlüsse der Kirche, nach Weise der Canonen, erklärt werden? Und wenn die Kirche entscheidet, daß die Beschlüsse der Concilien Regel unsers Glaubens sein müssen, dürfen wir da wohl, um uns diesen Beschlüssen zu unterwerfen, fordern, daß uns wiederum von allen einzelnen eine Erklärung gegeben werde? Wie abgeschmackt diese Forderung wäre, leuchtet schon daraus ein, daß sie in's unendliche fortgesetzt werden müßte. Wann erwarten wir nichtsdestoweniger in Betreff solcher Beschlüsse und Bekenntnisse eine neue Erklärung der Kirche? Wann über ihre Aechtheit oder über Auslegung im Innern der Kirche Zweifel herrschen. – Nun eben dies ist es, was wir von der Schrift und von den Vätern sagen: wenn der Sinn des göttlichen Wortes nicht klar ist, und in der Kirche verschiedene Ansichten über denselben aufgestellt werden; wenn die Uebereinstimmung der Väter nicht einleuchtet und auch von Rechtgläubigen bestritten wird; dann ja haben wir eine Entscheidung der Kirche abzuwarten.

---

22 Nec sufficit generali lege et declaratione Ecclesiae nobis proponi, Patrum consensum esse sequendum; nam ut ea, in quibus Patrum deprehenditur consensio, sint etiam fidei catholicae dogmata, in specie determinari debent. Et sane hactenus Ecclesia semper, antequam ad dogmatis definitionem procederet, sensum Patrum inquisivit, et nonnisi tunc ad fidem habendam obligavit, postquam sua sententia eum esse authenticum fidei sensum declaravit; quem admodum Scripturae sensus, nisi sigillatim interpretatione Ecclesiae fuerit indicatus, fide divina non creditur, licet etiam generatim omnes Scripturae libri tanquam divini fuerint proposti. Ibid.

69. Hieraus erkennt man denn auch, mit welchem Unrecht Chrismann und Blau sich auf das Verfahren der Kirche berufen. Dieselbe untersuche, was die Väter einstimmig lehrten, und dann erst, wenn sie hierüber sich ausgesprochen, verpflichte sie die Gläubigen, jene Lehren anzunehmen. So nämlich verfuhr die Kirche, wann sie über streitige Lehrpunkte Beschlüsse faßte: aber folgt daraus, daß wir auch bezüglich jener Wahrheiten, über die nicht gestritten wird, ihre Beschlüsse abwarten müssen? Wenn das, so waren die Christen, als es noch wenige Entscheidungen der Kirche gab, ja so sind auch wir immer noch, wie oben gezeigt wurde, für unser Glauben und Leben übel berathen. – Gar viele möchten die Zahl der Glaubenslehren so sehr als möglich vermindern, damit sie nicht genöthigt seien, die entgegengesetzten Meinungen für häretisch zu erklären, und insofern diese Abneigung aus milder Gesinnung für Andersdenkende entspringt, ist sie ohne Zweifel sehr löblich. – Aber es ist doch dabei zu erwägen, daß eine Lehre, deren Gegentheil nicht häretisch genannt werden darf, auch nicht mit Zuversicht geglaubt werden kann, und daß die Grundsätze, welche man aufstellt, nicht bloß auf jene Wahrheiten, die man bei jener Rücksicht auf Andere im Auge hat, sondern eben weil es Grundsätze sind, auf Alle Anwendung finden, daß es sich nicht bloß darum handelt, welche Lehren wir im polemischen Vortrag wider die Gegner vertheidigen müssen, sondern auch welche wir im catechetischen, homiletischen, ascetischen Unterricht den Gläubigen als geoffenbarte Wahrheiten vortragen dürfen. Wer diese wahre Sachlage erwägt, muß einsehen, daß man durch die Ansichten, welche wir bestreiten, um wider die Irrgläubigen milde zu sein, die Rechtgläubigen um einen Schatz der heilsamsten Wahrheiten bringt, und statt jene zur Erkenntniß der Wahrheit zurückzuführen, vielmehr diese mit ihnen zum Indifferentismus verleitet. Sind ja in der That diese neuen Meinungen über die Glaubensnorm in jener Zeit entstanden und verbreitet worden, als die Gleichgültigkeit in Sachen des Glaubens auch unter den Katholiken überhand nahm, und das christliche Leben, das all seine Nahrung aus dem Glauben erhält, mehr und mehr verkümmerte.

III. Was die Theologen einstimmig für ein Dogma erklären, ist als solches zu betrachten.

70. Bezüglich der eben entwickelten Lehre möchte man entgegnen, es sei freilich wahr, daß alles, was die ganze Kirche als geoffenbarte Wahrheit glaube, zum eigentlichen Dogma gehöre; aber ohne eine ausdrückliche Entscheidung der Kirche könne man diesen ihren allgemeinen Glauben nicht mit Gewißheit erkennen. Obgleich aus dem oben Gesagten sich schon ergiebt, daß dies wenigstens nicht in der Ausdehnung, in welcher man es behauptet, wahr ist; so

wollen wir doch hier noch auf einen kurzen und sicheren Weg, auch in schwierigen Fällen zu bestimmen, ob etwas zum allgemeinen Glauben der Kirche gehöre, aufmerksam machen. Es ist dies aber kein anderer, als jener, auf welchem man auch ermittelt, ob eine Lehre von der Kirche ausdrücklich entschieden sei, oder nicht. Wenn nämlich die angesehensten Theologen über die Aechtheit und den Sinn einer Entscheidung immer übereingestimmt haben; so sieht man, und gewiß mit vollem Rechte, die Sache als ausgemacht an. Nun aber kann man mit derselben Zuversicht sagen, was die angesehensten Theologen einstimmig für eine unzweifelhafte Glaubenslehre erklären, das ist Lehre der allgemeinen Kirche, auch wenn es nicht durch feierlichen Ausspruch entschieden ist. Man wolle nicht sagen, daß auf solche Weise die Unfehlbarkeit der Kirche auf die Theologen übertragen werde. Denn wir reden nicht von dem Falle, wenn die Theologen, sei es auch in Glaubenssachen, eine Meinung, die sie für gegründet halten, vertheidigen; sondern von jenem Falle, wenn sie etwas ausdrücklich und mit Zuversicht als einen Glaubenssatz vortragen. Indem sie dies thuen, behaupten sie, daß der Satz, von dem die Rede ist, von der allgemeinen Kirche als geoffenbarte Wahrheit gelehrt und geglaubt werde. Sie treten also als Zeugen dieser Thatsache auf, und es muß ihr Zeugniß, wenn es so ausdrücklich und einstimmig ist, als unverwerflich gelten. Angesehene Theologen nennen wir, die zu großem Rufe gelangt sind, und deren Rechtgläubigkeit unbestritten ist. Diese Männer lebten in verschiedenen Jahrhunderten und in verschiedenen Theilen der Kirche; sie folgten in ihrer Wissenschaft, so weit es erlaubt war, verschiedenen Richtungen, und sind deßhalb in sehr vielen Fragen nicht derselben Ansicht. Ihre Uebereinstimmung also, wenn sie dies oder jenes für eine Lehre der allgemeinen Kirche erklären, läßt sich nur aus der Evidenz der Thatsache, die sie bezeugen, erklären. Mangel an Kenntniß, an Aufrichtigkeit oder Ernst in der Untersuchung dieser Thatsache, läßt sich höchstens bei einzelnen, und auch bei diesen, nur in wenigen Fällen, voraussetzen. –

Aber mehr noch. Was die angesehenen Theologen einstimmig als Glaubenslehre vortragen, das wird auch thatsächlich in der ganzen Kirche gelehrt. Denn wenn wir jenes in der Kirche fortdauernde Apostolat nicht bloß in der Abstraction, sondern in der Wirklichkeit betrachten; so ist es doch nichts anders, als die Unterweisung, welche von den Lehrern, den Theologen, den Predigern, den geistlichen Vätern, den Katecheten, kurz von allen Dienern der Kirche unter der Aufsicht der Bischöfe und der Oberaufsicht des Papstes den Gläubigen ertheilt wird. Nun ist es aber gewiß, daß alles, was die Theologen einstimmig für eine Lehre des Glaubens erklären, in diese ganze Unterweisung übergeht, und als solche fast von allen diesen Dienern der lehrenden Kirche wiederholt wird. Die Hirten können aus gewissen Rücksichten die öffentliche Rüge einer Abweichung vom kirchlichen Lehrbegriffe zuweilen unterlassen; aber können sie dies auch, wenn Jahrhunderte lang in fast allen Theilen der Kirche von vielen Tausenden ihrer Diener ein Irrthum verbreitet wird? Man muß also in solchem Falle ihr Stillschweigen als Gutheißung erklären. Wir sehen aber auch, daß die Hirten der Kirche, ohne Zweifel aus dem eben angegebenen Grunde, mit ganz besonderer Sorgfalt, die Lehre, welche Theologen, die zu einigem Rufe gelangt sind, in Büchern oder durch mündlichen Vortrag verbreiten, überwachen; und fast alle Entscheidungen der Kirche sind das Ergebniß dieser Wachsamkeit. – Endlich scheint es auch hinlänglich klar zu sein, daß die Hirten der Kirche den Grundsatz, von dem wir reden, selbst anerkennen. Denn nicht nur wurde derselbe bis auf unsere Tage gelehrt, und auf besagte Weise in Anwendung gebracht; sondern es wurde und wird auch nach ihm in den geistlichen Gerichten über die Unschuld oder Schuld derer, welche der Ketzerei angeklagt werden, entschieden. Wer bestreitet, was sämmtliche Theologen als eine Glaubenslehre vortragen, wird für schuldig erklärt. Wie könnten nun Päbste und Bischöfe ein solches Verfahren dulden, wenn nicht auch sie in jener einmüthigen Lehre der Theologen eine sichere Regel, die Lehre der Kirche zu ermitteln, anerkännten?

71. Nichtsdestoweniger hat man dies in unsern Tagen und zwar mit Entrüstung angegriffen. Die Behauptung, welche wir aufgestellt, sei entweder bedeutungslos oder in hohem Grade anmaßend. Was die Theologen für Dogma erklären, solle darum als solches gelten, weil sie als Zeugen auftreten von dem, was allgemein als Dogma gelehrt und geglaubt werde. Wenn nun dem so sei, so bedürften wir dieses Zeugnisses nicht. Denn was allgemein von den Dienern der Kirche als Glaubenslehre vorgetragen werde, das könne uns ja auch jeder dieser Diener sagen. Und wenn er es nicht könnte, so wäre damit das Zeugniß der Theologen als falsch erwiesen. – Ferner soll aus unserer Behauptung folgen, daß man, um zu entscheiden, ob etwas Dogma sei oder nicht, gar nicht in die Vergangenheit zurückzugehen, sondern immer nur das dogmatische Bewußtsein der Kirche in der Gegenwart zu befragen brauche. Nun sei es aber unläugbar, daß die Kirche selbst, und zwar nicht bloß in Gerichten über einzelne Personen oder Bücher, sondern sogar auf den allgemeinen Concilien nicht unmittelbar aus ihrem Bewußtsein schöpfe, sondern vor der Entscheidung historische Forschungen und sonstige wissenschaftliche Erörterungen für nöthig erachte. Um wie viel mehr, schließt man, müssen demnach die Theologen also verfahren. Sie können nicht als unmittelbare Zeugen des dogmatischen Glaubens auftreten, sondern müssen ihre Aussage begründen. Eine Aussage aber, welche nur durch Begründung Gewicht habe, dürfe immer wieder der

Prüfung unterworfen werden, und ihr Inhalt niemals als Dogma, dem zu widersprechen Häresie sei, gelten. Werde nun dies dennoch behauptet, so sei das gräuliche Anmaßung.

Endlich aber will man noch dem Satze, den wir vertheidigen, seine ganze Unterlage nehmen. Jenes kirchliche Glaubensbewußtsein, aus dem die Theologen schöpfen sollen, sei in der Wirklichkeit gar nicht vorhanden. Um sich davon zu überzeugen, brauche man nur die einzelnen Theologen oder andere, welche das kirchliche Lehramt üben, ja selbst auch die einzelnen Bischöfe zu befragen; man werde finden, daß sie keinesweges mit Bestimmtheit anzugeben im Stande seien, was außer dem erklärten Dogma noch zur Glaubenslehre gehöre. Wenn also die Theologen über ein solches Bewußtsein Zeugniß geben wollten, so gäben sie Zeugniß von etwas, das gar nicht existire. Aber wenn man die Sache näher betrachte, so handele es sich in der übereinstimmenden Lehre der Theologen, wovon die Rede ist, nicht um Glaubenspunkte, die im allgemeinen Bewußtsein gegeben seien, sondern um nähere Bestimmung und Deutung der ausdrücklichen Dogmen, und es seien am Ende doch diese, welche sie eigentlich im Auge hätten. Und das würde bald zur Klarheit kommen, wenn man nur einmal Beispiele geben wollte, auf welche diese unsere Lehre Anwendung fände[23].

72. Um die Antwort von diesen letzten Einwürfen zu beginnen, so haben wir von keinem allgemeinen Glaubensbewußtsein, aus dem die Theologen oder gar die Hirten der Kirche schöpfeten, geredet. Vielmehr haben wir absichtlich eine Ausdrucksweise vermieden, welche die irrige Ansicht begünstigt, daß die lehrende Kirche nur ausspreche, was in dem Bewußtsein der hörenden enthalten sei. Wir also redeten von der *allgemeinen Lehre* der Kirche, und wenn wir neben ihr des *allgemeinen Glaubens* erwähnten, so haben wir schon bemerkt, daß sich die Theologen auf diesen insofern berufen, als aus ihm die Lehre der Kirche, wie aus der Wirkung die Ursache erkannt wird. Die hier zu stellende Frage ist demnach diese, ob es eine allgemeine Lehre der Kirche gebe, in welcher mehr als in ihren förmlichen Entscheidungen enthalten sei. Und um dies zu entscheiden, genügt es wirklich, diejenigen, welche das kirchliche Lehramt verwalten, einzeln zu befragen. Aber welche Fragen muß man zu dem Ende stellen? Nicht diese, ob etwas und was alles außer den förmlich erklärten Dogmen noch zum Glauben gehöre. Denn wir behaupten ja nicht, daß alle, welche in der Kirche lehren, die bewußte Ueberzeugung haben, daß es solche nicht förmlich erklärte Glaubenspunkte gebe; vielmehr wissen wir sehr wohl,

23 Athenäum Bd. 1. S. 306–311.

wie weit in unsern Tagen die entgegengesetzte Meinung, – freilich ohne daß man sich über dieselbe Rechenschaft gebe – verbreitet ist: noch weniger aber behaupten wir, daß alle im Stande seien, uns jene Lehren aufzuzählen. Um nichtsdestoweniger einen Prediger oder Theologen, der jener Meinung anhienge, zu überführen, daß er in einem Vorurtheile befangen sei, lege man ihm Punkte, welche von der Kirche bis jetzt nicht ausdrücklich entschieden sind, vor, und frage, ob er und seine Amtsgenossen dieselben als Lehren der christlichen Religion vortragen, und ob sie den, welcher sie läugnete, noch für einen rechtgläubigen Christen halten würden. Man frage ihn, ob er lehre, daß Gott seinem Wesen nach unendlich, daß er allgütig, allwissend ist, daß er auch die freien Handlungen der Menschen vorhersieht; daß er die Welt mit Freiheit erschaffen hat und regiert, daß die Geschöpfe durch ihn nicht nur das Dasein empfangen haben, sondern auch in demselben erhalten werden, daß seine Vorsehung sich über alles erstreckt. Man frage ihn ferner, ob er lehre, daß die gefallenen Engel alle verdammt sind, daß die Abgeschiedenen zwar im Fegfeuer ihre Sünden büßen, an Tugend und Verdienst jedoch nicht mehr wachsen können. Und um ihn mehr und mehr zu überzeugen, führe man ihn auf das Gebiet der Sittenlehre und erinnere ihn an jene Glaubenspunkte, deren wir oben erwähnten, ihn z.B. fragend, ob er Bedenken trage, alle acht Seligpreisungen als Lehren des Herrn zu wiederholen oder etwa aus ihnen jene zwei oder drei wähle, die sich – wenigstens einigermaßen – in kirchlichen Entscheidungen wiederfinden. Ebenso darf man ihn aufmerksam machen, daß er die Flucht nach Aegypten mit derselben Zuversicht wie die Geburt und die Kreuzigung Christi vortrage, daß er nicht bloß die Gottheit des h. Geistes, sondern auch seine wunderbare Sendung am Pfingsttage, und nicht bloß diese Sendung, sondern auch die vorhergegangene Verheißung derselben als geoffenbarte Wahrheiten verkündige. – Und wo würden wir ein Ende finden, wenn wir hier fortfahren wollten?

73. Es ist demnach unläugbar, daß die Kirche durch ihr ordentliches Lehramt eine Menge Wahrheiten als geoffenbarte verkündigt, über welche sie in keinen Beschlüssen sich ausgesprochen hat; und somit läßt sich gewiß nicht sagen, daß die Theologen, wenn sie diese allgemeine Lehre bezeugen, etwas das gar nicht vorhanden ist, bezeugen. – Aber, sagt man, um Wahrheiten, wie sie eben angeführt wurden, handelt es sich nicht: diese pflegen ja die Theologen wenig oder gar nicht zu besprechen, und folglich in Betreff ihrer kein Zeugniß von der allgemeinen Lehre abzulegen. Das ist, entgegnen wir, von vielen der zuletzt erwähnten Lehren und Thatsachen wahr. Aber was folgt daraus, wenn nicht, daß durch das ordentliche Lehramt der Kirche eine große Anzahl von Glaubenswahrheiten ohne förmliche Entscheidung so gewiß und so bekannt sind,

daß es nicht nöthig ist, sie in der Theologie zum Gegenstand besonderer Untersuchungen zu machen. Denn man wird doch nicht läugnen, daß jene sittlichen Wahrheiten und Thatsachen der h. Geschichte im vollsten Sinne des Wortes Gegenstand des christlichen Glaubens sind, und mit Recht als solche in der Unterweisung des christlichen Volkes vorgetragen werden. Immer also bleibt es wahr, daß es eine allgemeine Lehre der Kirche giebt, die sich viel weiter als ihre Entscheidungen ausdehnt.

Aber wenn von vielen der Wahrheiten, welche wir erwähnten, wahr ist, daß sie in der Theologie einzeln nicht behandelt zu werden pflegen; so ist dies darum nicht von allen und namentlich nicht von jenen wahr, auf die wir zuerst hinwiesen. Sie werden alle von den Theologen insbesondere untersucht, alle einstimmig für Glaubenspunkte erklärt, keine aber ist von der Kirche als solche ausdrücklich festgestellt, obschon man sich für eine oder andere einigermaßen auf gewisse Entscheidungen berufen kann. – Und haben wir nicht auch in unsern Tagen noch einige derselben als dogmatische Wahrheiten wider neue Gegner vertheidigen müssen? Man bemerke nun auch, daß es sich weder in diesen noch auch in den übrigen Punkten, deren wir gedachten, um nähere Bestimmung oder Deutung der ausdrücklich erklärten Glaubenslehren handelt. Ueber das Wissen Gottes, über seine Freiheit zu erschaffen, giebt es kein erklärtes Dogma, ebensowenig über seine allwaltende Vorsehung.

74. Indeß wurde etwa in den vorhergehenden Einwürfen mit Recht gesagt, daß wir, wenn es eine solche wahrhaft allgemeine Lehre gebe, um sie zu erkennen, nicht erst des einmüthigen Zeugnisses der Theologen bedürfen? Antworten wir durch ein Beispiel, das unserm Gegner nicht unwillkommen sein möchte. Der h. Hieronymus sagte dem Rufinus, er dürfe sich nicht wundern, daß seine Zweifel über den Ursprung der menschlichen Seele unter den Gläubigen Aergerniß errege[24]. Daraus geht hervor, daß in den Kirchen, mit welchen der h. Hieronymus in näherer Verbindung war, d. i. in jenen des Morgenlandes die Ueberzeugung herrschte, es sei geoffenbarte Lehre, daß die einzelnen Seelen der Menschen von Gott erschaffen werden. Nun erfuhr aber der h. Hieronymus, und zwar vorzüglich durch die Briefe des h. Augustin, daß im Abendlande sich vielmehr die Ansicht verbreitete, es lasse sich diese Frage aus der Offenbarung nicht mit Gewißheit lösen. Er änderte zwar deßhalb, so viel wir wissen, seine Ueberzeugung nicht, ließ aber von nun an die Sache auf sich beruhen. So dürfte es also wohl, um zu erfahren, was in der Kirche allgemein gelehrt werde, auch uns nicht genügen, den ersten besten Katecheten oder Prediger zu fragen; wie

---

24 Miraris, si contra te fratrum scandala concitentur, cum id nescire te jures, quod Christi Ecclesiae se nosse fatentur. Adv. Ruf. III.

es uns auch nicht in den Sinn kommen kann, die Allgemeinheit einer Lehre, welche die Theologen einmüthig bezeugen, deßhalb zu bezweifeln, weil wir in unserer Nähe einen unwissenden Katecheten finden.

Aber folgt nun daraus, wie behauptet wurde, daß man, um das Dogma zu erkennen, nicht mehr in die Vergangenheit zurückzugehen brauche? Vorerst müssen wir bemerken, daß die Kirche, um über eine Lehre zu entscheiden, jenes Zurückgehen keinesweges immer für nöthig erachtet hat. Oder lehrt die Geschichte der Concilien nicht, daß gar oft die Väter ohne geschichtliche Forschung und ohne wissenschaftliche Erörterung nach dem Bewußtsein ihres und des allgemeinen Glaubens über gewisse Irrthümer sofort das Urtheil sprachen? Haben aber wir etwa behauptet, daß die Theologen, wenn sie eine Lehre, über welche die Kirche sich nicht ausdrücklich ausgesprochen hat, als dogmatische Wahrheit vortragen, stets aus diesem unmittelbaren Bewußtsein schöpfen und von ihm Zeugniß ablegen? Hier kommen wir zu dem größten Mißverständniß. Als die Thatsache, welche die Theologen bezeugen, haben wir, wie gesagt, vorzüglich die allgemeine Lehre, dann auch den allgemeinen Glauben der Kirche angegeben. Wenn wir nun an dieser Stelle keine nähere Bestimmungen hinzufügen, so hatten wir es doch in dem unmittelbar vorhergehenden Abschnitt gethan. Die Kirche sagten wir, übe ihr ordentliches Lehramt, indem sie uns die von ihr für canonische anerkannten Bücher als Gottes Wort übergebe; was immer also in diesen klar ausgesprochen und von den katholischen Auslegern in derselben Weise erklärt werde, das gehöre zur allgemeinen Lehre der Kirche. Ferner weise uns die Kirche auf die in ihr fortdauernde Ueberlieferung, besonders auf jene der hh. Väter hin. Auch das also, was als Glaubenswahrheit von den Vätern mit Uebereinstimmung vorgetragen werde, sei in der allgemeinen Lehre der Kirche enthalten. Der Glaube der Kirche aber, bemerkten wir, werde vorzüglich aus ihrem Leben, ihren Gesetzen, Einrichtungen, Gebräuchen erkannt. Sehen wir nun, wie die Theologen von dieser Thatsache der allgemeinen Lehre in verschiedener Weise Zeugniß ablegen können.

75. Daß Gott unendlich, d. h. nicht bloß über Zeit und Raum erhaben, sondern seinem Sein und Wesen nach unbeschränkt sei, ist keines der ausdrücklich festgestellten Dogmen. Wenn nun die Theologen dies dennoch für eine Glaubenswahrheit erklären, so dürfen sie sich dafür unmittelbar auf das Bewußtsein der ganzen Kirche berufen. Oder kann es einen Augenblick zweifelhaft sein, daß die ganze Christenheit Gott als das absolut vollkommene und höchste Wesen bekennt und anbetet, und die auf seine Größe bezüglichen Schriftstellen in diesem Sinne versteht? – Auch die Freiheit des göttlichen Willens ist in keinem dogmatischen Beschlusse mit Bestimmtheit ausgesprochen. Nun läßt

sich dieselbe zwar aus den göttlichen Schriften mit aller Gewißheit darthun: nichtsdestoweniger würde man sie ohne eine Erklärung der Kirche wohl nicht mit so großer Entschiedenheit den Dogmen beizählen, wenn die Uebereinstimmung der Väter und aller späteren Ausleger nicht jeden Zweifel über die Weise, wie die Schrift zu verstehen sei, unmöglich machte. – Der h. Augustin erklärte die Erbsünde, ehe über dieselbe Concilien gesprochen, mit aller Zuversicht für eine Glaubenswahrheit: er bewies sie aus der Bibel, aber er berief sich zugleich mit allem Nachdruck auf die Ueberzeugung sämmtlicher Gläubigen. Denn weßhalb, sagt er[25], rings in der Kirche jene ängstliche Eile, den Unmündigen, wenn sie in Lebensgefahr kommen, das Sakrament der Wiedergeburt zu ertheilen? Wie er nun aus dieser Thatsache den allgemeinen Glauben nachwies, so zeigte er auch noch die allgemeine Lehre aus den Schriften der einzelnen Väter[26]. Weil jedoch diese fast alle seine Zeitgenossen oder doch von seinem Zeitalter durch wenige Jahrzehnte getrennt waren, so kann man immer sagen, daß er wie den Glauben so die Lehre der ganzen Kirche in der Gegenwart nachwies. – In andern Fällen muß man, um diese Thatsache zu erkennen, in die Vergangenheit zurückgehen. Keines der Wunder und keine der Weissagungen, die nach den Zeiten der Apostel stattgefunden haben, ist Gegenstand des Glaubens; aber daß Gott nicht bloß zur Zeit der Apostel, sondern auch später die Gaben der Wunder und Weissagungen verliehen habe und verleihe, ist durch den allgemeinen Glauben und die allgemeine Lehre der Kirche gewiß. Um jedoch diesen Glauben aus dem Leben der Kirche zu erkennen, möchte, was wir in der Gegenwart beobachten, nicht hinreichen. Denn jene Handlungen, wodurch dieser Glaube sich kund giebt, sind nicht so häufig, wie z.B. die Taufe der Unmündigen, auf welche Augustin sich berief. Um ihn also außer Zweifel zu stellen, weisen wir zugleich auf die Vergangenheit zurück, hervorhebend, daß die Concilien, die Päbste, die Bischöfe, die Gläubigen durch ihr Verfahren jenen Glauben unverkennbar an den Tag legten. Ebenso könnten wir auch in Betreff dieses Punktes die Allgemeinheit der Lehre in der Gegenwart nicht nachweisen. Denn manche Theologen reden gar nicht von demselben, andere mögen ihn wohl auch in Zweifel stellen. Aber, wie oben bemerkt wurde, damit etwas Lehre der allgemeinen Kirche sei, ist durchaus nicht nothwendig, daß es zu allen Zeiten allgemein gelehrt wurde. Es genügt, daß wir dies von irgend einer Zeit außer Zweifel stellen. So genügt es also auch in unserm Falle, daß die hh. Väter nicht bloß ihren Glauben an Wunder, die zu ihrer Zeit gewirkt wurden, an den Tag legen, sondern auch mit vollster Ue-

---

25   Epist. ad S. Hier. 166. (al. 28) n. 21.
26   Cont. Julian. l. 1.

bereinstimmung die Verheißung des Herrn, daß er den Seinigen diese Gabe verleihen werde, von allen Zeiten verstehen. – Man sieht also, daß die Thatsache der allgemeinen Lehre und des allgemeinen Glaubens in verschiedener Weise erkannt wird, und die Theologen, wenn sie dieselbe behaupten, keinesweges immer unmittelbar aus dem Glaubensbewußtsein der Gegenwart schöpfen.

76. Aber tritt nun eben dadurch nicht auch zu Tage, daß sie, um die Allgemeinheit der Lehre oder des Glaubens bezeugen zu können, in vielen Fällen Nachforschungen anstellen müssen? Wie kann man also ihr Zeugniß für ganz zuverlässig erklären, ohne auf sie die Unfehlbarkeit, welche nur der lehrenden Kirche verheißen ist, zu übertragen?

Wohl bedarf es, antworten wir, einer ernsten Untersuchung und das haben wir ja auch oben schon anerkannt. Weßhalb aber glaubten wir dennoch behaupten zu dürfen, daß die Uebereinstimmung der Theologen volle Gewißheit gewähre? Weil der Mangel dessen, was zu einer solchen Untersuchung erfordert wird, höchstens bei einzelnen in einzelnen Fällen angenommen, und deßhalb die fortdauernde Uebereinstimmung so vieler nur aus der Evidenz der Thatsache erklärt werden kann, besonders da eben diese Männer in so vielen andern Fragen sich widersprechen, und in ihrer Wissenschaft verschiedenen Richtungen folgen. Wir stellen gewiß nicht in Abrede, daß die sichere Erkenntniß jener Thatsache, der allgemeinen Lehre nämlich und des allgemeinen Glaubens der Kirche, auch für Männer vom Fache großen Schwierigkeiten unterliegen kann: aber in solchem Falle wird man auch, bevor die Kirche sich ausgesprochen hat, unter den Theologen jene Uebereinstimmung in der entschiedenen Behauptung, daß etwas Glaubenswahrheit sei, nicht finden. Denn möge immer der eine oder andere zu einer solchen Entschiedenheit mehr als billig ist, geneigt gewesen sein; im Ganzen war unter den Theologen von jeher der Grundsatz anerkannt und befolgt, daß man nichts für dogmatische Wahrheit ausgebe, was nicht mit voller Klarheit als Lehre der Kirche anerkannt werde.

Indessen was die Hauptsache ist, mit großem Unrecht betrachtet man hier immer nur, was nach dem gewöhnlichen Laufe der menschlichen Dinge zu erwarten sei, von der übernatürlichen Vorsehung, welche über die Kirche Christi waltet, absehend. Wurde denn vor uns nicht mit allem Nachdruck hervorgehoben, daß jene Lehren, welche die Theologen einmüthig für Glaubenswahrheiten erklären, auch als solche in der Kirche allgemein vorgetragen und gelehrt werden? Daß aber in der ganzen Kirche als geoffenbarte Lehre verkündigt werde, was nicht geoffenbart ist, streitet mit den Verheißungen ihres göttlichen Stifters. Und fügten wir nicht die Gründe bei, weßhalb man eben deßhalb für dieselben sich auch auf die Gutheißung der Hirten der Kirche berufen darf? Was alle Theologen und die ihnen folgenden Prediger oder Schriftsteller lehren, das lehren durch sie der Pabst und die Bischöfe. Es ist also nicht billig, wenn man unsere Beweisführung entkräften will, gerade dieses, wodurch sie unserer Absicht nach ihre Vollendung erhalten sollte, zu umgehen.

IV. Von der Eintheilung der Dogmen.

77. Man kann die Dogmen sowohl nach ihrem Inhalt, den Wahrheiten näm-lich, die sie ausdrücken, als auch nach dem, wodurch sie Dogmen sind, also nach ihren Ursachen eintheilen. Betrachten wir den Inhalt der Dogmen zu-nächst in sich selbst, so erhalten wir die bekannte, schon von den h. Vätern gebrauchte Eintheilung in *nothwendige* und *geschichtliche* Wahrheiten. Wäh-rend jene in der Natur Gottes und der Dinge ihren ewigen Grund haben, setzen diese das freie Wirken Gottes und der Geschöpfe in der Zeit voraus. – Zwar immer noch in sich selbst, aber doch auch mit Beziehung auf den Zweck, zu dem sie geoffenbart werden, betrachten wir die Glaubenslehren, wenn wir sie in *theoretische* und *praktische* eintheilen. Alle dienen dem einen Zwecke, uns zum ewigen Leben zu führen; jedoch einige dadurch, daß sie uns Wahrheiten deren Erkenntniß uns nothwendig oder heilsam ist, enthüllen, andere dadurch, daß sie uns über die Mittel und Wege, zu jenem unserm Ziele zu gelangen, belehren. Es kann nun ferner die Erkenntniß unbedingt nothwendig sein, so daß kein Mensch, der zum Gebrauch der Vernunft gelangt ist, ohne sie selig wird, und sie kann nur als Pflicht nothwendig sein, so daß, wer aus sträflicher Nachläßigkeit ihrer beraubt ist, vom ewigen Leben ausgeschlossen wird. Nach vieler Theologen Ansicht läßt sich jene unbedingte Nothwendigkeit nur von den beiden Grundwahrheiten, die man auch die Substanz des Glaubens nennt[27], behaupten. Sie werden vom Apostel mit den bekannten Worten ausgedrückt: „Wer zu Gott kommen will, muß glauben, daß er ist, und daß er denen, die ihn suchen, Vergelter ist." (Hebr. 11, 6.) Die Wahrheiten aber, deren Erkenntniß jedweder Christ sich zu erwerben streng verpflichtet ist, sind in jenen Formeln, welche nach Vorschrift der Kirche dem Volksunterricht zu Grunde gelegt werden müssen, dem apostolischen Glaubensbekenntniß, den zehn Geboten Gottes, den Sakramenten und dem Gebete des Herrn ausgedrückt. Und hier werden wir auf die schon oben erwähnte Eintheilung zurückgeführt. Es giebt nämlich Dogmen, welche als die Hauptpunkte der Heilslehre anzusehen, und es giebt andere, welche diesen untergeordnet und nicht von derselben Bedeu-tung sind. –

---

27 S. Thom. S. 2. 2ᵃᵉ q. 1. a. 7.

78. Obschon diese Eintheilungen, durch welche die Dogmen nach ihrem Inhalt unterschieden werden, zu ebenso wichtigen als schwierigen Fragen Veranlassung gegeben haben; so bieten sie doch in sich d. i. als Eintheilungen betrachtet, keine Schwierigkeit dar. In Betreff der letzten jedoch ist vor einem Mißverständniß zu warnen, dem wir bei Hirscher begegnen. Derselbe beantwortet nämlich die Frage: „Wie weit die Einheit der Ueberzeugung gehen müsse, um zur Gemeinschaft einer Kirche zu gehören" – in folgender Weise: „Ich glaube, daß man keinen Lehrsatz haben dürfe, welcher dem gemeinsamen Lehrbegriff der Kirche in einem wesentlichen Punkte widerspricht. Ein unentwickelter Glaube, ein einseitiger Glaube, ein in Außerwesentlichem irrender Glaube ist wohl ein Mangel, und das unvermeidliche Loos der menschlichen Schwachheit, aber kein Gegensatz gegen den gemeinsamen religiösen Glauben, und kein Abfall von demselben[28]."

Diese Antwort nun können wir nicht gelten lassen, ohne, was Hirscher vom Wesentlichen und Außerwesentlichen sagt, zu streichen. Allerdings ist die Einheit der Kirche im Glauben nicht nothwendig eine *materiale;* das heißt, damit die Kirche im Glauben einig sei, wird nicht erfordert, daß ihre Bekenner in allen und jeden religiösen Fragen dasselbe denken und sagen; aber sie ist nothwendig eine formale, das ist: alle, die zu ihr gehören, müssen das Princip der Einheit, ihr unfehlbares Lehramt anerkennen. Wer von diesem Prinzip abfällt, der fällt auch von der Gemeinschaft der Gläubigen ab. Nun aber giebt man doch offenbar dieses Prinzip ebenso wohl auf, wenn man in einem außerwesentlichen, als wenn man in einem wesentlichen Punkte dem kirchlichen Lehrbegriff widerspricht. Und eben deßhalb heißt es nicht *in parvis*, sondern *in dubiis libertas*. Wohl darf auch der Katholik zwischen wesentlichen und nicht wesentlichen (besser: zwischen wichtigen und minder wichtigen) Glaubenslehren insofern unterscheiden, als einige Glaubenswahrheiten ihrem Inhalte nach von größerer Bedeutung sind, als andere; aber nicht in jenem Sinne, daß man zur Annahme der einen verpflichtet, der Glaube an die andere aber frei gegeben sei[29]. Dies würde ja geradezu auf die protestantische Lehre von den Fundamentalartikeln führen. –

Wir klagen Hirscher deßhalb nicht an, daß er diese vorzutragen beabsichtigt habe, und wollen gern hierin nichts anders, als ein Versehen finden. – Vielleicht hat er auch, da er vom unvermeidlichen Loose der menschlichen Schwäche redet, an einen aus bloßer Unwissenheit Irrenden gedacht. Aber dann hat er erstlich die Frage: wie weit die Einheit der Ueberzengung gehen

---

28 Erörterungen. 14. Erört. S. 163.
29 Suarez. De fide Disp. 19. sect. 2. n. 7. – De Lugo. De fide. Disp. 3. sect. 1. n. 4. Disp. 20. sect. 1. n. 8.

müsse, um zur Gemeinschaft der Kirche zu gehören, in einem Sinne gefaßt, den sie weder ihrem Wortlaute, noch dem Zwecke der ganzen Abhandlung nach haben kann; und überdies in ihrer Beantwortung zu viel gefordert. Denn ein unschuldig Irrender fällt von der Einheit der Kirche nicht ab, wenn er gleich in einem wesentlichen d. h. höchst wichtigen Punkt irrt.

79. Was nun die Eintheilung der Dogmen nach dem, wodurch sie Dogmen sind, angeht; so wollen wir darüber zuerst *Hermes* vernehmen. Gewöhnlich, sagt er, verstehe man unter Dogma: „jede besondere theologische Lehre, welche erweislicher Maßen oder nach dem allgemeinen Dafürhalten von Gott übernatürlich geoffenbart sei;" von einigen Theologen jedoch werde außerdem noch eine ausdrückliche Erklärung der Kirche gefordert. Da nun aber ein vollendeter Beweis und der allgemeine Glaube *(traditio universalis)*, daß eine besondere Lehre geoffenbart sei, nach katholischen Grundsätzen ihre Offenbarung eben sowohl, als die ausdrückliche Lehre der Kirche verbürgen; so schlage er vor, statt Dogma in jenem ersteren Sinne *dogma revelatum, Offenbarungslehre*, und statt Dogma in dem zweiten Sinne *dogma declaratum v. definitum, erklärte Offenbarungslehre* zu sagen. Dieses stimme auch mit dem theologischen Sprachgebrauch überein; indem man unter *„dogma fidei"* oder es ist *„de fide,"* verstehe: *dogma fidei (declaratae)* und *de fide (declarata)*. Dann fügt er noch die Anmerkung hinzu: „Wer wissentlich einem *dogma declaratum* widerspricht, sagt sich von der Gemeinschaft der Kirche los, nicht so, wer dem *dogma revelatum* widerspricht, weil die *Allgemeinheit* der Annahme desselben gewöhnlich unbekannt ist[30]."

Wenn Hermes hier lehrt, ein vollendeter Beweis oder der allgemeine Glaube, daß eine Lehre geoffenbart sei, verbürge die Offenbarung derselben eben so gut, als eine ausdrückliche Erklärung der Kirche; so scheint das mit dem, was wir von der richtigen Auffassung der katholischen Glaubensnorm oben gesagt haben, übereinzustimmen. Dennoch können wir das nur zugeben, wofern er erstlich unter dem vollendeten Beweis einen solchen versteht, der entweder auf ganz klaren und unzweideutigen Stellen der Schrift, oder auf der einstimmigen Erklärung der Väter beruht; und der folglich auch in der katholischen Kirche keinen Widerspruch von Bedeutung findet; und wofern er zweitens in einem solchen Beweis oder jenem allgemeinen Glauben darum die gesagte Bürgschaft findet, weil so bewiesene oder so angenommene Lehren zu jenen gehören, die durch das öffentliche Lehramt der Kirche zu glauben vorgelegt werden. Denn dies ist durchaus fest zu halten, daß keine anderen

---

30 Dogmatik. Bd. I. Meth. §. 45.

geoffenbarten Lehren als jene, die uns als solche durch das Ansehen der Kirche verbürgt werden, zum katholischen Glauben gehören. Und eben deßhalb ist die erste Erklärung des Wortes Dogma, die Hermes als die gewöhnliche anführt, viel zu unbestimmt. Das *eigenthümlich* katholische Prinzip ist in ihr nicht ausgesprochen. Diesem Prinzip gemäß setzt das Dogma zwei Thatsachen, die *Offenbarung* und die *Vorlegung,* oder *Verkündigung durch die Kirche* voraus. Es läßt sich nun zwar nicht läugnen, daß man von der Wahrheit einer göttlichen Offenbarung auch auf anderm Wege, als durch die Lehre der Kirche Gewißheit erhalten kann; was nicht nur von den schon oben erwähnten Offenbarungen, die einzelnen Gläubigen zu Theil werden, sondern auch von der allgemeinen christlichen Offenbarung gilt. Denn durch Forschung in den Quellen derselben kann jemand zur klaren Erkenntniß gelangen, daß eine Wahrheit geoffenbart sei, welche als solche in der Kirche nicht allgemein angenommen wird. Aber wenn gleich deßhalb ältere und ausgezeichnete Theologen lehren, daß so erkannte Offenbarungslehren Gegenstand des übernatürlichen d. h. durch die göttliche Gnade verliehenen Glaubens sein können; so räumen sie doch ein, oder dringen vielmehr darauf, daß dieselben nicht zu den christkatholischen Glaubenslehren gehören, und unterschieden deßhalb zwischen *fides divina* und fides catholica[31]. Für jenen Glauben genügt es, von der Thatsache, daß eine Wahrheit geoffenbart sei, eine subjective Gewißheit zu haben, für diesen ist es nothwendig, daß wir davon durch das öffentliche Lehramt der Kirche versichert werden. Kann ich also nur nachweisen, daß eine Lehre in der Offenbarung enthalten ist, aber nicht zugleich, daß sie als solche von der Kirche allen zu glauben vorgelegt wird; so kann ich sie auch nicht für ein katholisches Dogma ausgeben. Hiermit streitet nicht, was oben gesagt wurde, nämlich die Erklärung der Kirche, daß die Schrift Gottes Wort sei, genüge, um auch einzelne in ihr enthaltene Lehren als solche zu betrachten, die uns von ihr als geoffenbarte zu glauben vorgelegt werden. Denn dies wurde nur behauptet und kann nur behauptet werden, wenn entweder die Worte der Schrift so bestimmt und klar sind, daß über ihren Sinn kein Zweifel sein kann; oder wenn die gelehrte Erklärung derselben, durch die jemand zu einer subjectiven Ueberzeugung kommt, in der allgemeinen Annahme ihre Bestätigung findet.

80. Es scheint, daß eben diese Unterscheidung Hermes vorschwebte, als er die Dogmen in Offenbarungslehren und erklärte Offenbarungslehren eintheilte. Denn unter jenen versteht er solche Lehren, die erweislicher Maßen in der

---

31 Bellarm. De justif. l. 3. c. 3. – Suarez. De fide D. 3. sect. 10. n. 2. – De Lugo. De fide. Disp. 1. sect. 11. Disp. 20. sect. 2. n. 60 seqq.

Offenbarung enthalten, aber uns als solche doch nicht durch das Ansehen der Kirche gewiß sind. Weil uns aber, wie er selbst bemerkt, diese Gewißheit ebensowohl durch die allgemeine Lehre, als durch die ausdrückliche Erklärung der Kirche gegeben wird, und jene Allgemeinheit keinesweges immer unbekannt ist; so hätte er auch nicht in *dogmata revelata et dogmata definita*, sondern *dogmata revelata et dogmata proposita* eintheilen sollen. Das wäre aber dann jene alte schon vom h. Thomas gebrauchte Eintheilung in dogma in se et dogma quoad nos[32]. Dadurch daß eine Lehre in der Schrift oder Tradition enthalten ist, hat sie in sich das, wodurch sie Gegenstand des allgemeinen christlichen Glaubens sein kann, – sie ist von Gott und zwar in der für die ganze Menschheit bestimmten Offenbarung bezeugt: aber erst dadurch, daß sie als solche von der Kirche verkündigt wird, erfüllt sich die Bedingung, ohne welche wir sie nicht als Gegenstand jenes Glaubens anerkennen dürfen[33]. Es bedarf aber kaum einer Bemerkung, daß Hermes, um die Eintheilung, welche er vorschlägt, zu rechtfertigen, mit Unrecht beifügt, die Ausdrücke *Dogma fidei* oder *Est de fide* seien unter den Theologen nur von Glaubenslehren, welche die Kirche ausdrücklich entschieden habe, gebräuchlich. Die Grundsätze, welche die Theologen aufstellten, haben wir mitgetheilt, es genügt aber die gebräuchlichsten Handbücher, Abelly's z.B. Antoine's, Charmes, aufzuschlagen, um sich zu überzeugen, daß sie diesen Grundsätzen zufolge gar viele Lehren, über welche die Kirche keine Beschlüsse erlassen hat, und namentlich die oben von uns angeführten, durch jene Ausdrücke für katholische Glaubenswahrheiten erklären. – Und eben deßhalb kann man auch nicht einräumen, daß nur derjenige sich von der Gemeinschaft der Kirche lossage, der einer feierlich entschiedenen Glaubenslehre widerspreche. Wer z.B. das göttliche Vorherwissen der freien Handlungen oder auch geschichtliche Thatsachen, wie die Verklärung des Herrn auf Thabor oder die Reise des Apostels Paulus nach Rom läugnete; würde eben so gut von dem Glauben der Kirche abfallen, als jener der die Menschwerdung des Sohnes Gottes anstritte und dies, wie oben bemerkt wurde, aus demselben Grunde, weßhalb Arius auch vor dem nicänischen und Nestorius vor dem ephesinischen Kirchenrath von einzelnen Bischöfen mit

---

32 In ep. ad Rom. c. 14. lect. 3. – Bestimmter bei Melch. Can. de S. theol. l. 12. c. 14.

33 Duo concurrunt in aliqua propositione, ut credi possit et debeat, scilicet testificatio divina et applicatio, seu ut sufficienter proponatur. Primum est per se et formale in propositione fidei et illud est simplex atque unius tantum rationis in omnibus fidei propositionibus. Secundum autem est quasi per accidens et tanquam conditio necessaria ex parte nostra. Suarez. De fide. Disp. 19. sect. 2. n. 8.

vollem Rechte als Ketzer bezeichnet und von der Gemeinschaft der Gläubigen ausgestoßen wurden[34].

Gleichwie dem Bisherigen zufolge eine Wahrheit von Gott geoffenbart sein kann, ohne katholisch zu sein, weil sie nämlich von der Kirche nicht als geoffenbarte Lehre verkündigt wird: also kann auch umgekehrt eine Lehre katholisch sein, weil sie von der Kirche vorgetragen wird, ohne deßhalb eine geoffenbarte zu sein. Diese Unterscheidung giebt uns aber nicht sowohl eine Eintheilung der Dogmen, als vielmehr der kirchlichen Lehren: denn eben deßhalb, weil etwas zwar von der Kirche gelehrt, aber nicht als geoffenbarte Wahrheit gelehrt wird, ist es auch nicht Dogma. Von dieser Unterscheidung der kirchlichen Lehren im folgenden Abschnitt.

V. Von den nicht dogmatischen Lehren der Kirche.

81. Es unterliegt keinem Zweifel, daß die Kirche ihr ordentliches Lehramt übend, manche Wahrheiten vorträgt, welche nicht als Glaubenssätze zu betrachten sind: die Auferstehung z.B. und die Himmelfahrt Maria's, die vollkommene Weisheit, welche der menschlichen Seele Christi im ersten Augenblick ihres Daseins verliehen wurde. Aber auch nicht alle Lehren, welche sie durch ausdrückliche Entscheidungen feststellt, werden von ihr für Glaubenswahrheiten erklärt. Am deutlichsten tritt dies bei Verwerfung falscher Lehren hervor. Denn die einen bezeichnet sie als häretische, die andern nur als der Häresie nahe liegende, irrthümliche, ärgerliche u.s.w. Weil also die Häresie in der Läugnung der Glaubenswahrheit besteht, so wird durch solche Verwerfung nur jene Lehre, mit welcher die als häretisch bezeichnete einen Gegensatz bildet, als dogmatische festgestellt. Und doch werden auch die Lehren, welche den in anderer Weise verurtheilten entgegengesetzt sind, durch diese Verurtheilung für kirchliche erklärt. Indem z.B. die Kirche den jansenistischen Satz, der Glaube sei die erste Gnade, als irrthümlich verwirft[35], spricht sie als ihre Lehre aus, der Glaube sei nicht die erste Gnade, weil nämlich andere, die zum Glauben führen, ihm vorhergehen. Und wenn sie die Behauptung, die Andacht zum Herzen Jesu sei eine, wenn nicht irrthümliche doch gefährliche Neuerung, als falsch, verwegen und die Frömmigkeit der Gläubigen verletzend untersagt[36]; so lehrt sie dadurch ohne Zweifel, daß jene Andacht ebensowenig gefährlich als irrthümlich sei. – Wie mit diesen verwerfenden Urtheilen, so verhält es sich auch mit jenen Entscheidungen, durch welche, was zu lehren sei,

---

34 Lugo. De fide. Disp. 3. sect. 1. n. 4. 5.
35 Bulla. Auctorem fidei n. 22.
36 Ibid. n. 62.

in positiver Weise bestimmt wird. Nur das wird durch dieselben als Glaubenswahrheit ausgesprochen, was in ihnen für eine solche in irgend einer unzweideutigen Weise (n. 46.) erklärt wird.

Aber könnte man nicht in Zweifel stellen, ob durch manche dieser kirchlichen Censuren über die Wahrheit oder Unwahrheit der Lehre ein bestimmtes Urtheil gefällt werde? Wenn eine Meinung gerügt wird, weil sie der Häresie sich nähere, dieselbe begünstige oder mit ihr verwandt sei, bleibt es da nicht unentschieden, ob sie der Wahrheit entgegenlaufe oder nicht? Und wenn sie gar nur als eine übellautende, ärgerliche und verführerische bezeichnet wird, so könnte sie doch deßhalb immer noch wahr sein.

Um diese Schwierigkeit zu lösen, müssen wir zuvor die verschiedenen Censuren, deren sich die Kirche bedient, näher ansehen[37]. Zwar sind die Theologen, wenn es darauf ankommt, die Bedeutung derselben scharf zu bestimmen[38], in Betreff einiger nicht derselben Ansicht; aber wir werden sehen, daß diese Verschiedenheit der Meinungen von geringer Bedeutung ist.

82. *Häretisch* wird nur jene Behauptung genannt, welche einem anerkannten Dogma geradezu entgegengesetzt ist, möge übrigens dieser Gegensatz ein contradictorischer oder conträrer sein. So widersprach Luther der Glaubenslehre, daß auch der gefallene Mensch noch freien Willen habe, nicht bloß indem er behauptete, daß durch die Sünde Adams der freie Wille zerstört worden, sondern auch und mehr noch durch die Lehre, daß alle Werke des gefallenen Menschen nothwendig Sünden seien.

Auf die schärfste Censur: *sententia haeretica* folgen zunächst diese beiden anderen: *sententia erronea, sententia haeresi proxima*. Nach der vorherrschenden Ansicht wird jene Meinung als *irrthümlich* bezeichnet, welche einer klaren und gewissen Folgerung aus dem Dogma und somit diesem nicht unmittelbar, aber doch mittelbar widerspricht. So wurden gewisse Sätze der Aftersynode zu Pistoia über die Vollmacht und Freiheit, womit die Bischöfe ihre Diöcesen verwalten dürften, für irrthümlich erklärt, weil durch dieselben geläugnet wird, was aus der göttlichen Einsetzung der bestehenden hierarchischen Ordnung folgt, daß nämlich die Bischöfe in jener Verwaltung einer höheren kirchlichen

---

37 Zuerst hat sich das Concil von Constanz dieser Censuren bedient, indem sie die Artikel Wikleff's verwarf als notorie haereticos et a SS. Patribus reprobatos, alios non catholicos, sed erroneos, alios scandalosos et blasphemos; quosdam piarum aurium offensivos, nonnullos temerarios et seditiosos. Sess. 8.

38 Melch. Can. De loc. theol. l. 12. c. 8. seqq. Bannes. In S. 2. 2ae – q. 11. a. 2. – Suarez. De fide. Disp. 19. sect. 2. – Lugo. Disp. 20. sect. 3. – Wurceburg. (Kilber) De virt. theol. Disp. 3. c. 3. a. 2. – Zacharias Thes. Vol. I. Diss. 2. c. 2.

Gewalt untergeordnet sind. – Welche Meinung verdiene *haeresi proxima* genannt zu werden, ergiebt sich aus der Erklärung der Häresie. Damit eine Meinung häretisch sei, sagt mit aller Kürze und Klarheit Suarez, werden zwei Stücke erfordert, daß nämlich erstlich die Lehre, welcher sie widerspricht, ohne allen Zweifel dogmatisch, und zweitens jene Meinung ebenso gewiß ihr entgegengesetzt sei. Wenn also das eine oder das andere nicht völlig erwiesen ist, und deßhalb innerhalb der Kirche ein gewisses Schwanken sich kund gibt, so ist die fragliche Meinung nicht häretisch; sie kommt aber der Häresie nahe, wenn an der vollen Uebereinstimmung und Entschiedenheit nur wenig mangelt. Die Lehre, daß Gott sich mit den Gerechten nicht bloß durch seine Gaben, sondern auch seinem Wesen nach vereinige, läßt sich aus dem göttlichen Worte mit triftigen Gründen beweisen. Dennoch pflegen die Theologen sie nicht für dogmatisch, wohl aber für *fidei proxima* zu erklären, und auch Hermes stimmt ihnen, wie wir sehen werden, darin bei. Die entgegengesetzte Behauptung wäre also *haeresi proxima*. – Da jedoch diese Censur nur sehr selten und erst in spätern Zeiten von der Kirche angewendet wurde[39], so begreift man, weßhalb einige Theologen nur von der *sententia erronea* reden und diese so erklären, daß sie die *sententia haeresi proxima* einschließt. Melchior Canus aber, welcher der Ansicht war, nicht bloß die Läugnung des Dogmas selbst, sondern auch der aus ihm mit Nothwendigkeit fließenden Sätzen sei eigentliche Häresie, giebt (a.a.O.) von der *sententia erronea* die Erklärung, welche wir der herrschenden Ansicht gemäß von der *sententia haeresi proxima*, deren er nicht erwähnt, gegeben haben.

83. Wie die *sententia erronea*, so steht auch die *sententia de haeresi suspecta* und noch mehr die *sententia haeresin sapiens* mit der Häresie in Verbindung, aber nicht in nothwendiger, so daß man also auch nicht mit Gewißheit, sondern nur mit Wahrscheinlichkeit behaupten kann, sie sei aus der Läugnung des Dogmas entsprungen. So wird von der Kirche die Lehre des Bajus, welche die Synode zu Pistoja erneuerte, daß die ursprüngliche Heiligkeit des Menschen eine Folge der Schöpfung gewesen sei, für einen Irrthum erklärt; die Lehre aber, daß Gott den gefallenen Menschen, ehe er den Erlöser sandte, seiner Schwäche überlassen habe, damit seine Verirrungen ihn dahin brächten, nach dem Erlöser zu verlangen, als der Häresie verdächtig bezeichnet, weil sie nämlich leicht dahin verstanden und ausgelegt wird, daß der Mensch aus sich selbst ein Verlangen nach dem Erlöser haben könne.

---

39 Prop. damnatae ab Alexandro VIII. d. 7. Dec. 1690. – Bulla Clementis VIII. Unigenitus.

Man hat in unsern Tagen wider den Gebrauch dieser Censur geeifert, weil dadurch sich die kirchlichen Behörden anmaßten, was auch den allgemeinen Concilien nicht gegeben sei, nämlich über die Absicht, in welcher eine Lehre vorgetragen sei und folglich über das Innere des Menschen zu urtheilen. Wir reden hier zwar nicht vom Gerichte über die Personen, sondern vom Urtheile über die Lehre; doch wollen wir eine Anklage der Kirche, zu der man die Veranlassung von unsern Worten genommen hat, nicht mit Stillschweigen übergehen. Es ist wahr, daß derjenige, welcher eine *sententia de haeresi suspecta* lehrt, von den kirchlichen Behörden für der Häresie verdächtig erklärt wird. Aber es ist so falsch, daß deßhalb diese Behörden sich anmaßen, über die Absicht, mit welcher jemand rede, zu entscheiden, daß sie gerade umgekehrt dies Verfahren beobachten, weil sie nicht über das Innere der Menschen urtheilen wollen. In allen Gerichten der Welt unterscheidet man diese drei Stufen: *angeklagt* heißt derjenige, wider welchen das gerichtliche Verfahren eingeleitet ist; der Angeklagte aber wird für *verdächtig* erklärt, wenn die Beweise seine Schuld wahrscheinlich machen; für *schuldig,* wenn sie ihn überführen. Wenn also ein kirchliches Gericht in dem Falle, von welchem wir reden, über jemand das Urtheil spricht, er sei der Häresie verdächtig; so erklärt es dadurch, die Lehre, welcher er anhange, mache es wenngleich nicht gewiß, doch wahrscheinlich, daß er der Häresie ergeben sei. Nämlich diese Lehre steht zwar mit der Häresie in Verbindung, jedoch nicht in nothwendiger, so daß jemand ihr anhängen kann, ohne zugleich der Häresie anzuhangen. Gerade deßhalb also, weil die Behörde über den Angeklagten nur nach seiner äußerlich vorliegenden Lehre urtheilt, erklärt sie ihn für verdächtig; denn maßte sie es sich an, über seine Gedanken und Absichten zu entscheiden, dann würde sie ihn für schuldig oder unschuldig erklären. – Indeß wie gesagt, wir reden hier vielmehr von dem Urtheil, das die Kirche über Lehren fällt, nicht bloß jene rügend und verbietend, welche den Irrthum aussprechen, sondern auch die, welche geeignet sind, zu demselben zu verleiten.

84. Aus eben diesem Grunde bedient sie sich auch der Censur *sententia male sonans.* Denn so heißt ein Satz, der zwar gut ausgelegt werden kann, aber dem Sinne zufolge, welchen die Worte gewöhnlich und besonders im Munde der Irrgläubigen haben, der reinen Lehre widerstreitet; wie wenn jemand sagte: „der Glaube ist's, der rechtfertigt." Umgekehrt giebt es auch Sätze, in welchen die Ausdrucksweise der rechtgläubigen Frömmigkeit mißbraucht wird, um dem Irrthum Eingang zu verschaffen. Dieser Art sind viele Lehren Quesnel's und der Synode von Pistoja wie: „Was anders bleibt der Seele, die Gott und seine Gnade verloren hat, als die Sünde und die Folgen der Sünde?" Werden diese Worte, die oft fromme Christen im Munde führen, im strengen Sinne genommen, wie

dies bei Quesnel der Fall ist; so enthalten sie den Irrthum, daß in einer Seele, welche der heiligmachenden Gnade beraubt sei, durchaus nichts Gutes sein könne. Mit Recht heißt also ein solcher Satz ein *verfänglicher (sententia captiosa)*.

Piarum aurium offensiva wird eine Lehre genannt, die wenn sie auch keinen ausdrücklichen Irrthum enthält, doch geeignet ist, die wahre Frömmigkeit und besonders die der Religion und der Kirche gebührende Ehrfurcht zu vermindern. Als eine solche Lehre wird von der Kirche die Behauptung gerügt, es sei zu wünschen, daß die Liturgie, damit sie nach den richtigen Grundsätzen geregelt sei, vereinfacht, daß in ihr der Gebrauch der Muttersprache eingeführt und alles mit lauter Stimme gesprochen werde[40].

Eine der gewöhnlichsten Censuren endlich ist *sententia temeraria*. Dem Wortlaute nach kann jede unbesonnene Behauptung also genannt werden: allein erstlich ist hier, wie bei allen diesen Censuren, nur von theologischen Lehren die Rede, und somit wird in der Sprache der Kirche nur eine solche Behauptung *temeraria* genannt, welche, wenn auch nicht in Glaubensfragen, aber doch in solchen, die mit diesen zusammenhängen, irgend etwas ohne Grund bejahet oder läugnet. Zweitens aber verdient, wenigstens der gewöhnlichen Ansicht nach eine solche Behauptung erst dadurch diese Censur, daß sie zugleich der in der Kirche herrschenden Lehre widerspricht. –

Noch manche andere Censuren sind gebräuchlich, die aber keiner weiteren Erklärung bedürfen, wie *sententia impia, scandalosa, blasphema, seditiosa, schismatica vel haeresin fovens* u.s.w.

85. Kehren wir nun zu der oben aufgestellten Schwierigkeit zurück. Es werde, sagt man, durch manche dieser Censuren über die Wahrheit oder Unwahrheit einer Lehre gar nicht entschieden. Und wäre dies, entgegnen wir, nicht bloß von manchen, sondern auch von allen wahr, so würde nichts desto weniger jede ein sehr bestimmtes Urtheil enthalten. Die Kirche verbietet nicht nur allen ihren Untergebenen, solche Meinungen zu hegen und zu verbreiten, sondern erklärt auch, daß dieselben, vor ihrem Richterstuhl *verwerflich* sind. Denn wenn sie dies auch nicht durch ausdrückliche Worte, wie da sind *Reprobamus, Damnamus*, ausspräche, so würde sie es durch die Censur selbst thun. Denn zu welchem anderen Zwecke werden dieselben verhängt, wenn nicht um den Grund, weßhalb, und mehr oder weniger den Grad, in welchem eine Lehre verwerflich sei, anzugeben? – Aber wird durch dieselben über die Wahrheit und Unwahrheit der Lehre wirklich nicht entschieden? Suarez im Gegentheil

---

40 Bulla. Auctorem fidei n. 33.

beginnt die oben angeführte Erörterung der Censuren mit der Bemerkung, daß jede Lehre, welche durch dieselbe verworfen werde, nothwendig falsch sei: denn es leuchte ein, daß eine wahre Lehre nicht verwerflich sei. Alle Meinungen also, welche die Kirche in solcher Weise verurtheile, seien falsch, aber durch die verschiedenen Censuren werde bestimmt, welche besondere Rüge sie über dies verdienen. Diese Lehre des Suarez scheint in dem Verfahren der Kirche selbst ihre Bestätigung zu erhalten. In späteren Zeiten haben nämlich die Päbste sich auch eben der Censur *sententia falsa* bedient; aber als den geringsten von allen, was namentlich in der mehr erwähnten Bulle *Auctorem fidei* bemerkbar ist. In derselben werden nämlich jedem einzelnen Satze die Censuren, die er verdient, beigefügt; wenn aber dieser mehrere sind, so ist fast immer eine derselben *sententia falsa*, und von ihr aus wird zu den oben erwähnten fortgeschritten[41].

86. Nichts desto weniger läßt sich nicht von allen Censuren in derselben Weise behaupten, daß in ihnen ein Urtheil über Falschheit eingeschlossen ist. Daß eine Lehre, die für häretisch oder irrthümlich erklärt wird, auch für falsch erklärt werde, leuchtet freilich ein. Ebenso kann kein Zweifel sein, daß jede Meinung falsch ist, die verdient gottlos, gotteslästerisch, die Ehre der Heiligen oder der Kirche verletzend genannt zu werden. Was ferner jene Sätze angeht, an welchen die verfängliche oder zweideutige Ausdrucksweise gerügt wird; so werden auch sie für irrthümlich erklärt, nicht zwar schlechthin, aber dem Sinne nach, in welchem die Worte gemeiniglich und besonders bei dem Schriftsteller, welcher sie gebraucht, verstanden werden. Wenn aber Lehren verworfen werden, weil sie den guten Sitten oder den Glauben gefährden, verderblich, ärgerlich, aufrührerisch seien, die Frömmigkeit der Gläubigen vermindern, das Schisma oder die Häresie begünstigen; so könnte man zweifeln, ob sie dadurch ohne weiteres für unwahr erklärt werden. Können ja auch wahre Lehren der Zeitumstände wegen in mancher Weise zur Störung des Friedens, zum Aergerniß der Gläubigen, zur Begünstigung der Unsittlichkeit und des Irrglaubens mißbraucht werden. – Indessen wird hingegen mit Recht bemerkt, daß die Kirche solche Urtheile nie für eine gewisse Zeit, sondern unbedingt und für immer ausspricht. Eine Lehre aber, welche zu allen Zeiten und unter allen Umständen verderblich, ärgerlich oder geeignet ist, die Frömmigkeit zu vermindern, zum Irrthum und zur Sünde zu verleiten, kann unmöglich wahr sein. – Es kann geschehen, daß die Kirche eine Lehre, weil sie zum Aergerniß gereicht, verhindern will, ohne sich über ihren Werth oder Unwerth auszusprechen; aber dann verbietet sie dieselbe, ohne ihr durch eine Censur das Siegel der

---

41   Prop. 9ᵃ falsa, temeraria, Episcopalis auctoritatis laesiva & Prop. 10ᵃ falsa, temeraria, [...] schisma fovens et haeresin. Prop. 12ᵃ falsae, captiosae, temerariae, scandalosae etc.

Verwerflichkeit aufzudrücken. So war die Lehre, daß auch die gebenedeite Mutter des Herrn in der Sünde empfangen sei, lange Zeit verboten, aber ohne irgend eine Censur: warum dies, wenn nicht, weil die Kirche über die Lehre selbst sich zu erklären nicht für gut fand?

87. Aus dem Gesagten läßt sich nun auch abnehmen, was von den Censuren *sentenia temeraria, sententia haeresi proxima*, den einzigen, welche in dieser Frage Schwierigkeit darbieten, zu urtheilen ist. Die erstere verdient eine Meinung, welche in theologischen Fragen ohne genügenden Grund dem allgemeinen Dafürhalten widerspricht. Durch diese Censur wird also erklärt, daß jenes Dafürhalten seine guten Gründe hat, der Widerspruch aber dieser entbehrt. Da es sich jedoch hier nicht um Glaubenslehren, noch auch um Sätze, welche als Folgerungen aus diesen mit aller Entschiedenheit festgehalten werden, handelt; so haben wir auch keine unfehlbare Gewißheit, daß die allgemeine Ansicht wahr sei. Somit könnte es geschehen, daß später Gründe entdeckt würden, welche sie als zweifelhaft oder unwahr erwiesen. Obgleich es demnach zur Zeit, wo die Kirche ihr Urtheil fällte, sträfliche Unbesonnenheit war, der herrschenden Ansicht zu widersprechen; so wäre es doch dies im Falle solcher Entdeckung nicht mehr. Allein auch hier gilt, daß die Kirche ein derartiges Urtheil nicht für eine Zeit, sondern für alle Zeiten fällt, und was von der Lehre an sich zu halten sei, entscheidet. Nur dies läßt sich sagen, daß sie streng genommen nicht über die Wahrheit oder Unwahrheit der Lehre sich ausspricht. Sie erklärt, daß die in ihr verbreitete Ansicht wohl gegründet, die entgegengesetzte ungegründet sei. Es ist aber nicht dasselbe, eine Lehre für wohlgegründet oder ungegründet, und sie für wahr oder unwahr zu erklären. – In ähnlicher Weise verhält es sich mit der Censur *sentenia haeresi proxima*. Dieselbe findet statt, wenn es nicht völlig gewiß ist, entweder daß die Lehre, welche geläugnet wird, eine Glaubenswahrheit, oder daß die Meinung, welche verurtheilt wird, ihr unmittelbar entgegengesetzt sei. So lange nun hierüber nur unter den Theologen gestritten wird, kann eine Veränderung nach beiden Seiten hin eintreten, so daß bei fortschreitender Forschung entweder alle Zweifel verschwinden, und die fragliche Lehre allgemein als Häresie anerkannt, oder umgekehrt die Zweifel zunehmen, und das Urtheil über jene Lehre gemildert wird. Aber anders verhält sich die Sache, wenn die Kirche über eine solche Lehre durch jene Censur ihr Urtheil spricht. Durch dasselbe wird freilich nicht entschieden, daß die Lehre häretisch sei, wohl aber, daß die Gründe, welche dafür sprechen, stark, die Gegengründe aber von geringer Bedeutung sind. Denn wenn keine sehr starke und fest entscheidende Gründe vorhanden sind, oder wenn Gegengründe von Bedeutung vorgebracht werden können; so läßt sich gewiß nicht mit Wahrheit sagen, daß etwas fast häretisch – *haeresi proxi-*

mum – sei. Hat nun die Kirche ein solches Urtheil gesprochen, so können zwar fortgesetzte Studien zu immer gewisserer Erkenntniß führen, daß die Lehre, um welche es sich handelt, mit der geoffenbarten Wahrheit in Widerspruch stehe, aber nicht umgekehrt dies immer zweifelhafter machen. Denn nicht in jenem, wohl aber in diesem Falle würde das Urtheil der Kirche aufhören wahr zu sein.

Der Cardinal Lugo sagt (a.a.O.), die Censur, von welcher wir reden, bedeute so viel als die Lehre werde, wenn auch nicht von allen, doch von den meisten Theologen als Häresie bezeichnet. Es scheint mir aber, daß er hiebei die Censuren, wodurch untergeordnete Behörden oder einzelne Censoren ihr Urtheil aussprechen, von jenen, die von der lehrenden Kirche mit einer die ganze Christenheit bindenden Vollmacht erlassen werden, nicht unterschieden hat. Jene Behörden und Censoren sollen, wie er mit Recht sagt, über die Lehren anderer nicht sowohl nach ihrem eigenen Gutachten, als vielmehr nach jenem der Theologie überhaupt urtheilen, und darum erhält in ihrem Munde der Ausspruch, eine Lehre komme der Häresie sehr nahe, den Sinn, sie gelte wenn auch nicht allen, doch den meisten Theologen für häretisch. Aber das läßt sich nicht von einem Ausspruch der lehrenden Kirche sagen. Derselbe ist keine bloße Bezeugung dessen, was die Theologen lehren, sondern ein Urtheil über die Sache selbst. Obgleich nun dieses in dem Fall, wovon wir reden, nicht in dem Sinne entscheidend ist, daß ein Dogma festgestellt werde; so läßt sich doch, wie wir gesehen haben, nicht behaupten, daß es keine oder nur eine zeitweilige Entscheidung sei.

88. Aus der falschen Voraussetzung, daß, so lange keine eigentlich dogmatische Entscheidung vorliege, so gut als nichts entschieden sei, ist denn auch die Meinung entstanden, daß der Katholik alles, was nicht häretisch sei, frei annehmen und lehren dürfe. Welches immer nun die Tragweite der einzelnen Censuren, die wir betrachtet haben, sein möge; durch die Thatsache, daß sie sich derselben bedient, legt die Kirche klar an den Tag, wie weit sie entfernt ist, jene Freiheit anzuerkennen. Wohl aber rechtfertigt sie durch eben jene ihre Urtheile die Unterscheidung, welche die Theologen zwischen Lehre der Kirche im engeren und weiteren Sinne machen. Zur Lehre der Kirche im engeren Sinne gehört, was von der Kirche als geoffenbarte Wahrheit geglaubt und bekannt wird; zur Lehre der Kirche im weiteren Sinne, was in ihr außerdem, sei es nun in Folge der erwähnten Erlasse oder auch ohne dieselben mit Uebereinstimmung angenommen und vorgetragen wird. Es versteht sich, daß dies nur von Lehren gilt, welche sich auf die christliche Religion beziehen, und daher mit der geoffenbarten Wahrheit in Verbindung stehen. –

Durch das Bisherige wird nun auch ein Mißverständniß beleuchtet, zu welchem Werke, wie die *Regula fidei* des Veronius, Veranlassung geben. Die

Verfasser bemühen sich zu zeigen, daß gar vieles, was von Katholiken gewöhnlich angenommen und gelehrt wird, doch nicht zum eigentlichen Dogma gehöre. Es ist gewiß nicht zu tadeln, daß man das Gebiet des Dogmas so genau als möglich zu bestimmen sucht, aber man darf deßhalb nicht so reden, als wenn, wo dieses Gebiet aufhöre, sofort das Gebiet der freien Ansicht beginne, und alles, was nicht Glaubenssatz ist, als Schulmeinung betrachtet oder, wie dies von Chrismann geschieht, den *adiaphoris* beigezählt werden dürfe. – Wenn man ferner jene Ausscheidung des dogmatischen und nicht-dogmatischen zu dem Ende unternimmt, das Joch des Gehorsams gegen die lehrende Kirche zu erleichtern; so waltet darin durchgängig eine wahre Täuschung ob. Denn was hat man für jenen Zweck gewonnen, wenn man von einer in der Kirche verbreiteten Ansicht nachgewiesen hat, daß sie nicht Dogma sei; dann aber, (was freilich die erwähnten Schriftsteller gewöhnlich unterlassen) hinzusetzen muß, es hange jedoch diese Ansicht mit dem Dogma so innig zusammen, daß die entgegengesetzte Lehre mit einer oder mehreren der erwähnten Censuren entweder belegt sei oder nach der allgemeinen Ansicht der katholischen Gelehrten belegt zu werden verdiene? – Dies ist aber in solchen Fragen fast immer der Fall. Der ganze Trost, den sie einem Protestanten, der sich bekehren, oder einem Katholiken, der so frei als möglich denken möchte, bieten können, wäre also dieser: die Kirche verpflichte ihn nicht, diesen oder jenen Satz als eine geoffenbarte Wahrheit, sondern nur als eine durch ihre Verbindung mit dem Geoffenbarten bewährte und allein fromme und heilsame Lehre festzuhalten; wenn er dieses nun nicht thue, so mache er sich zwar einer schweren Sünde, aber doch nicht des Abfalls vom Glauben schuldig, und gelte in der Kirche nicht für einen Ketzer, sondern nur für einen unbesonnenen, ärgerlichen aufrührischen, dem Irrthum anhängenden oder auch der Häresie verdächtigen Menschen. –

89. Obschon nun die Kirche seit Jahrhunderten ihr Urtheil über Lehren oder Bücher fast immer mit Anwendung verschiedener Censuren ausspricht; so hat man doch in unsern Tagen dies Verfahren als unangemessen dargestellt, und ganz besonders getadelt, daß kirchliche Behörden angewiesen seien, zu urtheilen, nicht nur ob eine Schrift häretische, sondern auch ob sie Lehren enthalte, welche eine der übrigen Censuren verdienen. Allein was man wider die Anwendung der Censuren überhaupt vorgebracht hat, wurde schon bei Erörterung derselben von uns berücksichtigt, die Declamationen aber wider das den Censurbehörden vorgeschriebene Verfahren bedürfen bei keinem bedachtsamen Leser der Widerlegung. Sie beruhen sammt und sonders auf der Voraussetzung, daß die Theologen und selbst die höchsten Würdenträger der Kirche, welche jene Behörden bilden, von Partheisucht geleitet und unfähig seien,

wissenschaftliche Werke zu beurtheilen. Es ist aber bekannt, daß zu allen Zeiten die Freidenker sich allein reine Liebe zur Wahrheit und wissenschaftliche Befähigung zugeschrieben haben.

90. In eine Frage von größerer Bedeutung einzugehen, werden wir durch *Chrismann* genöthigt. Von der Lehrgewalt der Kirche redend, behauptet er, daß die Unfehlbarkeit derselben auf die ausdrücklich geoffenbarten Wahrheiten beschränkt sei, so daß die Kirche nicht bloß irren könnte, wenn sie über Personen und Thatsachen, über die nichts geoffenbart ist, sondern auch wenn sie über Lehren, die aus den geoffenbarten Wahrheiten durch Vernunftschlüsse hergeleitet werden, urtheilt[42]. Demzufolge würden fast alle Entscheidungen der Kirche, von welchen hier die Rede ist, insbesondere aber jene, wodurch eine Meinung für *erronea, temeraria* oder *falsa* erklärt wird, also gerade jene, welche die gewöhnlichsten und für die Wissenschaft von großem Interesse sind, dem Irrthum unterworfen seien. Dahingegen haben sämmtliche Theologen, wie sich unsere Leser aus den (n. 81) angeführten Werken überzeugen können, von jeher gelehrt, daß die Kirche in allen diesen Entscheidungen ebenso unfehlbar sei, als in den eigentlichen Glaubensbeschlüssen. Nur darauf kommt es an, ob das Urtheil, wodurch eine Lehre mit einer Censur belegt wird, eine Entscheidung der lehrenden Kirche, also von den Trägern der höchsten Lehrgewalt für die ganze Christenheit ausgesprochen sei. So gewiß es ist, daß eine Meinung häretisch ist, welche durch ein solches Urtheil für häretisch erklärt wird; so gewiß ist es, daß jene irrthumlich, ärgerlich, falsch sind, welche in demselben als solche bezeichnet werden.

Um sich hiervon zu überzeugen, bemerke man zuvörderst, daß die Lehrvollmacht der Kirche unmöglich auf den Inhalt der Offenbarung in der Weise beschränkt sein kann, daß ihr nichts anders obliege, als die ausdrücklichen Lehren der Offenbarung zu verkündigen. Der Zweck der Offenbarung wird nämlich dadurch noch nicht erreicht, daß wir die Wahrheiten, welche sie ausdrücklich enthält, mit frommem Glauben annehmen; es sollen diese Wahrheiten wie unser Handeln und Wirken, so unser Denken und Dafürhalten, wenigstens in so weit es sich einigermaßen auf die Religion bezieht, ordnen, unser ganzes innere und äußere Leben durchdringen. Dies kann aber nicht geschehen, ohne daß bald die geoffenbarten Lehren näher bestimmt, bald ihr Inhalt entwickelt, bald Folgerungen aus ihnen hergeleitet und vielerlei Gegenstände nach ihnen wie nach Principien beurtheilt werden. Ist also die Kirche

---

42 Ecclesia non gaudet infallibiliter assistentia Spiritus S. in docendis recte veritatibus, quae ratione tantum ex revelatis licet evidenter concluduntur: nam nulla conclusio, quatenus praecise conclusio est, sufficit fundando articulo fidei catholicae. Sect. 3. c. 3. §. 99.

kraft ihres Hirtenamtes bestellt, das göttliche Licht, so weit als der Zweck der Offenbarung es fordert, zu verbreiten; so sind wir auch bei dieser Bestimmung, Entwicklung, Anwendung und Benutzung der geoffenbarten Wahrheit für das Leben und die Wissenschaft auf sie als unsere Lehrerin angewiesen. Und weil sie in eben der Sphäre, in welcher sie die Wahrheit verbreiten soll, auch den Irrthum abwehren muß; so hat sie die Gewalt, nicht nur jene Lehren zu verbieten, welche der geoffenbarten Wahrheit direkt widerstreiten, sondern auch diejenigen, welche auf dem Gebiete sei es der praktischen, sei es der theoretischen Wissenschaften im Lichte der Offenbarung als irrig, gottlos, verführerisch und schädlich erkannt werden.

Obgleich die christliche Religion in dem Sinne über die Natur erhaben ist, daß keine natürlichen Kräfte uns in den Besitz dessen, was sie verleiht, setzen können: so ist es doch nicht in diesem andern, daß, was sie verleiht, in uns ohne Verbindung mit dem, was wir durch die Natur vermögen, bleiben könnte. Das christlich religiöse Leben ist ja kein von dem natürlichen getrenntes und ausgeschiedenes, sondern das durch ein göttliches Element erhöhte und verklärte natürliche Leben. So wenig wir deßhalb bei der Feier des Gottesdienstes zwar fromme Christgläubige, in unserm Hause aber weltlich gesinnte Ungläubige sein dürfen; so wenig können wir in der Religionslehre den geoffenbarten Wahrheiten folgen, in der Natur- oder Rechtslehre aber ihnen widersprechen. Ja, wenn zwischen den Wahrheiten, welche die Kirche als geoffenbarte verkündigt, und den Lehren der Wissenschaften keine nothwendige Verbindung statt hätte, dann wäre es möglich, daß die Kirche ihre Lehrthätigkeit ganz auf die Erklärung und Bestimmung der ersteren beschränkte. Da nun aber vielmehr eine solche Verbindung durch die Natur der Sache besteht; so kann weder die Kirche ihrem Lehramt, noch können wir der Benutzung des uns gewordenen Lichtes solche Gränzen setzen. Dies hat auch Günther eingesehen. Er schreibt: „Jene (göttliche) Leitung offenbart sich als Unfehlbarkeit in der lehrenden Kirche [...] Diese *Unfehlbarkeit* ist mehr negativer oder abwehrender als positiver und direct bestimmender Natur [...] Ihr *Veto* aber hat die Kirche nicht bloß in Bezug auf Theologie, sondern auch in Bezug auf *alles Wissen* einzulegen; weil *kein* Wissen in der Menschheit bei dem *organischen Verband aller* Wissenschaften von der Art ist, daß von ihm ein absoluter *Separatismus* prädicirt werden könnte. Ist aber dies der Fall, so ist die Möglichkeit einer feindlichen Stellung gegen das Object der Theologie gegeben, und im Fall der Wirklichkeit ihr Veto zugleich, ja selbst das Anathem, das mit jenem nicht zu verwechseln ist[43].

---

43 Peregrin's G. S. 365.

91. Wenn nun aber dem zufolge die *Lehrgewalt* der Kirche nicht auf die ausdrücklich geoffenbarten Wahrheiten eingeschränkt, sondern auf alles, was die Erfahrungs- und Vernunft-Wissenschaften lehren, insofern es mit den geoffenbarten Wahrheiten zusammenhängt, ausgedehnt ist: so ist dasselbe auch, wie es eben von Günther geschah, von der *Unfehlbarkeit* zu behaupten[44]. Oder würden die Verheissungen ihres göttlichen Stifters noch wahr sein, wenn die Kirche in den Entscheidungen, welche sie *kraft ihres Lehramtes* erläßt, dem Irrthum unterläge? Hat die Kirche Gewalt, nicht bloß jene Lehren, durch welche die geoffenbarte Wahrheit geradezu und ausdrücklich geläugnet wird, sondern auch diejenigen, welche ihr mittelbar widersprechen oder wie immer mit ihr unvereinbar sind, zu verwerfen und zu verbieten: so ist auch die ganze Christenheit verpflichtet, dieselben mit ihr zu verwerfen und als schlechte Lehren zu meiden. Wenn also, was die Kirche für irrthümlich, folglich für solches erklärt, das mit der Glaubenslehre, wenn auch nur mittelbar streitet, mit der Glaubenslehre vereinbar und daher nicht irrthümlich, wenn, was sie für falsch erklärt, wahr, wenn was sie als den Glauben und die guten Sitten gefährend bezeichnet, eine gesunde und heilsame Lehre wäre: so würde die ganze Christenheit und zwar gerade dadurch, daß sie der ihr Lehramt rechtmäßig übenden Kirche Gehör gäbe, in Irrthum geführt. Und wäre dann diese Kirche noch die Säule und Grundfeste der Wahrheit? wäre sie noch das auf den Felsen gegründete Gebäude, welches die Mächte der Finsterniß nicht zu erschüttern vermögen? Sie hat die Verheißung, daß der Geist Gottes sie alle Wahrheit lehre, in alle Wahrheit einführen werde: ist denn diese Verheißung nicht von all der Wahrheit zu verstehen, über welche sie uns belehren soll, und wir um dem Zwecke der Offenbarung zu entsprechen, der Belehrung bedürfen?

Aber sagt man denn nicht allgemein, daß die Lehrgewalt und daher auch die Unfehlbarkeit der Kirche auf die *Glaubenssachen* beschränkt sei? Allerdings, aber darin liegt der Irrthum anzunehmen, nur dann handle es sich um Glaubenssachen, wenn die geoffenbarte Wahrheit selbst geläugnet wird. So wie nur die geoffenbarte Wahrheit ihrer selbst wegen, aber doch auch alles, was mit ihr in nothwendiger Verbindung steht, mittelbar zum Glauben gehört; so gehört auch nicht bloß, was der geoffenbarten Wahrheit geradezu entgegengesetzt ist, sondern alles, was mit ihr unvereinbar ist, wenigstens mittelbar zur Irrlehre. Ferner genügt es nicht, daß der Glaube nur eben nicht zerstört werde, er muß auch gesund und lebenskräftig sein, damit aus ihm wie aus ihrer Wurzel die christliche Gerechtigkeit Nahrung erhalten könne. Wie er nun aber durch die Läugnung der geoffenbarten Wahrheit zerstört wird; so wird er durch alle

---

44 Zacharias. l. c. cap. 3 a. 2 et 4.

irrigen Meinungen, welche auf jene Beziehung haben, siech und kraftlos, und je näher diese Beziehung ist, desto größer ist die Gefahr, daß er ganz ersterbe. Wie also der Arzt den, welcher seiner Pflege sich übergiebt, nicht bloß vor allem, was tödliche Krankheiten, sondern auch vor dem, was Schwäche und Siechthum hervorbringt, warnet; also muß die Kirche, deren Obhut Gott uns übergeben hat, nicht bloß die Häresie, welche dem Gifte gleich das geistige Leben in seiner Wurzel ertödtet, sondern auch die mit ihr verwandten Irrthümer, welche den Glauben schwach und unwirksam machen, von uns fern halten[45]. Und dies führt uns auf einen andern Grund, aus dem man die Unfehlbarkeit der Kirche in solchen Entscheidungen erkennen kann.

92. Es ist außer allem Zweifel, daß die Kirche ebenso wohl in der *Sittenlehre* als in der Glaubenslehre unfehlbar ist, so zwar daß sie nicht irren kann, wenn sie z.B. einen Vortrag für unerlaubt erklärt, oder was das göttliche Gesetz für den würdigen Empfang eines Sakramentes vorschreibe, bestimmt. Weil sowohl dies positive als auch das natürliche Gesetz in der Offenbarung enthalten ist, so gehört auch die Sittenlehre zur Glaubenslehre, und die Unfehlbarkeit der Kirche in der Erklärung derselben läßt sich aus ihrer Lehrgewalt, wie es oben geschehen ist, herleiten. Aber sie ergiebt sich auch als eine nothwendige Folge aus jener *Heiligkeit,* welche wir im Glaubensbekenntniß selbst als eine wesentliche Eigenschaft ihr beilegen. Denn diese fordert doch gewiß vor allen Dingen, daß die Lehre der Kirche heilig sei, daß sie also nie etwas für Tugend oder Laster erkläre, was es nicht ist. Nun aber enthalten die Entscheidungen, von denen wir reden, die Erklärung, daß es sündhaft sei, den Meinungen, welche in ihnen verworfen werden, anzuhangen. Denn, wie oben schon bemerkt wurde, die Kirche verbietet nicht bloß dieselben vorzutragen, sondern verwirft sie, und bezeichnet sie durch die Censuren als solche, die wir aus Liebe und Hochschätzung der reinen Lehre des Glaubens meiden und fliehen sollen. Oder welchen andern Sinn können jene Benennungen: *sententia temeraria, scandalosa, de haeresi suspecta, haeresin sapiens* u.s.w. haben? Verdiente also eine Meinung diese Benennung nicht, welche die Kirche ihr giebt; so wäre dies derselbe Fall, als wenn ein Vertrag, den die Kirche für ungerecht erklärt, gerecht oder eine sinnliche Handlung, die sie für unkeusch erklärt, keusch wäre[46].

93. Was nun insbesondere die Behauptung Chrismann's angeht, die Kirche sei nicht unfehlbar, wenn sie lehre, was aus geoffenbarten Wahrheiten durch

---

45 Cf. Melch. Can. de loc. theol. l. 12. c. 10.
46 Cf. Lugo l. c. n. 109 etc.

Vernunftschlüsse gefolgert wird; so muß er zu derselben dadurch verleitet worden sein, daß er eine unter den Theologen schwebende Streitfrage mißverstand. Damit die Bestimmung der Vernunft, womit wir einen Satz für wahr halten, ein Glaubensact sei, muß sie das Ansehen Gottes zum Beweggrunde haben. Wenn wir aber aus einer geoffenbarten Lehre vermittelst einer natürlichen Erkenntniß Folgerungen herleiten; so stützt sich das Fürwahrhalten dieser Folgerungen nicht einzig auf Gottes Ansehen, sondern zugleich auf menschliche Einsicht oder menschliche Erfahrung. Daher sind fast alle Theologen der Ansicht, daß dies Fürwahrhalten keine Beistimmung des Glaubens *(assensus fidei)*, sondern des aus dem Glauben entspringenden Wissens *(assensus theologiae)* sei[47]. Doch lehren, die älteren wenigstens, gemeiniglich, daß solche Folgerungen durch die Entscheidung der lehrenden Kirche zu eigentlichen Glaubenssätzen werden: weil nämlich in diesem Falle es nicht die menschliche Vernunft, sondern der die Kirche leitende Geist Gottes ist, der uns die Richtigkeit jener Folgerungen verbürgt. Nichts desto weniger haben Molina[48] und später einige andere Theologen dieses geläugnet; aber nicht etwa weil die Kirche in solchen Entscheidungen des göttlichen Beistandes, der sie unfehlbar mache, entbehrete, sondern weil durch diesen Beistand jene Sätze zwar unfehlbar gewiß, aber deßhalb nicht zum *Worte Gottes* würden, vielmehr immer aus diesem Worte abgeleitete Folgerungen blieben. Dies also muß Chrismann nicht beachtet und gemeint haben, auch darüber werde gestritten, ob die Unfehlbarkeit der Kirche sich auf diese Lehrsätze ausdehne.

94. Wohin aber seine wahrhaft unerhörte Behauptung führe, läst sich schon daraus allein erkennen, daß sehr viele Concilienbeschlüsse, auch solche, die in der strengsten Form der Canonen erlassen sind, Wahrheiten feststellen, die ganz gewiß nicht unmittelbar geoffenbart, sondern aus geoffenbarten hergeleitet sind. Dahin gehören, daß der h. Geist vom Vater und Sohne nicht wie von zwei Prinzipien, sondern wie von einem und durch eine Hauchung hervorgeht; daß die göttliche Wesenheit nicht zeugt, noch gezeugt wird; daß im Menschen die vernünftige Seele durch sich selbst d. h. unmittelbar die Form des Leibes ist; daß in der h. Eucharistie eine Verwandlung des Brodes und Weines vor sich geht, die mit Recht Transsubstantion genannt wird; daß in derselben die Accidenzen des Brodes und Weines ohne Subject bleiben; daß Messen, in welchen nur der Priester den Leib und das Blut des Herrn genießt, erlaubt sind u.s.w. Alle solche Entscheidungen würden also, wenn Chrismann's Grundsatz gälte, ungewiß werden. Aber was von noch größerer Bedeutung ist, auch die

---

47   Suarez. De fide. Disp. 3. sect. 11. Lugo De fide disp. 1. sect. 13. n. 269 seq.
48   In Summam S. Thom. p. 1. q. 1. a. 2. Disp. 1 & 2.

Gewißheit der übrigen wäre in den meisten Fällen von unserm Ermessen abhängig. Wenn nämlich die Kirche nicht in allen Lehrbestimmungen, sondern nur in jenen unfehlbar ist, welche in sich selbst *(explicite)* geoffenbarte Wahrheiten feststellen; so müssen wir doch diese Bestimmungen von den übrigen unterscheiden können. Nun ist es wahr, daß die Kirche zuweilen in ihren Beschlüssen selbst sich hierüber erklärt, namentlich dadurch, daß sie die Worte der Schrift, worin die Lehre enthalten ist, anführt: aber in den meisten Fällen begnügt sie sich, was ihre Lehre sei, ohne Zusätze auszusprechen. Um also auch dann ihrer Entscheidung uns mit Zuversicht unterwerfen zu können, müßten wir fast immer nach eigenem Urtheile entscheiden, ob der Inhalt derselben in sich selbst geoffenbart sei, und folglich jene Kenntniß der Offenbarung, welche wir durch die unfehlbare Kirche erhalten sollen, schon besitzen.

95. Hätten wir aber nicht auch volles Recht, über das Verfahren der Kirche Klage zu führen? Sie verpflichtet uns mit Strenge, und meistens unter Androhung schwerer Strafen zur Annahme der Lehre, über welche sie entscheidet. Wenn sie also nicht in allen Entscheidungen gleich unfehlbar wäre; so müßte sie, um sich nicht der ungerechtesten Willkür schuldig zu machen, die fehlbaren von den unfehlbaren Entscheidungen sondern.

Man kann nicht entgegnen, daß die Concilien ihren Beschlüssen allgemeine Erklärungen vorausschicken, in denen hinlänglich ausgesprochen sei, was Chrismann zufolge nothwendig ist, damit etwas Gegenstand der unfehlbaren Lehrgewalt sei. Denn ihm zufolge ist hiezu nothwendig, daß die Lehren in sich selbst geoffenbart seien. Nun sind aber erstlich, wie oben gezeigt wurde, unter den Sätzen, welche auf jene Erklärungen folgen, sehr viele enthalten, die ganz gewiß nicht also geoffenbart sind. Wenn daher die Erklärungen, was Chrismann will, aussprächen, so würden sie falsch sein. Aber sie sprechen es auch nicht aus. Sehr oft sagen die Väter nur, daß sie, „was der Heilslehre," „was der katholischen Wahrheit gemäß" sei, bestimmen, und wenn sie auch ausdrücken, daß sie „die von den Vätern überlieferte," „die in der h. Schrift enthaltene," „die von Gott geoffenbarte Lehre" vorlegen, so hat man kein Recht, dies, wie Chrismann's Grundsatz fordern würde, zu deuten. Denn was aus dem Worte Gottes unter dem Beistande des h. Geistes gefolgert wird, von dem kann mit aller Wahrheit gesagt werden, daß es in dem Worte Gottes enthalten, daß es geoffenbart ist. – Endlich aber, was in unserer Frage ganz und gar entscheidend ist, im Beschlusse des Kirchenrathes zu Constanz wider Wiklef und in den dogmatischen Bullen der Päbste wider Bajus und Quesnel werden ganze Reihen von Sätzen durch die oben betrachteten Censuren verworfen, so jedoch daß nicht bestimmt wird, welche der verschiedenen Censuren jeder Satz verdiene; umgekehrt wird in der Bulle wider die Jansenisten zu Pistoja den einzelnen

Sätzen die betreffende Censur beigefügt. Was haben wir also nun nach Chrismann's Grundsatz über diese kirchlichen Entscheidungen zu urtheilen? Er mag mit einigen Theologen dafür halten, daß auch die Kirche nur jene Wahrheiten, welche in sich selbst geoffenbart sind, für Glaubenspunkte, und folglich nur die Behauptungen, welche solchen Wahrheiten direkt entgegenstehen, für häretisch erklären könne. Wenn aber die Kirche, was er allein behauptet, nur in der Bestimmung dieser Wahrheiten unfehlbar ist; so folgt, daß wir nur diejenigen Sätze der Wiklefiten und Jansenisten zu verwerfen verpflichtet sind, welche in den genannten Denkschriften als häretisch bezeichnet werden. So müßten wir also unter den Paragraphen der Bulle *Auctorem fidei* eine Auswahl machen, die einen als Bestimmungen der unfehlbaren Kirche annehmend, die andern dahin gestellt sein lassend. Die Beschlüsse wider Wiklef, Bajus und Quesnel aber würden höchstens noch eine ernste Warnung, keine Entscheidung der Kirche sein. Denn in ihnen bleibt es ungewiß, welchen Sätzen die Benennung häretisch zuzueignen ist. In der allgemeinen Lehre, die wir vertheidigen, bietet dieses keine Schwierigkeit dar. Denn ihr zufolge sind wir durch das unfehlbare Ansehen der Kirche gewiß, daß alle die verurtheilten Sätze der Lehre des Heiles widerstreiten, und es bleibt nur unentschieden, in welchem Grade sie ihr widerstreiten.

96. Aus allem Gesagten folgt, daß wir, um uns den Entscheidungen der Kirche mit aller Zuversicht zu unterwerfen, nichts anderes zu erkennen brauchen, als daß es *Entscheidungen über die Lehre* sind. Auch jener Satz, daß die Kirche in ihrem Urtheile über Personen und Thatsachen irren könne, hat seine Ausnahmen, und durch die triftigsten Gründe läßt sich darthun, daß die Kirche in der Heiligsprechung und der Bestimmung des Sinnes, welchen gewisse Sätze bei einem Schriftsteller haben, keinesweges dem Irrthume unterworfen ist. Indeß begreift man, daß hierüber auch unter Rechtgläubigen Zweifel entstehen konnten. – Aber daß die Kirche, auch wenn sie über Lehren entscheidet, nicht immer vom h. Geiste geleitet sei, ist vor Chrismann, so viel ich weiß, noch keinem Katholiken in den Sinn gekommen. Wohl ist es wahr, daß die Lehrgewalt der Kirche ihre Gränzen hat: denn sie ist gegeben, um die Religion Jesu Christi und nicht um alles, was von Menschen gewußt werden kann, zu lehren. Aber was folgt daraus, wenn nicht, daß die Kirche nichts lehrt, und über nichts entscheidet, als was zur Religion Jesu Christi gehört? Wäre ihr nicht die unfehlbare Einsicht verliehen, wie weit sich ihre Vollmacht zu lehren erstrecke, dann wäre ja offenbar die Unfehlbarkeit selbst nichtig und bedeutungslos. Wenn immer also der Träger dieser Vollmacht über eine Lehre so urtheilt, daß er die ganze Christenheit verpflichtet, seinem Urtheil sich zu unterwerfen, so ist auch die Untrüglichkeit dieses Urtheils außer Zweifel.

BIBLIOGRAPHY

Ecclesiastical Documents

Agatho, Pope. Apostolic Letter *Omnium bonorum spes*. 680.
Alexander VIII, Pope. Constitution *Inter multiplices*. 4 Aug. 1690.
Benedict XII, Pope. Bull *Benedictus Deus*. 29 Jan. 1336.
Benedict XIV, Pope. Encyclical Letter *Vix pervenit*. 1 Nov. 1745.
Boniface VIII, Pope. Bull *Unam sanctam*. 18 Nov. 1302.
Catechism of the Catholic Church. 15 Aug. 1997.
Clement XI, Pope. Apostolic Constitution *Unigenitus Dei Filius*. 8 Sep. 1713.
___, Apostolic Constitution *Vineam Domini Sabaoth*. 16 Jul. 1705.
Code of Canon Law. 25 Jan. 1983.
Code of Canon Law. 27 May 1917.
Code of Canons of the Eastern Churches. 18 Oct. 1990.
Congregation for the Doctrine of the Faith. Declaration *Mysterium Ecclesiae*. 24 Jun. 1973.
___, Instruction *Donum veritatis*. 24 May 1990.
___, *Professio fidei*. 17 Jul. 1967.
___, *Professio fidei*. 29 Jun. 1998.
___, *Responsum ad dubium*. 28 Oct. 1995.
Council of Chalcedon. Definition of Faith *Sancta et magna*. Session V. 22 Oct. 451.
Council of Constantinople III. Definition of Faith *Unigenitus Dei*. Session XVIII. 16 Sep. 681.
Council of Florence. Bull of Union with the Armenians *Exsultate Deo*. Session VIII. 22 Nov. 1439.
___, Bull of Union with the Copts and Ethiopians *Cantate Domino*. Session XI. 4 Feb. 1442.
___, Bull of Union with the Greeks *Laetentur caeli*. Session VI. 6 Jul. 1439.
Council of Trent. *Decree on Original Sin*. Session V. 17 Jun. 1546.
___, *Decree on Scripture and Tradition*. Session IV. 8 Apr. 1546.
___, *Decree on the Sacraments*. Session VII. 3 Mar. 1547.
Council of Vatican I. Dogmatic Constitution *Dei Filius*. Session III. 24 Apr. 1870.
___, First Dogmatic Constitution *Pastor Aeternus*. Session IV. 18 Jul. 1870.
Council of Vatican II. Declaration *Nostra aetate*. Session VII. 28 Oct. 1965.
___, Decree *Orientalium Ecclesiarum*. Session V. 21 Nov. 1964.
___, Decree *Unitatis redintegratio*. Session V. 21 Nov. 1964.
___, Dogmatic Constitution *Lumen gentium*. Session V. 21 Nov. 1964.
Gregory XVI, Pope. Brief *Dum acerbissimas*. 26 Sep. 1835.
___, Encyclical Letter *Commissum divinitus*. 17 May 1835.
Innocent X, Pope. Apostolic Constitution *Cum occasione*. 31 May 1653.
Innocent XI, Pope. Bull *Caelestis Pastor*. 20 Nov. 1687.
Innocent XII, Pope. Brief *Cum alias*. 12 Mar. 1699.

John Paul II, Pope. *Address to Congregation for the Doctrine of the Faith*. 24 Nov. 1995.

___, Apostolic Constitution *Pastor Bonus*. 28 Jun. 1988.

___, Apostolic Letter *Ordinatio sacerdotalis*. 22 May 1994.

___, Encyclical Letter *Evangelium vitae*. 25 Mar. 1995.

___, *General Audience on the Divine Assistance in the Magisterium of the Successor of Peter*. 17 Mar. 1993.

___, *General Audience on the Divine Assistance in the Magisterium of the Successor of Peter*. 24 Mar. 1993.

___, *General Audience on the Doctrinal Mission of the Successor of Peter*. 10 Mar. 1993.

___, Motu Proprio *Ad tuendam fidem*. 18 May 1998.

John XXIII, Pope. Encyclical Letter *Aeterna Dei*. 11 Nov. 1961.

Leo I, Pope. Apostolic Letter *Lectis dilectionis tuae*. 13 Jun. 449.

Leo X, Pope. Bull *Exsurge Domine*. 15 Jun. 1520.

Leo XIII, Pope. Bull *Apostolicae curae*. 15 Sep. 1896.

___, Encyclical Letter *Annum sacrum*. 25 May 1899.

___, Encyclical Letter *Immortale Dei*. 1 Nov. 1885.

___, Encyclical Letter *Inscrutabili Dei*. 21 Apr. 1878.

___, Encyclical Letter *Sapientiae christianae*. 10 Jan. 1890.

___, Encyclical Letter *Satis cognitum*. 29 Jun. 1896.

___, Encyclical Letter *Testem benevolentiae*. 22 Jan. 1899.

Nicholas V, Pope. Bull *Romanus Pontifex*. 8 Jan. 1454.

Paul VI, Pope. Apostolic Constitution *Regimini Ecclesiae Universae*. 15 Aug. 1967.

___, Encyclical Letter *Humanae vitae*. 25 Jul. 1968.

Pius IV, Pope. Bull *Iniunctum nobis*. 13 Nov. 1565.

Pius V, Pope. Bull *Ex omnibus afflictionibus*. 1 Oct. 1567.

Pius VI, Pope. Apostolic Constitution *Auctorem fidei*. 28 Aug. 1794.

Pius IX, Pope. Apostolic Letter *Tuas libenter*. 21 Dec. 1863.

___, Brief to the Archbishop of Cologne *Eximiam tuam*. 15 Jun. 1857.

___, Bull *Ineffabilis Deus*. 8 Dec. 1854.

___, Letter *Quanta cura*. 8 Dec. 1864.

___, Encyclical Letter *Qui Pluribus*. 9 Nov. 1846.

___, *Syllabus of Errors*. 8 Dec. 1864.

Pius X, Pope. Apostolic Letter *Notre Charge Apostolique*. 15 Aug. 1910.

___, Apostolic Letter *Sacrorum antistitum*. 1 Sep. 1910.

Pius XI, Pope. Encyclical Letter *Casti connubii*. 31 Dec. 1930.

___, Encyclical Letter *Divini illius Magistri*. 31 Dec. 1929.

___, Encyclical Letter *Miserentissimus Redemptor*. 8 May 1928.

___, Encyclical Letter *Mortalium animos*. 6 Jan. 1928.

Pius XII, Pope. Apostolic Constitution *Munificentissimus Deus*. 1 Nov. 1950.

___, Encyclical Letter *Ad apostolorum principis*. 29 Jun. 1958.

___, Encyclical Letter *Ad sinarum gentem*. 7 Oct. 1954.

___, Encyclical Letter *Haurietis aquas.* 15 May 1956.

___, Encyclical Letter *Humani generis.* 12 Aug. 1950.

Sixtus IV, Pope. Bull *Licet ea.* 9 Aug. 1479.

Collections of Ecclesiastical Documents

Abbott, Walter M., ed. *The Documents of Vatican II.* Chicago: Association Press, 1966.

Carlen, Claudia, ed. *The Papal Encyclicals, 1740–1981,* vol 1. Ypsilanti, MI: Pierian Press, 1990.

Migne, J. P., ed. *Patrologiae cursus completus, series latina.* Paris, 1844ff.

Tanner, Norman P., ed. *Decrees of the Ecumenical Councils.* London: Sheed and Ward; Washington, D.C.: Georgetown University Press, 1990.

Theological Literature

Antón, Angel. "*Ordinatio Sacerdotalis:* Algunas reflexiones de 'gnoseología teológica'." *Gregorianum* 75 (1994): 723–42.

Aubert, Roger. *Le Problème de l'Acte de Foi.* Louvain: Wainy, 1945.

Bainvel, Jean V. *De magisterio vivo et traditione.* Paris: Beauchesne, 1905.

Ballerini, Pietro. *De potestate ecclesiastica.* Rome: Propaganda Fide, 1850.

___, *De vi ac ratione primatus romanorum pontificum et de ipsorum infallibilitate in definiendis controversiis fidei.* Ed. Elbert W. Westhoff. Westphalia: Deiters, 1845.

Balthasar, Hans Urs von. *The Office of Peter and the Structure of the Church.* Trans. Andrée Emery. San Francisco: Ignatius Press, 1986.

Bate, Herbert N. ed. *Faith and Order: Proceedings of the World Conference.* London: Student Christian Movement, 1927.

Baum, Gregory. "Doctrinal Renewal." *Journal of Ecumenical Studies* 2 (1965): 365–81.

Beinert, Wolfgang. "Unfehlbarkeit." In *Lexicon für Theologie und Kirche,* vol. 10. 3rd ed. Ed. Walter Kasper. Freiburg im Breisgau: Herder, 2001.

Belair, Raymond W. "A Recent History of the Ordinary Universal Magisterium." *American Theological Inquiry* 1 (2008): 68–77.

Bellamy, Julien M. *La théologie catholique au XIXᵉ siècle.* 2nd ed. Paris: Beauchesne, 1904.

Bellarmine, Robert. *De controversiis christianae fidei adversus hujus temporis haereticos.* In *Opera omnia,* vol. 1. Ed. Xisto Riario Sforza. Naples: Giuliano, 1856.

Benard, Edmond D. "The Doctrinal Value of the Ordinary Teaching of the Holy Father in View of *Humani Generis.*" *Proceedings of the Catholic Theological Society of America* 6 (1951): 78–107.

Bertone, Tarcisio. "Magisterial Documents and Public Dissent." *L'Osservatore Romano,* English Edition (29 Jan. 1997): 6–7.

Betti, Umberto. "Considerazioni dottrinali." *Notitia* 25 (1989): 321–25.

___, "Qualification théologique de la Constitution." In *L'Église de Vatican II*, vol. 2. Ed. Guilherme Baraúna. Unam Sanctam 51b, 211–18. Paris: Cerf, 1967.

Beumer, Johannes. "Die Regula Fidei Catholicae des Ph. N. Chrismann OFM und ihre Kritik durch J. Kleutgen SJ." *Franziskanische Studien* 46 (1964): 321–44.

___, "Sind päpstliche Enzykliken unfehlbar?" *Theologie und Glaube* 42 (1952): 262–69.

Billot, Louis. *Tractatus de Ecclesia Christi sive continuatio theologiae de verbo incarnato*, vol. 1, 3rd ed. Prati: Giachetti, 1909.

Boyle, John P. "The 'Ordinary Magisterium': Towards a History of the Concept." *Heythrop Journal* 20 (1979): 380–98; 21 (1980): 14–29.

___, "The Natural Law and the Magisterium." *Proceedings of the Catholic Theological Society of America* 34 (1979): 189–210.

___, *Church Teaching Authority: Historical and Theological Studies*. Notre Dame: University of Notre Dame Press, 1995.

Brinkmann, Bernhard. "Gibt es unfehlbare Äußerungen des 'Magisterium Ordinarium' des Papstes?" *Scholastik* 28 (1953): 202–21.

Butler, Cuthbert. *The Vatican Council: The Story Told from Inside in Bishop Ullathorne's Letters*, vol. 2. New York: Longmans, Green and Co., 1930.

Cartechini, Sixtus. *De valore notarum theologicarum et de criteriis ad eas dignoscendas*. Rome: Gregorian University Press, 1951.

Caudron, Marc. "Magistère ordinaire et infaillibilité pontificale d'après la constitution *Dei Filius*." *Ephemerides Theologicae Lovanienses* 36 (1960): 393–431.

Chirico, Peter L. "Infallibility: A Reply." *The Thomist* 44 (1980): 128–35.

___, "Infallibility: Rapprochement between Küng and the Official Church?" *Theological Studies* 42 (1981): 529–60.

Choupin, Lucien. *Valeur des décisions doctrinales et disciplinaires du Saint-Siège*. 2nd ed. Paris: Beauchesne, 1913.

Chrismann, Philip Neri. *Regula Fidei Catholicae*. Lingg, 1792.

Ciappi, Luigi. "Crisis of the Magisterium, Crisis of Faith." *The Thomist* 32 (1968): 147–70.

Congar, Yves. "A Semantic History of the Term 'Magisterium'." In *The Magisterium and Morality*. Readings in Moral Theology, vol. 3. Ed. Charles E. Curran and Richard A. McCormick. 297–313. New York: Paulist Press, 1982.

___, "En guise de conclusion." In *L'Église de Vatican II*, vol. 3. Ed. Guilherme Baraúna. Unam Sanctam 51c, 1365–73. Paris: Cerf, 1967.

___, "Saint Thomas Aquinas and the Infallibility of the Papal Magisterium." *The Thomist* 38 (1974): 81–105.

___, *Fifty Years of Catholic Theology: Conversations with Yves Congar*. Ed. Bernard Lauret. Philadelphia: Fortress, 1988.

_____, *The Meaning of Tradition*. New York: Hawthorn, 1964.

Connell, Francis J. "Theological Content of *Humani generis*." *American Ecclesiastical Review* 123 (1950): 321–30.

Connery, John R. "The Non-Infallible Moral Teaching of the Church." *The Thomist* 51 (1987): 1–16.

Costanzo, Joseph F. *The Historical Credibility of Hans Kung: An Inquiry and Commentary*. North Quincy: Christopher, 1979.

Costigan, Richard F. *The Consensus of the Church and Papal Infallibility: A Study in the Background of Vatican I*. Washington, D.C.: Catholic University of America Press, 2005.

Curran, Charles E. "Pluralism in Catholic Moral Theology." In *The Magisterium and Morality*. Readings in Moral Theology, vol. 3. Ed. Charles E. Curran and Richard A. McCormick. 364–87. New York: Paulist Press, 1982.

_____, ed. *Contraception: Authority and Dissent*. New York: Herder and Herder, 1969.

_____, et al. "Statement by Theologians." *New York Times*. 31 July 1968.

_____, et al. *Dissent In and For the Church*. New York: Sheed and Ward, 1969.

_____, et al. *The Responsibility of Dissent: The Church and Academic Freedom*. New York: Sheed and Ward, 1969.

_____, *Faithful Dissent*. Kansas City: Sheed and Ward, 1986.

_____, *Loyal Dissent: Memoirs of a Catholic Theologian*. Washington, D.C.: Georgetown University Press, 2006.

D'Ormesson, Wladimir. *The Papacy*. Trans. Michael Derrick. Twentieth Century Encyclopedia of Catholicism, vol. 81. Ed. Henri Daniel-Rops. New York: Hawthorn Books, 1959.

De Guibert, Joseph. *De Christi Ecclesia*. 2nd ed. Rome: Gregorian University Press, 1928.

Diekamp, Franz. *Die origenistischen Streitigkeiten im 6. Jahrhundert und das 5. allgemeine Konzil*. Münster: Aschendorff, 1899.

DiNoia, J. A. "Communion and Magisterium: Teaching Authority and the Culture of Grace." *Modern Theology* 9 (1993): 403–18.

Dublanchy, Edmond. "Infaillibilité du Pape." In *Dictionnaire de théologie catholique*, vol. 7. 1638–1717. Paris: Letouzey et Ané, 1927.

Dulles, Avery. "Newman on Infallibility." *Theological Studies* 51 (1990): 434–49.

_____, *Magisterium: Teacher and Guardian of the Faith*. Naples, FL: Sapientia Press, 2007.

Epting, Karl-Christoph. "Lausanne 1927: The First World Conference on Faith and Order." *The Ecumenical Review* 29 (1977): 167–81.

Ernst, Harold E. "The Theological Notes and the Interpretation of Doctrine." *Theological Studies* 63 (2002): 813–25.

Fenton, Joseph C. "Infallibility in the Encyclicals." *American Ecclesiastical Review* 128 (1953): 177–98.

———, "John Henry Newman and the Vatican Definition of Papal Infallibility." *American Ecclesiastical Review* 113 (1945): 300–20.

———, "*Magisterium* and Jurisdiction in the Catholic Church." *American Ecclesiastical Review* 130 (1954): 194–201.

———, "The Doctrinal Authority of Papal Allocutions." *American Ecclesiastical Review* 134 (1956): 109–17.

———, "The Doctrinal Authority of Papal Encyclicals." *American Ecclesiastical Review* 121 (1949): 136–50, 210–20.

———, "The *Humani generis* and its Predecessors." *American Ecclesiastical Review* 123 (1950): 452–58.

———, "The *Humani generis* and the Holy Father's Ordinary Magisterium." *American Ecclesiastical Review* 125 (1951): 53–62.

———, "The Lesson of the *Humani generis*." *American Ecclesiastical Review* 123 (1950): 359–78.

———, "The Local Church of Rome." *American Ecclesiastical Review* 122 (1950): 454–64.

———, "The Necessity for the Definition of Papal Infallibility by the Vatican Council." *American Ecclesiastical Review* 115 (1946): 439–57.

———, "The Papal Allocution *Si diligis*." *American Ecclesiastical Review* 131 (1954): 186–98.

———, "The Question of Ecclesiastical Faith." *American Ecclesiastical Review* 128 (1953): 287–301.

———, "The Religious Assent Due to the Teachings of Papal Encyclicals." *American Ecclesiastical Review* 123 (1950): 59–67.

———, "The Requisites for an Infallible Pontifical Definition according to the Commission of Pope Pius IX." *American Ecclesiastical Review* 115 (1946): 376–84.

———, "Two Solemn Pontifical Definitions." *American Ecclesiastical Review* 124 (1951): 52–61.

Fessler, Joseph. *The True and the False Infallibility of the Popes: A Controversial Reply to Dr. Schulte*. 3rd ed. Trans. Ambrose St. John. London: Burns and Oates, 1875.

Figueiredo, Anthony J. *The Magisterium Theology Relationship: Contemporary Theological Conceptions in the Light of Universal Church Teaching since 1835 and the Pronouncements of the Bishops of the United States*. Serie Teologia, vol. 75. Rome: Gregorian University Press, 2001.

Ford, John C., and Germain Grisez. "Contraception and the Infallibility of the Ordinary Magisterium." *Theological Studies* 39 (1978): 258–312.

Ford, John T. "Infallibility: A Review of Recent Studies." *Theological Studies* 40 (1979): 273–305.

___, "Küng on Infallibility: A Review Article." *The Thomist* 35 (1971): 501–12.

Franzelin, Johann Baptist. *Tractatus de divina traditione et scriptura.* Turin: Marietti, 1870.

Fuchs, Josef. "Sittliche Wahrheiten – Heilswahrheiten?." *Stimmen der Zeit* 200 (1982): 662–76.

Gaillardetz, Richard R. "The Ordinary Universal Magisterium: Unresolved Questions." *Theological Studies* 63 (2002): 447–71.

___, *By What Authority? A Primer on Scripture, the Magisterium, and the Sense of the Faithful.* Collegeville, MN: Liturgical Press, 2003.

___, *Teaching with Authority: A Theology of the Magisterium of the Church.* Theology and Life Series, vol. 41. Collegeville, MN: Liturgical Press, Michael Glazier, 1997.

___, *Witnesses to the Faith: Community, Infallibility, and the Ordinary Magisterium of Bishops.* New York; Mahwah, N.J.: Paulist Press, 1992.

Galvin, John P. "Papal Primacy in Contemporary Roman Catholic Theology." *Theological Studies* 47 (1986): 653–67.

Gams, Pius, ed. *Verhandlungen der Versammlung katholischer Gelehrten in München vom 28. September bis 1. Oktober 1863.* Regensburg: Manz, 1863.

George, Francis. "God's Point of View: Apostolicity and the Magisterium. A Lecture Delivered to the St. Anselm Institute at the University of Virginia." *Nova et Vetera* 6 (2008): 271–90.

Gleeson, Brian. "Commemorating *Lumen Gentium*: A Short History of a Ground-breaking Charter." *Australian eJournal of Theology* 3 (Aug. 2004): 1–5.

Goyau, Georges. "Johann Baptist von Hirscher." In *The Catholic Encyclopedia*, vol. 7. 363–65. New York: Robert Appleton, 1910.

Granderath, Theodor. *Geschichte des Vatikanischen Konzils: von seiner ersten Ankündigung bis zu seiner Vertagung: nach den authentischen Dokumenten*, vol. 3. Ed. Konrad Kirch. Freiburg: Herder, 1906.

Gres-Gayer, Jacques M. "The Magisterium of the Faculty of Theology of Paris in the Seventeenth Century." *Theological Studies* 53 (1992): 424–50.

___, "The *Unigenitus* of Clement XI: A Fresh Look at the Issues." *Theological Studies* 49 (1998): 259–82.

Grisez, Germain. "Infallibility and Contraception: A Reply to Garth Hallett." *Theological Studies* 47 (1986): 134–45.

___, "Infallibility and Specific Moral Norms: A Review Discussion." *The Thomist* 46 (1985): 248–87.

___, "Response to Francis Sullivan's Reply." *Theological Studies* 55 (1994): 737–38.

___, "The Ordinary Magisterium's Infallibility: A Reply to Some New Arguments." *Theological Studies* 55 (1994): 720–32.

Gutwenger, Englebert. "The Role of the Magisterium." *Concilium* 1.6 (1970): 43–55.

Hallett, Garth L. "Contraception and Prescriptive Infallibility." *Theological Studies* 43 (1982): 629–50.

———, "Infallibility and Contraception: The Debate Continues." *Theological Studies* 49 (1988): 517–28.

Harrison, Brian W. "The *Ex Cathedra* Status of the Encyclical *Humanae Vitae*." *Living Tradition* 43 (Sep.–Nov. 1992).

Hennessy, Paul K. "Episcopal Collegiality and Papal Primacy in the Pre-Vatican I American Church." *Theological Studies* 44 (1983): 288–97.

———, "Infallibility in the Ecclesiology of Peter Richard Kenrick." *Theological Studies* 45 (1984): 702–14.

Hettinger, Franz. *Supremacy of the Apostolic See in the Church*. Trans. George Porter. London: Burns and Oates; New York: Catholic Publication Society, 1889.

Hirscher, Johann Baptist von. *Die kirchlichen Zustände der Gegenwart*. Mainz: Kirchheim and Schott, 1849.

Hodgson, Leonard, ed. *Convictions: A Selection from the Responses of the Churches to the Report of the World Conference on Faith and Order, Held at Lausanne in 1927*. New York: Macmillan, 1934.

———, ed. *The Second World Conference on Faith and Order: Held at Edinburgh, August 3–18, 1937*. New York: Macmillan, 1938.

Horst, Ulrich. *Papst-Konzil-Unfehlbarkeit: Die Ekklesiologie der Summenkommentare von Cajetan bis Billuart*. Mainz: Matthias-Grünewald, 1978.

———, *Unfehlbarkeit und Geschichte: Studien zur Unfehlbarkeitsdiskussion von Melchior Cano bis zum I. Vatikanischen Konzil*. Mainz: Matthias-Grünewald, 1982.

Hughes, Gerald J. "Infallibility in Morals." *Theological Studies* 34 (1973): 415–28.

Hughes, John J. "Hans Küng and the Magisterium." *Theological Studies* 41 (1980): 368–89.

———, "Infallible? An Inquiry Considered." *Theological Studies* 32 (1971): 183–207.

Hünermann, Peter, and Dietmar Mieth, eds. *Streitgespräch um Theologie und Lehramt: Die Instruktion über die kirchliche Berufung des Theologen in der Diskussion*. Frankfurt: Knecht, 1991.

Hünermann, Peter. "Schwerwiegende Bedenken: Eine Analyse des Apostolischen Schreibens 'Ordinatio Sacerdotalis'." *Herder Korrespondenz* 48 (1994): 406–10.

———, "Theologischer Kommentar zur dogmatischen Konstitution über die Kirche *Lumen gentium*." In *Herders Theologischer Kommentar zum Zweiten Vatikanischen Konzil*, vol. 2. Ed. Bernd Hilberath and Peter Hünermann. 263–582. Freiburg; Basel; Vienna: Herder, 2009.

Hurley, Denis E. "Population Control and the Catholic Conscience: Responsibility of the Magisterium." *Theological Studies* 35 (1974): 154–63.

Journet, Charles. *The Primacy of Peter: From the Protestant and from the Catholic Point of View.* Trans. John Chapin. Westminster: Newman Press, 1954.

Joy, John P. *Cathedra Veritatis: On the Extension of Papal Infallibility.* Licentiate Thesis. International Theological Institute, 2012.

Kasper, Walter. *Die Lehre von der Tradition in der römischen Schule.* Freiburg, 1962.

Kenrick, Francis. *Theologiae dogmaticae tractatus tres: de revelatione, de Ecclesia, et de Verbo Dei.* Philadelphia: Johnson, 1839.

Kleutgen, Joseph. *Die Theologie der Vorzeit verteidigt*, vol. 1. 1st ed. Münster: Theissing, 1853. 2nd ed. Münster: Theissing, 1867.

Komonchak, Joseph A. "*Humanae vitae* and its Reception: Ecclesiological Reflections." *Theological Studies* 39 (1978): 221–57.

___, "Ordinary Papal Magisterium and Religious Assent." In *Contraception: Authority and Dissent.* Ed. Charles E. Curran. 105–16. New York: Herder and Herder, 1969.

Küng, Hans. *Fehlbar? Eine Bilanz.* Zurich: Benzinger, 1973.

___, *Unfehlbar?Eine Anfrage.* Zürich: Benzinger, 1970.

Kwasniewski, Peter A. "The Authority of Papal Encyclicals." *Lay Witness* (March/April 2007): 54–55.

Lamont, John R.T. "Determining the Content and Degree of Authority of Church Teachings." *The Thomist* 72 (2008): 371–407.

Landgraf, A. M. "Scattered Remarks on the Development of Dogma and on Papal Infallibility in Early Scholastic Writings." *Theological Studies* 7 (1946): 577–82.

Lécuyer, Joseph. "La triple charge de l'évêque." In *L'Église de Vatican II*, vol. 3. Ed. Guilherme Baraúna. Unam Sanctam 51c, 891–914. Paris: Cerf, 1966.

Levillain, Phillipe, and John W. O'Malley, Editors. *The Papacy: An Encyclopedia.* New York: Routledge, 2002.

Lio, Ermenegildo. *Humanae Vitae e Infallibilità: il Concilio, Paolo VI e Giovanni Paolo II.* Vatican City: Libreria Editrice Vaticana, 1986.

Lutheran-Roman Catholic Dialogue. "Teaching Authority and Infallibility in the Church." *Theological Studies* 40 (1979): 113–66.

MacIntyre, Alasdair. *Three Rival Versions of Moral Enquiry: Encyclopaedia, Genealogy, and Tradition.* Notre Dame, IN: University of Notre Dame Press, 1990.

Manning, Henry Edward. *The Centenary of St. Peter and the General Council: A Pastoral Letter to the Clergy.* London: Longmans, Green, and Co., 1867.

___, *The Oecumenical Council and the Infallibility of the Roman Pontiff: A Pastoral Letter to the Clergy.* 2nd ed. London: Longmans, Green, and Co., 1869.

___, *The True Story of the Vatican Council.* London: Henry King, 1877.

___, *The Vatican Council and Its Definitions: A Pastoral Letter to the Clergy.* London: Longmans, Green, and Co., 1870.

___, *The Vatican Decrees in Their Bearing on Civil Allegiance.* London: Longmans, Green, and Co., 1875.

May, William E. "The Cultural and Ecclesial Situation 1964 to 1967: Paving the Way for Dissent From Church Teaching on Contraception." *Nova et Vetera* 7 (2009): 711–29.

May, William W., ed. *Vatican Authority and American Catholic Dissent: The Curran Case and Its Consequences.* New York: Crossroad, 1987.

McCool, Gerald A. *Nineteenth-Century Scholasticism: The Search for a Unitary Method.* New York: Fordham University Press, 1989.

Melina, Livio. "The Role of the Ordinary Magisterium: On Francis Sullivan's *Creative Fidelity.*" *The Thomist* 61 (1997): 605–15.

Merry del Val, Raphael. *The Truth of Papal Claims.* London: Sands; St. Louis: Herder, 1904.

Mettepenningen, Jürgen. *Nouvelle Théologie – New Theology: Inheritor of Modernism, Precursor of Vatican II.* London: T&T Clark, 2010.

Morris, Eugene S. "The Infallibility of the Apostolic See in Jaun de Torquemada O.P." *The Thomist* 46 (1982): 242–66.

Müller, Gerhard L. *Katholische Dogmatik: Für Studium und Praxis der Theologie.* Freiburg: Herder, 2005.

Nau, Paul. "Le Magistère pontifical ordinaire au premier concile du Vatican." *Revue Thomiste* 62 (1962): 341–97.

———, "The Ordinary Magisterium of the Catholic Church." In *Pope or Church? Essays on the Infallibility of the Ordinary Magisterium.* Trans. Arthur E. Slater. Kansas City: Angelus Press, 2006.

Naud, André. *Devant la nouvelle profession de foi et le serment de fidélité.* Montreal: Fides, 1989.

———, *Le magistère incertain.* Montreal: Fides, 1987.

Newman, John Henry. *A Letter Addressed to His Grace the Duke of Norfolk on Occasion of Mr. Gladstone's Recent Expostulation.* London: Pickering, 1875.

Nichols, Aidan. *The Shape of Catholic Theology.* Edinbourgh: T&T Clark, 1991.

O'Connor, James T. *The Gift of Infallibility.* San Francisco: Ignatius Press, 2008.

O'Meara, Thomas F. "Divine Grace and Human Nature as Sources for the Universal Magisterium of Bishops." *Theological Studies* 64 (2003): 683–706.

Oeing-Hanhoff, Ludger. "Ist das kirchliche Lehramt für den Bereich des Sittlichen zuständig?" *Theologische Quartalschrift* 161 (1981): 56–66.

Orsi, Giuseppe-Agostino. *De irreformabili romani pontifici in definiendis fidei controversiis judicio.* Rome: Junchius, 1771.

Örsy, Ladislas. "Magisterium: Assent and Dissent." *Theological Studies* 48 (1987): 473–97.

———, *Receiving the Council: Theological and Canonical Insights and Debates.* Collegeville: Liturgical Press, Michael Glazier, 2009.

———, *The Church: Learning and Teaching.* Wilmington: Glazier, 1987.

Ott, Ludwig. *Fundamentals of Catholic Dogma.* Ed. James Bastible. Trans. Patrick Lynch. Rockford: Tan Books, 1974.

Palmieri, Dominico. *Tractatus de romano pontifice cum prolegomeno de Ecclesia.* Prati: Giachetti, 1891.

Perrone, Giovanni. *De romani pontificis infallibilitate, seu Vaticana definitio contra novos hereticos asserta et vindicata.* Turin: Marietti, 1874.

____, *Praelectiones theologicae.* 26ᵗʰ ed. Paris: Leroux, Jouby, et Cie, 1854.

Pesch, Christian. *Compendium theologiae dogmaticae,* vol. 1. Fribourg: Herder, 1913.

Pottmeyer, Hermann J. *Der Glaube vor dem Anspruch der Wissenschaft: Die Konstitution über den katholischen Glauben "Dei Filius" des 1. Vatikanischen Konzils und die unveröffentlichten theologischen Voten der vorbereitenden Kommission.* Freiburg: Herder, 1968.

____, *Towards a Papacy in Communion: Perspectives from Vatican Councils I and II.* Trans. Matthew J. O'Connell. New York: Crossroad, Herder and Herder, 1998.

Powell, Mark E. *Papal Infallibility: A Protestant Evaluation of an Ecumenical Issue.* Grand Rapids: Eerdmans, 2009.

Prendergast, R. S. "Some Neglected Factors of the Birth Control Question." *Sciences Ecclesiastiques* 18 (1966): 218–19.

Quinn, John R. *The Reform of the Papacy: The Costly Call to Christian Unity.* New York: Crossroad, Herder and Herder, 1999.

Rahner, Karl. "Basic Observations on the Subject of Changeable and Unchangeable Factors in the Church." In *Theological Investigations,* vol. 14. Trans. David Bourke. 3–23. New York: Seabury, 1976.

____, "Dogmatic Constitution on the Church, Chapter III, Articles 18–27." Trans. Kevin Smyth. In *Commentary on the Documents of Vatican II,* vol. 1. Ed. Herbert Vorgrimler. London: Burns and Oates; New York: Herder and Herder, 1967.

____, "Magisterium." In *Sacramentum Mundi: An Encyclopedia of Theology,* vol. 3. Ed. Karl Rahner. 351–58. New York: Herder and Herder, 1968.

____, "On the Relationship between the Pope and the College of Bishops." In *Theological Investigations,* vol. 10. Trans. David Bourke. 50–70. New York: Herder and Herder, 1973.

Raming, Ida. "Endgültiges Nein zum Priestertum der Frau? Zum Apostolischen Schreiben Papst Johannes Pauls II. Ordinatio Sacerdotalis." *Orientierung: Katholische Blätter für weltanschauliche Information* 58 (1994): 190–93.

Ratzinger, Joseph, and Tarcisio Bertone. *Doctrinal Commentary on the Concluding Formula of the Profession of Faith.* 29 Jun. 1998.

Ratzinger, Joseph. "Cardinal Frings's Speaches during the Second Vatican Council." *Communio* 15 (1988): 131–47.

____, "Letter Concerning the CDF Reply Regarding *Ordinatio Sacerdotalis.*" *L'Osservatore Romano,* English Edition (19 Nov. 1995): 2.

____, "The Limits of Church Authority." *L'Osservatore Romano,* English Edition (29 Jun. 1994): 6–8.

Reed, John J. "Natural Law, Theology and the Church." *Theological Studies* 26 (1965): 40–64.

Sala, Giovanni. "Fallible Teachings and the Assistance of the Holy Spirit: Reflections on the Ordinary Magisterium in Connection with the Instruction on the Ecclesial Vocation of the Theologian." *Nova et Vetera* 4 (2006): 29–54.

Salaverri, Joseph. "Valor de las Encíclicas a la luz de 'Humani Generis'." *Miscelánea Comillas* 17 (1952): 135–72.

___, *Tractatus de Ecclesia Christi*. In *Sacrae theologiae summa*, vol. 1. 5th ed. Madrid: Biblioteca de Autores Cristianos, 1962.

Santogrossi, Ansgar. "*Ordinatio Sacerdotalis*: A Definition *ex cathedra*." *Homiletic and Pastoral Review* (Feb. 1999): 7–14.

Schatz, Klaus. *Der Päpstliche Primat: seine Geschichte von den Ursprüngen bis zur Gegenwart*. Würzburg: Echter, 1990.

___, "Welche bisherigen päpstlichen Lehrentscheidungen sind 'ex cathedra'? Historische und theologische Überlegungen." In *Dogmengeschichte und katholische Theologie*, 404–22. Ed. Werner Löser, Karl Lehmann, and Matthias Lutz-Bachmann. Würzburg: Echter, 1985.

Scheeben, Matthias J. *Theologische Erkenntnislehre*. In *Handbuch der Katholischen Dogmatik*, vol. 1. 3rd ed. Ed. Martin Grabmann. Freiburg: Herder, 1959.

Schmaus, Michael. *Katholische Dogmatik*, vol. 1. 6th ed. Munich: Hueber, 1960.

___, *The Church: Its Origin and Structure*. Volume 4 of *Dogma*. London: Sheed and Ward, 1972.

Schmied, Augustin. "'Schleichende Infallibilisierung': Zur Diskussion um das kirchliche Lehramt." In *In Christus zum Leben befreit: Festschrift für Bernhard Häring*. Ed. Josef Römelt and Bruno Hidber. 250–72. Freiburg; Basel; Vienna: Herder, 1992.

Seckler, Max. "Die Theologie als kirckliche Wissenschaft nach Pius XII. und Paul VI." *Theologische Quartalschrift* 149 (1969): 209–34.

Sesboüé, Bernard. "Magistère 'ordinaire' et magistère authentique." *Recherches de science religieuse* 84 (1996): 267–75.

Spohn, William C. "The Magisterium and Morality." *Theological Studies* 54 (1993): 95–111.

Stirnimann, Heinrich. "'Magisterio enim ordinario haec docentur.' Zur einer Kontroversstelle der Enzyklika 'Humani generis'," *Freiburger Zeitschrift für Philosophie und Theologie* 1 (1954): 17–47.

Sullivan, Francis A. "Infallible Teaching on Moral Issues? Reflections on Veritatis Splendor and Evangelium Vitae." In *Choosing Life: A Dialogue on* Evangelium Vitae. Ed. Kevin W. Wildes and Alan C. Mitchell. Washington, D.C.: Georgetown University Press, 2007.

___, "New Claims for the Pope." *The Tablet* 248 (18 Jun. 1994): 767–69.

___, "Recent Theological Observations on Magisterial Documents and Public Dissent." *Theological Studies* 58 (1997): 509–15.

___, "Reply to Germain Grisez." *Theological Studies* 55 (1994): 732–37.

___, "Reply to Lawrence J. Welch." *Theological Studies* 64 (2003): 610–15.

___, "Some Observations on the New Formula for the Profession of Faith." *Gregorianum* 70 (1989): 549–58.

___, "The 'Secondary Object' of Infallibility." *Theological Studies* 54 (1993): 536–50.

___, "The Doctrinal Weight of *Evangelium Vitae*." *Theological Studies* 56 (1995): 560–65.

___, "The Meaning of Conciliar Dogmas." In *The Convergence of Theology: A Festschrift Honoring Gerald O'Collins, S.J.* Ed. Daniel Kendall and Stephen T. Davis. , 73–86. Mahwah, N.J.: Paulist Press, 2001.

___, "The Ordinary Magisterium's Infallibility: A Reply to Germain Grisez." *Theological Studies* 55 (1994): 732–37.

___, "The Teaching Authority of Episcopal Conferences." *Theological Studies* 63 (2002): 472–93.

___, "The Theologian's Ecclesial Vocation and the 1990 CDF Instruction." *Theological Studies* 52 (1991): 51–68.

___, *Creative Fidelity: Weighing and Interpreting the Documents of the Magisterium.* Eugene, OR: Wipf and Stock, 2003.

___, *Magisterium: Teaching Authority in the Catholic Church.* Eugene, OR: Wipf and Stock, 2002.

___, *Quaestiones theologiae fundamentalis.* In *De Ecclesia*, vol. 1. Rome: Gregorian University Press, 1963.

___, *Salvation Outside the Church? Tracing the History of the Catholic Response.* Eugene, Ore.: Wipf and Stock, 2002.

Tanquerey, Adolphe. *Sysnopsis theologiae dogmaticae fundamentalis.* 24th ed. Paris: Desclée, 1937.

Thils, Gustave. "Truth and Verification at Vatican I." *Concilium* 3/9 (1973): 27–34.

___, *L'infaillibilité pontifical: Source, conditions, limites.* Gembloux: Duculot, 1969.

Tierney, Brian. "Infallibility in Morals: A Response." *Theological Studies* 35 (1974): 507–17.

___, "John Peter Olivi and Papal Inerrancy: On a Recent Interpretation of Olivi's Ecclesiology." *Theological Studies* 46 (1985): 315–28.

___, *Origins of Papal Infallibility, 1150–1350: A Study on the Concepts of Infallibility, Sovereignty and Tradition in the Middle Ages.* Leiden: Brill, 1972.

Topmoeller, William C. "Faith and Order on Unity of Doctrine." *Proceedings of the Catholic Theological Society of America* 19 (1964): 119–30.

Torrell, Jean-Pierre. *La théologie de l'épiscopat au premier concile du Vatican.* Paris: Cerf, 1961.

Ullathorne, William. *Mr. Gladstone's Expostulation Unravelled.* New York: Catholic Publication Society, 1875.

Vacant, Jean-Michel-Alfred. *Etudes théologiques sur les Constitutions du Concile du Vatican d'après les Actes du Concile.* Paris: Delhomme et Briguet, 1895.

___, *Le magistère ordinaire de l'Eglise et ses organes.* Paris: Delhomme et Briguet, 1887.

VanderWilt, Jeffrey Thomas. *Communion with Non-Catholic Christians: Risks, Challenges, and Opportunities.* Collegeville, MN: Liturgical Press, 2003.

Veron, François. *De regula fidei catholicae seu de fide catholica.* Madrid: Fuentenebro, 1839.

Vollert, Cyril. "*Humani generis* and the Limits of Theology." *Theological Studies* 12 (1951): 3–23.

Vorgrimler, Herbert, ed. *Commentary on the Documents of Vatican II*, vol. 1. Trans. Lalit Adolphus et al. New York: Herder and Herder, 1967.

Weigel, Gustave. "Gleanings from the Commentaries on *Humani generis.*" *Theological Studies* 12 (1951): 520–49.

____, "The Historical Background of the Encyclical *Humani generis.*" *Theological Studies* 12 (1951): 208–30.

Welch, Lawrence J. "Reply to Richard Gaillardetz on the Ordinary Universal Magisterium and to Francis Sullivan." *Theological Studies* 64 (2003): 598–609.

____, "The Infallibility of the Ordinary Universal Magisterium: A Critique of Some Recent Observations." *Heythrop Journal* 39 (1998): 18–36.

Wilson, George B. "The Gift of Infallibility: Reflections Toward a Systematic Theology." *Theological Studies* 31 (1970): 625–43.

Wolf, Hubert. *Die Nonnen von Sant'Ambrogio. Eine wahre Geschichte.* Munich: Beck, 2013.

STUDIA OECUMENICA FRIBURGENSIA

(= Neue Folge der ÖKUMENISCHEN BEIHEFTE)
(= Nouvelle Série des CAHIERS OECUMÉNIQUES)

Mit den Unterreihen

GLAUBE UND GESELLSCHAFT (G&G)
hg. von Walter Dürr und Stefan Wenger

und

SEMAINES D'ÉTUDES LITURGIQUES SAINT-SERGE (SÉtL)
hg. von André Lossky und Goran Sekulovski

69 André Lossky / Goran Sekulovski (Hg.): Liturges et liturgistes : fructification de leurs apports dans l'aujourd'hui des églises. 59ᵉ Semaine d'études liturgiques. Paris, Institut Saint-Serge, 25-28 juin 2012, 372 S., 2015.

68 Michael Quisinsky: Katholizität der Inkarnation – Catholicité de l'Incarnation. Christliches Leben und Denken zwischen Universalität und Konkretion „nach" dem II. Vaticanum. Vie et pensée chrétiennes entre universalité et concrétion (d')après Vatican II, 474 S., 2016.

67 Will Cohen: The Concept of "Sister Churches" in Catholic-Orthodox Relations since Vatican II. Prefaces by Metropolitan Kallistos (Ware) and Cardinal Kurt Koch. 303 S., 2015.

66 Daniel Eichhorn: Katholisches Schriftprinzip? Josef Rupert Geiselmanns These der materialen Schriftsuffizienz. 316 S., 2015.

65 Walter Dürr / Stefan Wenger (Hg.), Theologische Bildung und Spiritualität. Wie akademische Theologie kirchliche Praxis inspirieren kann (G&G 1), 176 S. Münster 2015.

64 André Lossky / Goran Sekulovski (Hg.): Jeûne et pratiques de repentance : dimensions communautaires et liturgiques (SÉtL 58), 322 S., 2015.

63 Nicolas Thomas Wright: Rechtfertigung. Gottes Plan und die Sicht des Paulus, hg von Barbara Hallensleben und Simon Dürr. Übersetzt von Rainer Behrens, 274 S., 2015.

62 Viorel Ionita: Towards the Holy and Great Synod of the Orthodox Church. The Decisions of the Pan-Orthodox Meetings since 1923 until 2009, 211 S., 2014.

61 Uwe Wolff: Iserloh. Der Thesenanschlag fand nicht statt, hg. von Barbara Hallensleben. Mit einem Geleitwort von Landesbischof Friedrich Weber und einem Forschungsbeitrag von Volker Leppin. 267 S., 2013.

60 Nikolaus Wyrwoll: Ostkirchliches Institut Regensburg. Studierende und Gäste 1963–2013. 283 S., 2013.

59 Jürg H. Buchegger: Das Wort vom Kreuz in der christlich-muslimischen begegnung. Leben und Werk von Johan Bouman. 322 S., 2013.

58 Christof Betschart: „Unwiederholbares Gottessiegel". Zum Verständnis der personalen Individualität in Edith Steins philosophisch-theologischem Horizont. 378 S., 2013.

57 Ernst Christoph Suttner: Einheit im Glaube – geistgewirkte Vielfalt in Leben und Lehre der Kirche. 151 S., 2013.

56 Christoph Schwyter: Das sozialpolitische Denken der Russischen Orthodoxen Kirche. Eine theologische Grundlegung auf der Basis offizieller Beiträge seit 1988. VIII + 375 S., 2013.

55 Franck Lemaître : Anglicans et Luthériens en Europe. Enjeux théologiques d'un rapprochement ecclésial. IV + 356 p., 2011.

54 Ernst Christoph Suttner: Quellen zur Geschichte der Kirchenunionen des 16. bis 18. Jahrhunderts. Deutsche Übersetzung der lateinischen Quellentexte von Klaus und Michaela Zelzer mit Erläuterungen von Ernst Christoph Suttner. IV + 292 S., 2010.

53 Marie Louise Gubler: Befreiung verkündigen. Eine Auslegung der Sonntagsevangelien. 466 S., 2010.

52 Ernst Christoph Suttner: Kirche und Theologie bei den Rumänen von der Christianisierung bis zum 20. Jahrhundert. 258 S., 2009.

51 Augustin SOKOLOVSKI: *Matrix omnium conclusionum*. Den *Augustinus* des Jansenius lesen. VIII + 322 S., 2013.

50 Cyril PASQUIER osb : Aux portes de la gloire. Analyse théologique du millénarisme de Saint Irénée de Lyon. 176 p., 2008.

49 Ernst Christoph SUTTNER: Staaten und Kirchen in der Völkerwelt des östlichen Europa. Entwicklungen der Neuzeit. 484 S., 2007.

48 Barbara HALLENSLEBEN und Guido VERGAUWEN (Hg.): Letzte Haltungen. Hans Urs von Balthasars „Apokalypse der deutschen Seele" – neu gelesen. 360 S., 2006.

47 Hilarion ALFEYEV : Le mystère sacré de l'Église. Introduction à l'histoire et à la problématique des débats athonites sur la vénération du nom de Dieu. 448 p., 2007.

46 Urs CORRADINI: Pastorale Dienste im Bistum Basel. Entwicklungen und Konzeptionen nach dem Zweiten Vatikanischen Konzil. 560 S., 2008.

45 Gottfried Wilhelm LOCHER: Sign of the Advent. A Study in Protestant Ecclesiology. 244 S., 2004.

44 Mariano DELGADO und Guido VERGAUWEN (Hg.): Glaube und Vernunft – Theologie und Philosophie. Aspekte ihrer Wechselwirkung in Geschichte und Gegenwart. 248 S., 2003.

43 Hilarion ALFEYEV: Geheimnis des Glaubens. Einführung in die orthodoxe dogmatische Theologie. 280 S., 2003; 2. Auflage 2005.

42 Jorge A. SCAMPINI o.p. : „La conversión de las Iglesias, una necesidad y una urgencia de la fe". La experiencia del *Groupe des Dombes* como desarrollo de un método ecuménico eclesial (1937–1997). 672 p., 2003.

41 Iso BAUMER: Von der Unio zur Communio. 75 Jahre Catholica Unio Internationalis. 536 S., 2002.

40 Adrian LÜCHINGER: Päpstliche Unfehlbarkeit bei Henry Edward Manning und John Henry Newman. 368 S., 2001.

39 Klauspeter BLASER : Signe et instrument. Approche protestante de l'Eglise. Avec la collaboration de Christian Badet. 216 p., 2000.

38 Kurt STALDER: Sprache und Erkenntnis der Wirklichkeit Gottes. Texte zu einigen wissenschaftstheoretischen und systematischen Voraussetzungen für die exegetische und homiletische Arbeit. Mit einem Geleitwort von Heinrich Stirnimann o.p., hg. von Urs von Arx, unter Mitarbeit von Kurt Schori und Rudolf Engler. 486 S., 2000.

37 Marie-Louise GUBLER: Im Haus der Pilgerschaft. Zugänge zu biblischen Texten. 300 S., 1999.

36 Iso BAUMER: Begegnungen. Gesammelte Aufsätze 1949–1999. 356 S., 1999.

35 Barbara HALLENSLEBEN und Guido VERGAUWEN o.p. (éd.) : *Praedicando et docendo*. Mélanges offerts à Liam Walsh o.p. 345 p., 1998.

34 Son-Tae KIM: Christliche Denkform: Theozentrik oder Anthropozentrik? Die Frage nach dem Subjekt der Geschichte bei Hans Urs von Balthasar und Johann Baptist Metz. 626 S., 1999.

33 Guido VERGAUWEN o.p. (éd.) : Le christianisme : Nuée de témoins – beauté du témoignage. 152 p., 1998.

32 Marcelo Horacio LABÈQUE : Liberación y modernidad. Una relectura de Gustavo Gutiérrez. 444 p., 1997.

31 Bernd RUHE: Dialektik der Erbsünde. Das Problem von Freiheit und Natur in der neueren Diskussion um die katholische Erbsündenlehre. 296 S., 1997.

30 Marek CHOJNACKI: Die Nähe des Unbegreifbaren. Der moderne philosophische Kontext der Theologie Karl Rahners und seine Konsequenzen in dieser Theologie. 448 S., 1996.

29 Carlos MENDOZA-ÁLVAREZ o.p.: *Deus liberans*. La revelación cristiana en diálogo con la modernidad: los elementos fundacionales de la estética teológica. XVI + 478 p., 1996.

28 Iso BAUMER und Guido VERGAUWEN o.p. (Hg.): Ökumene: das eine Ziel – die vielen Wege. Œcuménisme : un seul but – plusieurs chemins. Festschrift zum 30jährigen Bestehen des Institutum Studiorum Oecumenicorum der Universität Freiburg (Schweiz). 340 S., 1995.

27 Odilo Noti: Kant – Publikum und Gelehrter. Theologische Erinnerung an einen abgebrochenen Diskurs zum Theorie-Praxis-Problem, 256 S., 1994.

26 Charles MOREROD: Cajetan et Luther en 1518. Edition, traduction et commentaire des opuscules d'Augsbourg de Cajetan. 2 tomes, 708 p., 1994.

25 Gheorghe SAVA-POPA: Le Baptême dans la tradition orthodoxe et ses implications œcuméniques, 312 p., 1994.

24 Guy BEDOUELLE / Olivier FATIO (éd.): Liberté chrétienne et libre arbitre. Textes de l'enseignement de troisième cycle des facultés romandes de théologie, 212 p., 1994.

23 Wolfgang BIALAS: Von der Theologie der Befreiung zur Philosophie der Freiheit. Hegel und die Religion, 172 S., 1993.

22 Philip KENNEDY OP: Deus Humanissimus. The Knowability of God in the Theology of Edward Schillebeeckx, 460 p., 1993.

21 Martin HAUSER: Prophet und Bischof. Huldrych Zwinglis Amtsverständnis im Rahmen der Zürcher Reformation, 292 S., 1994.

20 Martin HAUSER (Hg.): Unsichtbare oder sichtbare Kirche? Beiträge zur Ekklesiologie. In Zusammenarbeit mit Ulrich Luz, Hans Friedrich Geißer, Jean-Louis Leuba und Anastasios Kallis, 104 S., 1992.

19 Felix SENN: Orthopraktische Ekklesiologie? Karl Rahners Offenbarungsverständnis und seine ekklesiologischen Konsequenzen im Kontext der neueren katholischen Theologiegeschichte, 820 S., 1989.

18 Maria BRUN: Orthodoxe Stimmen zum II. Vatikanum. Ein Beitrag zur Überwindung der Trennung. Mit einem Vorwort von Metropolit Damaskinos Papandreou, 272 S., 1988.

17 Bruno BÜRKI: Cène du Seigneur - eucharistie de l'Eglise. Le cheminement des Eglises réformées romandes et françaises depuis le XVIIIᵉ siècle, d'après leurs textes liturgiques. Volume A: Textes, 176 p. Volume B: Commentaires. 224 p., 1985.

16 Paul Patrick O'LEARY O.P.: The Triune Church. A Study in the Ecclesiology of A.S. Chomjakov, 257 p., 1982.

15 Joseph RITZ: Empirie im Kirchenbegriff bei karl Barth und Hans Küng, 285 S., 1981.

14 Richard FRIEDLI: Frieden wagen. Der Beitrag der Religionen zur Gewaltanalyse und zur Friedensarbeit, 252 S., 1981.

13 Johannes FLURY: Um die Redlichkeit des Glaubens. Studien zur deutschen katholischen Fundamentaltheologie, 325 S., 1979.

12 Jean-Jacques VON ALLMEN: Pastorale du baptême, 197 S., 1978.

11 Pietro SELVATICO: Glaubensgewissheit. Eine Untersuchung zur Theologie von Gerhard Ebeling, 183 S., 1977.

10 Jean-Jacques VON ALLMEN: La primauté de l'Église de Pierre et de Paul. Remarques d'un protestant, 125 S., 1977.

9 Johannes Baptist BRANTSCHEN: Zeit zu verstehen. Wege und Umwege heutiger Theologie. Zu einer Ortsbestimmung der Theologie von Ernst Fuchs, 292 S., 1974.

8 Richard FRIEDLI: Fremdheit als Heimat. Auf der Suche nach einem Kriterium für den Dialog zwischen den Religionen, 214 S., 1974.

7 Zukunft der Ökumene. Drei Vorträge von Heinrich Stirnimann, Willem Adolf Visser't Hooft, Hans Jochen Margull, 42 S., 1974.

6 Hildegar HÖFLIGER: Die Erneuerung der evangelischen Einzelbeichte. Pastoraltheologische Dokumentation zur evangelischen Beichtbewegung seit Beginn des 20. Jahrhunderts, 224 S., 1971.

5 Heinrich STIRNIMANN (Hg.): Interkommunion. Hoffnungen – zu bedenken. Mit Beiträgen von H. Helbling, O.K. Kaufmann, J.-L. Leuba, P. Vogelsanger, H. Vorgrimler, D. Wiederkehr. Internationale Bibliographie, zusammengestellt von J.B. Brantschen und P. Selvatico, 150 S., 1971.

4 Heinrich STIRNIMANN (Hg.): Ökumenische Erneuerung in der Mission. Studien von I. Auf der Maur, P. Beyerhaus, H. Rickenbach, E. Wildbolz, Fribourg 1970, 102 S.

3 Heinrich STIRNIMANN (Hg.): Kirche im Umbruch der Gesellschaft. Studien zur Pastoralkonstitution „Kirche in der Welt von heute" und zur Weltkonferenz „Kirche und Gesellschaft". Mit Beiträgen von F. Böckle, E.-J. Kaelin, H. Ruh, K. Stalder. Internationale Bibliographie, zusammengestellt von Ph. Reymond, 132 S., 1970.

2 Einheit und Erneuerung der Kirche. Zwei Vorträge von Karl Barth und Hans Urs von Balthasar, 37 S., 1968.

1 Heinrich STIRNIMANN (Hg.): Christliche Ehe und getrennte Kirchen. Dokumente. Studien von J.-J. von Allmen, G. Bavaud, A. Sustar. Internationale Bibliographie, zusammengestellt von J.B. Brantschen, 124 S., 1968.